BUZZ ME IN

MARTIN PORTER & DAVID GOGGIN

BUZZ ME IN

Inside the Record Plant Studios

This book is dedicated to every runner, general, bookkeeper, studio manager, assistant engineer, receptionist, gofer, tape operator, driver, session musician, maintenance tech, and studio rat who made this all happen.

The musical selections in the Tape track sheets to follow have been selected as the soundtrack to each section and are available on playlists at www.recordplantdiaries.com. They were all recorded, mixed, mastered, released, or charted during the period of the section or were part of the narrative.

First published in the United Kingdom in 2025 by
Thames & Hudson Ltd, 181A High Holborn, London WC1V 7QX

First published in the United States of America in 2025 by
Thames & Hudson Inc., 500 Fifth Avenue, New York, New York 10110

Buzz Me In: Inside the Record Plant Studios © 2025
Thames & Hudson Ltd, London

For image copyright information, see pages 375–377

Text by Martin Porter and David Goggin © 2025 RPD Partners, LLC

All Rights Reserved. No part of this publication may be reproduced or transmitted in any form or by any means, electronic or mechanical, including photocopy, recording or any other information storage and retrieval system, without prior permission in writing from the publisher.

British Library Cataloguing-in-Publication Data
A catalogue record for this book is available from the British Library

Library of Congress Control Number 2024950054

ISBN 978-0-500-02869-8

Impression 01

Printed in China by RR Donnelley

Be the first to know about our new releases, exclusive content and author events by visiting
thamesandhudson.com
thamesandhudsonusa.com
thamesandhudson.com.au

CONTENTS

Prologue 6

1 **LIVING ROOM STUDIO** 10
1966–1970

2 **MASTER CONTROL** 76
1970–1971

3 **SECOND HOME** 108
1971–1974

4 **VIP CLUBHOUSE** 204
1974–1975

5 **HOTEL CALIFORNIA** 266
1975–1977

6 **SANCTUARY OF SOUND** 340
1977–1980

Epilogue 365

TEXT SOURCES 368
ILLUSTRATION CREDITS 375
INDEX 378
ACKNOWLEDGMENTS 384

Prologue

> Once upon a time, rock and roll was the primal scream of adolescence. Rock grew so big, so fast, that the businessmen who controlled it couldn't keep up with it. But then it grew so big that the people who made the music, the rock stars, the producers, the audience, couldn't keep up with it, either. So, they got stoned. Or died. Or went straight. Rebellion made rock music go, but the final rebellion was against your own body.
>
> Lucian K. Truscott IV, "Inside the Real Hotel California,"
> *New Times* magazine, August 5, 1977

ELECTRA GLIDE NAILS

It began with Jimi.

Gary Kellgren built the world's first living-room-style recording studio on the West Side of Manhattan in 1968, and the success of the album Jimi Hendrix worked on there, *Electric Ladyland*, launched a recording-studio empire. Music industry demands quickly fueled the studio's expansion out west. And a fleet of concert recording trucks soon followed.

Kellgren's Record Plant studios in New York, Los Angeles, and Sausalito owned the top of the *Billboard 200* album chart for ten months in 1977, with discs they recorded for Stevie Wonder, the Eagles, and Fleetwood Mac. The unique creative environments he built to manufacture music combined a residential vibe with the best gear and five-star customer service. The technology was groundbreaking. The parties were notorious. And the combination helped make music history.

Coming off this winning streak, Kellgren was now planning his greatest Record Plant of all, a rock and roll resort on a four-acre estate in the Hollywood Hills. And yet, nobody outside of the

Record Plant studio co-founder Gary Kellgren vamped for the camera on the steps of the front entrance to his old Hollywood mansion in 1977 for an article for *New Times* magazine. The piece labeled the Record Plant studio as "the Real Hotel California."

inner-inner-circle of the rock and roll elite had ever heard of Gary Kellgren or ever been inside one of his high-security studios.

Lucian K. Truscott IV from *New Times* magazine was assigned to find out who this "Kellgren guy" was, after he had been spotted working the crowd at the Rainbow Bar & Grill on Sunset Boulevard. His editor told him that "Kellgren was surrounded by rock stars trying to convince him to listen to their tapes and they were literally begging to get into his studio. They're saying Record Plant is the 'Real Hotel California.'"

Truscott wasn't known for this type of story. But then the editor added something that piqued his interest: "Lucian, this story is about the death of rock and roll."

By 1977, there were signs that the seventies rock and roll party was coming to an end. The record-label bean counters were starting to tighten recording budgets. The gear was getting more affordable, leading to more low-overhead studio competitors. The new bands were looking for a big, live studio sound, which didn't fit Record Plant's acoustical formula. And it was starting to look like Gary Kellgren's new resort-studio venture was dead on arrival.

If this was the "death of rock and roll," Kellgren was going down in style—with his name and reputation part of the public record. He told Truscott:

> When I go, I'm going in class. I'm going to call a limousine, have it pull right up outside here in the parking lot, and I'm gonna climb in the back seat and tell the driver to take me down to the beach. It's gonna be one of those limousines with the smoked glass, so you can see out but they can't see in. I'm gonna sit back there with my feet up, with a tape on the eight-track, and I'm gonna polish my nails as we drive down to the beach. I'm gonna polish them, shine them, and polish them until they seem like chrome. When I go, I'm gonna have Electra Glide nails, man . . . When they catch the light, they're gonna be as bright as chrome. They're gonna blind you, man. I'm gonna have Electra Glide nails when I die. Let those fuckers try to take that from me, man, just let them.

PROLOGUE

Truscott returned to New York and wrote the story, which the *New Times* editor headlined "Inside the Real Hotel California." Then, three days before the magazine shipped, Kellgren was dead.

July 22, 1977, *Los Angeles Times*

The owner-operator of a West Los Angeles recording studio and his secretary drowned in his swimming pool in Hollywood in what police called a double-accidental death. Just before the drowning, Gary Kellgren, 38, was swimming in the deep end of the pool and Kristianne Gaines, 34, of Los Angeles was sitting on a raft, according to a business associate of Kellgren who told police he was in the house when the incident occurred. Police said Kellgren had recently undergone surgery and Miss Gaines could not swim. "Nothing we have found at this point indicates there was any foul play," said one investigator.

1

LIVING ROOM STUDIO

1966–1970

"We wanted to jam somewhere, so we went to [Record Plant], the best place to jam, and brought about 50 of our friends along."

JIMI HENDRIX
first client

TAPE 1

STUDIO	MAYFAIR STUDIOS, NY / APOSTOLIC STUDIOS, NY	
ARTIST	TITLE	FORMAT
Velvet Underground & Nico	"Sunday Morning"	Single
Frank Zappa	Lumpy Gravy	Album
Frank Zappa	We're Only in It for the Money	Album
Jimi Hendrix	"Burning of the Midnight Lamp"	Single
Jimi Hendrix	"The Stars that Play with Laughing Sam's Dice"	Single
Velvet Underground	White Light / White Heat	Album

NAIL POLISH

Chris Stone knocked on the frosted glass door of an ordinary-looking office in a Times Square tower. It was the summer of 1967, and he was dressed in his black business suit even though this wasn't a sales call. He had met an audio engineer named Gary Kellgren the night before and been invited over to see how music was made.

    Stone's wife, Gloria, had just given birth to their first child and Kellgren's wife, Marta, was nervous about her own first pregnancy. The women became friends and they made an excuse for the couples to get together one night for dinner. Gary was quiet at first, concerned that he was missing a recording session, but he grew animated when their conversation turned to business. Kellgren made Stone feel like the rock star in the room, complaining about his base pay, which was for forty hours regardless of how many hours he worked. Money was something Stone understood. He offered to help.

    Stone was a regional sales manager at Revlon and spent his days making sure that the shelves at Macy's were stocked with nail polish; this was clearly not what he had been expecting when his college roommate helped land him a job with Revlon founder, Charles Revson.

LIVING ROOM STUDIO

After work the next day, Stone went to visit Kellgren at Mayfair Studios. Nobody answered the door when he knocked, so Stone walked right into a studio with a shiny black linoleum floor and filled with folding chairs, microphone stands, wires, and instruments, where somebody was banging away from under the lid of a grand piano. Stone walked up and tapped him on the leg and said, "Hi. I'm Chris. I'm here to see Gary."

Stone was greeted with a "looks-can-kill" stare from this hippie with a big head of hair, Fu Manchu mustache, and soul patch who demanded, "Who the hell are you?"

Stone assumed that this was Kellgren's boss and repeated that he was looking for Gary.

"Listen, I'm Frank Zappa. I'm recording here, so get the hell out," he was told.

Stone didn't know who Frank Zappa was, so he carried on, "I'd like to talk to you about giving Gary a raise."

Zappa lit a cigarette, took a sip of coffee from a cardboard cup, then shrugged his shoulders and muttered, "Get lost," before diving back into the piano.

This Zappa guy wasn't Kellgren's boss; he was a client—a famous one—which would have been obvious to anyone but Stone who had missed out on most of the sixties music scene. Stone had taken a straight and narrow path to business, first getting his MBA at UCLA, then entering the business-development training program at General Electric, followed by a junior-marketing-executive stint at Mattel.

> # "Listen, I'm Frank Zappa. I'm recording here, so get the hell out."
>
> Frank Zappa, musician

Zappa was working at Mayfair on the aptly titled album, *We're Only in It for the Money*. And after Kellgren showed him the studio's finances, Stone realized that not only was his new friend underpaid, but this studio was a damn profitable business.

Kellgren and Stone continued their conversation over the next few nights in the bar across the street. They talked about starting their own studio and Zappa, who was there for some of the meetings, tried to warn them off: he had owned a studio in Cucamonga, California, where he had worked eighteen-hour days, eventually went broke, and even ended up, for a short period of time, in jail.

Kellgren, who was quoted in the article, read out loud from that week's issue of *Billboard* magazine:

> The talk of the industry is the amount of time being spent in the studio and the astronomical studio costs that have resulted from the Beatles and the Beach Boys setting a new standard for creative record making with *Pet Sounds* [Beach Boys, 1966] and *Sgt. Pepper's Lonely Hearts Club Band* [Beatles, 1967]. These artists have inspired others to experiment in the studio and take whatever time is necessary to realize their creative vision.

Kellgren explained that the more tracks the musicians had to work with, the more hours they spent in the studio, which meant more money for the studio owner. The Beatles had recorded *Sgt. Pepper's* using four-track tape machines, Mayfair Studios had an Ampex eight-track, and there was an upstart competitor named Scully demonstrating twelve-tracks around town. Musicians were becoming hooked on multitrack recording, which allowed them to add layers of instruments and endlessly mix their sounds. And controlling this transformation, much like a future generation of tech superstars, were the recording engineers.

Kellgren's talk was way too technical for Stone to understand. He only knew what he had read in a *Time* magazine cover story about this crazy new hippie subculture that had emerged. And so much of that subculture revolved around music.

Which Kellgren knew how to make.

And which Stone knew he could market.

Chris Stone learned his craft as a marketer first at Trader Vic's in Emeryville, California, where owner Victor Bergeron, the master drink-mixer himself and inventor of the Mai Tai, taught him how to pour. Stone shared his favorite story with Kellgren and Zappa: "Trader Vic's was the last place an army man stopped in for a drink before he went overseas. You know, fucking lines around the block. But they were there for more than a drink. That drink was the magic that was going to keep them alive and get them back home in one piece."

Stone then looked at Kellgren and said, "You've got the magic, Gary."

"And so?"

"So, how much does it cost to build a studio?"

Zappa told them about a brand-new room called Apostolic on Tenth Street in Greenwich Village with a hippie-vibe, twelve-track recorder, and one of the first solid-state consoles. Apostolic had cost $85,000 to build. The price seemed so unobtainable that Kellgren couldn't contain a smile.

Stone looked past Kellgren's expression though, did some quick math and saw his ticket out of Revlon. For safety's sake, he rounded the price up to $100,000, and he knew exactly where to get it.

THE COUNTESS

Ancky Revson had always liked Stone and his wife, Gloria. Her soon-to-be husband, Ben Johnson, was Stone's college roommate, who had a thing for rich, older women.

Johanna Catharina Christina (Ancky) de Knecht was the former wife of a French count who escaped the Nazis on a private yacht in 1939, when a storm diverted them to Monte Carlo and then to Cuba, where Johanna disembarked and subsequently made her way to New York. She sat out the war in America with nothing but the clothes on her back and the money she won playing mahjong during the passage.

To make ends meet, the twenty-five-year-old ex-countess modeled for Saks Fifth Avenue, where she was solicited by one of Charles Revson's assistants to meet their boss. Revlon executives were always on the lookout for attractive young models for the cosmetics mogul to meet, but this one he married. The couple bought a mansion in Rye, New York, had two sons and rarely saw each other. Revson ran the business and ran around, while Ancky raised the boys and managed their mansion before the inevitable divorce.

Suddenly rich and single from her settlement, Ancky explored the nearby Manhattan nightlife that she had missed out on as a suburban housewife. An investment in the Off-Broadway rock musical *Hair* paid off handsomely, so Ancky was looking for another hippie venture

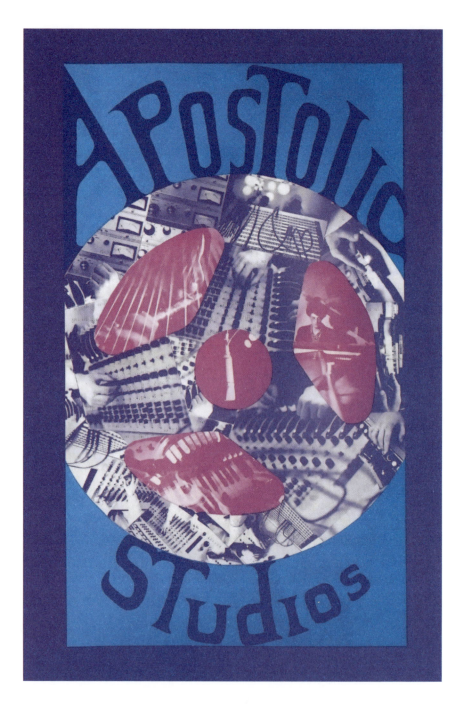

An Apostolic Studios poster from 1967 featuring a revolutionary new console design that would become the API, the premier US-made studio mixer of the seventies. Gary Kellgren discovered the Greenwich Village recording studio with the first twelve-track tape recorder.

to fund. Stone's timing was perfect when he paid her a visit at her twelve-acre estate in the early fall of 1967.

Ancky greeted Stone with a European-style kiss on both cheeks and invited him to join her out on the veranda. He had prepared a one-page business proposal for the "Recording Studio of Tomorrow," which he planned to franchise in New York, Nashville, Los Angeles, and London. Hotel rooms for traveling musicians were part of the original strategy.

Ancky didn't look at the paper, preferring to let Stone tell the story himself. His pitch went on for a half hour before she asked for her ledger and wrote a check to Stone for $100,000. Stone immediately excused himself and went off in search of a telephone. He got Kellgren on the line at Mayfair right away and couldn't contain himself: "I've got the money. Let's go."

Kellgren replied, "First, we need to talk to Wilson."

WILSON

Kellgren was setting up for a Velvet Underground session and, like everyone else at Mayfair Studios, he was waiting for the band's producer, Tom Wilson, to show up and get things rolling. Kellgren was planning to tell Wilson about his deal with Stone. But he was having a hard time organizing his thoughts amidst all the noise that was coming off the recording console. Lou Reed was distorting sounds with fuzz boxes plugged into his Gretsch guitar. The whole studio was a battle between distortion and feedback. Then, as if a fuse had just blown, everything went silent; and all eyes turned to the door where Tom Wilson had just entered.

A tall, handsome, Black man with mustache and goatee, wearing an antelope-suede overcoat, bell bottoms, and purple crepe shirt, Wilson made the rounds in the room; he slapped every palm before sitting down at the board and greeting Kellgren with his usual nickname: "So, what's happening here, Wiz?"

Wilson was a Texas-born, Harvard-educated producer, who had originally built his pop music credibility over at Columbia Records, where he was responsible for turning Bob Dylan onto folk rock with his breakthrough album, *Bringing It All Back Home*. Without their knowledge, Wilson also took Simon and Garfunkel's *Sounds of Silence* back into the studio after it initially failed and, by adding electric instruments and a subtle layer of echo, turned the folk song into a popular hit. He then moved to MGM/Verve, where he recorded an eclectic mix of jazz, folk, and rock, moving from Sun Ra, John Coltrane, and Herbie Mann to Pete Seeger, Connie Francis, and Hugh Masekela, to the Blues Project, Frank Zappa, and the Velvet Underground.

"The music was changing and Tom's ears were open," explained keyboardist Al Kooper, who Wilson paired with Dylan and the Blues Project.

In a *New York Times* profile, Kellgren was by Tom Wilson's side in all the pictures—the young, good-looking kid with bangs who was seated in front of a command center of blinking meters, dials, and plugs. Wilson originally defined the producer's role as part creative partner, part manager, part psychoanalyst, and part technical translator for artists who needed a parent around.

Finding a studio like Mayfair in those days was no easy feat, and once you found one you liked you never left for fear that a competing band would lock you out of the room. An industry connection introduced Wilson to Clair Krepps, a former Capitol Records engineer, who had built Mayfair, a new studio on the northeast side of Times Square and Forty-Seventh Street. Krepps had gained industry notoriety with the release of the loudest single ever manufactured, Manfred Mann's "Doo Wah Diddy." He was also the first recording engineer to import rich-sounding vocal mics and massive plate reverbs from Germany. But his real claim to fame was discovering young talent like Gary Kellgren who swept the floors, kept the bathroom tidy, and never let the producers down when he was behind the console.

For someone with so many hits, Wilson was uncharacteristically hands-off in the studio. Some of his artists had no idea what he did all day; he allowed them endless takes, while sitting there with a phone pressed to his ear doing business or sending flowers to last night's date. As usual, Wilson let Kellgren run the late-1967 sessions with the Velvets that would result in their classic proto-punk album, *White Light/White Heat*.

It was a challenging assignment. The band had worked at Mayfair and with Kellgren once before on the single "Sunday Morning" from their *Banana* album with Andy Warhol. This time, as if rebelling against that song's pop sentiment, the band members were continuously yelling to crank it up. Kellgren was struggling to get more than just the noise onto tape and because of the tension, he even missed a few cues. Band member John Cale wrote in his autobiography, "it was all this noise just smashing into more noise, but we felt that if we caught the excitement of a live performance on tape, we'd have achieved our one aim. We never quite realized that there were technical problems involved in turning [the volume] up past nine."

Kellgren sat with cigarette filters in his ears, struggling to separate the instruments, while trying to convince the band to turn things down. Out of frustration, he finally twirled the console knobs to the max, let the VU meters crash into the red zone, and exclaimed, "Go ahead . . . you do this. When you're done, just give me a call." He then abruptly left the room.

Kellgren had to go back into the studio with Frank Zappa that same night, anyway, though neither customer knew Kellgren's full schedule. Zappa and the Velvet Underground had a running feud in the music business during those years, which made this juggling act especially challenging for the young engineer. Working multiple studios, with multiple

> **"Go ahead ...
> you do this.
> When you're
> done, just give
> me a call."**
>
> Gary Kellgren,
> studio co-owner

artists at one time, was perhaps Kellgren's greatest talent and it became the secret sauce of the recording-studio conglomerate he would build.

Kellgren never got the chance to talk to Wilson about his new project that day and didn't take it to him later either. Starting right then and there, he always left all the business up to Stone.

MONEY

A soaking wet Frank Zappa walked into Mayfair Studios wearing his favorite monkey-fur jacket, with a stack of tape boxes in his arms. In those days, musicians protected their recordings like newborns, never leaving them in the studio overnight for fear that they'd be

CHAPTER ONE

stolen, confiscated for unpaid bills, or worse, recut by the label execs without permission. It was pouring outside, with lightning scorching the Times Square skies.

Kellgren and Zappa had been collaborating for two and a half months during the Summer of Love in this steamy midtown office building, with Kellgren bouncing between Frank Zappa's caffeine-charged tape constructions and the Velvet Underground's meth-fueled noise. At Zappa's request that night, Kellgren grabbed a metal microphone and stuck it out of the window like a human lightning rod to record the thunder. Dissatisfied with the results, Zappa urged the engineer to get even closer to the noise. Without hesitating, Kellgren crawled out the window and onto the ledge, seven stories above the pavement, to capture the unobstructed storm. The engineer's job was to help realize the art, while always making sure his client (Tom Wilson) looked good in front of his artists.

"In the studio, Tom Wilson was always bullshitting and laughing and joking, while Gary was focusing, focusing, focusing," Wilson's friend John Richo remembered.

Zappa and Kellgren had been "focusing" together for endless hours—creating a mash-up of original takes, orchestral leftovers, assorted voices, and tape machinations for what would become Zappa's tandem album release *We're Only in It for the Money* and *Lumpy Gravy*. With the artist seated cross-legged by his side, Kellgren cut and pasted the composition together bar by bar. In the studio, tape splicing was the pre-digital way to (literally) assemble a song from a musician's greatest licks. You could draw blood and accidentally obliterate genius, but this new tape-and-blade art form was ideal for making weird sounds, getting a decent or unique recording out of untrained musicians, and, oftentimes, covering up for their mistakes.

Gary and Frank, like everyone else, were both obsessed with what Beatles producer George Martin and his studio engineers had achieved with only four tracks of tape on *Sgt. Pepper's*. That summer at Mayfair, they copied the album onto a reel-to-reel so they could start and stop, rewind, and replay it to figure out exactly how Martin and his team had doubled the vocals, sped up (or slowed down) the band's instruments, and spliced in backward recordings.

Above and below: Musician Frank Zappa (far left), Gary Kellgren (seated), and bassist Roy Estrada (standing), listen to a playback of *We're Only in It for the Money*, while (above only) music producer Tom Wilson takes a phone call at Mayfair Studios, New York, in 1967.

CHAPTER ONE

The recording studio was the "new instrument." And many musicians couldn't keep their hands off the dials. Artists and producers alike now wanted to wrest control of their sound from the label-owned studios and their union engineers. This power play ultimately led to the opening of a new wave of independent recording studios like Mayfair, staffed by a younger, more compliant generation of audio freaks, who would do anything to get close to the music.

"The youth cultural revolt of the 1960s played out in the studio," wrote studio historian Susan Schmidt Horning. "Whereas the best hands in the profession had developed their expertise through years of experience, rock and roll was about youth, inexperience and experimentation."

Kellgren gave Zappa room to experiment. He was willing to spend endless hours in an airless, soundproof room, consuming a variety of stimulants, all to satisfy the creative whims of the musical maniac he was working for. And even in those early days, Kellgren's body was paying the price; Frank told *EQ Magazine* that the young engineer was "a suffering individual . . . he was recording 18 hours a day, and he had no private life, no social life. He was just run down . . . He would do maybe three or four bands per day, and it was just grinding him down. He was living on leapers [amphetamines] and beer."

Kellgren was responsible for the creepy whispering on the song "Are You Hung Up," where he threatened to "erase all the tape in the world." He didn't appear in the album's *Sgt. Pepper's*-homage cover that featured his clients Jimi Hendrix and Tom Wilson. However, a lightning bolt prominently blazes across the blue-black sky at the top of *Money*'s famous photo-composite as a possible nod to that rainy night in Times Square when Gary Kellgren proved he'd do anything, even risk electrocution, to capture his client's sound.

TAPE 2

STUDIO MAYFAIR STUDIOS, NY / RECORD PLANT NY

ARTIST	TITLE	FORMAT
Eric Burdon	"Sky Pilot"	Single
Fraternity of Man	"Don't Bogart Me"	Single
Soft Machine	*The Soft Machine*	Album
Traffic	*Traffic*	Album
Jimi Hendrix	*Electric Ladyland*	Album
Jimi Hendrix	"All Along the Watchtower"	Single
Jimi Hendrix	"Voodoo Chile"	Single
The Fool	*The Fool*	Album
Jimi Hendrix, John McLaughlin	*The Record Plant Sessions, 3/25/1969*	Bootleg Album

THE SCENE

Kellgren rode his Harley through the mid-sixties Manhattan streets. He was the image of hip, youthful confidence at all the city's cool music hangouts, with his Midwestern good looks and smile, long straight black hair and bangs. For someone who made his mark because of his ears, Kellgren's allure was really all about the eyes: they sparkled incandescent green.

Two years earlier, twenty-six-year-old Kellgren had ridden that bike from his home in Shenandoah, Iowa, to New York City. The former air force pilot had skipped out on a pregnant girlfriend at the altar and planned to save up money to go to the Sorbonne in Paris to study writing and art. Music was a way of reinventing himself at the time, and recording was only a way to make a living. He had sung in the high school choir and, like everyone else from his hometown, he regularly listened to the town's country radio stations, and

CHAPTER ONE

personally knew the two local brothers who had become rock stars, Don and Phil Everly.

Gary rode that bad bike everywhere—it was his trademark. He would park it outside of the clubs down in the Village where he would hang with the musicians during their twenty-minute-on-twenty-minute-off breaks, before heading over to the Albert Hotel to hear a basement jam and finishing the night on the West Side at Steve Paul's The Scene.

Located downstairs in a dilapidated tenement building on West Forty-Sixth Street and Eighth Avenue, The Scene nightclub attracted jet-setters, Broadway types, bikers, and Manhattan's moneyed elite. Unknowns like Pink Floyd, Jeff Beck, Traffic, Fleetwood Mac, the Chambers Brothers, and Johnny Winter played the club before their glory days. Linda (McCartney) Eastman was the house photographer. Tiny Tim, with his trademark ukulele, often opened the show.

Jimi Hendrix played at The Scene late into the night after most customers had been ushered out the doors. The nightclub's stage hosted a famous jam and bootleg featuring Hendrix, Jim Morrison, Johnny Winter, Buddy Miles, and members of the McCoys—a precursor to the Sunday night super-jams at Record Plant LA.

The Scene made a big impression on both Hendrix and Kellgren. Gary studied the way the owner personally catered to the celebrities, and Jimi decided that he wanted a club of his own. But first, Hendrix needed to finish his new record, and Tom Wilson suggested that he ask Kellgren for help.

Hendrix (or Hendricks as his name was misspelled on the tape box) and Kellgren had already worked together for four hot and humid sessions at Mayfair during July 1967. It was the first time Hendrix recorded on an eight-track and experimented with a wah-wah pedal that Frank Zappa had left in the room. Hendrix drank strawberry shakes while Kellgren showed off his tape tricks on the song "Burning of the Midnight Lamp" and the B-side, "The Stars that Play with Laughing Sam's Dice." Gary was always willing to stay late into the night to turn Jimi's hallucinations into music.

One night, Kellgren and Hendrix were in the middle of a "Star-Spangled Banner" sound experiment when Mayfair owner, Clair

Krepps, heard the console burning up with distortion and ran into the studio: "I saw this left-handed guitar player in there playing like mad. My first reaction was anger. Then I said to myself, 'What the hell.'"

Hendrix archivist and historian John McDermott explained: "There were a lot of talented engineers in town, but they weren't pulling up to the studio on a motorcycle and happy to go all night long if you were in the flow. Hendrix was treated like shit every time he had been at a recording studio. Gary was the first guy to make the artist feel like this was his domain. If you're an artist and you finally have an opportunity to create your sound in a professional recording studio, in a supportive environment, that's a very big deal."

Keyboardist Al Kooper added: "At the time, there were no available studios in New York. If you were going to get in, you needed to own the place. Like I said to Hendrix, 'You want in, you want to run it, you got to own it.'"

Hendrix didn't want to own a studio (at least not yet), but he needed a place to work on his new album that was as comfortable as The Scene; somewhere he could play loud, late into the night, and hide out from the Warner Bros. executives, somewhere he could experiment and jam.

While seated in one of The Scene's private banquettes, Kellgren and Wilson told Hendrix about their plans for a new type of recording studio, one that was more like a living room than a lab. Hendrix seemed interested and said he'd be happy to check it out when it was ready.

Stone arrived just as Hendrix got up to take the stage, and he took the opportunity to chat privately with Wilson about cutting him in on their new studio venture; a steady stream of business was worth, at least, a 10 percent under-the-table ownership. Kellgren and Stone had rehearsed the pitch, but just as with Ancky Revson, Wilson didn't need to be sold. Having first dibs on the studio and access to Kellgren's ears mattered more to him than the money.

Stone and Kellgren went right to work, forming their first corporation, which they called Abaddon, after the Angel of the Abyss. One night Gary and Marta were sitting across from each other at the kitchen table, brainstorming names for the studio. With a nod

Above: Jimi Hendrix with Band of Gypsy's drummer Buddy Miles at Record Plant NY in 1968.
Below: Artist Joan Baez backstage with Jimi Hendrix on August 12, 1968 at the "Operation Airlift Biafra Benefit" held at Steve Paul's The Scene nightclub in Manhattan.

LIVING ROOM STUDIO

to Andy Warhol's art studio, "The Factory," they started playing around with the names "Record Factory" and "Music Factory," as a clear indication that the room would be primed for production.

"How about the word 'Plant'?" Marta asked, looking for a word that was synonymous with "factory."

Gary liked it, and he spent the rest of the night designing the studio's soon-famous bubble-type logo.

The name "Record Plant" was often assumed to be a double-entendre for marijuana, which Wilson/Kellgren had just taken mainstream with the Fraternity of Man hit single, "Don't Bogart Me." During 1967, Wilson had eight records in the *Billboard 100,* five at one time, and on average he was producing two albums a week.

If Andy Warhol could mass-produce art with a silkscreen in Midtown Manhattan, Tom Wilson could create a factory for sound nearby.

FORTY-FOURTH STREET

Late one night, after a series of press interviews for his first US tour, Gary Kellgren asked Jimi Hendrix if he wanted to grab a drink at The Scene. Eager to get away from the media, Hendrix agreed.

They hailed a cab and raced crosstown through the wintry streets of the West Side. The cab passed The Scene and, instead of stopping, turned a few corners and pulled up in front of 321 West Forty-Fourth Street, an early-1930s office building, west of Times Square, that had audio in its bones. The building was the original East Coast corporate headquarters of Vitagraph Studios, which pioneered sound-on-film before Warner Bros. acquired them to produce the world's first talkie, Al Jolson's *The Jazz Singer*.

A security guard waved them through a lobby door and into a large, empty retail space. Kellgren lit a cigarette while threading a tape reel onto a portable Sony recorder that was sitting atop a scuffed, metal office desk. It was apparent that this had all been staged. Having planned it out earlier that day on the phone with his partner, Kellgren wanted to make sure that Hendrix was committed to booking the studio before they signed the lease.

Kellgren pressed play, turned up the volume, and the room rang out with the sounds of "Burning of the Midnight Lamp," which they had finished at Mayfair the prior summer, and which later ended up

CHAPTER ONE

on the B-side of the US release of the Hendrix's single "All Along the Watchtower." Hendrix told a biographer about the mood the song put him in: "I think [every musician] can understand the feeling when you're traveling, that no matter what your address, there is no place you can call home."

"Burning" failed to chart when it was released in the UK in August 1967, but that didn't make a difference to Hendrix. The recording touched him so deeply that he invited Kellgren to work with him on his next LP. With Gary by his side, he didn't need a producer anymore. He would make all the decisions, book all the studio time that he wanted, and work with any musician who stopped by to jam.

Kellgren and Hendrix talked about sound the same way. They both knew airplanes. Kellgren had flown in the air force and Hendrix had served in the army's revered 101st Airborne, so when Hendrix said he was looking for "air sounds" Kellgren knew exactly what he meant. The engineer also shared Hendrix's way of describing sound in terms of colors, clinically called "synesthesia," which some scientists say is the "hidden sense."

Now five months later, Hendrix was watching Gary build him an imaginary studio. With a fat piece of chalk in hand, Kellgren added white lines to the drips of paint that covered the concrete floor. He helped Hendrix visualize the space by explaining that "this was the studio lounge," which would be decorated with pillow chairs, and art by Warhol and Dali, making it a perfect place to crash, relax, and listen to playbacks.

He then walked Hendrix's imagination into an enormous control room, which was large enough to turn any recording session into a happening for friends. He sketched out where he would put one of the new twelve-track tape machines and fill most of the space with a long mixing console with English-style sliders and controls.

Then, quietly constructing the largest box of all, Kellgren surrounded Hendrix with draped walls, each covered with imported Moroccan cloths, and all up-lit with psychedelic lighting. This was Studio A, he added, while chalking out a small box in the corner for a booth where Jimi could record his vocals in privacy.

Kellgren told Hendrix the details—how he had money coming in from a cosmetics millionaire, the same person who was behind *Hair*.

He also reminded Hendrix that Bob Dylan's producer Tom Wilson was a partner in the studio.

Kellgren then handed Hendrix an acoustic guitar and walked him into the far corner of the abandoned space where he used his shoulder to open a heavy, metal fire door. There by the garbage cans, Hendrix played a few riffs that reverberated up the stairwell and the guitarist smiled, loving what he heard.

With a private performance by the biggest rock star of the day bouncing to the rooftops of Times Square, Kellgren went in for the close:

"Welcome to your new studio, Jimi. Welcome home."

WHERE'S JIMI?

The opening of Record Plant NY was intended to be a music industry extravaganza. Tom Wilson called every musician and producer in town to stop by; Stone invited the money guys; and Kellgren worked with a team of after-hours Broadway carpenters to complete the job on time. They mailed out a Victorian-style, opium-themed invitation:

> HIPSTERS AND OLD HITTITES
> YOU ARE INVITED TO A POPPY PARTY
> RECORD PLANT RECORDING STUDIO
> OFFICIAL OPENING CELEBRATION
> TUESDAY, MARCH 19, 1968, 6 PM

As the date approached, Kellgren finally broke the news to Stone that the studio wasn't ready. Hendrix had asked to use the room, but even he had to be turned away. Kellgren promised that he could make all the lights on the console work, play loud music, and spin the reels on the tape machines, though no live session work was possible. The opening was still on.

Stone arrived late from a business appointment, dressed in his Revlon uniform—black suit and black tie. Marta had sewn Gary a shirt with a ruffled collar and cuffs, and satin tunic; his hair was slicked across his forehead and, as always, a cigarette was lodged between his fingers. Kellgren was uncharacteristically outgoing as a parade of business types came in for a drink and a tour. Everyone was

CHAPTER ONE

there except for Jimi. Nobody had the guts to tell Gary that Hendrix had a gig up in Ottawa.

As the evening wore on, Kellgren became agitated by the absence of his prized customer. He wondered if he was over at the Fillmore East, which had just opened ten days earlier. Gary kept asking, "Where's Jimi?"

Stone finally broke the news that Hendrix was on tour, but quickly added that Ancky was on her way over with an acceptable substitute— Beatle George Harrison. Kellgren was more than satisfied but, unfortunately, Stone had heard her wrong. Ancky showed up a half-hour later with ersatz celebrity George *Hamilton*, who toured the studio wearing an open-necked Nehru jacket.

George Hamilton was no George Harrison, and this put Kellgren into a tailspin. He pulled his partner aside and blamed him for driving Hendrix away with his accountant friends, investors, and business-suit attire. Stone fought back, saying: "You're lucky Hendrix isn't here. He doesn't know your living room studio sounds more like a basement . . ."

Confrontations were few and far between for the partners over the years. Besides, it was really Kellgren's business; at the time, Stone and Wilson each only had 10 percent of the new venture, with the remaining 80 percent split evenly between Ancky and Gary.

The party was energized by the arrival of the cast of *Hair* who stopped by to bless Record Plant as hippiedom's new creative home. Wilson trotted executives from Warner Bros., ABC/Dunhill, CBS, and MGM/Verve around the facility, pointing out the comfortable and casual vibe that Kellgren had created. Someone had a copy of the Beatles' new single, "Lady Madonna," which had just been released in the UK, and Kellgren demoed it over the control room's assortment of Tannoy and JBL loudspeakers.

It was really Ancky's party. Dressed elegantly in white, she reveled in the attention. The studio opening came right after the cast album of *Hair* had won a Grammy and the rock musical was scheduled to

Opposite: Invitation to the first gala opening party for Record Plant NY on March 19, 1968 (above). Photographs from the party (below) show founders Chris Stone and Gary Kellgren, music producer Tom Wilson, celebrity guest George Hamilton, Hendrix producer Chas Chandler, and Gary's wife Marta.

hit the Broadway stage. While her ex, Charles Revson, was busy building a bigger yacht and flaunting his new trophy wife, Ancky was in the vortex of this colorful, high-energy youth culture. She owned a recording studio, so now all the handsome, young rock stars came to her.

Once everyone left, Kellgren asked Stone to join him for a drink in the control room. Stone mixed himself a gin and tonic, while Kellgren cracked open a beer.

"Great party . . ." Chris said.

"Except for Jimi."

"Well, I gave you a Beatle," Stone laughed.

"Listen Stone, these parties are very important."

"Parties? What 'other' parties?"

"With all those stereos they're selling, they're going to need more records. They're going to need more record plants to keep up with all the business."

"How about getting this studio working first?"

Kellgren noticed a clock on the control room wall and pulled it down, as if it didn't belong—this was the first and last clock ever to hang in a Record Plant studio. Casually tossing it into the trash, Kellgren remarked: "We've got all the time in the world."

JUST A PHASE

It wasn't the new studio that made Gary Kellgren famous. It wasn't even the word on the street that Jimi Hendrix had block-booked an unproven room to record his new album.

Kellgren's audio-engineering street cred took off during the spring of 1968 because of the aggressive, acid rock "swooshing sound" he created on the Eric Burdon anti-war anthem, "Sky Pilot." The air force pilot-turned-recording engineer made an analog tape machine sound like a jet hurtling through space on the seven-minute, two-sided single. This technique involved playing two identical tapes simultaneously on two machines, while slowing down the tempo on one of the reels with a hand on the metal rim of the tape called the flange (hence, the technique was sometimes called "flanging"). Much like a sculptor shapes clay, Kellgren shaped sounds.

LIVING ROOM STUDIO

Gary Kellgren didn't invent "phasing" (another name for the technique). The sound effect was reportedly first developed by Les Paul, before it made the circuit out to Gold Star Studios in Los Angeles, then over to Olympic Studios in London, where it was famously used on Small Faces' "Itchycoo Park." The EMI engineers at Abbey Road in London automated the process with a still secret device that John Lennon was the first to call "the flange." Kellgren's "Sky Pilot" mix made the sound effect famous again and, in the process, it brought industry attention to its creator and his new studio.

It was because of that phasing sound that Bill Szymczyk (pronounced *sim-zick*), then chief engineer at the Hit Factory in New York, gave his old friend Gary Kellgren a call. "I heard this record that Kellgren engineered that had phasing on it, and for the life of me I couldn't figure out how to do it. So, tail between my legs, I called him up and asked, 'I want to bring over a tape and I want you to help me phase it,' and he goes, 'Okay, fine, bring it over.'"

Szymczyk and Kellgren first met in 1964 at a small songwriter's studio, Dick Charles Recording, in the United Artists Building on Forty-Ninth Street and Seventh Avenue. Dick Charles was where the Gerry Goffin–Carole King hit "The Locomotion" was initially recorded, and Neil Diamond also made a demo there that became the final release of "Cherry, Cherry." The songwriters used the monaural discs that Szymczyk and Kellgren cut for them to sell their songs to the music publishers. Kellgren and Szymczyk made $70 per week sitting in front of two mono tape machines and a console with two big knobs, trying to keep the VU-meter needle from going into the red. The fledgling engineers hustled the songwriters out of a nickel for every extra dub they sold. Szymczyk continued:

> So, I went over to Record Plant and Gary's there plugging
> eight million things into this box. It's got ins and outs, dials
> and shit, and I'm looking at it going, "What the fuck is this?
> What's he doing?" Then he does the sound just like this
> [vocalizing a jet engine noise] and gives me exactly what I
> want, right? I go, "Oh, man" and I was hooked, I said, "Okay,
> I got to have one of those boxes."

Then, Gary started to laugh. He had had his maintenance guy throw a bunch of shit together in a box that did absolutely nothing. Nothing was inside. Behind my back, Kellgren had secretly been slowing down the tape, playing with the tape reel to get the phasing sound. Kellgren was an artist at phasing, and I learned how to do it from him.

Years later, as a tip of the hat to his friend, Szymczyk would place Kellgren's phasing stamp on the finale of the Eagles' song "Life in the Fast Lane" on the band's fifth studio album, *Hotel California*.

FIRST JAM

Eddie Kramer emerged from the terminal at JFK Airport in New York like rock royalty: his flowing, black fireman's jacket was draped on his shoulders like a cape and it made it clear that he was not just an ordinary recording engineer in from London. The South African studio superstar was Stone and Kellgren's first hire. Gary had chased him over the phone for months and Tom Wilson closed the deal while he was in London working at Olympic Studios with the Animals. Stone hired a prestigious Wall Street law firm to expedite his visa.

After building Studio A and shaking it down with Jimi Hendrix's opening act, Soft Machine, Kellgren was burned out. He needed someone to back him up with their growing list of clients—especially Jimi. And there was nobody more proven and trusted than Kramer, with whom Jimi had worked on his first two albums.

Kramer took a cab into Manhattan and stayed at Gary's apartment that night. His first day in America, Kellgren drove him down to Record Plant and surprised Jimi with his new engineer. "I walked in the studio and Jimi looked at me and he says, 'Where the hell have you been?'" Kramer remembered.

Turning to the Scully twelve-track machine, Jimi then added, "Hey man, check this out. We've got four more tracks we can mess with."

"I'm the one who's got to mix it, Jimi," Kramer replied.

Later known for his work with the Rolling Stones, Led Zeppelin, and Kiss, Kramer had just recorded Jimi Hendrix's second album *Axis Bold as Love* at Olympic Studios and was a fixture in the London studio scene in the late sixties.

"The whole concept of me coming over to the States was to continue my work with Hendrix," Kramer added.

Stone remembered it this way: "We were building a second room (Studio B) and it needed to be more than just Gary. Kellgren did this many times over the years as we got busier and busier. Gary would bring the customers in, then turn them over to somebody like Eddie Kramer, and then he'd go work with somebody else. It was the way we built the business. It was all about him. Everyone wanted to work with Kellgren."

Hendrix's sound-effects designer, Roger Mayer, made this comparison: "Jimi worked with Kramer. He fell in love with Kellgren."

He also fell in love with Kellgren's twelve-track tape machine and living room studio design which, if anything, was what ultimately broke up his band, the Jimi Hendrix Experience.

"We just opened the studio up and all our friends came down," Jimi explained to a journalist, "We wanted to jam somewhere, so we just went to the studio, the best place to jam [laughs], and brought about fifty of our friends along."

Kramer was there on the night of April 18, 1968, for the first *Electric Ladyland* recording session at Record Plant, when thirteen takes of the song "Long Hot Summer Night" turned into what Hendrix's bass-player Noel Redding called "marathon twiddling sessions." Hangers-on from The Scene stopped by and the scene in Record Plant Studio A soon got out of hand. Unlike other places in town, you could openly smoke pot during Record Plant sessions; there was always a bowl of rolled joints on the console when Jimi was in town.

"Jimi would turn up in the studio with a dozen hangers-on who you've never seen before in your life. I just couldn't communicate with him. I felt like an alien," Hendrix's producer, Chas Chandler, was quoted as saying.

If any session defined the new Hendrix in-studio experience, it was the recording of "Voodoo Chile" in early May, which featured a constant, all-night back and forth between Record Plant and The Scene. Musicians carried their drinks and the nightclub atmosphere into the nearby studio, where the final mix included clinking cocktail glasses, chatter, and party sounds. "Hendrix got everybody around a microphone and we started talking as if we were in a club.

CHAPTER ONE

That's when Jimi started using the recording studio in a creative way—as his new instrument," Jefferson Airplane bass player Jack Casady remembered.

Noel Redding looked back: "I came into the studio [Record Plant] and there were thirty people in the booth when we were trying to work, and I said, 'Can I sit down? I'm just the bass player.' You couldn't even move; it was a party, not a session. I took it out on Jimi. I told him to get all the people out. He just said, 'Relax man.' I had a big go at him and I walked out in front of all those people."

Within a month, Redding and Chandler were both gone. And the jam sessions at Record Plant continued for two more years.

Even Eddie Kramer couldn't keep up with all the work that Hendrix was generating. So, Kellgren raided the other studios in New York for engineers. He hired Roy Cicala (the eventual owner of Record Plant NY) from A&R Recording; Bob Hughes and his wife, Fran, came over from Mirasound; R&B engineer Jack Adams worked and partied with Hendrix by night and somehow managed to stay awake for advertising jingle dates first thing the next morning. Kellgren turned a generation of young, hungry kids such as Todd Rundgren, Thomas Erdelyi (aka Tommy Ramone), and John Lennon's future producer, Jack Douglas, into the leading producers, artists, and engineers of their day.

"Jimi Hendrix offered me a joint in the studio," Douglas told an interviewer. "I thought, 'This is unbelievable! What a great job.'"

The recording of Jimi's biggest hit single, Dylan's "All Along the Watchtower," was a studio-wide effort. Originally recorded in England, "Watchtower" was reworked countless times at Record Plant throughout the summer of 1968, with Hendrix trying out numerous engineers and laying down multiple versions of the song's famed guitar solo. Kramer's name is on the tape box of the final mix, though Jimmy Robinson, Kellgren's confidant and Band of Gypsys' sax player, believed that "Gary's sounds are all over that record."

"I'd say there was a lot of Gary and a lot of me," Kramer remarked.

Hendrix's *Electric Ladyland* topped the charts for thirty-seven weeks when it first debuted in the fall of 1968. The guitarist was now more motivated than ever to start using Gary's living room studio as his "second instrument."

Gary Kellgren with Jimi Hendrix at the Datamix console in the original Studio A at Record Plant NY, August, 1968. With an engineer like Kellgren by his side, Hendrix no longer needed a producer and could finally take control of his music.

CHAPTER ONE

FOXY LADIES

It was around that time that the relationship between Hendrix and Kellgren worsened. Some say it had to do with Jimi's groupies.

"I have a feeling that Gary had a relationship with [Jimi's girlfriend] Fayne Pridgeon," archivist and historian John McDermott said. "I just have a feeling that there was a little bit of sandpaper between Jimi and Gary as a result that never got cleared up."

Stone put it this way: "No matter how close we were to our customers—and we were very close—there was still this line that needed to be respected. His ladies were getting uncomfortably close."

Hendrix walked into The Scene one night with Devon Wilson and spotted Fayne Pridgeon at a table snuggling up close to his engineer. Jimi had already had words with Devon about the way she flirted with Gary behind the console. But Hendrix was even more possessive with Fayne—she was his real "Foxy Lady."

Determined to break things up, Jimi jumped into Fayne's lap while Devon moved in on Kellgren. The two couples laughed, touched, and exchanged sexual innuendos. Then the women made eye contact, shared a sly whisper, and excused themselves to the ladies' room. There, they dusted their noses with blow, gossiped about Jimi and his engineer, and Fayne chuckled about what just happened: "Did you see Gary's face when Jimi sat in my lap? I nearly died. Jimi's always doing something like that. You never know what he's gonna do next."

On the way out of the bathroom, they ran into Eric Clapton, who had been waiting for Devon. She enjoyed the attention, grabbed the rising-star guitarist by the arm, and swept him back to the table, where she made it clear that she had other intentions. With Clapton, Hendrix, and Kellgren talking shop, Devon whispered into Fayne's ear and she nodded with a wink that it was time for them all to leave.

Hendrix and his two "Electric Ladies" ultimately exited arm in arm to spend the night together at his Greenwich Village apartment. Kellgren and Clapton were left alone with the shared realization that Devon, not Hendrix, had just shown them who was in charge.

MUSIC TELEVISION

Another factor played a role in the eventual split between Kellgren and Hendrix—money.

LIVING ROOM STUDIO

A widely circulated Hendrix interview in *Rolling Stone* magazine described a two-hour drive in his Aston-Martin from Woodstock, New York, to Record Plant, where he was scheduled to record that afternoon. Jimi complained to the interviewer that he was paying the studio owners an exorbitant $200 per hour and that they "take advantage of long-hair musicians."

The publicity hurt Kellgren's feelings more than the studio's business. Record Plant's reputation was so strong and the number of available studios in New York was so limited, that the controversy quickly passed. The studio charged Hendrix top dollar for his studio time and his block-booking meant Hendrix could be billed even when he was not there. Despite the $200 number he cited in *Rolling Stone*, Hendrix was actually paying Record Plant $160 per hour for sixteen-track recording, with tape running another $120 per reel. A night of experimentation in the studio could cost up to $2,500. But, Chris Stone argued, "There was always a room for Jimi anytime he needed it and those sessions got him his first hit single and his first number one album in the US."

Even though *Electric Ladyland* was the only album Hendrix completed while there, the Record Plant sessions ultimately gave the Hendrix estate an endless source of post-mortem material, offering historians a treasure trove of insights into the creative process of Hendrix's short but inspired recording career. One of his biographers equated the inventiveness of Hendrix's Record Plant sessions to "Charlie Parker's alternative takes for Savoy and to Picasso's studies."

> **"There was always a room available for Jimi anytime he needed it ..."**
>
> Chris Stone,
> studio co-owner

One popular bootleg of Jimi jamming with jazz guitarist John McLaughlin was recorded there in March 1969, with Buddy Miles on drums and Dave Holland on bass. Miles Davis stopped by Record Plant NY Studio A for a high-volume playback of his recently recorded album, *In a Silent Way*.

"Back then it seemed to me that they [Kellgren and Stone] were taking advantage of Hendrix. They would let the tape run, or they'd

CHAPTER ONE

just let him jam, and do whatever he did. Which is great. Thank God they did. Thank God that somebody ran those tape recorders," engineer Eddie Kramer said.

Eddie Kramer never fit in with Gary Kellgren's crew. Studio employees remembered him as demanding and (rightfully) critical of the finicky Scully twelve-track recorder and noisy Datamix console. Studio A's hollow walls and thin control room glass weren't the quality soundproofing he was used to.

"I came from a school of thought in England where the engineers were strict; they knew their shit. And if you grow up in that atmosphere where it's got to be done right, this whole noise thing is not an option. So yeah, I am afraid I was a bit demanding," Kramer said.

Kramer had a vision for "what's next." He pushed (against Stone's objection) to buy their first Ampex sixteen-track recorder to keep Jimi happy. He wanted them to build a room with better acoustics. And he felt he was being financially short-changed by his employers. Not surprisingly, he didn't stick around very long. "I was at Record Plant slightly less than a year, and then I realized, 'Wait a minute. I'm getting paid what?' I took a leaf out of a few engineers' books, about not being tied to any studio, and went out on my own."

Kramer also encouraged Jimi to build his own studio, one that would make Record Plant pale in comparison. It was no secret how successful Record Plant had become and other music business execs, including Hendrix's management team, wanted in on the action. Future Electric Lady Studios president Jim Marron told an interviewer that, in 1968 alone, Hendrix spent $300,000 on studio time at Record Plant NY. A feasibility study concluded that it would be cheaper in the long run for Jimi to own his own studio.

The business side of music was never of much interest to Hendrix, though the idea of being able to come and go in the studio as he pleased was appealing. Hendrix agreed to spend up to $500,000 on a room of his own as designed by an inexperienced twenty-one-year-old nightclub architect, named John Storyk.

"At the time, it was unheard of that an artist would own their own studio, let alone one south of Forty-Second Street. To build a studio of that magnitude and of that professionalism, was something extremely new," Storyk said. "The actual creation of Electric Lady—its size, its scope, its feeling, its look, its concept—came about because Jimi rejected the studios he was working in [i.e., Record Plant] and wanted to have something that was very, very different. He wanted to have one where the atmosphere could change and become very personalized. He wanted it to be very private and very safe."

Kellgren worked hard to keep Hendrix's business, but the big change at Record Plant, and what ultimately ended Hendrix's long-term residence there, came fifteen months after the studio first opened, when Chris and Gary were approached by a buyer and sold out. Kellgren told his former employer, Clair Krepps, that he was now a millionaire.

The birth of Record Plant in the late sixties coincided with the birth of cable television. It was one of the largest cable companies, Television Communications Corp. (TVC), that made the unexpected offer to buy out Kellgren and Stone. Long before MTV, the company wanted to add a music channel to their new pay-TV programming mix, which was why buying Record Plant appeared to make sense.

"Yeah, it was a real fairy tale that all of this happened. In those days, very few people knew anything about cable TV. It was kind of a rich man's toy and was just starting to grow. TVC came to us, and we thought, what the hell, let's build a studio in LA with their money," Stone recalled.

The timing was right. Kellgren was becoming hesitant about his partnership with Stone. He was also spending most of his time in LA looking for space for the next Record Plant, while Stone was still running the New York studio for TVC. The partners never told their new owners that they were about to lose their prized client and that the recording industry was undergoing a seismic geographic shift.

TAPE 3

STUDIO	RECORD PLANT LA	
ARTIST	TITLE	FORMAT
Hedge & Donna	*All the Friendly Colours*	Album
The Flying Burrito Brothers	"Wild Horses"	Single

GO WEST

Chris Stone said it was Hendrix who started them thinking about making a move out to LA: "Jimi came in one day jumping up and down because he'd been to LA on tour and visited this studio with [Animals vocalist] Eric Burdon. Zappa was working there too. He had no idea where it was or even what it was called, but he said they had something that made his guitar sound amazing. He told Gary, 'You gotta hear it!' So, Kellgren told me, 'Stone, we gotta go to LA.'"

Recording studios were in the middle of a technology arms race and an obsessive audio whiz kid named Tom Hidley, out in Los Angeles, had cracked the code for a speaker box and studio-control-room design that could approach what musicians and engineers were hearing on stage.

LA hi-fi magnate Earl "Madman" Muntz first discovered Hidley in the late-fifties and put him to work building the first car stereo for Frank Sinatra. For a time, he worked in maintenance at A&R Recording in New York before returning to LA to build TTG (Two Terrible Guys) Studios to service Tom Wilson's acts.

"In the early days, most studios were built for orchestral things, instrumental things, big bands, and so on," Hidley remembered. "Our first clients at TTG were Eric Burdon and the Animals, and Frank Zappa, and they loved noise, lots of noise. And, of course, the rooms couldn't handle all the reflections, and there simply was not enough control of the extreme bottom end."

So, Hidley went to work. He built an even larger speaker box and packed it with two large woofers, then experimented with circuitry tricks. Most importantly, he and Kellgren endlessly listened. He

LIVING ROOM STUDIO

calculated that he could squeeze an extra 10 percent out of the box by building the speakers into the wall soffit, and that's when he discovered the real, audacious bass that the rock and rollers were missing.

"The difference was so apparent that, suddenly, every musician had to hear my new speakers. The news in the industry traveled fast in those days. And soon everyone heard about us because of Hendrix," Hidley recalled.

Hidley's loudspeakers became the centerpiece of a legendary control-room design that was ultimately key to Record Plant's success. With just the right measurements and a ceiling that directed the sound behind the console, Hidley created a new and transformative listening experience for musicians. "The name of the game in the seventies in terms of the control room was loud, clean, and punchy," he told an interviewer.

Kellgren's wife, Marta, worked at American Airlines, and Kellgren and Stone used her perks to fly first class out to the West Coast. This was the first of innumerable transcontinental flights for the partners. Stone saw a big change in Kellgren during those trips—he loved acting rich.

Once the partners landed at LAX, they grabbed a cab to TTG Studios, near the crossroads of Sunset and Highland in Hollywood, to hear what all the excitement was about. If Record Plant was a living room, TTG was more of a finished basement. But Hendrix was right—the control room speakers were exceptional, with full, round bass, and clean high-end.

Stone couldn't hear the difference but he could see the excitement in Kellgren's eyes. And when Hidley gave them a tour of his shop and showed them a prototype twenty-four-track tape machine he was building, Kellgren couldn't contain himself. "We've gotta have this guy," Kellgren exclaimed, leaving it up to Stone to figure out how to pay the bill.

As if Hidley's technical prowess wasn't enough reason for the studio millionaire to move out west, a visit to Monkee Peter Tork's party house with a panoramic view of the San Fernando Valley closed the deal. The house was built for fun. Guests dove out of the upstairs window into a backyard pool filled with naked swimmers.

CHAPTER ONE

Gary was obsessed with Peter Tork's pool, and his comment the next morning would haunt Stone for years: "Record Plant LA is going to be just like that house—music, parties, a sauna, and a big, bad, naked pool. There's gotta be a pool."

HIPPIE HEF

The Record Plant partners toured the Troubadour and Whisky a Go Go, and other LA musician hangouts to get a taste of the local scene. None of the spaces gave Kellgren the design direction he was looking for. The house parties in the Hills were "The Scenes" in LA in 1969—that is, until the Manson Murders scared everyone into hiding later that summer.

There was one more Sunset Boulevard night spot the partners still needed to check out. Kellgren's sister, Aleda Michelle, was a Playboy Bunny and she had invited them over to the LA Playboy Club, which was becoming a hot spot for the city's rockers. Hugh Hefner's *Playboy After Dark* TV series first aired that summer, featuring intimate, living room performances by the Grateful Dead, Steppenwolf, Iron Butterfly, Ike & Tina Turner, and other bands.

If The Scene was the inspiration for the first Record Plant in New York, the Playboy Club on Sunset Boulevard in Los Angeles was the actual blueprint for how Kellgren and Stone turned their original NY living room studio into an LA penthouse pad. Gary once told Chris that he wanted to be the "Hippie Hef."

A fan of the *Playboy* centerfolds since high school, Kellgren admired how Hefner integrated a revolving party into his business lifestyle, offering his guests a chance to share his home—a place where they could talk, screw, or get stoned. The LA Playboy Club featured a game room and bowling alley, twenty-four-hour kitchen, a Jacuzzi, and a high-decibel, custom-crafted stereo. It was all super-locked-down secure.

The Playboy Club had everything Kellgren wanted in his exclusive rock-star studio. And Record Plant LA's interior would use similar hardwood walls, stonework, mirrors, sliding glass doors, and decorative art—features that were more characteristic of a home in the Hollywood Hills than a recording facility.

"It was all about mood, environment, relaxation of the musicians for their creative ideas," Tom Hidley recalled. "This was all Gary. We built him all the stuff that he asked for and sat back and wondered 'Is this really going to work?'"

THIRD STREET

Kellgren had a knack for finding the right spaces. The former film studio that he leased for Record Plant LA at 8456 West Third Street near La Cienega Boulevard had long, winding hallways and thick, Mexican-stucco walls. There was a large dirt parking lot and a warehouse that was being used to produce a Saturday-morning TV show for kids.

Kellgren and Stone flew in and out of town to check on the state of the studio construction. They hired anyone who could wield a sledgehammer and work for $1.25 an hour; some of this early crew stayed on long enough to learn how to record. Construction didn't always go smoothly. Kellgren once walked into a nearly completed room and ordered the crew to start over. Another time, Chris's nephew, Mike D. Stone, and his friends removed a bearing beam and brought the roof down on their heads.

"Once everything was down to the studs, Tom Hidley joined Kellgren to handle the acoustical design and together they built the recording studio of their dreams," Mike D. Stone remembered.

With so much of the music now being assembled on tape as opposed to performed live, the need to isolate the instruments from one another in an open-air studio became the primary acoustical challenge. Hidley's breakthrough was first to deaden the sound in the room to minimize unwanted reverberation, and then to trap the instrument sound waves in place with moveable half-walls, called "gobos," which, in keeping with the aesthetics of the times, were elaborately tie-dyed.

It was up to inexperienced techs to arrange the gobos and mics, and to figure out how to make finicky analog audio electronics work. Record Plant was built on a generation of kids with blind ambition and no need for money, who would do anything to get close to the musicians.

Phil Schier was Lou Reed's Syracuse University roommate and a former Velvet Underground roadie who, by chance, ran into Gary Kellgren on Sunset Boulevard while delivering pastrami sandwiches

CHAPTER ONE

for Greenblatt's Deli. Gary hired him on the spot to join the underpaid-but-happy Record Plant LA construction/engineering crew. Schier recalled Studio A's first paying customer: "We finally got the Quad Eight console and Ampex tape machines all wired up in Studio A, and turned it all on, and started to get things right. We did a few test sessions and then, just as we were figuring out the console, just as it was all running for the very first time . . . somebody came into the room and gave us the news: 'We just booked the Flying Burrito Brothers and they're on their way!'"

Gary didn't know the console. The room was never used. But still somehow they got the session onto tape.

"And what did we record?" Schier asked rhetorically. "We recorded 'Wild Horses.' Yes, that first session in Studio A was a version [not the final version] of 'Wild Horses'."

> # "Here was Hollywood with its luxurious lifestyle and—can you believe it—just a bunch of shitty, jive-ass studios!"
>
> Gary Kellgren,
> studio co-owner, engineer

The band was oblivious to the drama inside the control room and liked what they heard, so much so that band leader, Gram Parsons, called Keith Richards of the Rolling Stones—in town after the disastrous concert at Altamont Speedway—to come over and check the studio out.

"The fucking Rolling Stones!!!" was how Chris Stone first heard the news from Kellgren.

"Are we ready?" Stone asked his partner from a temporary desk in his new corner office.

"You just head out to the clubs to spread the word that Mick Jagger will be recording here tonight . . . and Stone . . ."

"Yes?"

"If you see a couple of big, ugly Colombians at the front door, make sure to let them in."

ALWAYS UNDER CONSTRUCTION

A red brick with Jimi Hendrix's name on it arrived in a brown-paper

LIVING ROOM STUDIO

package at the front desk of Record Plant NY where he was still working. The silk-screened message on the brick announced:

RECORD PLANT OPENING NITE PARTY
LA'S 1st HUNCHY PUNCHY RECORDING STUDIOS
8456 W. 3RD ST. L.A.
DEC. 4, 1969, 6-11 P.M.
BRING YOUR BRICK AND BUILD OUR WALL
DRESS . . . BELLS & RIBBONS, SATIN AND SPANGLES

The brick invitation was the talk of the music business and caused pandemonium at the post office. It was proudly displayed on executive desks and fancy coffee tables awaiting the big night. Over the phone, Phil Spector freaked out the new LA receptionist when he threatened to kill the person who had misspelled his name "Specter" on his brick invitation.

Hendrix called the LA office to congratulate Gary on the new studio, trying to patch things up after having trashed Record Plant in *Rolling Stone* magazine. Chris Stone was the one who took the call. He remembered talking business with the rock legend: "His manager owed us $36,000 and wasn't answering the phone . . . his bookkeeper was giving us some bullshit. So, I told Jimi to dump the whole Electric Lady thing and come in with us, instead."

Hendrix didn't show up for the December 4, 1969, opening, although everyone else who was anyone in LA rock and roll spent the night popping back and forth between Record Plant and Beach Boy Dennis Wilson's twenty-fifth birthday party. The Woodstock tapes had arrived earlier that week from New York and even though Jimi wasn't there, his "Star-Spangled Banner" pushed the limits of Tom Hidley's monitors in Studio A.

Stone and Kellgren dressed like pirates for the affair, with large-collared open-neck shirts, tunics, and oversized belt buckles. Backer Ancky Revson and producer Tom Wilson posed with the group cutting a celebratory cake. The opening of Record Plant LA heralded the dawn of a new era of major studio construction in Los Angeles. Within a year there would be fifteen major recording studios in town, and within ten years there would be fifty.

Above: Gary Kellgren transformed a television production studio on Third Street into Record Plant LA. Below: The famous brick invitation to the LA studio's opening party on December 4, 1969. Music producer Phil Spector threatened to kill the receptionist for misspelling his name on his brick.

The celebrities all came with their brick invitations in hand. They were led into the front office where a tuxedoed mason cemented them on the Record Plant's own Wall of Fame to celebrate the studio's opening and immortalize its clientele.

Lee Kiefer, who assisted Gary on many of his studio designs, recalled standing with his boss in front of the brick wall when it was finished that night: "Gary always had an eye for that 'special something' that people would talk about. We were always looking to add to the experience, to build something new. Gary once told me his credo. He said, 'At Record Plant, we're always under construction!'"

TAPE 4

STUDIO	RECORD PLANT LA	
ARTIST	TITLE	FORMAT
James Gang	*James Gang Rides Again*	Album
Frank Zappa	*Chunga's Revenge*	Album
Jackson 5	"ABC"	Single
Frank Zappa	*Funky Nothingness*	Posthumous Album
Denny Doherty	*Watcha Gonna Do*	Album

GI-NORMOUS

Guitarist Joe Walsh remembered walking into Record Plant LA for the first time: "It was a brand-new studio and it was state-of-the-art. Being in that environment creatively was like a B-12 shot. We didn't know how to record, but we could do anything we wanted, so we did."

CHAPTER ONE

Studio A was booked for Walsh and the James Gang's second album by Kellgren's friend from his Dick Charles Recording days, producer Bill Szymczyk, who had just landed in Los Angeles to work as a staff producer at ABC/Dunhill Records. Even with hits by B. B. King (*The Thrill Is Gone*) and The J. Geils Band (*The J. Geils Band*) under his belt, Szymczyk remembered, "I was envious as hell of Gary. It was like, 'Damn, look at what he did. Son of a bitch. And here I am.'"

Szymczyk's recording style became more aggressive as he made the transition from engineer to producer. His business cards read, "Made Loud to be Played Loud," which also became the motto for the now legendary *James Gang Rides Again* sessions at Record Plant LA in early 1970 that transformed the way studio playbacks were monitored.

Szymczyk and the band wanted their ears to bleed during playback. So, Kellgren provided Szymczyk with a daisy chain of UK-made Tannoy loudspeakers that were stacked on a shelf above the console. Szymczyk recalled, "So, it was maybe the second or third month that the studio was open, and we were doing 'The Bomber,' which was just *gi-normous*. There's a big, big guitar solo and then a huge drum break at the end, and I heard it coming; and that's when I slammed the faders so loud that I literally blew out eight of the speakers."

"Bill [Szymczyk] used to play the tunes back in the control room at ear-shattering volume and we really got psyched!" James Gang bassist, Dale Peters, concurred.

"That was part of the deal at Gary's studio," Szymczyk added as backstory. "You could break anything if you wanted to. It didn't matter to Chris and Gary. The label paid the bills. So, what did I know? The speakers just couldn't handle it. Not my fault. But here's what happened next: he [Gary] goes to Tom Hidley and he says, 'Build me a monitor system that Szymczyk can't blow up.'"

Stone filled in the rest: "We made money on every one of those Tannoy speakers that the artists used to blow up. I remember when Kellgren first told Hidley to build a pair that Szymczyk couldn't blow up; I said, 'Wait a minute . . . you sure that's a good idea?'"

The original pair of loudspeakers that Tom Hidley built for Bill Szymczyk on a test platform on Record Plant's rooftop were the

Above: Bill Szymczyk and Gary Kellgren seated (bottom right) on the Studio A shag carpet floor in Record Plant LA in 1970 while working on Denny Doherty's album *Watcha Gonna Do*. Below: Szymczyk and B. B. King were among the first to make use of Studio A when they recorded the album *Indianola Mississippi Seeds* in May 1970.

CHAPTER ONE

historic Westlake Monitors. Recognizable by their laminated "monkey-lips" protrusion on the front, Hidley's innovative loudspeakers became the primary listening device of thousands of recording studios around the world, and their clear-but-muscular punch helped define the sound of classic rock and roll.

Szymczyk helped further Record Plant LA's street cred with B. B. King's *Indianola Mississippi Seeds* sessions that introduced Kellgren (who co-engineered) to Walsh (who sat in) and the unique Record Plant vibe to a host of LA-influencers, including Carole King, Leon Russell, and session men like Russ Kunkel, and Hugh McCracken. With so many musicians working on B. B. King's first rock and roll album there, the word spread quickly around town that Record Plant Studio A on Third Street was making some great sounding records.

Szymczyk got what he wanted in the studio in those days. ABC/Dunhill paid full rate and always on time. And important for Record Plant, he was building its brand with his hits. "I was their new bread and butter. And Chris [Stone] knew how to spread the butter around," Szymczyk said.

> When I first moved out to LA and I was having some success, Chris came to me one day and asked: "What are they paying you royalty-wise?"
>
> "I'm not getting any royalties because I'm staff," Szymczyk remembered saying.
>
> [To which Stone said,] "That's a fucking crime. How can we fix that? What do you need in your house?"
>
> "Well, I really wouldn't mind having a kick-ass stereo."

Two days later, a pair of JBL studio monitors, McIntosh receiver, and Thorens turntable arrived at Szymczyk's house courtesy of Record Plant. And unbeknownst to Szymczyk at the time, Stone billed it all back to ABC/Dunhill as "equipment rentals."

"Classic Chris Stone move," Szymczyk recalled.

TAPE 5

STUDIO   RECORD PLANT NY / RECORD PLANT LA

ARTIST	TITLE	FORMAT
Jimi Hendrix	*Paper Airplanes*	Bootleg Album
Mountain	*Climbing!*	Album
Various	*Woodstock: Music from the Original Soundtrack*	Album
Jimi Hendrix	"Star-Spangled Banner"	Single
Love, with Jimi Hendrix	"Everlasting First"	Single
Todd Rundgren	*Runt*	Album

SEX, DRUGS, & ROCK AND ROLL

Stone admired the midtown Manhattan skyline from the executive boardroom of Warner Bros. Kellgren and his chief engineer, Jack Adams, were supposed to have met him in a nearby coffee shop earlier that morning to discuss the strategy for the meeting, but they never showed. It wasn't often you got facetime with Steve Ross, the Wall Street whiz kid who had turned a funeral business into a rental-car empire, and now into the world's largest entertainment company. For years, he owned the parking lot across the street from Record Plant on Forty-Fourth Street.

Just months after the Record Plant acquisition, Television Communications Corp. (TVC) was already negotiating its own sale to Ross's Warner Cable Division, and the company wanted to show off its new rock and roll property. TVC knew that the Warner Music Division was a profit-machine for Ross and thought that Record Plant would sweeten the deal.

Ross originally thought the place was a "record-pressing plant" that could help him expand manufacturing and distribution for his labels. Instead, he saw the recording studio that TVC had just

CHAPTER ONE

acquired as a small, high-risk venture with weird line items that the bookkeepers couldn't categorize. So, either Stone and Kellgren were going to impress him with a "Big Idea" or he wanted out.

Stone didn't have a "Big Idea." He stood there with his TVC bosses checking their watches, hoping that his partner would sweep into the room with a vision for the Record Plant's future. But when Kellgren and Jack Adams finally stumbled in, he saw that they had been up all night drinking.

Popular with the R&B set, Adams was a notorious carouser. He once drove his motorcycle onto the Record Plant elevator and up to the tenth floor where he terrorized the talent and the tenants before crashing through the building's glass front door on his way out. Kellgren drank more when he was around Adams, who had also become his boss's docent to the sex clubs in New York's Meatpacking District.

Stone was pissed off by how disheveled they looked, but there wasn't time for words between him and his partner. Just as Kellgren and Adams took their seats, kicking four badly scuffed boots up on the conference table, Ross and his team walked in.

Stone began talking about all the obvious things they were doing to grow the business, how there was room for further expansion into film and TV in LA, and that they were scouting locations for a third studio in either San Francisco, Nashville, or London. He talked about a fleet of recording trucks they were going to build to turn concerts into sellable vinyl. But Stone knew from the look on Ross's face that he didn't want to hear from the numbers guy. Stone turned to Kellgren to help with some vision.

Kellgren was a born salesman and his best product was himself. While Stone was all about the money, Kellgren's primary desire was to be admired and loved. He was ready with his "Big Idea." He talked about turning Record Plant into more than just a chain of recording studios in every music market. He described, "Record Plant, The World's First Chain of Five-Star, Rock Star Hotels."

And speaking for the first time, engineer Jack Adams interjected: "Yeah, Sex, Drugs, and Rock and Roll!"

Everyone around the conference table smiled politely; it wasn't their first meeting with music types. The accountants asked for the numbers and Steve Ross introduced Stone to Abe Silverstein, one of his lieutenants, who he said would be following up.

On the way down the elevator, Kellgren asked Stone, "So, how do you think it went?"

"Where the hell did you come up with a rock and roll hotel?" Stone asked.

"You should see some of those rooms they've got in the Hellfire Club downtown; every room's a different fetish."

At that moment, Stone wasn't questioning what Kellgren had been doing at the Hellfire Club that night. He was fixated on Kellgren's "Big Idea"—and he liked it: a hotel serving time and tape at $150 per hour, twenty-four hours a day, seven days a week.

As a sober counterpoint to the partners' excitement, back upstairs Steve Ross instructed his lieutenants to sell off the recording studio as soon as the deal was closed.

ROY

Gary Kellgren left New York later that month. He drove cross-country in his Cadillac Eldorado convertible with his three-year-old son, pregnant wife, Marta, and her parents in the back seat, leaving his first studio and adopted city in the rearview mirror. Chris Stone flew back and forth to manage the New York business for the new Warner owners for several years. Tom Hidley visited for a series of renovation marathons to bring the New York rooms up to LA standards. After 1970, Kellgren never worked at Record Plant NY ever again.

Stone needed someone else to be Kellgren in New York. The billings were trailing off and they needed advertising business to fill the morning slots. Though Hendrix was still working in the studio and Stone was desperately trying to keep him there, down deep Chris knew that as soon as Electric Lady was up and running later that year the magical run of high-rate, middle-of-the-night bookings would come to an end.

Hidley told Stone about a hot engineer named Roy Cicala, who had just been fired from A&R Recording. He had made a name for himself by turning a late-night demo session with the Young Rascals into the final mix of their first album. In due time, every studio owner in New York knew that Roy Cicala had it all—he could engineer, mix, fix the gear and, most importantly, manage a team of assistants.

CHAPTER ONE

Kellgren may have built Record Plant NY, but from that point forward, it would always be Roy Cicala's studio. And much to the credit of the respective management teams, few clients ever realized that Record Plant NY (East) and Record Plant LA (West) were separate business entities. Cicala and Kellgren's individual personalities and recording styles would define their respective studios on opposite coasts throughout the seventies.

While Kellgren was the son of the town car mechanic in a Midwestern farm community, Cicala was an Italian kid from Connecticut, who repaired the organ for his family's Catholic church. Still, the two engineers were strikingly similar. Both loved to go hands-on with tape recorders and consoles like they worked on carburetors, fan belts, and brakes when they were teens. They were fearless inventors and passionate about capturing a sound. Kellgren may have been the life of the party, and Cicala the father figure, but they created their own unique work universes, each with their own tribe of acolytes.

Stone knew how to motivate them both. "Everywhere Kellgren went, it was a party. Everywhere Cicala went was a sitcom. But they both wanted cars, boats, and fancy homes. All I had to do was teach them how to sell," he explained.

Roy Cicala became Roy Cicala because of his high-school sweetheart, Lori Burton. Songwriter of the hit "I Ain't Gonna Eat Out My Heart Anymore" for the Young Rascals, Lori cut her song demos in the basement of her family house with her boyfriend rolling the tape, which the young lovers would then run down to New York City to peddle. Through Lori's connections, Roy got his first real studio job at A&R Recording, where he worked all day alongside Tom Hidley in maintenance, then recorded Lori's friends throughout the night, only to go home, shower, and return to the studio again when it opened the next morning.

Almost overnight, Roy was in demand by music celebrities, including Dionne Warwick; Frankie Valli and the Four Seasons; and Peter, Paul and Mary. He gained a reputation as a fearless audio experimenter, once even dropping a water-cooler bottle down seven flights of stairs to record the crashing glass. He was becoming the studio's number-one engineer, which, for some reason, didn't go over

LIVING ROOM STUDIO

well with A&R owner and chief engineer, Phil Ramone, who, around that same time, decided it was time for Roy to leave. A notice was unceremoniously posted on the A&R bulletin board: "Sorry to see Roy go!"

"Roy found out that he was fired from that notice Phil posted for everyone to read on the studio bulletin board," said Lori Burton.

The timing was perfect for Record Plant NY, which was struggling to keep up with demand. Studios A and B were working around the clock and they had just taken out a lease on a tenth-floor office to build Studio C. Three studios required a new business plan.

Stone realized that if they were going to keep manufacturing hits, he needed to make his star engineers more productive; everyone wanted to work with Cicala or Kellgren but they couldn't be everywhere at once. He found the solution while sitting in the dentist's chair, watching his Fifth Avenue dentist maximize his billings by having his hygienists do all the dirty work while he bounced from room to room. "Cicala understood the 'studio bait and switch.' Just like Kellgren, he was more valuable starting the session and then handing it off to some assistant, which was the only way he could keep multiple studios going and multiple artists happy, all at the same time," Stone said.

> # "Roy Cicala was not very talkative, so not that many people may have heard of him."
>
> Yoko Ono,
> artist, musician

This business model relied on a steady flow of young kids who were hungry to work in the music business, would do anything to keep their clients happy, and were willing to work for just $1.25 an hour. Cicala especially enjoyed the sweet revenge of stealing his future assistants from A&R Recording. In fact, Roy Cicala built Record Plant NY and, some say, New York's seventies rock and roll, by poaching the best young talent from his former employer. Not surprisingly, the best thing any aspiring engineer could say on their Record Plant application was that they had been fired by A&R's owner, Phil Ramone. "I don't know what it was, but Roy just had that

CHAPTER ONE

intuitive feeling about those young engineers. He just saw it. He knew if they were serious because he'd put them through such hell," Burton remembered.

Roy's first disciple was his A&R assistant engineer, Shelly Yakus. He taught the curly-haired kid from Boston that the only rules were that there are no rules in recording and to always trust his ears. After Roy left A&R, it was only a matter of time before Shelly got the call.

"Roy rang me up maybe a month after he landed at Record Plant and he said, 'Listen, you've got all my clients; if you don't come over here, I'm going to have to kill you.' And he meant it . . . or at least it sounded like it. So, I gave my notice and I came over to Record Plant," Shelly Yakus said, recalling how he started his career making records for the likes of John Lennon, Tom Petty, U2, the Ramones, Patti Smith, Alice Cooper, Don Henley, and Stevie Nicks, among others.

Another Cicala pupil and future hitmaker, Jack Douglas, first applied for a job at A&R and was told he'd have a better chance getting his start over at Record Plant where everyone was going to work anyway. Douglas walked through the Record Plant lobby door and up to the front desk, where he told the receptionist:

"I'm looking for a job."

"We need a janitor," the receptionist said.

To which Douglas replied, "I'm your guy."

"Okay. You start tomorrow."

Fortunately, that young janitor had connections in the New York City rock and roll scene. Douglas had played guitar on the road with Chuck Berry and other headliners, and he knew all the bands over at Max's Kansas City. More importantly, he had grown up in an Italian neighborhood in the Bronx.

"It was a big plus to be Italian at Record Plant in those days," studio manager Arlene Reckson remarked, listing a host of future Record Plant employees with vowels at the end of their names: Jay Messina, Jimmy Iovine, Thom Panunzio, Carmine Rubino, Paul Prestopino, Steve Marcantonio, Dennis Ferrante, and Eddie "Jason" Germano.

All the engineers who made the cut with Roy went through the same rigorous Record Plant training program, first starting as a janitor, then a gofer (or "general" as they were called), tape librarian, assistant engineer, and finally having the ultimate "trial-by-fire" moment alone with a famous client in session. The Record Plant school of recording launched a studio career for Douglas that included records with the James Gang, Alice Cooper, The Who, Patti Smith, the New York Dolls, Cheap Trick, but most notably Aerosmith, and John and Yoko. "Record Plant was more fly by the seat of your pants, more adventurous than the other studios, you know. It was a bit more helter-skelter and crazy and wild; maybe because there were more drugs involved," Douglas recalled.

Roy flourished in the free-for-all freedom of TVC's hands-off management style and, oftentimes, pushed it past its limits. Arlene Reckson remembered it this way: "When Chris [Stone] left and Roy was running the show by himself, the inmates took over the asylum."

Cicala was a complicated character: creative, nurturing, generous, fair, and often wildly unpredictable. If he didn't like the way a piece of gear was behaving, he'd hurl it across the room. He once rolled a condom onto a microphone and dropped it into water to create an underwater sound.

Under his regime, Jack Douglas was duct-taped to a desk chair and then rolled out into traffic in the middle of Forty-Fourth Street. Another engineer rigged a blast cap to the tape machine to make it look like the multitrack had just blown up mid-session. There were plenty of pie fights. And then there was this thing with the fire extinguishers.

It all started one night back at A&R. Shelly was pretending to be grooving with his eyes closed to the band playing live on the other side of the glass. Cicala knew his act; Yakus was just catching a nap, holding onto the console for dear life while dozing off, with the console meters crashing into the danger zone.

Cicala needed to shake the kid up, so he reached for the nearest thing, which in this case was a fire extinguisher, and he aimed and fired it at Yakus to wake him up. The gush of CO_2 made a startling blast, left a vapor trail, and taught Cicala that the red canisters could come in handy for keeping sleepy engineers in line.

The fire extinguisher gag became a rite of passage for countless assistant engineers at Record Plant NY.

CHAPTER ONE

PAPER AIRPLANES

The tenth-floor studio where John Lennon and Roy Cicala eventually worked was built as a last-ditch attempt to keep Jimi Hendrix's business.

As early as January 1970, Stone heard that Jimi was getting cold feet about finishing Electric Lady Studios. Construction was running way over budget, and the project had mushroomed from a club with a private studio to a multi-room complex. Kellgren knew Jimi and knew he needed something small.

While a team of engineers was struggling to build Hendrix his dream studio in Greenwich Village, Roy Cicala and Tom Hidley built Studio C just for Jimi up on the tenth floor of 321 West Forty-Fourth Street, entirely on spec and in just seventy-two hours. The room kept Jimi Hendrix working at Record Plant for almost the rest of his life.

Like every other worker, this rock god took the elevator up to his office, did his job, then went home. Upstairs at Record Plant NY, there was no cross-traffic between studios. No distractions. The upstairs control room was smaller than the original, main-floor Studio A and, as a result, there was no room for the posse that usually tagged along. Up on the tenth floor, Hendrix wasn't being hassled by policemen, managers, reporters, and fans. He was focused and in command. And the change of locale gave him renewed energy to create.

And then, of course, there was the tenth-floor roof.

Down the hall from the new studio was a tar-beach rooftop where Hendrix would go outside to smoke and look down upon the early morning streets of Times Square. Up on that same roof over the coming years, songs would be written, bands would break up, and Record Plant staffers would fall in love, and some of the most iconic rock portraits were photographed.

One morning the janitor told Chris Stone that he had found the tenth-floor roof littered with Record Plant stationery, and much of it had blown out into the streets. Jimi was the only one working upstairs the night before, so Stone knew engineer Jack Adams must have somehow been involved.

Adams explained that "it had been one of those nights" with Jimi. They had mixed a song "for ten hours straight, after three hundred mixes" of the same song earlier that week. And a big part of the problem was that Hendrix, "like Captain Video at the space deck," wouldn't take his hands off the dials. Others believed that all the high-volume recording had damaged Hendrix's hearing, as evidenced by piles of overloaded headphones that he left discarded after every session.

Taking a break from the madness, Jack and Jimi went out on the roof to fly paper airplanes. Adams grabbed a ream of letterhead from the office and, just like kids, the guitarist and his engineer folded fighter jets with the colorful Record Plant logo emblazoned along the side and launched them into the early morning skies. They competed for hours to see whose projectile could fly further before they spiraled to crash landings in the streets below.

STAR-SPANGLED BANNER

In contrast to the creative calm on Jimi's floor, the two downstairs studios had become a veritable supply chain of engineers and assistants working around the clock on the Woodstock concert tapes.

For his first job at Record Plant, Jack Douglas unloaded hundreds of rain-drenched Woodstock tape boxes from a delivery truck. Staff engineers auditioned the master tapes for the first time only to find that the greatest rock concert of all time was an audible mess.

Eddie Kramer had recorded the festival from an isolated backstage trailer, where he struggled to capture what was happening onstage in the middle of a near-hurricane. He and his assistant engineers communicated with the stage, which was hundreds of feet away, using hand signals. The cables had been connected backwards and out of phase, which resulted in a high-frequency squeal on some performances. With a small twelve-track console borrowed from the Fillmore East and only seven tracks of tape to work with (the eighth was a sync track for the film), many instruments had to be recorded together, making it difficult to fix them later in the mix. These were the early days of live concert recording; it was not yet the art and business that Record Plant would eventually perfect.

Much of the final *Woodstock* album either had to be fixed, mixed, or entirely replaced. Master tapes shuttled around the country for months, so the artists could work with their own engineers and musicians to enhance their performance before sending them back to Record Plant to be stitched into the final LP set.

CHAPTER ONE

Sly Stone paid his first visit to a Record Plant studio to mix his Woodstock stage performance, only to learn that his famed anthem, "I Want to Take You Higher," was marred by a high-pitched signal. The famed crossfade of the audience rain chant leading into Santana's "Soul Sacrifice" was manufactured in the studio to obscure the fact that chunks of the original performance were marred by a sixty-cycle buzz.

Eventually, the *Woodstock* album project moved to Record Plant LA where the original eight-track tapes were transferred to sixteen-track so the bands or their surrogates could come in and lay down entirely new parts. "Some of the instruments you hear on the Woodstock album was some guy we found in Hollywood who could duplicate the original performance. We spent months on that stuff," engineer Phil Schier said.

Kellgren used Jimi's Woodstock performance of "Star-Spangled Banner" to demo the new Hidley speaker system for the guitarist when he recorded at Record Plant LA for the first and only time in early June 1970. Hendrix was in LA to jam with local legend Arthur Lee and his band Love, playing his V-shaped Gibson guitar with Kellgren behind the console for the album *False Start*, which included the single "Everlasting First." It was the last time Gary and Jimi worked together.

"Gary was excited to have Jimi in LA that last time. All the old business from back in New York was water under the bridge," Stone observed.

Kellgren demoed a few mixes of the Woodstock performance to see which one Hendrix preferred. He pushed Hidley's loudspeakers to their max and Hendrix liked what he heard. Ultimately, the final version of the "Star-Spangled Banner," the defining cut of the three-album *Woodstock* album release, was selected by a couple of the film's sound engineers without Hendrix's approval.

By the time the *Woodstock* album was released a month later, the legendary guitar solo had taken on an even greater meaning in a country at war.

TAPE 6

STUDIO	RECORD PLANT LA	
ARTIST	**TITLE**	**FORMAT**
Crosby, Stills, Nash & Young	"Ohio"	Single
Crosby, Stills, Nash & Young	"Find the Cost of Freedom"	Single

FOUR DEAD

The last time Jimi Hendrix worked at Record Plant NY was May 15, 1970, the same date that the shootings at Kent State appeared on the cover of *Life* magazine. The photographs startled a nation and changed the course of the Vietnam War.

Neil Young's response to the images was to grab a guitar, walk out into the woods, and write "Ohio," one of the greatest protest songs of all time. In his biography, Graham Nash wrote what happened next:

> [David Crosby] immediately called me and said, "We need to be in the studio right now."
> "What is this all about?" I asked him.
> "It's a song we've got to cut immediately," he insisted. "Round up the guys . . ."

The "guys" were all planning to be together in LA to rehearse for their next tour. Stills was already down there working on his debut solo LP at Record Plant Studio A with Crosby, Stills, Nash & Young's regular engineer, Bill Halverson, behind the console. CSNY was not a Record Plant client, though their first session as a band actually took place at Record Plant NY. Once out in LA, they preferred the more low-key Wally Heider Studios, which had originally been built for the Beach Boys to evade their corporate overseers at Capitol. In comparison to the scene at Record Plant, Nash recalled, "Heider's was a beautiful little dump of a place. We recorded there because it was private, off the beaten track."

CHAPTER ONE

Unfortunately, Heider's was booked the night of the "Ohio" session, so they used Stills's time at Record Plant Studio A instead. Halverson rented one of his preferred 3M tape machines from Heider, raided the Record Plant microphone closet for the best German vocal mics, and hired a rhythm section.

"They each came into the studio individually. They all seemed so isolated from each other, until they sang," assistant engineer, Mike D. Stone, remembered.

"The mood was very intense," engineer Halverson added, "I've been around those personalities for a long time, and the four of them take over a room. That night they were bent on getting it right and were on a mission."

It only took three takes, with live vocals, live harmonies, and live instruments, to get "Ohio" right. The band picked "Find the Cost of Freedom" for the B-side and to record the song Halverson arranged four folding chairs facing each other just inches apart so the band could sing a cappella into a single microphone. In the control room, Halverson doubled their voices and applied EQ filtering to even it all out. Together, they "gang mixed" both songs with all hands on the console at once and had the entire single completed by dawn.

In June 1970, "Ohio" hit the FM radio airwaves. Along with Jimi's "Star-Spangled Banner," the synergy of the two songs amped up the anti-war movement in America.

Later that summer, a band of anti-war demonstrators somehow got into the Record Plant's tenth floor and rappelled off the roof to raid the Selective Service records office that was located several floors below. Nobody ever found out who at the studio let them in.

TAPE 7

STUDIO RECORD PLANT LA

ARTIST	TITLE	FORMAT
B. B. King	*Indianola Mississippi Seeds*	Album
Dave Mason & Cass Elliot	*Dave Mason & Cass Elliot*	Album
Wes Farrell	"The Partridge Family"	TV Show Theme Song

GREED AND DEDUCT

GREED was everywhere on the Sunset Strip in 1970.

GREED was the license plate on Gary Kellgren's sparkling-purple Rolls-Royce. The stately British limousine shuttled its owner, customers, and friends from party to party and back and forth between the studio and the clubs. It served double duty as the Record Plant house car to pick up producers at LAX or to send a runner up the hill to Tower Records for a stash of LPs. When it wasn't cruising the streets, GREED was parked by the Record Plant front door.

Gary had his own studio arrival routine. He'd pull GREED into the yellow-walled parking lot with the radio blaring, get out and leave the door open with the motor still running. He'd then take his ice cooler filled with Korbel Brut champagne and orange juice from the back seat and walk inside, knowing one of the runners would park it for him. He never needed to ask.

"It was gorgeous. It was the most amazing color—a combination of blue and purple," Marta Kellgren remembered. "When it came time to get the license plates, he came up with the word, 'GREED.' I said, 'Gary, that is so tacky. Why don't you use your initials?' Later, I understood what he was saying."

GREED was a rolling Record Plant billboard. In a frontier town built on new money, where one couldn't tell the difference between the artists, the businessmen, and the freaks, the car made a splash and contributed to the Gary Kellgren mystique. GREED was everywhere musicians were in the winter of 1970. George Harrison loved the car,

CHAPTER ONE

often borrowing it to go play tennis with friends in Bel Air. Even with Gary at home with Marta and the kids, GREED cruised the clubs, bringing musicians and their entourages over to Record Plant or back to Kellgren's house to party.

The first house Kellgren picked out for his family was at 1735 Camino Palmero in Hollywood, an exclusive, residential artery, where MGM's Samuel Goldwyn once lived. Coincidentally, the Tudor-style mansion that he purchased was originally built by Vitagraph founder, Albert E. Smith, the same movie mogul who also built the Record Plant office building in New York. A former Canadian consulate, it was across the street from songwriter Jimmy Webb's compound and down the hill from the real home of the Ozzie and Harriet (Nelson) television family. The property came furnished with antique furniture and Tiffany lamps, tennis court and swimming pool.

> **"They were like the Gatsbys of rock and roll."**
>
> Grange Rutan, friend of Marta Kellgren

The Kellgrens brought an odd mix of cultures to the white, conservative neighborhood. Marta's parents were Black Puerto Ricans from Manhattan's Hell's Kitchen. Gary was a doting hipster of a dad who came home early in the morning when the rest of the neighborhood was just waking up. "They were like the Gatsbys of rock and roll," said Marta's longtime friend, Grange Rutan.

It was a new Jazz Age and the LA rock scene was filled with Gatsby-like song peddlers who had reinvented themselves as hippie record-industry impresarios. Kama Sutra Records founder, Artie Ripp, set up a suite of offices at Record Plant where he worked with Tom Wilson and, one year later, would bring a newbie New Yorker named Billy Joel into the LA studio to finish his first LP. Songwriter Wes Farrell ("Hang on Sloopy"), who made it big in television with the early-seventies TV show *The Partridge Family*, was a frequent customer and close friend of Kellgren's. Though Motown was still technically based in Detroit, the record label owner, Berry Gordy and his production team were already camped out at Record Plant LA to mix singles with the Jackson 5.

Vehicle license plates GREED and DEDUCT, belonging to Gary Kellgren and Chris Stone respectively, were fixtures in the Record Plant LA parking lot, and provided rolling billboards for the studio on the streets of LA in the seventies.

CHAPTER ONE

Kellgren and Stone catered to these producers. If a producer had a favorite engineer, he was hired. If they needed a piece of gear, they bought it. Dope and women fueled their twenty-four-hour marathon recording sessions. Stone, like any skilled concierge, knew who liked what, made no judgments, and found a way to get the label to cover the bill.

Kellgren's artistry moved from creating new sounds to choreographing new experiences. He met the Dutch hippie artist collective known as The Fool, which had given John Lennon's piano and Rolls-Royce the psychedelic treatment and had put their Flower Power stamp on the Beatles' London headquarters. (Eddie Kramer had worked with the collective at Record Plant NY on an album, with Graham Nash producing.) Emulating their designs, the studio owner began adding artistic details to his new studio's façade and interior, including mirrors, lights, fabrics and murals.

"Gary was an artist. He was really a genius at making ambiance and color and, always, a party. Everything was totally different than what you'd find in most studios. He would take simple plywood and wrap it in beautiful fabrics and use it for baffling the sound, and at the same time he was assembling bright colors to make everything look so festive," recording engineer Lillian Davis Douma recalled.

Kellgren was also always coming up with new ways to cater to the clientele. Record Plant LA was the first studio to add a canteen with candy machines selling rolling papers, free pinball, and a Coca-Cola machine filled with twenty-five-cent beers. There was a telephone in the men's bathroom within reach of the toilet. A shower and sauna were installed, eventually making room for the famed Record Plant Jacuzzi.

Though hot tubs were already common around town, the new jet-stream Jacuzzi was one of the first units large enough for a party. The bare asses of countless rock stars and their dates soaked in that tub. The room itself had a prism-like skylight and was decorated with flags from cocaine-exporting nations. It would always get the studio mainstream press attention, with its good-looking studio owner smiling out from the pages like some hipster Hef in a chlorinated stew.

Kellgren originally wanted a pool in the studio's back parking lot. It was Stone who talked him out of it and into buying a Jacuzzi instead to save room for customers' cars; however, he didn't make a habit of saying "no" to his partner.

Gloria Stone remembered:

> We gave Gary a safety net so that he could do what he did best. Gary wanted a boat, so we got him the boat. He wanted a new console, a tape machine, a new piece of gear, we had to figure out how to make it work. He needed to be flamboyant and we didn't. He had big houses, big parties, friends like Jack Nicholson and Anjelica Huston, all having fun until the early morning. He attracted a lot of people. He was very charismatic. He loved that lifestyle . . .

To which Chris Stone added, ". . . and that lifestyle made our image."

The Jacuzzi made the studio even more famous. But the recording gear was what generated the hits. Beneath the hood of this record factory, Tom Hidley and his team of maintenance engineers kept a very complicated, high-performance hit-making machine running around the clock.

The labels were beginning to look beyond stereo at quadraphonic sound, so Kellgren and Hidley outfitted Studio B with the first recording-studio quadraphonic speakers. Sixteen-track tape was now the industry standard and selling stacks of two-inch tapes was a prime studio profit center. A slanted "compression" ceiling in every control room created the trademark loud and punchy Record Plant sound. But it was the recording console that was becoming the main studio attraction, the command center for producers who wanted to get their hands on the music. Kellgren made sure that the Record Plant consoles sounded clean and had acres of blinking lights, sliders, and knobs that few customers understood how to control. They came with inlaid mirrors for snorting cocaine, which were cleaned and outfitted daily with fresh razors and straws.

> **"[Gary] attracted a lot of people. He was very charismatic. He loved that lifestyle ..."**
>
> Gloria Stone, wife of co-founder Chris Stone

CHAPTER ONE

Keeping up with Kellgren's demands for the latest audio gear was financially challenging. In those early analog days, hand-assembled studio equipment costs were skyrocketing. Hidley was using his successful LA designs on an expensive Record Plant NY upgrade, and TVC's bean counters were unwilling to spend any more than they had to. It was never easy being first. But being first was what gave Record Plant its edge.

"There was always some new microphone or piece of gear to buy. It was my job to find the money to pay for it," Stone said. "I remember, I was shopping for my first Mercedes and the sales guy started talking to me about leasing the car instead of buying it. I asked him about leasing studio equipment, and he introduced me to this guy who would lease anything; nobody had done it before."

Stone leased $500,000 worth of studio gear for New York and LA that year, in addition to a silver Mercedes 280SL for himself with its own vanity license plate—DEDUCT. It was Stone's first personal extravagance and he strategically parked DEDUCT alongside GREED in the Record Plant lot. It was a joke. And then again it wasn't.

TAPE 8

STUDIO	RECORD PLANT NY / RECORD PLANT LA	
ARTIST	**TITLE**	**FORMAT**
Jimi Hendrix	Band of Gypsys	Live Album
Buddy Miles	We Got to Live Together	Album

TEN WEEKS

When Jimi Hendrix finally moved his operations out of Record Plant and downtown to Electric Lady Studios in early summer 1970, the staff gathered in the lobby to say goodbye to the recordings that he had made there over the past two years. Everyone stood in silence as eighty marked-up tape boxes, including the makings of Jimi's fourth, unfinished album, were rolled out of the building into a panel truck that took them downtown to their new home in Greenwich Village.

"It felt like a funeral when they came and collected Jimi's tapes. There were piles and piles of boxes on that truck. It felt sad and empty when they came and took them all away," said Lillian Davis Douma who worked with Hendrix at Record Plant and is considered to be the first woman rock and roll recording engineer.

Studio manager Fran Hughes gave Jimi a pound of weed as a going-away present and she remembered that he acted like "nobody had ever given him a gift and the concept that it was a giving gesture made him break down in tears."

Electric Lady Studios' opening had been long delayed. A stream that ran underneath the studio caused occasional flooding; expensive soundproofing had to be added to block the rattle and hum of the subway; and Hendrix had to borrow $300,000 against future royalties from Warner Bros. Records to finish the job. Despite these problems, after his first session with Steve Winwood in mid-June, Hendrix recorded exclusively at Electric Lady. He would spend only ten weeks there, though, before he died.

Both Record Plants paled in comparison to Electric Lady Studios' extravagant, proto-hippie designs. Architect John Storyk reimagined

CHAPTER ONE

the Eighth Street building's brick façade as the side contour of a guitar sunken into the sidewalk; its colored lighting was adjustable to suit any mood; the studio walls were curved and painted with psychedelic sci-fi murals. Still, as Hendrix guitar-effects designer, Roger Mayer, said, technically the studio with its own Datamix console "was a tip of the hat to Record Plant."

Jimi was conspicuously absent at both Record Plant opening-night parties, but he wasn't going to miss his own studio's August 26 debut. He even helped put the finishing touches to the paint job. Throughout the party, Jimi kept an extremely low profile and spent much of the time seated in the barber's chair in the studio lounge with a close circle of friends. It was clear to everyone that he wanted to be left alone; the reality of being a business owner was starting to sink in. Jimi had recently been blocked from recording in his own room because of a conflict with a commercial gig, and, to pay the bills, he was leaving for a tour in Europe even though he just wanted to stay home and record.

> **" Jimi Hendrix came up the stairs and found me sitting there like some hick wallflower and grinned."**
>
> Patti Smith, musician

Future Record Plant NY artist Patti Smith remembered meeting the guitarist alone in the studio stairwell that night. "Jimi Hendrix came up the stairs and found me sitting there like some hick wallflower and grinned," she wrote in her memoir. "When I told him I was too chicken to go in, he laughed softly and said that contrary to what people think, he was shy and parties made him nervous."

Three weeks later, on September 18, 1970, in London, Hendrix died.

As soon as the news broke in New York, a mob of fans and the media crowded the street outside the new Eighth Street studio, while inside the engineers recorded audio off the TV news on a brand-new, $40,000 Ampex multitrack machine. Though he wanted to close Record Plant for the day out of respect, Roy Cicala had morning sessions with advertising clients who had deadlines to meet. Over at Mediasound, Roger Mayer was working with Stevie Wonder

LIVING ROOM STUDIO

when the news broke and Wonder, who would soon take up residence at Electric Lady Studios, choked back tears and sent everyone home. Jimi's girlfriend, Devon Wilson, fled the Greenwich Village apartment she shared with him and hid out with Kellgren's sister, Aleda Michelle, and other Playboy Bunny friends in an Upper West Side apartment. Aleda Michelle called to break the news to Gary, who was in session out in LA.

Kellgren was in the studio with former Hendrix drummer Buddy Miles, who was recording his solo LP, *We Got to Live Together*, when he received the call. Kellgren poured a glass of champagne from his cooler and nodded a toast to his friend.

Kellgren knew how much he owed Hendrix, but their relationship had never been the same since the disparaging quote in *Rolling Stone* magazine. Jimi's studio was now the competition and Electric Lady made his brand-new LA studio look plain and dated in comparison. To Kellgren and Stone the name "Hendrix" had become shorthand for any wealthy musician who had unlimited funds to burn through studio time and tape: "Get me another Hendrix" was how Stone used to goad Kellgren into going out to the clubs to find Record Plant's next studio cash cow.

With his emotions whirling, Kellgren called off the session. On the way out of reception, he fielded a call from Stone, who he told, "There wouldn't have been a Record Plant without Jimi." He then climbed into the backseat of GREED, poured another drink, and had a runner drive him home to Marta, their son Mark, and newborn daughter Devon.

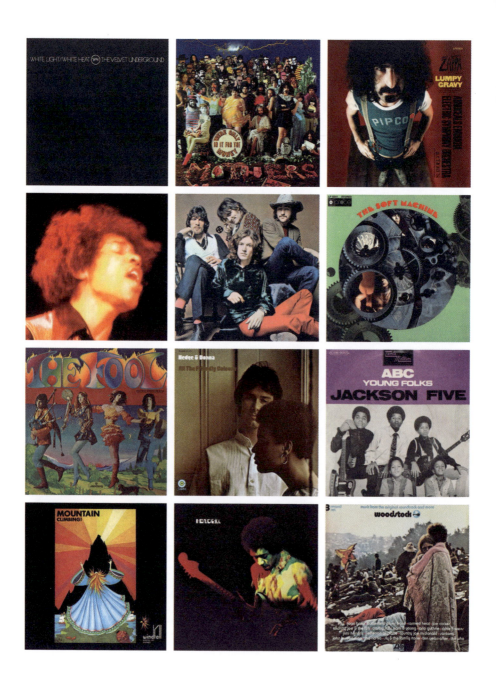

From top left: *White Light/White Heat*, the Velvet Underground, 1968; *We're Only in It for the Money*, Frank Zappa, 1968; *Lumpy Gravy*, Frank Zappa, 1968; *Electric Ladyland*, Jimi Hendrix, 1968; *Traffic*, Traffic, 1968; *The Soft Machine*, Soft Machine, 1968; *The Fool*, The Fool, 1968; *All the Friendly Colours*, Hedge & Donna, 1969; "ABC," Jackson 5, 1970; *Climbing!*, Mountain, 1970; *Band of Gypsys*, Jimi Hendrix, 1970; *Woodstock: music from the Original Soundtrack*, 1970.

From top left: *James Gang Rides Again*, James Gang, 1970; *Runt*, Todd Rundgren, 1970; *Chunga's Revenge*, Frank Zappa, 1969; *Indianola Mississippi Seeds*, B. B. King, 1970; *We Got to Live Together*, Buddy Miles, 1970; *Watcha Gonna Do*, Denny Doherty, 1971; *Dave Mason & Cass Elliot*, Dave Mason & Cass Elliot, 1971; *Paper Airplanes*, Jimi Hendrix, 1995; *Funky Nothingness*, Frank Zappa, 2023.

2

MASTER CONTROL

1970–1971

" Custom speakers, custom console, everything brand-sparkling-new. Everybody couldn't wait to get in."

TODD RUNDGREN
musician, assistant engineer

TAPE 9

STUDIO RECORD PLANT NY

ARTIST	TITLE	FORMAT
Jimi Hendrix	Cry of Love	Posthumous Album
Jimi Hendrix	Rainbow Bridge	Posthumous Album
Jimi Hendrix	Nine to the Universe	Posthumous Album
Jimi Hendrix	Valleys of Neptune	Posthumous Album
Jimi Hendrix	People, Hell and Angels	Posthumous Album
Jimi Hendrix	Both Sides of the Sky	Posthumous Album

ANOTHER HENDRIX

All the late nights that Hendrix spent recording at Record Plant resulted in decades' worth of posthumous albums and, once he was gone, Chris Stone needed "another Hendrix." Tom Wilson found him one, and coincidentally his name was Stone.

Wilson knew Sly Stone through David Kapralik, the former Columbia and Epic Records A&R executive who discovered Sly and his band in a Bay Area nightclub and became their manager and producer.

Wilson only produced two albums in 1970 (by Albino Gorilla and Country Joe and Fish), neither of which generated a hit. The industry now branded Wilson as a Black rock and roll producer even though he was eager to break into R&B. According to musician and Tom Wilson documentarian Marshall Crenshaw, "Rock music started closing itself off racially during the seventies; that might have had something to do with how his career went."

Wilson was still very well connected. "He seduced the clients like he seduced the women," Chris Stone said.

Wilson took Kellgren and Stone over to David Kapralik's bungalow at the Beverly Hills Hotel; it was the Liz Taylor and Richard Burton honeymoon suite, though its current occupant was a short, record company space-case. Right away, Kapralik began fast-talking about why he had invited them over for a chat.

Sly was out of control, he said. He had just moved into the former home of John and Michelle Phillips of the Mamas and the Papas in Beverly Hills; it was a stately Tudor mansion with a secret recording studio. With a studio one flight up from his bedroom, it was hoped that Sly would, once again, start generating hits; but to the contrary, he was working around the clock and still getting nothing done.

The home studio had all the gear that Sly needed and, after years of working at CBS-owned studios where the union always prevailed, he was finally free to control his own sound, which was taking a darker, murkier tone. He worked for unprecedented stretches at home, at Record Plant LA, and in his Winnebago studio-on-wheels, but because of his drug intake the new album was two years late. "There was really no separation between life and drugs. Life was drugs and music," Sly's assistant, Stephani Owens, said in an oral biography. "They would spend so many hours—thirty-six to forty-eight hours— in one session at Record Plant, wearing out the engineers. And to keep up, the engineers were doing drugs, too."

Sly carried a violin case filled with his stash wherever he went, and he helped introduce the animal tranquilizer angel dust (PCP) to the LA music scene. As the apostle of this powerful new, designer drug, Sly's sessions became even more erratic and confused.

Sly's behavior was breaking up his band, the Family Stone. As a result, Sly had to play all the instruments on *There's a Riot Goin' On*. And when drummer Greg Errico eventually quit, Sly began using one of the first drum machines, the Maestro Rhythm King MRK-2 or "Funk Box," which quickly became the R&B recording-artist rage.

Despite the innovation and the fact that his *Greatest Hits* album was generating plenty of cash, Sly's career was in trouble without new material and a tour. Kapralik hired Sly Stone's future manager Ken Roberts to get him back on stage at a time when no other promoter trusted him to show up. Similarly, Kapralik was hoping that Tom Wilson and the owners of Record Plant could help his artist finish his

CHAPTER TWO

record. Kapralik said, "Build him a damn studio at Record Plant if that's what it takes."

"We know how to work with talent," Chris Stone assured him.

Later that afternoon, the Record Plant partners piled into the back seat of GREED and headed over to Sly Stone's $12,000-per-month rental in Beverly Hills. Sly's fleet of collectible cars lined the driveway. His prized pit bull, Gun, was barking by the front door, and there were other dogs roaming the property. Sly lived on the second floor in a room with its own Jacuzzi and with the hidden studio one flight up.

Sly barely acknowledged Kellgren and Stone when they emerged from the staircase into the control room where he worked. Kellgren noticed that the adjacent studio was being used for storage, not recording. In this new era of electronics, artists like Sly were bypassing the studio acoustics by plugging directly into the console.

Kellgren told Sly how he had originally built Record Plant for Jimi Hendrix as a place to jam. But since he wasn't recording live, Sly simply needed a control room where he could create with the machines.

Sly liked Kellgren's idea but told the Record Plant partners he already had plenty of places to record; what he really needed was an engineer who could keep up with his production style.

Kellgren replied that he had someone in mind.

"Who's that?"

"The same guy who saved your Woodstock performance—Tom Flye. You worked with him in New York," Kellgren replied.

"Get him over here tonight."

As it turned out, Tom Flye was scheduled to start sessions with singer-songwriter Don McLean at Record Plant NY and Roy Cicala was unwilling to let him go. Kellgren never built Sly his private studio in LA either. It wasn't until Record Plant Sausalito opened in 1972, with Tom Flye in charge as chief engineer, that Kellgren would finally build Sly Stone the control-room-only studio of his dreams.

At Record Plant, rock and roll dreams often came true.

TAPE 10

STUDIO RECORD PLANT NY

ARTIST	TITLE	FORMAT
Coca Cola	"It's the Real Thing"	Jingle
The Who	Who's Next (Lifehouse)	Album
Don McLean	American Pie	Album / Single
Patti LaBelle	Labelle	Album

NAKED DRUM BOOTH

Jack Douglas's mind was blown.

The rock and roll bass player from the Bronx, who just months earlier was cleaning toilets at the hippest studio in New York, was alone behind a newly purchased, $80,000 ultra-audiophile Spectra Sonics console, getting ready to work with The Who. On the band's second night of recording at Record Plant NY, Douglas set up the studio microphones, aligned the tape machines, and tested the monitors in quad. Then he waited for their engineer Jack Adams to show up.

Douglas had moved up quickly at Record Plant NY. He started as a janitor, advanced to the tape library and the dubbing room, then cut demos for unknowns like Patti LaBelle and Billy Joel. Just a few days earlier he was called up to assist Adams on The Who's new concept LP.

"Jack Douglas . . . he had smarts. Caught on right away. When he was around Roy [Cicala], he was all ears," Lori Burton recalled.

When the band finally arrived ready to work, nobody questioned the fact that the kid who ran out for burgers the night before was now behind the board. Douglas focused his eyes on the controls, tried to remember which buttons and sliders did what, and was determined not to fuck things up. The last time he had worked alone with Patti LaBelle's new vocal trio, a cup of coffee had spilled on the console electronics.

CHAPTER TWO

The Who was at Record Plant NY to work on new songs for an unfinished rock theater production called *Lifehouse* that would never materialize but would evolve into *Who's Next*. They were among the first to work in the recently upgraded Studio A, an East Coast replica of Kellgren and Hidley's now popular design for Studio A in LA that, ahead of its time, was equipped for surround-sound recording. Sadly, the Studio A where Jimi Hendrix had made history was now forever downgraded to Studio B.

Jack Adams, Douglas's boss, was not particularly fond of The Who's music. The studio's colorful gay chief engineer wasn't even sure who the band was, according to Douglas: "I had to tell him about *Tommy*. As far as [Adams] was concerned, that music did not have a groove."

In contrast, working with one of the great British-invasion bands was mind-blowing for Douglas. And The Who's arrival on Forty-Fourth Street was a signal to the local studio market that Record Plant was back on top.

The Who's producer Kit Lambert had worked at Record Plant NY earlier that year with Patti LaBelle; he fell in love with the studio's loud and loose style and its chief engineer with whom he explored the city's post-Stonewall gay nightlife. Adams became famous for working with Hendrix, but he was essentially an R&B engineer whose prominent high-hat sound became his signature on many of the R&B records of the era. And though he hated waking up early in the morning, Adams was also a go-to engineer at the McCann-Erickson ad agency for their popular R&B series of "It's the Real Thing" jingles for Cola.

Like The Who band members themselves, Adams lived on the edge. The drinking, drugging, and partying were starting to show and, even worse, affect his work, which explained his disappearances during The Who's sessions. Former Hendrix saxophone player and assistant engineer, Jimmy Robinson told a writer: "I used to call him 'Merlin' because he would disappear a lot during sessions. He would literally say 'Jimmy, take the board,' and then he would disappear. We'd eventually find him in the broom closet or in the bathroom stall with a half-empty bottle of Scotch, the door locked, passed out."

Jack Adams's drinking gave Jack Douglas his star-is-born moment during the *Who's Next* sessions; like so many other assistants under

Roy Cicala's tutelage, he was thrown into the deep end and left to either sink or swim.

At the time, the Record Plant NY regime was in transition—from Kellgren's original crew to Cicala's A&R Recording recruits—and the recording philosophy was changing as well. "These guys coming over from A&R, they were from the [A&R owner] Phil Ramone school of recording," Douglas said. "And that was—you get it to sound exactly like it sounds out in the room, and then you make it sound like a record; you add the magic. The Kellgren guys were all about feel—'How did it feel? Did it feel good?'—Jack Adams was very much about how something felt; he especially liked to feel the full blast of the quad monitors in the control room."

The Who wanted to play loud, fast, and live. The finely tuned, control room playbacks at Record Plant reminded the band how a studio album should sound, although they struggled to play live in the sound-deadened room.

At the same time, Mountain was recording their classic *Climbing!* in the Hendrix room across the hall, and Jack Douglas invited guitarist Leslie West to sit in and jam with the band on the Marvin Gaye tune, "Baby Don't You Do It."

While Roger Daltrey was recording his vocals on "Won't Get Fooled Again," Kit Lambert threw himself across the console to adjust the room lighting and badly bruised his ribs. During a microphone change, Douglas found Keith Moon sitting naked in the drum booth.

During one of those sessions, Douglas rolled in a beat-up, old upright piano he had first discovered as a janitor in a tenth-floor storage closet. Made by New England Piano Company out of Boston, this tall, oak instrument had a rich, bright, and percussive sound. The piano remained in the studio for decades. It was eventually dubbed "the John Lennon Piano," due to its constant use as the former Beatle's in-studio songwriting instrument.

Pete Townshend loved pounding away on that keyboard, too. He liked the way it added a percussive R&B sound when mixed with his guitar. Unfortunately, the band's two-week Record Plant NY booking only lasted three days. Disgusted by Lambert's drugged-out behavior, Pete abruptly returned to London where he replaced him with the Rolling Stones' and Led Zeppelin's producer, Glyn Johns. The Record

CHAPTER TWO

Plant recordings were eventually thrown into an Olympic Studios dumpster as part of a studio housecleaning (though backup tapes were later discovered and used for a box-set release).

Ultimately, Record Plant's main contribution to The Who's catalog was as the first-time Townshend experienced the quadraphonic sound effect that inspired the title of his next rock opera, *Quadrophenia*.

While The Who's sessions were career-making for Jack Douglas, they marked the beginning of the end for Jack Adams in New York. His drinking was getting in the way and young up-and-comers like Douglas could fill the void less expensively. Kellgren and Stone were eager to hire Adams to move out to LA anyway, so he could help bring in the R&B dates. And, uncharacteristically, Cicala agreed to let LA poach one of his New York engineers.

Anybody but Tom Flye. Roy was still mad at Gary for suggesting he loan him Flye for Sly out in LA, and specifically told Chris that he was off-limits.

Good thing. If Tom Flye hadn't been in New York that spring, there would never have been an *American Pie*.

THE DAY THE MUSIC DIED

Record Plant was staffed by musicians in service of musicians. For every band that worked in the studio, there were dozens of staff engineers, assistants, runners, and receptionists who also had been in bands. They all went to work every day to serve the musicians and took any job to get a foot in the door. Where else would you meet a night-maintenance engineer who had played with the Chad Mitchell Trio, a front-desk receptionist who had his own album deal, or a drummer for an electronic-psychedelic band who became a world-class engineer?

Tom Flye was the drummer of that band, Lothar and the Hand People. In the late sixties, they were a house fixture at Bob Margouleff's Forty-Seventh Street loft, a low-rent, high-tech version of Andy Warhol's Factory; it was a popular hang-out for musicians, there to explore early electronica while doing their fair share of drugs to fuel their experimentation.

"Lothar" was the band's pet name for its theremin, an electronic instrument played without physical contact by the performer, which they had assembled from a kit. The "Hand People" became the first band to tour with a Moog synthesizer after Margouleff introduced them to the instrument. Margouleff's own creative obsession was *Ciao! Manhattan*, an avant-garde film about the rise and fall of Warhol starlet Edie Sedgwick, and the Moog was an inexpensive way for him to score the movie's music. Lothar musicians, including Tom Flye, were immortalized as characters in the arthouse film classic.

When the movie bombed and Margouleff's audio collective went bust, the musicians scattered in search of a paycheck. Margouleff bought his own Moog to work on ad-agency jingles. Tom Flye and his band made a second album for Capitol Records over at Record Plant in 1969—where he stayed and never left.

Like so many "could-have-been" bands, Lothar had legal problems and struggled to pay its bills. Fortunately, Chris Stone had an eye for talent and told the tech-savvy drummer to call him if he ever wanted a job. Flye had learned recording basics over at Margouleff's loft and needed work. But, as usual, Record Plant was looking for someone who could build, not just record. Studio C was under construction for Jimi Hendrix and the contractor needed someone to cover dozens of sound-deadening panels with felt; the contractor gave Flye a week to get the job done but Flye figured out how to cut the material all at once and was done in less than a day.

Within a month, Flye was doing his own sessions for $15 per hour (plus a percentage of the tape he sold to his artists). He assisted Eddie Kramer with Jimi Hendrix, learned analog tape delay from Roy Cicala, and demonstrated his artistry making a "live album" out of the mangled *Woodstock* album tapes.

The music business was changing in the spring of 1971. The unprecedented success of Carole King's *Tapestry* set the stage for other singer-songwriters, which was why United Artists was putting its money behind Don McLean and his producer, Ed Freeman.

A roadie for the Beatles' 1966 US tour, Freeman did early recordings for Tim Hardin and Carly Simon, and produced Tom Rush's 1970 album for Columbia Records, which led him to Don McLean. It was the first record he was doing outside of the Columbia Records system and, thus, he needed an independent studio to record it in.

"Columbia was a union shop and the studio all looked very

CHAPTER TWO

institutional. You know, white walls, linoleum floors, fluorescent lights," Freeman recalled. "The tape op[erator] had complete control over the session. When he said, 'It's lunch,' you had to take an hour break. That was it. You couldn't say, 'Hey, we're really in the middle of a hot take' or 'Let's just go and order out something.' No, it didn't work like that. If the tape op said it was lunch, the whole machine got shut down. It wasn't a very music-friendly environment for this new generation of musicians."

Then Ed Freeman walked into Record Plant. "It was all padded walls and everything was colorful. The place was just swarming in drugs, many of which I was taking. It was all very hip; I think the word was groovy at the time. I was completely enamored with it right off the bat," Freeman said, adding, "I also had a good stroke of luck to work with Tom Flye."

> ## "The place was just swarming in drugs, many of which I was taking."
>
> Ed Freeman,
> record producer

Freeman rehearsed the musicians for two weeks before heading into the studio, where Flye tracked McLean and the band exclusively live. They recorded "American Pie" from start to finish more than twenty times on a sixteen-track, two-inch tape machine, never delivering the perfect take they were after. McLean refused to fix a performance by overdubbing, which caused friction between Freeman and his artist. But as Freeman told *Sound on Sound* magazine, "[Flye] was endlessly patient, and his personality was so perfect for the position, sitting there between these two monster egos—the producer and the artist. He was like the glue that held the whole thing together."

McLean and his band recorded "American Pie" and two other songs on May 26, 1971; but the real work on "American Pie" began once the recording sessions were over.

"I was a monster when it came to editing tape," Freeman recalled, instructing Flye to cut and paste the best licks into the final song. The song's famous vocal-and-piano-only introduction was actually made up of eight different tape edits. A single, three-syllable word was reconstructed from three different tapes. Freeman even had Flye cut a drum fill into individual beats so he could shuffle them into a new arrangement.

"No matter what crazy idea I came up with, he would do it," Freeman said about his engineer.

Musicians in service of other musicians—that was the staffing formula for the Record Plants on both coasts; it was a unique support system that was built on committed and adoring, low-wage workers with their own musical ambitions who were the core capital of every studio in town.

While a drummer turned engineer (Flye) and a roadie turned record producer (Freeman) were wrapping up a hit record at Record Plant NY, a similar scenario was unfolding at another studio, Mediasound on Fifty-Seventh Street. There, Flye's former producer turned filmmaker turned Moog programmer (Bob Margouleff) was about to embark on a five-year hit-making ride alongside a bass player turned electronics wizard (Malcolm Cecil) and an energized twenty-one-year-old song machine named Stevie Wonder.

TONTO

Stevie Wonder wanted to meet TONTO. He was flush with cash from Motown Records and had songs and sounds in his head that he was unable to get onto tape. A friend had loaned him a copy of a recently released album called *Zero Time: TONTO's Expanding Head Band* that had been recorded using the world's largest music synthesizer named TONTO—an acronym for The Original New Timbral Orchestra. He hadn't heard anything like it.

The mastermind behind TONTO was an afro-haired, English bassist named Malcolm Cecil who worked at Mediasound, a midtown-Manhattan advertising recording studio. The album—which was named by Cecil's music partner, Bob Margouleff, while on a peyote trip—was a breakthrough for electronic music when it was first released in March 1971. "[It's] like taking acid and discovering that your mind has the power to stop your heart . . ." a *Rolling Stone* magazine reviewer wrote.

To create the album, Cecil and Margouleff cobbled together synthesizers from Moog and ARP along with a mix of custom modules from a Russian electronic composer and Jimi Hendrix's guitar tech.

Above: Bob Margouleff (left) and Malcolm Cecil at Record Plant LA. Below: Malcolm Cecil pictured with the behemoth synthesizer of his creation. He and Margouleff named it TONTO, an acronym for The Original New Timbral Orchestra, and Stevie Wonder fell in love with it.

The resulting instrument was a behemoth electronic-music control center that, for the first time, allowed incompatible synthesizers to play together like an orchestra.

Late in May 1971, Cecil heard a ring at the studio door and stuck his head out of the window to see someone in a chartreuse jumpsuit out on the street waving with a copy of the TONTO album under his arm. Cecil walked down the stairs, opened the door and discovered that it was Stevie Wonder who wanted to "meet" the synthesizer he and Margouleff had used to make the record.

"Hey man, is this a keyboard instrument?" Wonder asked.

"Yes, it has a keyboard and knobs and patch cords," Cecil replied.

"Show me," Wonder said.

Cecil led Wonder into the studio, sat him down and placed his hands on the keyboard. Wonder's fingers went to work, but he was surprised that TONTO could produce only one note at a time, and that it required two assistants working the dials and patch cords in real time with the performer to create sounds, chords, and orchestration. Cecil demonstrated what he meant, played him a demo tape of something new he and Margouleff were working on, and Wonder immediately heard the potential. That night, Cecil called Margouleff into the session, and suddenly Stevie, Cecil, Bob, and TONTO were all making music.

> ## "I had ideas in my head, and I wanted those ideas to be heard."
>
> Stevie Wonder, musician

A former radar technician for the Royal Air Force, Cecil's career always straddled the worlds of music and engineering. In England, at the same time as he was tinkering with plans for a voice-activated typewriter, he was a principal bassist with the BBC Radio Orchestra and was playing bass guitar with Keith Richards, Mick Jagger, Rod Stewart, and Jimmy Page. He recorded the original demo for "The House of the Rising Sun" with the Animals.

Cecil's technical skills eventually led him to Los Angeles, where he was hired to build one of the city's first Ampex sixteen-track studio for singer Pat Boone. In those early days of multitrack recording,

CHAPTER TWO

tape machines would frequently malfunction and munch tape, which made the maintenance engineer a studio's most valued employee. Cecil had the "analog touch," and it was at Boone's studio that he was discovered by Tom Hidley, who quickly hired him for a short-term project at Record Plant NY.

The tape machines were failing frequently in the Record Plant NY studios and, coincidentally, it was all happening at the same time as Kellgren and Stone were selling the studio to TVC. The studio's engineers were concerned that the union might come for their jobs, now that it was owned by a television company, and Stone was suspicious that somebody was sabotaging the gear. Stone had Hidley call Cecil in to troubleshoot the problem.

> ## "I'm talking to George Harrison about his next project..."
>
> Gary Kellgren, studio co-owner

Cecil worked undercover in maintenance at Record Plant NY for six weeks; he met Hendrix up on the tenth floor and frequently saw Phil Spector who was there trying to date the studio's receptionist. Cecil fingered the culprit who was sabotaging the equipment for Stone who, as a thank you, agreed to sign Cecil's application for an immigration green card and referred him to a friend for a full-time job at Mediasound.

Mediasound was no Record Plant. Housed in a midtown church and built by several founders of the Woodstock Festival, the studio was geared mostly to daytime, Madison Avenue work. Margouleff landed at Mediasound after the *Ciao! Manhattan* fiasco, selling himself to the studio as a one-person jingle machine. He bought one of the first three Moogs in town and began assembling an assortment of keyboards, electronic modules, and patch cords on a gurney that he rolled from room to room to score jingle dates. At the time, the $35,000 Moog was an esoteric piece of musical gear favored only by academics and experimental composers.

That night at Mediasound in 1971 changed the course of music history. TONTO's collaboration with Stevie Wonder would prove, for the first time, the crossover potential of electronic music for a mainstream audience. During a sweltering Memorial Day weekend in the studio one week later, Wonder and TONTO recorded seventeen songs.

At the time, TONTO looked nothing like the command-and-control center it would become when Wonder, Cecil and Margouleff took up residence at post-Jimi Electric Lady Studios in Greenwich Village, where John Storyk installed the instrument in an orb-like wooden case. They were burning up studio time night after night, keeping the studio alive after its owner's death. The team of Stevie Wonder and TONTO was every studio owner's dream—including Chris Stone's.

"Go to New York to see if you can steal Little Stevie?" Stone told Gary.

"I'm talking to George Harrison about his next project . . ."

Stone wanted a block-booking, not a Beatle. "Malcolm [Cecil] owes me a favor . . ."

Kellgren ignored him and continued: ". . . and Tom Wilson is talking to Phil Spector about bringing John Lennon out to finish his new solo album."

"I'd rather have Stevie."

Stone eventually got his wish. The following year, Record Plant LA Studio B became Stevie Wonder's headquarters for virtually his entire classic period, where he composed, recorded and/or mixed *Music of My Mind*, *Talking Book*, *Innervisions*, *Fulfillingness' First Finale*, *Songs in the Key of Life*, plus over two hundred other songs, many still unreleased.

But Kellgren was also correct. During that early summer of 1971, Record Plant was about to re-establish its reputation as the studio of the stars by booking not one, but two former Beatles, in two studios, on two coasts at the same time.

TAPE 11

STUDIO	WALLY HEIDER STUDIOS, LA / RECORD PLANT LA	
ARTIST	**TITLE**	**FORMAT**
George Harrison and Ravi Shankar	"Bangla Desh"	Single
George Harrison	"Deep Blue"	Single

CALL WALLY

George Harrison's name had become a running joke between the Record Plant partners ever since Stone mistook George *Hamilton* for him at the New York studio's opening-night party in 1968. But when Marta answered the phone in the spring of 1971, it was the real George Harrison who was calling, looking to come over to the house to see Gary.

"Oh, God! Needless to say, the Beatles were THE BEATLES at that time. The two of us were like groupies, for lack of another word. So, shy," Marta Kellgren remembered.

Harrison was in LA putting the finishing touches on the soundtrack to the Ravi Shankar documentary *Raga* that he was producing. While working on the movie, Harrison learned about the mass starvation in Bangladesh and decided to do something about it. He scheduled two celebrity charity concerts for August 1st at Madison Square Garden and had Apple Records management cut deals for a film and triple-album to maximize donations.

Harrison visited Kellgren to ask for Record Plant's help recording a live album for the upcoming concert. His people were negotiating with Wally Heider to use his remote truck for the show but the studio owner wouldn't budge on the price. Heider wanted to get paid for the remote recording, especially since "that pain in the ass," Phil Spector, was producing.

Record Plant didn't own a truck, at least not yet, but with the disastrous Woodstock tapes as his studio's only live-show experience, Kellgren still took the assignment. Without asking Stone's permission, he even volunteered to do it for free.

Kellgren had an assistant drive George back home in the backseat of GREED and then called Stone right away. Kellgren updated him on their "donation" and, true to the character of someone with a car named DEDUCT, Stone calculated the tax savings. "But where the hell are we going to get a truck?" he then asked.

"We'll build one," was Kellgren's reply

"In three weeks?"

Separately, they came to the same conclusion: "Let's call Wally."

Everybody in LA did business with Wally Heider. In addition to owning studios in LA and San Francisco, the overweight recording engineer with a merciless stutter was one of the pioneers of remote recording. As a kid, he traveled around the country recording big-band concerts and built a legendary collection of live performances from that era.

Wally was also a businessman. He and Stone, both straights in a field of freaks, talked the same language. When Stone gave him a call, Heider said that he was expecting a purchase order any minute from Apple Records for the live concert album in New York, though he complained about the cost of moving the truck and its crew cross-country.

Heider's white panel truck was one of the first real studios-on-wheels. Outfitted and finished like a modern, miniature control room, it came with heavy-duty insulation, wood paneling, recessed lighting, and a flush-mounted speaker system, all of which made the vehicle heavy and cramped. Two tape machines took up half the space. It also needed a generator. And by the time it was roadworthy, Heider and his design engineer, Tom Scott, were already talking about tearing it apart and starting from scratch.

Then Chris Stone called and changed their plans. As Heider told *Mix* magazine: "We built a truck in 1970 that didn't work out too well, so we sold it to one of our competitors in the east."

Stone didn't buy the truck, he leased it. And Heider had one stipulation—the Record Plant remote would only record shows on the East Coast, leaving Heider all the West Coast concerts for himself. Stone agreed, as long as Heider handed over the keys to the truck in time for Record Plant to do the *Concert for Bangladesh*. Knowing what they were in for, Heider sent Tom Scott to babysit the production and teach Kellgren and the New York team everything they needed to know about remote recording.

Heider told Stone to always run two tape machines. As his tech Tom Scott explained, "Running two machines meant running twice the amount of tape. Wally was good at explaining to customers that, 'Oh, well, my gosh, if something happens to one machine, or if we need to change the tape in the middle of a song, you might lose a precious performance, so you always need to run a backup.' And that worked pretty well; we sold a huge amount of tape. And Chris Stone learned that lesson well."

Before heading to New York for the concert, George Harrison and Phil Spector recorded the "Bangla Desh" single at Wally Heider Studios in Los Angeles. Drummer Jim Keltner, who worked on those dates, remembered: "Phil was on his toes in those days . . ." Allen Steckler, head of A&R at Apple Records, added: "Phil was Phil. Phil was . . . he was crazy. But he was an amazing producer. When Phil got into the studio, it was Phil's studio."

With the tracks for the "Bangla Desh" single in the can, Spector handed George Harrison over to Lillian Davis Douma to complete the single's B-side "Deep Blue" at Record Plant LA. Spector booked a room for horn overdubs and mixdowns the following week. And then suddenly, with the Capitol Records vinyl pressing plant constantly calling for updates, Spector disappeared. Harrison thought he had checked himself into rehab, but the producer actually had another Beatle to record.

Phil Spector had headed east with a suitcase filled with cherry brandy to join John and Yoko Ono for an Independence Day weekend of string overdubs on "Imagine" at Record Plant NY.

TAPE 12

STUDIO RECORD PLANT NY / REMOTE

ARTIST	TITLE	FORMAT
Yoko Ono	*Fly*	Album
John Lennon	*Imagine*	Single / Album
George Harrison	*Concert for Bangladesh*	Album / Soundtrack

CRAZY YANK

John Lennon checked into Record Plant NY on July 4, 1971, and left on December 8, 1980, the night of his death. He collaborated with Roy Cicala and his team of engineers on his entire post-Beatles catalog: *Imagine* (1971), *Some Time in New York* (1972), *Mind Games* (1973), *Walls and Bridges* (1974), *Rock 'N' Roll* (1975), and *Double Fantasy* (1980). He even found a home at a Record Plant during the "Lost Weekend," his eighteen-month-long bender out in LA.

Not to be ignored, Record Plant NY was also the site of Yoko Ono's solo work from the period, including *Fly* (1971), *Approximately Infinite Universe* (1973), *Feeling the Space* (1973), and *A Story* (released in 1997, recorded in 1974). Though she continued recording after John's death, Ono never recorded at Record Plant NY ever again.

Jack Douglas was there from the beginning (*Imagine*) to the end (*Double Fantasy*). His relationship with John and Yoko began that Independence Day weekend when Lennon arrived at the studio to finish "Imagine," still unaware that this "protest song" would become the biggest commercial hit of his solo career.

Lennon was up on the tenth floor looking for some privacy and walked in on Douglas who was in Studio C editing tapes. After his brief star-is-born moment with The Who earlier that spring, Douglas was back in the tape library and assisting the staff engineers.

"Can I sit down?" John asked while seating himself on the other side of a small console.

CHAPTER TWO

Douglas was one of the first people in the world to hear Lennon's new solo album; as an assistant, it was his job to transfer the eight-track *Imagine* tapes onto sixteen-track so that Roy and Shelly Yakus could build up the sound once John arrived. "You know, I've visited Liverpool," Douglas told Lennon, breaking the ice.

The comment piqued Lennon's interest, "Why would anyone go to Liverpool?"

Douglas told him that he took a freighter to the UK to meet the Beatles back in the mid-sixties, and that he and a bandmate snuck into the country without the necessary papers. They were arrested and made headlines in the local newspapers, and eventually got deported, which caused a local stir and gave him a great tale to tell everyone back in New York.

"You were that crazy Yank?" Lennon asked, telling Douglas that he and McCartney had both read the article and had admired the Les Paul guitar that Jack was holding in the photograph. Then Lennon had an idea:

"Let's go downstairs and meet Yoko."

Lennon and Douglas took the elevator downstairs to Studio A where the *Imagine* team was hard at work. Shelly Yakus was a knob-whirling dervish. Spector worked the faders on the console with his black-leather-gloved hands, Dr. Strangelove-style. Roy Cicala was sitting alongside Yoko and, when interrupted, turned in his swivel chair and asked Douglas what he was doing there.

"John invited me," Douglas replied

Before Roy could object, Lennon intervened: "Hey Roy, give the kid a chance."

IMAGINE

What was supposed to be a weekend of string and sax overdubs evolved into four days of recording, and a summer-long sonic overhaul.

John and Yoko fell in love with Manhattan. John loved walking around the city streets without anyone asking for an autograph. He also got a kick out of the quintessential New York characters like this Italian engineer named Roy Cicala.

"John wanted to work in the hippest studio in town. And everybody knew the guy who had to do those dates was Roy," Jack Douglas said.

In a book about the making of *Imagine*, Shelly Yakus described the vibe in the room when John first arrived:

> I'm twenty-five years old. We have John Lennon and Phil Spector—two giants of the music business—who represent every reason I got into this business—sitting at the console. Roy Cicala, Jack Douglas, and I are all at attention, all our senses heightened beyond belief. I sat there saying to myself, "OK, what is it going to take so that this session doesn't go wrong? Is the tape machine going to stop? Is it gonna eat the tape? Is the board gonna crackle? Is someone going to knock a cup of coffee into the board?" All of us wanted to be sure that when the sessions were over John was going to say, "This was really great. I got what I came for. This really works for the song. Thank you."

John, Yoko, Phil, Roy, and Shelly kicked off their Record Plant sessions with a playback of the stereo tapes from the UK. Assistant engineer Dennis Ferrante remembered, "[John] said he hated the vocals. He called them 'too syrupy' and wanted them redone." John also told Phil he didn't want a "Ronettes record" this time, and the comment enraged Spector. (The vocals that ultimately ended up on the album's multitrack master were originally recorded back at Lennon's Tittenhurst home studio).

Fortunately, Roy Cicala was there to get the two raging egos under control. Allan Steckler (A&R, Apple Records NY) remembered Roy's calming influence on the creative process, "Roy commanded authority, but he did it in a fairly quiet way."

Spector respected his engineers and Cicala's team was tops. Shelly's job was to control the compressors and equalizers and to make sure that the assistants, Jack Douglas and Dennis Ferrante, placed the microphones correctly and kept the tape machines running. Yoko Ono's commemorative *Imagine John Yoko* book describes a scene where Roy was at the console, making his moves with Lennon and Spector talking into each ear at the same time:

"The mix isn't quite right."

"Let's try to make it sound like this . . ."

CHAPTER TWO

"We need a little more of that . . ."

"A little more violin . . ."

"A little more viola . . ."

Jack Douglas noticed, "It was like Roy immediately and instinctively knew exactly what John wanted to hear."

At one point, John asked for an Automatic Double Tracking (ADT) device, a legendary EMI Studios invention that was not commercially available and that remained a studio secret for many years. Lennon liked the way it filled out the sound of his voice. Roy told an interviewer what happened next:

"What's an ADT?" the Record Plant engineers wondered.

"I don't know but go make me one," Roy demanded of his tech staff.

A few days later, maintenance tech (and world-class banjo player) Paul Prestopino rolled out a hot-rodded tape machine with big knobs into Studio A, which delivered the desired effect. He recalled: "It came close to the sound of an ADT. I mean, not knowing exactly what they did, this came pretty close."

John was impatient in the studio and drove the engineers to complete a song a day. Disciplined by the EMI Records Studio school of recording, he came to work and didn't waste time. That first day they added strings—soft, subtle pads of background sound—with members of the New York Philharmonic. R&B sax player King Curtis, who had opened for the Beatles at Shea Stadium, came in on July 5 to add some soulful sax. They didn't have time to do much more.

Lennon was notoriously insecure about his vocals. He usually turned them down on the console (while Yoko would turn them back up when he was out of the room). Whatever happened, it worked.

Shelly Yakus explained: "When you listen to the vocals on 'Imagine,' his feet weren't even touching the ground. He sang it from the deepest part of him. And when you listen, you can hear that it wasn't planned. It was all by the feel, you know. And hearing that stuff over the big studio speakers, it just took you over."

It was during those sessions that John first played the John Lennon Piano, the old oak upright that Jack Douglas rolled into Studio A. In an auction catalog years later, Douglas recalled, it "had a certain nostalgic sound that John associated with early American Rock and Rhythm and Blues." (The piano parts that ended up on the final song were also those he had recorded back in England.) Very few people even knew Lennon was in New York at the time, let alone on Forty-Fourth Street. The studio had two entrances, and John used to enter with the freight. Late-night sessions often took place up on the tenth floor, using a secret work tape that neither Spector nor Yoko knew about. Shelly cryptically said: "After everybody left, we would go upstairs to Studio C, sometimes with John and sometimes not, and we would add things there; there was this work tape that nobody knew about. It was so John could work on stuff with us alone, and uh, without certain input, you know? I'm not going to talk about which take the final song ['Imagine'] was mixed from; I'm just going to say that there was a work tape where stuff was added." Those who have studied the "Imagine" tapes firsthand maintain there is "zero evidence" of this tape existing.

By the end of the month, John and Yoko were ready to listen to the newly sequenced album for the first time. Phil Spector was manic and drunk. John's mind was somewhere else, still unconvinced that "Imagine" was the title cut. Cicala reminded everyone that Apple Records had ordered a quadraphonic mix. But it was time to stop, sit back, and listen.

They invited the Record Plant staff into the studio to hear the just-sequenced album start to finish. Studio manager, Arlene Reckson, remembered: "The studio was pretty filled, mostly with people who worked on the album. John was very anxious, very impatient. We were smoking these thin joints I had rolled, one for everyone in the room, since that was how John liked it. And I remember saying, 'It doesn't get better than this.'"

Everyone assumed that John would be sticking around Record Plant for George Harrison's charity show at Madison Square Garden the following week, while in fact, that night he was giving his work in progress a farewell listen. The next day, without Yoko and without finishing *Imagine*, John took off for England to avoid having to join half of the Beatles on stage at the Concert for Bangladesh.

THE GARDEN

Gloria Stone carried a red leather clutch bag that Tom Wilson had given her for Christmas to the Concert for Bangladesh. She and Chris

CHAPTER TWO

had arrived early at Madison Square Garden on Sunday, August 1, 1971, to keep an eye on their new recording truck and to hobnob with the TVC and Warner executives, who they had treated to passes for the super-session of the decade.

The press had already leaked that the show's line-up included Bob Dylan, Eric Clapton, Ringo, Leon Russell, Billy Preston, Ravi Shankar, and John Lennon. But unfortunately, Lennon skipped out at the last minute, Bob Dylan was still missing in action, and Eric Clapton was going through heroin withdrawal. "It was all one big fat risk," was how Apple Records' Allen Steckler described it. And most of that risk was going on backstage.

Record Plant wasn't the only tech company Harrison had tapped for a favor. Concert sound was borrowed from The Band. Additional equipment was loaned by Stephen Stills, who later grumbled that Harrison never thanked him for his help. Woodstock master of ceremonies and lighting wizard, Chip Monck, worked the lights. There were so many separate companies working for free that it was bedlam behind the scenes.

During setup, a massive speaker cabinet fell to the floor, wiping out the first few rows of seats where the audience would be seated the next day. The stage wiring was so shoddily run that it could have electrocuted one of the stars at any moment. One of the documentary cameras was out of focus and the film audio was not properly synced. A rigger fell off his scaffolding and died. Finally, as if defining this a shit show, an oversized tour truck tore the fire sprinkler heads from the loading ramp ceiling, flooding the backstage and leaving a stink in the arena air.

"I worked on *Woodstock* and we know how those tapes turned out, and these guys weren't nearly as prepared. They didn't know how to deal with all these different companies coming in. They had all these cables laid out on the stage and you had to be escorted by a guide to get you through the maze," engineer Lillian Davis Douma recalled.

George Harrison was oblivious to the chaos; his only concern was getting the performance onto tape. The recordings would make the albums that would make the money to feed millions of starving people. This life-and-death chain of events was all riding on a team of audio engineers who had never before recorded a live concert.

It was trial by fire for Gary Kellgren, Tom Flye, Lillian Davis Douma, and several other hand-picked members of the Record Plant crew who were being trained on the job by Heider tech Tom Scott. The concert gig marked the first pairing of "Tom & Tom" as Flye and Scott would eventually be known. Together, they would both work at the third Record Plant studio in Sausalito, California, less than fourteen months later.

Harrison had handpicked Spector to produce the charity album and Kellgren to engineer. Being Cicala territory, Kellgren's arrival in New York caused friction on Forty-Fourth Street as to who would get credit for the show. Stone assured Cicala that the truck was for the exclusive use of the New York operation; their agreement with Wally Heider restricted the vehicle from recording west of the Mississippi.

Cicala inspected his new truck and realized that the console was too small for the forty-five microphones and cables they had loaded it up with to satisfy Spector's demand for a live Wall of Sound. And since Heider leased it without tape machines, Cicala rolled a pair of sixteen-track Ampex recorders inside, leaving barely enough room in the box for two operators.

Kellgren knew that Spector wanted to party in the truck during the show, so he told the New York studio techs to move one of the machines out onto the street to make room. Two hours before show time, the Record Plant engineers lowered the second Ampex on the truck's tailgate and the six-hundred-pound tape machine accidentally toppled to the ground.

"Go back to the studio and roll us another one," Kellgren snapped.

"We're not going to get it here in time for the show," someone replied.

"So, you better jump for your job . . ."

As if on cue, and with the guts of the $40,000 tape machine strewn on the ground outside, Phil Spector showed up to see what was going on. It was late morning; he had already been drinking and he had only one question for the crew: "George wants to know if everything's okay."

Kellgren was too busy to engage, "Sure, tell him we're set."

Spector walked off satisfied without mentioning the mangled machine. The replacement recorder arrived in time and it taped both shows from outside the truck.

CHAPTER TWO

"Thank God George didn't know," the show's stage manager, Jonathan Taplin, said. "He had his own problems."

Backstage, Bob Dylan had unexpectedly arrived with a new song list. The record-label lawyers were already fighting over album royalties. And Eric Clapton was in a stupor. "Eric came into New York and didn't have a connection. He eventually found 'something' but you could see he was a little 'not all there' on stage," Taplin added.

Chris Stone was with a group of Clapton's handlers who were trying to revive him for the show. Gloria Stone was sitting with the TVC and Warner brass, when her husband rushed in with panic written all over his face.

"Is everything all right?" she asked.

"Usual rock star shit," Chris replied. "Give me your bag."

Gloria emptied the purse of its belongings and handed it over. Less than an hour later she spotted it in the hands of a young woman wandering, as if lost, backstage, obviously looking for someone to hand it to.

Gloria never saw her red bag again, and Chris would never tell her exactly what had happened. Like everyone else, she had her suspicions when she saw Clapton emerge semi-sober from his dressing room and being led on stage.

At the end of the afternoon performance, Phil Spector returned to the truck, asking Kellgren only one question: "Did we get it?"

Kellgren hadn't had time to review the tapes, but he wasn't worried. Flye had reminded him how much work had gone into *Woodstock* after the fact and how every live concert recording can be fixed, especially with two performances to draw from. So, Kellgren smiled and gave the producer the thumbs up, which seemed to assuage any concerns.

Jonathan Taplin remembered what happened next: "Phil Spector came backstage after the first show and told George 'I think we've

> # "Phil [Spector] was at the front dancing when it was being recorded. Gary Kellgren did all the work."
>
> George Harrison, musician, concert promoter

got it,' which was a great relief because everyone knew Phil was a little crazy in those days."

Things went more smoothly for the evening show, which is recognized as the better of the two performances. Afterwards, the cast and crew headed uptown to a West Side club to keep their stage-buzz going. There, Dylan hugged Harrison and encouraged him to do a third show. Ravi Shankar scolded Clapton for being a "chickenshit junkie." Keith Moon demolished a drum set. And Phil Spector did a drunken rendition of "Da Doo Ron Ron." The producer had been drinking all day while all the performers had assumed he was in the truck. But Harrison knew better. "Phil was at the concert dancing in the front when it was being recorded," he told a magazine reporter. "Gary Kellgren did all the work."

The next afternoon, Kellgren toured Cicala's Record Plant NY for the first time. He felt like a stranger in the studio he had built just three years earlier. Many of the assistant engineers didn't even know who he was. He noted how much "straighter" New York had become with so many ad-agency types working there just to see John Lennon. With the *Concert for Bangladesh* in the can, Kellgren split for LA and left the cleanup work to the New York engineers.

For the next two weeks, Flye and several other *Woodstock* album veterans worked with Harrison on the *Concert for Bangladesh* tapes. There were simply too many microphones fighting for the same sounds on stage. Many of the acoustic guitar parts needed to be replaced. And, as Flye predicted, some of the finished songs had to be pieced together from the two performances. Steckler remembered: "George was working a couple of weeks in New York, trying to get the sound right, and he just couldn't do it. They had mixed the whole album and listened to it and hated it. Then out of frustration George said, 'Let's go back to LA and we'll do it there.'"

Spector was out in LA. And under pressure to get the triple-album box set released by Christmas, Harrison flew out west the next day to work with the producer at his preferred LA studio, A&M. On the first night of those sessions, Phil said to George, "Listen. Give me an hour, and then come back in." So, George and everyone else went out for dinner and when they returned, Phil was ready. He pressed play on the tape machine, slowly raised the volume on the faders and said,

George Harrison with Phil Spector (above) at a mixing session for the *Concert for Bangladesh* album in August, 1971. Track sheets with the Record Plant logo are visible on the control panel (below). The pair produced the live album together after the concert.

"Listen to this," as he debuted the new concert mix. Bangladesh was now bathed in the "big" Phil Spector sound that matched the size of the performance. "It was just amazing. We were just absolutely destroyed by how much better it all sounded," Allen Steckler said.

Record Plant's first live recording would win the 1973 Grammy for Album of the Year, even though it took almost a month of work in studios on both coasts to get it to sound "live."

RIPP-OFF

Not every producer was Phil Spector. Not even Spector's friend, Artie Ripp.

A former song publisher, who cut demos with Gary Kellgren over at Dick Charles Recording, Ripp competed with Spector on the *Billboard* charts throughout the sixties. Like all the other Tin Pan Alley West Coast expats, he was jealous that Spector had landed two Beatles and, hoping to catch up, signed a twenty-two-year-old, dewy-eyed Long Island singer-songwriter named Billy Joel. The deal was so exploitative that music-biz associates assumed the term "rip-off" had been coined in Artie Ripp's honor.

Ripp was Gary and Chris's back-office tenant during their first two years of operation in LA. Working out of his sparsely furnished Record Plant digs in 1970–71, he helped make a lasting change to the studio while there—the infamous "buzz lock."

In post-Manson LA, the musicians sought security wherever they worked and played. The walls that isolated the Record Plant parking lot from the Third Street traffic made a secure impression, but in those early days, once someone got through the Record Plant parking lot-gate, they could freely walk into the studio complex. It took the first of several drug busts to change all that. A session drummer working for Artie Ripp was arrested for marijuana possession after accidentally setting off Record Plant's silent alarm and causing a police raid. A second wooden door entrance was soon added inside with a loud buzz lock that could only be opened via a button under the reception desk. *"Buzz me in"* became the Record Plant LA password for years to come.

Billy Joel's first album, *Cold Spring Harbor*, was mixed to death for nearly a year in Record Plant LA Studio B by Ripp, Kellgren, and

CHAPTER TWO

former Record Plant NY engineer, Bob Hughes, who was brought out to LA expressly to work on the project. Hughes had helped Ampex build its first sixteen-track tape machine for Tommy James and the Shondells. Ampex was financing much of the recording and wanted Hughes to help them market their new tape machine's special features.

With Bob Hughes behind the console and with financial backing from Ampex, Ripp burned through a massive studio budget to break this new singer-songwriter. Billy Joel told his biographer that, "I believe that Artie saw me as his opportunity to be a musical impresario, some sort of studio wizard, and not just a cigar-chomping producer."

Engineer Lee Kiefer remembered the night that the producer and artist arrived at the studio for the first time. He was handed a stack of white tape boxes that were prepared by Jack Douglas on Forty-Fourth Street in New York and told to "Take these to the trash."

Ripp's technical incompetence nearly ended the singer-songwriter's recording career before it started. Bob Hughes introduced Ripp to a new control that allowed him to speed up or slow down the tape reels as they spun past the magnetic heads. Ripp became obsessed with this new Ampex "Varispeed" feature that allowed engineers to dial in the perfect tempo, though he was oblivious to the fact that, in the process, he was making Joel's voice sound like Alvin and the Chipmunks. When Billy auditioned a test pressing of the album at his Long Island home, he was so embarrassed that he snatched the acetate off the turntable, ran outside and flung it like a Frisbee down the street.

Ripp told Billy that he was out of money and couldn't afford a remix. With the project completed and Ripp already running late on his rent, the producer's Record Plant residence soon came to an end. And Gary Kellgren knew exactly what to do with the vacant space.

From top left: *Cry of Love*, Jimi Hendrix, 1971; *Who's Next*, The Who, 1971; *Labelle*, Patti Labelle, 1971; *Imagine*, John Lennon, 1971; *Fly*, Yoko Ono, 1971; *American Pie*, Don McLean, 1971; *Rainbow Bridge*, Jimi Hendrix, 1971; *Concert for Bangladesh*, George Harrison, 1971; *Nine to the Universe*, Jimi Hendrix, 1980; *Valleys of Neptune*, Jimi Hendrix, 2010; *People, Hell and Angels*, Jimi Hendrix, 2013; *Both Sides of the Sky*, Jimi Hendrix, 2018.

3

SECOND HOME

1971–1974

"John didn't have Paul and the boys in the group anymore, so the Record Plant family became a substitute. It became John's second home."

Arlene Reckson
Record Plant NY studio manager

TAPE 13

STUDIO	RECORD PLANT LA / RECORD PLANT NY	
ARTIST	**TITLE**	**FORMAT**
Stephen Stills	*Stephen Stills*	Album
Billy Joel	*Cold Spring Harbor*	Album
The J. Geils Band	*The Morning After*	Album

THE ACCOMMODATIONS

Everybody was having sex: "In those days, Record Plant was like a sex dispensary," keyboardist and producer Al Kooper recalled.

"If there was a room in the Record Plant where somebody didn't have sex at one point or another, I would be absolutely shocked," engineer Michael Braunstein said.

The Record Plant LA hot tub was the hotbed of the sybaritic activity at the studio. Drummer Buddy Miles used to joke about all the kids he birthed in that bubbling bath. Sly Stone and a girlfriend walked in to have sex one night and cleared the tub by saying, "Hi everyone. I'm Sly. Now everyone, get the fuck out." Mark Mothersbaugh of Devo brought his own towel, skeeved by the unsanitary conditions. Stevie Wonder made use of the facilities, as did Rod Stewart. Frank Zappa used to surreptitiously record the activities inside. Gary interviewed new female applicants in the tub, impressed most by the ones who rebuffed his come-ons.

The Jacuzzi was often too crowded to accommodate everyone, especially after it was discovered by the strippers from a club up the street, so building the long-planned and promised bedrooms became the next construction project for Kellgren and his team of hippies with hammers. In a studio that defined the counter-cultural sacraments of sex, drugs, and rock and roll, the Record Plant LA bedrooms were designed to serve up all three. For $50 per hour, customers and their crews could book a room to sleep, screw, rehearse, or write songs. Exhausted engineers could crash there between sessions.

Kellgren built three rooms, all inspired by theme rooms he had visited with Jack Adams at the Hellfire Club back in New York:

THE RACK ROOM was straight out of the New York City S&M scene. Its centerpiece was a rack-like bed with fur-covered shackle restraints. The ceiling and walls resembled a dungeon. The bathroom had bars on the windows. It was Gary's favorite room.

THE SISSY ROOM featured a huge white wicker bed with a canopy in the middle of the room, and with a shaft going up to a skylight on the roof. All the walls were airbrushed sky-blue with white clouds.

THE BOAT ROOM was set up like the cabin of a ship, with portholes in the walls and a king-sized bed in a loft with a full-size mirror overhead. Under the bed, accessible via a hidden panel, was a tiny hideaway called the Anne Frank Room.

"As soon as Artie Ripp moved out of the studio, Gary moved in on the space," Kellgren's design partner Lee Kiefer remembered. "He said he wanted to have a place where the musicians didn't ever have to go home. The rooms had beautiful showers, nice bathrooms. All three were different. If you were a New York player and you came to LA, it was very expensive to find a hotel. Record Plant was the best place you could stay if you were a player and working there."

In a disturbing comment from the period, Howard Kaylan (co-founder of the Turtles, Eddie in Flo & Eddie) told his biographer, "You could take a groupie girl in [one of the Record Plant bedrooms] and she wouldn't emerge for days. They would feed her, they would drug her, they would pass her around, and several days later she would emerge, probably the worse for wear. It was the last of the great, decadent studios."

In contrast, back at home Gary was a loving father. He built his son, Mark, a yellow bunk bed shaped like a sports car. He'd take the family up north to teach the kids how to fish. He even dressed like Santa Claus one Christmas, though Mark and Devon could tell it was their father because of his Iowa accent.

The Sissy Room (above left) at the LA studio was one of the "theme rooms" that Gary Kellgren built for musicians to crash in. The Boat Room (above right) came complete with a loft bed and mirrored ceiling. The Rack Room (below) was a fantasy escape.

Gary's job was to party and much of his extracurricular activity took place in Tom Wilson's rented bungalow, up in Beachwood Canyon. Stone went up to the house one night when the studio's Ampex sales rep installed one of the first VCRs in the living room and used the prototype machine to show them porn. With everyone's eyes glued to the screen, Stone had some business to discuss with his partner.

"I've been talking to Ancky . . ." Stone told Kellgren, explaining that she said the sale to Warner was imminent—and that Warner's CEO, Steve Ross, was planning to sell off Record Plant. Despite booming studio revenues, Warner needed a "record-pressing plant" not a "recording plant." A price-fixing scandal in Ross's parking lot division had made him extremely anxious about the casual way the studio did business.

Kellgren knew their founding investor, Ancky Revson, had connections inside TVC, so he declared, "As long as we get our money."

"We're going to need that money."

"What for?"

"For buying our studio back," Stone replied.

BIG DADDY

Raechel Donahue was sitting sandwiched between her husband, Tom, and Buddy Miles in one of the wooden, wave-shaped tables at the Trident Restaurant in Sausalito when Chris and Gary walked in. She was more than just arm candy for her 350-pound husband Tom "Big Daddy" Donahue, the father of underground radio. "She had talent, brains and a lightning wit to match her Veronica Lake-style of beauty," Los Angeles DJ Jim Ladd wrote.

The Donahues were the local San Francisco music-scene dealmakers. They presented the Rolling Stones at the Cow Palace and the Beatles at Candlestick Park and were the first to discover and record pre-Jefferson Airplane Grace Slick. They ran an independent record label whose executive producer was a DJ named Sylvester Stewart, who became Sly Stone. Each of them had their own radio programs in both LA and San Francisco.

"Tom Donahue was the man who stole the keys to FM radio's glass booth and opened it up to an entirely new generation of radio pioneers—long-haired, barefoot, tie-dyed dreamers, who came to their tiny, run-down, and woefully ill-equipped stations, filled with the rhythm of adventure, and the melody of revolution," Ladd wrote.

The Record Plant partners had just arrived on the PSA regional shuttle flight from Los Angeles, before hopping a twenty-minute helicopter ride over the Golden Gate Bridge and into the waterfront town that Otis Redding immortalized with his song, "[Sittin' On] The Dock of the Bay." Buddy Miles had called Gary up to Sausalito for a meeting.

Sausalito was in the middle of everything, Raechel recalled: "In the early seventies, everyone was moving to Marin County. That's where Janis was, that's where the [Grateful] Dead were. All the drug dealers lived in the area. All the session musicians that mattered lived in Sausalito. It was private and it had the best pot."

The Trident restaurant had its own musical pedigree. The waterfront eatery on Bridgeway was owned by the manager of the Kingston Trio. David Crosby called the Trident, "Ground zero for sex, drugs, and rock and roll!" Janis Joplin had her own table. The Rolling Stones launched national tours there. Robin Williams was one of the busboys. A couple of its bartenders invented the Tequila Sunrise, the drink that inspired the Eagles song of the same name.

Miles and the Donahues had a business proposition for the Record Plant partners to consider. Raechel remembered, "We were sick and tired of having to record in LA. We wanted a studio like the LA Record Plant nearer to where we all lived. So, we met with Chris and Gary to make a deal."

Alternative radio and the modern recording studio grew up together in the late sixties and early seventies; both were byproducts of a record industry that had tripled in size in just three years, requiring a "record plant" to manufacture the hits and an album-oriented radio station to sell them.

The technology of the average radio station control room paled in comparison to the recording studio. They were especially ill-equipped for live radio concerts, a new format that Tom Donahue had also pioneered.

"[Live remotes] meant sending a stereo signal from the concert back to the radio station over unreliable telephone lines. It meant keeping both channels in phase and properly balanced, using equipment never intended for the job. It meant creative engineers and it meant lots and lots of duct tape," Ladd explained.

Using a recording studio as both the concert hall and control room solved a lot of these problems. Down in LA, Donahue produced several concerts from Record Plant Studio A and liked what he heard. The shows sounded like live albums, clearer and more polished than the first "from the studio" radio concerts he had produced from Pacific High Recording, San Francisco's then premier studio facility.

Wally Heider owned the only other serious studio in San Francisco and introduced sixteen-track recording to the city. Located next door to a methadone clinic, it was nothing like the world-class room he owned in LA. Fantasy Records had also just opened its own in-house studio in nearby Berkeley for Creedence Clearwater Revival and the label's roster of jazz artists.

When Stone and Kellgren sat down with the Donahues and Miles at the Trident, it was Raechel who got everyone focused on the business at hand. "There's really no hip place to record in Sausalito," she said. "What's it going to take to get you to open a Record Plant up here?"

"It's going to take $500,000, plus a whole lot of business," Stone said.

Tom Donahue replied in his "made-for-radio" voice, "I can't help you with the cash, but I can deliver a whole lot of business."

Stone and Kellgren didn't need the cash. Once TVC sold out to Warner, their stock would be worth millions. Stone knew that their days with the new ownership were numbered and he was already planning to dump their stock for cash and reopen in a fresh new music market.

Stone watched Kellgren's keen green eyes darting around the Trident, taking in the inlay floor designs, psychedelic ceiling murals, and panoramic views of the Bay. The Trident was everything this kid from Iowa farm country wanted in his next studio, down to the sexy, braless waitresses and hefty portions of organic food. It was the local musicians' hangout, and Gary needed to find a space to record nearby.

Tom Donahue detailed his plan: KSAN, his radio station in San Francisco, was going into business with Bill Graham who had just closed both his theaters—Fillmore East and Fillmore West. They were going to launch an entirely new radio format built on marathon,

CHAPTER THREE

live-concert broadcasts. "The promotion is going to be priceless for the right studio," Donahue said.

The conversation bored Miles, and Kellgren wanted to scout the Trident's carvings, murals, and décor; the pair quickly left the table. Stone got down to business. He wanted to know why Wally Heider was having so much trouble with the building authorities. He wanted to know how reliable the helicopter flight was from San Francisco Internation Airport to Sausalito. And he wanted to know if there was any local musician with enough money to block-book a room.

"What about Sly?" Donahue suggested.

Now Stone was interested. Between gin and tonics, he shared his story about visiting Sly Stone's mansion with Tom Wilson, and how he and Kellgren had offered to build him a room in LA. Donahue had some inside information that suggested that this might be the right time to reapproach the artist.

Buddy Miles came through the door from the outside and grabbed a breadbasket off someone's table. Stone waited a few seconds for Kellgren to follow from behind. He waited some more and then went outside to look for his partner. With the city skyline as the backdrop, he followed the sound of a small speedboat racing from the dock and out into the open water. Kellgren was driving and howling at the top of his lungs as the boat skipped full-throttle across the whitecaps.

That was when Stone knew they were moving to Sausalito. He knew he'd never get Gary away from the water again.

Stone went back inside, pressed himself next to Raechel, and told the Donahues that they had a deal. He would give them a "Wilson," which was Record Plant shorthand for a 10 percent commission on every paying customer they brought in, and he would barter the studio time in exchange for *Live at the Record Plant* branding and co-ownership of the tapes.

"And while we're at it, find me the best pot connection in town," Stone added.

TAPE 14

STUDIO RECORD PLANT NY

ARTIST	TITLE	FORMAT
Laura Nyro & Patti LaBelle	*Gonna Take a Miracle*	Album / Single
Todd Rundgren	*Something/Anything?*	Album
John Lennon & Yoko Ono	*Some Time in New York City*	Album
David Peel & The Lower East Side	*The Pope Smokes Dope*	Album / Single

GIMME SOME TRUTH

Stone spiffed the Record Plant staff with stock options to drive revenues before the anticipated January 1972 TVC sale to Warner. All employees, from the top engineers to the front desk, were given shares in the business in exchange for building business and, thus, the value of the company for Kellgren and Stone. It worked. The studio had never been busier.

Record Plant engineers were mixing *Gonna Take a Miracle* with Laura Nyro and Patti LaBelle. Former assistant engineer Todd Rundgren was back at Roy's recording his double album *Something/Anything?* The Raspberries booked a room with Shelly Yakus to record their debut LP. Allen Ginsberg and Bob Dylan spent a few days in the studio with incense burning and an oddball orchestra playing tamburas, sitars, and finger cymbals. A yogi rented a studio simply to meditate in the nude. Carly Simon was singing with Elephant's Memory. There were dozens of no-name bands with budgets, hoping that the John Lennon magic would rub off with a hit.

The only one who didn't get a piece of the company, and who probably deserved it most, was Lennon, who was now camped out nights working on his next album. Roy Cicala regularly loaned the millionaire musician cash whenever he ran short.

CHAPTER THREE

Studio manager Arlene Reckson said: "John liked being around musicians. He didn't have Paul and the boys in the group anymore, so the Record Plant family became a substitute. It became John's second home; he really loved it there. Remember, he and Yoko didn't have a real home yet; they were a little nomadic at that time. The studio was built to be a comfortable hangout. So, he was there constantly working."

Late fall 1971 was a particularly productive period for Lennon at Record Plant NY. He arrived most evenings to rework his songs. He remixed his concerts, rehearsed his vocals, and auditioned cassette tapes for the most un-Beatle-like backup band possible for his next solo album (*Some Time in New York City*). Planning to stay for a while, he had his Mellotron keyboard (used on "Strawberry Fields") shipped over from his home in the UK, along with boxes of master tapes. And he let Yoko be Yoko. Roy Cicala's very first credit with the couple was a stereo recording of a toilet flush for Yoko's album "Fly," which used $7,000 worth of microphones.

> ## "Roy disrespected Yoko in the studio and John seemed to put up with it."
>
> Arlene Reckson,
> NY studio manager

In the studio, John and Yoko were a package deal. But Roy only had one client and he had no problem letting them both know.

"Roy disrespected Yoko in the studio, and John seemed to put up with it," Arlene Reckson said.

Contrary to his enlightened public image, in the privacy of the control room Lennon was just one of the guys. Several engineers remember John uncontrollably laughing at one of Yoko's takes, hiding his reaction from her by ducking under the console.

Elephant's Memory bassist, Gary Van Scyoc, recalled another encounter:

> Yoko was out in the studio and [assistant engineer] Dennis
> Ferrante went out to fix her microphone or something else.
> He tried to have a decent civil conversation with all the artists.
> He was just doing his thing, and somehow, for some reason,

Yoko turned to him and said, "Fuck you." So, Dennis is a tough kid. He points a finger back at Yoko Ono and, with the mics still on, he goes, "Well, fuck you, too."

John's at the console with Roy, smoking, taking this whole thing in. So, when Dennis goes back into the control room, knowing John has heard the whole thing, he apologizes to his boss first thing, "I'm sorry, Roy, I'm really sorry."

Roy looks at John and John turns to Dennis and smiles. "Anybody who can tell my old lady to go fuck herself is okay with me," Lennon said.

Over the last four days of October, John and Yoko resurrected their 1969 anti-war billboard message ("War is Over!") as a holiday radio perennial that was the last successful Lennon-Spector collaboration. Unlike the raw sound that marked the Lennon and Cicala mixes that ended up on *Some Time in New York City*, "Happy Xmas (War is Over)" was a classic Phil Spector Wall of Sound production. The "Happy Xmas" sessions in Record Plant NY Studio A reunited Lennon with his *Imagine* band: Nicky Hopkins, Jim Keltner, and Klaus Voormann. Spector also added a squad of five guitarists. And, on the final day, Arlene Reckson bussed in a Harlem children's choir complete with thirty singers and their mothers; they each got a McDonald's hamburger for their time (Yoko ordered blintzes). The photo session for the single's package was of the entire cast and crew, including a young secretarial assistant for the Beatles' manager, Allen Klein, named May Pang.

The "Happy Xmas" session at Record Plant NY was Lennon's second solo hit in a row with Phil Spector and, still, he couldn't get away from him fast enough.

Once the song was in the can and acetates were distributed to FM radio stations, John went back to work on *Some Time in New York City* with Cicala and Elephant's Memory. Known for their shows at New York anti-war rallies, the band wasn't up to Phil Spector's usual Wrecking Crew standards but they were the right, down-and dirty rock band for the political street-music sound John and Yoko were after.

"Elephant's Memory was an experiment with John," Roy Cicala told a PBS interviewer. "We were trying to get the dirtiest sound we

Above: John Lennon, Yoko Ono, and engineer Roy Cicala at Record Plant NY during a tequila-fueled recording session with Elephant's Memory in 1972. Below: Mick Jagger dropped by the NY studio to jam with John Lennon and Yoko Ono the same year.

could get. Very raw, very raw. John was even open to accentuating his and the band's mistakes. Elephant's was great, but we had to catch them during the first two hours of recording, because they were in never-never land after that."

"It was only when our friend Phil Spector came in that those sessions got weird," Elephant's bassist Gary Van Scyoc recalled. "I remember when Phil came in and put that silver revolver on the [mixing] console along with a fucking ounce of cocaine. Stan [Bronstein], the sax player, and I went, 'Oh boy, this is going to be a hell of a night.' They were just at each other's throats the whole time. Phil hated us; he didn't think we were worthy of John. Then he bailed. John gave him credit for the whole album, but he was never around after the first few nights."

Something else significant happened during those Elephant's Memory sessions: Roy rewired an old Ampex tape machine to add slapback, analog tape-delay echo, to Lennon's vocals, in exactly the same way an earlier generation of audio engineers did for Buddy Holly and Elvis.

"At the beginning, Phil was like giving him a dry vocal. And you know, it was all right," Van Scyoc recalled. "But then Roy put that tape echo on his voice right as he was doing the take and he loved it. I don't know whether he had ever done it before like that, but that became John's thing. He needed that echo on there from then on."

Lennon was looking for a new voice. Roy Cicala helped him find it. And with the right engineer by his side, he no longer needed Phil Spector around.

"John wanted a real, truthful sound, and he wanted real, truthful people around him. He didn't like people kissing his ass. He didn't want you to 'yes' him. He needed to know, especially when it came to his work, that he was getting a good opinion—and he certainly valued Roy's opinion. Roy was brilliant at it; he captured him the best anyone could. And that's when John started to rely more on Roy than Phil Spector. Whether it was the right amount of echo, whether it was the right microphone to use, John knew that Roy knew exactly what to do," Arlene Reckson said.

Cicala and his assistant, Shelly Yakus, had amazing ears, for sure, but an early-seventies boom in studio technology also played

CHAPTER THREE

its part in the process. Racks of new equipment were now stacked to the ceilings in each of the control rooms, enabling the engineers to expand, compress, distort, or delay the audio signals. A new limiter from Hendrix's effects wizard, Roger Mayer, created a sound that made a hit out of "Go All the Way" for the Raspberries. Down in the basement, the Record Plant maintenance staff were testing a prototype from a digital start-up called Eventide that emulated Gary Kellgren's famed phasing sound with a push of the button.

With Stone across the room in the tenth-floor office, Cicala called Kellgren to tell him about the Eventide invention he had just demoed. He and Gary gossiped briefly about the New York studio scene. The phone annoyingly clicked, but Cicala blamed it on the cross-country connection.

"Stevie Wonder is leaving Electric Lady to move out west," Cicala told his boss.

"Where's he working in LA?" Kellgren asked.

"Any place that will make room for that monster synthesizer of his."

"Wish we had space," Kellgren replied, "I'm spending more time in Sausalito than LA these days anyway"

"What's up there?"

"We're opening another studio up north."

Cicala stared across the room at Stone, surprised that he hadn't heard the news from him first. At least it meant that the partners were going to be preoccupied with this new project and thus out of his hair.

Kellgren then dropped the bomb on Cicala: "We've hired Tom Flye for our new studio . . ."

A screaming match ensued over the telephone, but Roy had lost the fight before it even began.

TAPPED!

For some reason, the suits from Warner and TVC didn't want to meet Stone at the Forty-Fourth Street studio. Lennon was working in Studio A, the other rooms were booked around the clock, and Stone had been hoping to impress them with all the activity.

Amidst the screaming between Cicala and Kellgren, Stone took a call from Steve Ross's assistant, who told him that the CEO and his

SECOND HOME

Warner team would be in a car across the street in the Kinney lot in ten minutes for their meeting. Stone also heard the clicking on the line and told one of his assistants to get the telephone company over right away. Then, avoiding Cicala's stare, Stone ducked out the door.

Across Forty-Fourth Street, the silver-haired Ross was waiting in a black stretch limousine filled with executives in overcoats. Stone sat down in the backseat, acting as if there was nothing unusual about the meeting location. He encouraged Ross to come inside for a tour but was waved off; Stone even offered to introduce him to John Lennon and mentioned that Jackie O and Rudolf Nureyev might be stopping by. Ross accommodated Stone's name dropping, then got down to business. With the limo's heat to the max and the engine idling, he confirmed that as soon as the TVC deal was closed he would be selling off the studios.

Stone had been rehearsing his answer for months. "I know just the right customer," he said. "Me and Gary."

"That might work." Ross said before changing the subject, "And Stone . . . be careful. The Feds have an eye on Lennon and you're right in the middle."

That's when it dawned on Stone that the clicking sound he had been hearing meant Record Plant's phones were being tapped. He thought about all the drugs that were being consumed across the street. John and Jack Douglas were working with radical street-musician David Peel on a song that was bound to stir controversy called "The Pope Smokes Dope." An FBI bust in New York would put Record Plant out of business on both coasts. "I'll be careful," Stone reassured everyone in the car, including himself.

◎

TAPE 15

STUDIO	ELECTRIC LADY STUDIOS, NY / RECORD PLANT LA	
ARTIST	**TITLE**	**FORMAT**
Stevie Wonder	*Music of My Mind*	Album
America	*Homecoming*	Album
America	"Ventura Highway"	Single

ELECTRIC LADY WEST

Stevie kept Electric Lady Studios alive after Jimi's death. Where else could a blind man get lost in his music while still having absolute command over his environment?

In early-1970s New York, the hits were just pouring out of him, fueled in part by TONTO and its Kemosabe production partners, Bob Margouleff and Malcolm Cecil. At twenty-one years of age and with millions in his bank account, Wonder was enjoying single life in New York City and a short stint of Motown independence. But sooner or later everyone goes home.

Home for Stevie Wonder was Motown and in 1972 the iconic label moved from Detroit to LA. Owner Berry Gordy closed the original Motown Hitsville studio called "the Snakepit," and was sampling all the LA rooms for a place that could capture the Motown sound.

He mixed the Jackson 5's "ABC" at the Third Street studio himself, with the engineers always tamping down his notoriously loud, kick-drum sound.

Stevie also moved his operation out to Los Angeles. Margouleff and Cecil found Stevie a temporary home at Crystal Recording Studios where he competed with the Laurel Canyon crowd for time. Just like Electric Lady, Crystal didn't have room for TONTO. Its enormous and eye-catching road cases always made finding a studio that could house it a logistical problem.

As a result, block-booking a studio became an expensive necessity for Stevie and his sonic space station. Margouleff and Cecil cut a

SECOND HOME

deal for an exclusive one-year residency at Record Plant Studio B, a relatively small room with a quirky Quad Eight console, right across the hall from the Jacuzzi. Billy Joel had worked there on his ill-fated first album prior to Stevie moving in. Bill Cosby rented it out for private jazz cigar parties with friends like James Brown and Muhammad Ali. Record Plant Studio B was nobody's favorite room.

Margouleff remembered:

> Of course, we were big shots at that point. We were just finishing up *Music of My Mind*, which we had started in New York. We negotiated and ended up with what we considered a very favorable deal, because we were, at that point—just think of it—booking a studio by the year . . . not by the hour, by the minute, or the day, or the week.
>
> So, we went to Gary's house on Camino Palmero to celebrate the deal. Gary, of course, was always very ceremonial; he brought out a bottle of Courvoisier that was so old that it had spider webs on it. He poured four pony glasses and we stood up around this long oak dining-room table and toasted the deal. When we clinked our glasses, suddenly the house started to shake. Really. It was an earthquake—my very first earthquake. I looked out through the kitchen, and I could see a wave coming down the swimming pool towards the house. It was a little, tiny tsunami basically, and that's how our relationship with Record Plant began.

As part of their deal, Chris Stone gave Bob and Malcolm an isolation booth for TONTO, a private vault for Stevie's tapes, and a carte-blanche budget to "Electric-Lady-fy" the room. Electric Lady Studios designer John Storyk himself drove out west in his hippie van to supervise a six-week build-out of the new Record Plant LA Studio B.

"There was a lot of Electric Lady in Record Plant Studio B . . ." Bob Margouleff said.

"Gary suffered from Electric Lady envy," Stone added. "I was just looking for 'another Hendrix.'"

Studio B underwent a modest renovation, featuring a saddle-shaped, redwood ceiling that emulated the acoustics of Electric

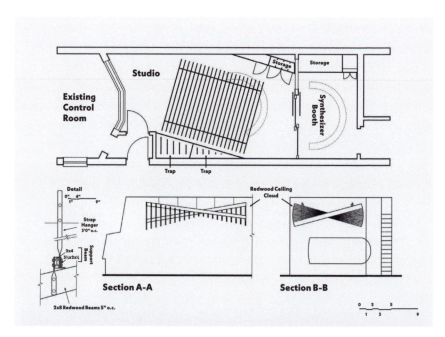

Above: Schematic of the new Studio B planned for Record Plant LA, showing the studio floorplan and Electric Lady studio-inspired redwood ceiling detail. Below: The studio was designed by John Storyk for Stevie Wonder and was fitted with quadraphonic sound.

SECOND HOME

Lady Studio A. One of the artists who decorated the walls at Jimi Hendrix's studio came out to do his mural magic on TONTO's music room. Anticipating the "next big thing" in home audio (that never happened), Studio B was outfitted for quadraphonic-sound recording, with the rear speakers jutting out of the back wall of the control room and into the hall.

The team picked up where they had left off in New York. Typically, Stevie came in around six thirty or seven o'clock at night and they recorded and mixed until five the next morning. Wonder was often two hours late for his sessions.

Regardless of when he arrived, the studio was ready. A song was always cued up on the tape machine for him to work on. TONTO's tubes were warm and ready to oscillate. His piano, clavinet, Rhodes, synthesizers, and drum kit were carefully arranged in a large circle so Stevie could confidently move around the room to play every instrument.

Everything was recorded in quad and mixed down to stereo, which created the underlying aural palette of Stevie Wonder's Record Plant sound. "By recording in quad, Stevie occupied the same space as the music. It wasn't in front of him like a picture frame. He was literally inside the music," Margouleff explained.

During session breaks, Stevie made use of the facilities. "Little Stevie" had grown into a six-foot-tall man, a star, and there was no shortage of young women willing to join him in the Jacuzzi. Somehow, he was always able to pick out the prettiest ones. A favorite prank was freaking them out by removing his sunglasses to reveal two unnerving, clouded pupils.

All the twenty-something shenanigans didn't impact their work. *Music of My Mind* was released in early March 1972, and *Talking Book* came out seven months later in October. Margouleff detailed their production workflow: "We really never cut songs for an album. It was more like cutting material for a library than an album. We would keep a long list of projects and songs we were working on. We would keep them in a little loose-leaf binder, and we would keep track of where we were with each specific song. Making the albums was simply an ongoing process of picking the right songs. It was a wonderful, creative, very inspiring place. We could do no wrong in Studio B. Every record we touched turned to gold."

CHAPTER THREE

Stevie was generous with both his time and talent while out in LA. He produced the first album by his wife, Syreeta Wright. "Tell Me Something Good" was originally written for Rufus and Chaka Khan by Wonder in Studio B. The TONTO team collaborated with the Isley Brothers ("That Lady") and Minnie Riperton ("Lovin' You") in Stevie's room. Ravi Shankar and George Harrison stopped by to experiment with TONTO. Wonder even helped shape the sounds of the rock-band America's famous cut "Ventura Highway" down the hall in Studio A. And the specter of Phil Spector was also always lurking about.

An assistant once led Stevie into the men's room and noted someone's feet in the stall next to a stack of master tapes. When Stevie started to sing, testing the echo chamber of tile, the occupant of the toilet started banging crazily on the wall, yelling, "Hey Stevie, shut the fuck up." It was Phil Spector, who flung open the stall door and, with a tape box under one arm, rushed out of the bathroom while pointing a revolver at the back of Stevie Wonder's head.

> # "Hey Stevie, shut the fuck up."
>
> Phil Spector,
> record producer

Fortunately for Stevie, he never sensed the danger. And unlike Spector, he wasn't worried about protecting his master tapes. Bob and Malcolm had the only keys to the vault shelves that were now packed with more than two hundred songs in various stages of completion.

"It was a period of total loyalty, total trust, and total belief," Margouleff reminisced: "It was a time that we thought would last forever."

TAPE 16

STUDIO RECORD PLANT NY / REMOTE

ARTIST	TITLE	FORMAT
Yoko Ono	"Sisters O Sisters"	Single
Alice Cooper	School's Out	Album / Single
The Raspberries	"Go All the Way"	Single
Elvis Presley	Elvis as Recorded at Madison Square Garden	Live Album

DAMN DOLBY

While Gary was scouting locations for his new studio and living on a houseboat in Sausalito, Stone was commuting between Los Angeles and New York, and working on a buyout plan with Warner.

On one of his many cross-country flights to New York in late spring 1972, Stone grabbed a copy of *Rolling Stone* magazine off the newsstand at LAX to learn a few things about the record business before meeting up with the clients and staff. There was one article that caught his eye:

> N.Y. RECORDING SCENE SEETHES, SITS, CHECKS ITS BOOKS
> All does not glisten in the Beau Monde of New York's recording studios. Business is off 60 percent. Manhattan is the center of the industry but a costly boom in building studios here during the last few years has not met with corresponding enthusiasm to record in them. There are more than 200 studios in the city of New York. Last year, 14 went out of business . . . Capitol has dropped its million-dollar studio plans and moved its recording operations to LA. RCA and A&R both laid off staff. One big factor is the sheer cost of all the glistening new hardware a top studio needs to stay competitive.

Reading the news while sipping a gin and tonic at 35,000 feet was not

CHAPTER THREE

what really upset Stone. It was the fact that Record Plant received a mere mention in the article, compared to lengthy descriptions of the goings-on at the other studios around town. The reporter gushed about what Eddie Kramer was doing over at Electric Lady. Mediasound was described as a hotbed of commercial advertising work. Hit Factory was portrayed as the best studio in town. And the only thing the journalist wrote about Record Plant NY was that it was "decorated with the frenzied taste of a whorehouse."

It was at that moment, with the newsprint rock and roll magazine folded neatly in his lap and a second round on his tray table, Stone realized that Gary was right. He was done with New York, too. Stone had enough of the red-eye flights and the power struggles with "the Italians!" and he was determined not to get caught up in a New York City studio downturn. Stone knew what he had to do— convince Roy Cicala that New York was his for the taking.

He made up his mind for sure as the cab pulled up outside 321 West Forty-Fourth Street. Rushing out of the building's front door was a gang of longhairs, pushing one of the bookkeepers wrapped mummy-style with duct tape to a rolling office chair, and launching her out into the middle of the street. A car swerved as the chair came to a halt and Roy Cicala was right in the middle of the mêlée. The man Stone had put in charge of running the New York business was wildly spraying the crowd with a fire extinguisher.

The commotion came to a halt when they spotted Stone getting out of the cab and everyone but Cicala quickly dispersed back into the building. Like a scene out of the movie *One Flew Over the Cuckoo's Nest*, he stood his ground all alone with the fire extinguisher in his arms.

Stone ordinarily would have dressed down his chief engineer, but with a bigger mission in mind all he did was grab his valise out of the trunk, head into the studio, and go right to work in his upstairs office. His usual routine was to review the bookings, check receivables, and look at the bills. This time he was gobsmacked by an invoice from a company named Dolby for $100,000 worth of "noise reduction equipment." He didn't know what noise reduction was or did, and he didn't care; the press was saying that studios all over town were going belly up, so it was an extravagance they couldn't afford.

Stone tucked the invoice into his breast pocket and walked out of his office to find Roy. He stopped by the studio manager's desk and glanced at the schedule book, noting that the chief engineer was in Studio A with producer Al Kooper. Kooper was an old client of Tom Wilson's from the early Hendrix days who, unlike most of the musicians, appreciated the talents that a hardcore numbers guy like Stone brought to the business.

When Stone walked into Studio A, Roy was behind the console with Shelly Yakus and their client, Canadian producer Bob Ezrin. Stone looked through the control-room glass and into the studio that was occupied by a strange and stringy rock and roller with smudged mascara who was madly conducting a choir of kids.

"Where's Al?" Stone asked.

The engineers stifled their laughs while Roy introduced his boss to the band, Alice Cooper, who were there recording *School's Out.*

Stone surveyed the studio while the engineers went back to work. The control room was a mess; it looked like a cake fight had just taken place. And even more bizarre, one of the maintenance engineers was sitting cross-legged on the floor, handcuffed to the door.

"What's with him?" Stone asked Cicala.

Ezrin snapped the retort: "The kid's not going anywhere . . ."

Ezrin had kidnapped the tech just in case the tape machines stopped working. It was the kind of studio shenanigans that only Bob Ezrin could get away with.

Stone moved on and asked Roy if he wanted to grab a bite.

Cicala knew something was up. He and Stone had never sat across a table outside of the studio before. "Sure," he replied, asking Shelly to finish the session. "Meet you at Smith's for a burger in half an hour?"

"Make it Downey's for steak," Stone replied, referring to the more upscale hangout on Eighth Avenue.

Walking down Forty-Fourth Street alone towards Eighth, Stone was shocked by how much the Times Square neighborhood had deteriorated since he moved to the West Coast. The scene made him even further determined to get out of town for good. He brought it up with Roy when they were ordering drinks several minutes later:

"No wonder Tom Flye wants out of here . . . what's happened to this city?" Stone began.

"The business is really tough here these days . . ."

CHAPTER THREE

"If business is so tough . . . what was that scene with the chair out in the street before?"

Cicala laughed. "We were just blowing off some steam."

"And if business is so tough, what the hell is a 'Dolby?'" Stone asked.

"It's something that makes a hit record," Cicala explained.

"Roy, I'm going to make you an offer you can't refuse," Stone joked, using the line from the new *Godfather* movie. "Warner is trying to unload Record Plant. Gary and I are buying LA and we're building up in Sausalito. New York's up for grabs if you want it . . ."

". . . Roy, if you own this place, you can buy as many damn Dolbys as you like."

TAPE 17

STUDIO	RECORD PLANT LA	
ARTIST	**TITLE**	**FORMAT**
Bill Withers	*Still Bill*	Album
Bill Withers	"Lean on Me"	Single

PSYCHEDELIC STUDIO

Kellgren was sitting cross-legged on the front hood of GREED when Stone's helicopter hovered over Richardson Bay and landed at the Sausalito Heliport. Gary was wearing a colorful open-necked polyester shirt, leather pants, and Italian loafers without socks, looking out of place amidst a crowd of half-clad hippies who were sunning themselves on the nearby dock.

Stone had just returned from his trip to New York and made the PSA Airlines regional connection at LAX directly to San Francisco

SECOND HOME

without stopping at home to see Gloria and the kids. Before leaving New York, Gary had called to say he had found the perfect space for their new Northern California studio and that he wanted him to see the place and sign the lease.

There was a 10,000-square-foot building in the Marinship district of Sausalito, currently occupied by a landscape-architecture firm that needed to sublet most of its space. The windowless building was right by the waterfront where ships had been built at a breakneck pace by Rosie the Riveters during World War II. The neighborhood had deteriorated over the past twenty-five years and was now the site of abandoned warehouses and mounds of debris that squatters used to build makeshift houseboats and huts.

Gary and GREED drove Stone down Bridgeway, the main drag along the waterfront, and wound up in a crowded neighborhood of houseboats where Gary was staying. He entered a small houseboat with a twenty-foot skiff tied to an adjacent dock.

Inside, a party was going on. A woman turned to Gary when he entered and exclaimed, "The no-socks fox is back!"

No matter where Gary went, a party always followed. He had been in Sausalito just three weeks and already his living room was the epicenter of fun. Another woman dropped the needle on the recently released Bill Withers song "Lean on Me" that had been recorded at Record Plant LA that spring. Oddly out of place, there was also a thin, balding man seated in the corner.

"Who's that?" Stone whispered to Kellgren.

"That's Myron . . . from Ampex," Kellgren replied.

Stone smelled money. He knew that the tape manufacturer from nearby Redwood City was investing in music: they had funded Artie Ripp's work with Billy Joel, paid for Todd Rundgren's second album, and helped bankroll Bob Dylan-manager Albert Grossman's new Bearsville Studio up in Woodstock, New York. Ever the salesman, Chris approached the guy from Ampex: "So Myron, has Gary been talking to you about our new studio?"

"I've been studying how he thinks . . . ."

Myron Stolaroff built the first magnetic tape recorder at Ampex Corporation, which was sold to Les Paul. In the mid-sixties he started taking LSD and envisioned Ampex becoming a "psychedelic

133

CHAPTER THREE

corporation." His team of tripping techs at Ampex eventually disbanded and Stolaroff left the company to study psychedelic compounds and the creative process.

"We've been talking about making Sausalito the first psychedelic recording studio," Kellgren said, pulling Stone back outside where Myron was waiting behind the wheel of GREED.

Myron slowly drove Kellgren's Rolls-Royce around the potholes, out of the village of houseboats, and back onto Bridgeway. Kellgren pointed up the hill where there were plenty of houses for rent where the artists could stay while they were recording.

Destination studios were just becoming a "thing" in the record business. Bearsville Studios in upstate New York had a nearby barn where artists stayed; bands were living by the beach while recording down at Criteria Studios in Miami; and Bill Szymczyk was at a new studio resort called Caribou Ranch, outside of Boulder, Colorado, where he and Joe Walsh were recording.

Kellgren continued: "When the musicians burn out on LA, they will love coming up here . . . it'll be like being in LA without all the craziness."

GREED pulled up to a windowless, redwood-sided building at 2200 Bridgeway. The three men walked inside the dark building and stood in a massive open space filled with abandoned drafting tables. Kellgren pulled a fat stick of chalk out of his pants pocket and took Stone on a virtual tour. Like that night in the fall of 1967, when he sold Hendrix on block-booking an imaginary studio on Forty-Fourth Street in NY, Gary sketched two mirror-image control rooms and studios with walls, floors, and ceilings all decorated with swirling puzzle-pieces of wood and padded, teardrop-shaped wall coverings.

"Welcome home, Chris," he said. "Welcome to the greatest Record Plant of all."

TAPE 18

STUDIO RECORD PLANT LA

ARTIST	TITLE	FORMAT
Sly and the Family Stone	There's a Riot Going On	Album
Black Sabbath	Vol. 4	Album
Bee Gees	Life in a Tin Can	Album

TWIN PALMS

Ancky was coming to Los Angeles and it was a very big deal, especially for Stone. As the matriarch of the Record Plant family, she always commanded his respect. Ancky was looking for a house in LA, and Stone and Gloria offered to give her a tour of the prospective neighborhoods. Besides, they had some business to discuss.

Stone drove her past the hedges of Bel Air and by the palisade cliffs of Malibu. From behind the wheel of DEDUCT, he had plenty of time to talk to Ancky about the deal he was cooking up with Warner.

The year 1972 was very good for the stock market. At $50 a share, their Warner stock had skyrocketed, due in large part to the well-received launch of Steve Ross's cable TV business. Stone had cut a deal for a stock-only buyout for both West Coast studios. One of Ross's lieutenants, Abe Silverstein, tried to throw in New York as well, but Stone wasn't interested.

"You want in on the deal?" Stone asked Ancky at one point during the afternoon tour.

Always a shrewd investor, Ancky replied, "I think I'll hold onto my shares." Then she changed subjects, asking, "What is up with Gary?"

Stone didn't know what she was talking about and didn't ask. "You know, he's talking about moving up north."

"You need to keep an eye on him, Stone . . . make sure he stays here in LA," she warned before suddenly asking him to stop the car, exclaiming:

"That's the house."

CHAPTER THREE

Stone pulled DEDUCT over to the curb and focused his eyes on a tall salmon-colored Hollywood mansion with twin palm trees overlooking Sunset Boulevard. A realtor's sign was on the corner and Ancky had her husband call the number from a nearby pay phone. Within the hour, the two couples were touring a mansion with a stately dining room and seven terraces, each with a view all the way to Catalina Island. The center hall staircase was right out of *Sunset Boulevard*. And it became even more appealing when they learned the property was going through foreclosure. Ancky made a $90,000 cash bid right on the spot, and the realtor said she'd approach the bank with the offer.

Stone needed Ancky's money. He ran the numbers in his head. They were already putting $500,000 into Sausalito, they needed three new consoles at about $100,000 each, not to mention the cool million dollars in Warner stock they would be shelling out in just a few weeks. Kellgren and Stone were putting everything on the line for this new business. Reaching out again to Ancky to chip in was worth another try.

The next day, the partners had an assistant drive them up the hill toward the house on Sunset, with Stone using the time to prep Gary for their next meeting.

"Convince her that we're on our game, that this is our biggest deal ever!"

The purple Rolls-Royce passed through the wrought-iron gate on 2331 Miller Drive, drove up the driveway and parked alongside the house's own gas pump. Inside, Ancky was going through paperwork with the realtor at the grand dining-room table. She brushed the boys off with a flick of her wrist, leaving them alone to tour each of the floors, including the large basement wine cellar.

When they re-entered the dining room, Ancky inquired, "So, what do you think?"

"It needs a pool . . ." was Gary's only response.

The three partners walked through a commercial-grade kitchen, then out to the terrace to admire the view.

"Why not help us buy out Warner with some of your stock?" Stone asked.

"Not this time, Christopher. I'm going to pass."

Studio co-founder and co-owner Chris Stone pictured in 1975 standing outside of the Third Street side of Record Plant LA. Keeping an increasingly lawless clientele under control became part of his job.

CHAPTER THREE

Before Stone could counter, Gary came up with an unexpected request: "If that's the case Ancky . . . let me at least buy this house."

Ancky and Stone both laughed. Gary was dead serious. He went on to say that the family was planning to move out of the house on Camino Palermo, and he needed a place to live that was closer to the Rainbow. And, as if he had somehow been eavesdropping on Ancky and Stone's earlier conversation, Kellgren then added:

"This place will keep me in LA, Ancky . . . it's where I belong."

Ancky didn't need much convincing. She knew that keeping Gary in LA was best for the business. "It's your house Gary," she replied, without hesitating, ". . . but please behave."

Several weeks later, right after Stone and Kellgren closed their deal with Warner, Gary's life changed.

Stone remembered: "Gary had his accident early that summer. He was up in the party house with Tom Wilson, and he passed out. Someone put him in the shower and left him there to go call 911. Then they heard a crash and rushed back in. Gary had fallen through the plate-glass shower door and nearly amputated his right arm. It was ripped to the bone. Blood was everywhere. Fortunately, a microsurgeon sewed him back together, but the pain was terrible."

Lee Kiefer added: "The first time I saw him after the accident, he had this rig on, wires through his fingers, and screws and stuff sticking out. His hand was, like, floating in the middle of this cage-like contraption. In every picture afterwards, you'd see Gary resting his right arm over his head. It was as if it was the only way for him to alleviate the pain. But one thing was for sure, he never stopped working, and he never stopped being in control of his dream."

Marta Kellgren concluded: "Gary was stoic and never complained about the pain."

Raechel Donahue said: "He worked the console like it was a piano keyboard. So, he must have felt like any musician would feel after losing the ability to play their instrument. The picture is very vivid in my mind, watching him mix with one arm, gently moving one hand with the other. He was struggling to perform. And that was so painful to watch."

LOWER DRAWER

Everyone knew that Chris Stone kept a gun locked in the lower right-hand drawer of his desk in LA. They knew because he reminded them of it all the time.

There was nothing in the lower drawer. But Stone created the mystique of the lower drawer as a deterrent against the fringe element that was starting to hang around the LA studio during the summer of 1972.

Kellgren was still recuperating from his near-amputation. He wore the Frankenstein-like brace on his arm and was usually stoned on painkillers but, amazingly, somehow could still pull off even the most complicated mix.

"After the accident, Stone needed him back in the studio right away," Marta Kellgren remembered. "It was much too fast, much too early . . ."

Stone needed Gary back in the studio right away because he had his hands filled with too many demanding clients who only wanted to work with his partner.

Black Sabbath was self-producing for the first time in Studio A, shuttling massive quantities of marching powder in road cases between their Bel Air mansion and Record Plant. Their resulting fourth album, *Vol. 4,* cost $65,000 in studio time and an additional $75,000 paid to an "equipment rental company" owned by the studio's preferred dope dealer.

Sly Stone brought his band and his blow to Studio A after his thirty-six-foot Winnebago recording studio was busted by LAPD in July 1972. Sly and friends like Bobby Womack had been cruising through the streets of LA in an enormous house-on-wheels, writing and recording away from the mansion, which had been overrun with dealers and pimps. After the bust, his RV was targeted by the cops and Sly needed a safe place to park it—and that's how he ended up back at Record Plant LA.

After discovering the Record Plant Jacuzzi, Sly moved out of the parking lot and into one of the hotel rooms where he stationed an XXL-sized sentry and entertained a revolving door of freeloaders and friends. Like Hendrix, time was just money and Sly acted like he still had plenty of both to burn.

CHAPTER THREE

Sly had somebody else's money to burn. His original manager, David Kapralik, was recovering from a suicide attempt, and concert promoter Ken Roberts was now running his affairs.

Roberts, a native of Hoboken, New Jersey, had already struck it rich with Frankie Valli and the Four Seasons. He was a larger-than-life record-business tummler, and the only concert promoter willing to take a risk on an unreliable artist like Sly Stone, who had already missed half of his shows that year. Roberts was putting up his own money on Sly in the hope that, unlike Kapralik, he could somehow get him to finish his next album.

Sly was in the Record Plant Rack Room when Stone was summoned to meet with him and his manager. The artist was stirring lazily on the fur bedspread, while seated across the room was possibly the whitest white guy Chris Stone had ever seen. Sly's new manager Ken Roberts was sitting with a stack of invoices on his lap, meticulously preparing for their meeting.

"It says here we're paying $175 per hour for Studio A," Roberts began. "We're paying for a studio. We should be getting some product," he reasoned.

Stone shook his head. "You're not paying for product. You're paying for time. You're paying for an engineer, an assistant, and the lease payments on all that expensive gear that is sitting there waiting for Sly to record."

"And an additional $50 per hour for this whorehouse hotel room?"

Again, Stone deadpanned, "Right. You booked both Studio A and the Rack Room. It's not our fault that Sly is spending his time here—getting 'inspired.'"

"We need a record Stone . . ."

"Take it up with your client."

Roberts's client appeared to be sleeping, so he was free to come clean. He explained that Sly's just-signed contract with Epic Records called for a $500,000 advance, which was already spent, and another $500,000 upon acceptance of the final masters. Clive Davis had just sent the tapes back marked "unlistenable," at about the same time as Sly's bass player and drummer both quit and his assistant suffered a mental breakdown. Sly was reworking the album so much that it was nicknamed *Overdub City*.

SECOND HOME

"I'm sending him back to his mother's house up in San Francisco; she's the last hope I have to get this album done," Roberts said.

Chris saw an opening. He told him that Record Plant was building a two-room outpost up in Sausalito for artists like Sly who needed to get away from the craziness in LA. Stone explained that he had just hired Tom Scott, Wally Heider's top remote engineer, who could put together a studio-to-go to follow Sly around town, ready to record anytime, anywhere. "And I just hired the perfect engineer to go along with the rig," Stone added.

Tom Flye and his wife had just visited Gary and Chris in LA. They were both spooked by Gary's Frankenstein-like condition, but they were sold on the idea of moving to Northern California. Back in New York, Flye was working as many as a hundred hours a week. That summer, he had recorded two huge live-recording remotes at Madison Square Garden with Elvis, and John and Yoko. In the studio, he worked alongside Yoko on her solo album, *Approximately Infinite Universe*, with Jack Douglas assisting, Elephant's Memory backing her up, and celebrities like Mick Jagger stopping by to jam. Tom Flye had made out well with the studio's stock incentives and agreed to take the job offer as Sausalito's chief engineer.

With Tom Scott "the fixer" and Tom Flye "the mixer," Record Plant Sausalito had the talent pool it needed to take on Wally Heider in San Francisco. And it was that team that would get Roberts his next Sly Stone album.

"So, what are we going to do about these invoices, Stone?" Ken Roberts demanded to know.

"You're going to pay them. I'll build Sly that portable studio and have Tom Flye finish the job.

Ken and Chris both smiled at the absurd way they both made a living and shook hands on the deal.

The very next day, Chris bought a gun for his lower drawer.

TAPE 19

STUDIO   RECORD PLANT NY / REMOTE / RECORD PLANT SAUSALITO

ARTIST	TITLE	FORMAT
Elephant's Memory	Elephant's Memory	Album
John Lennon and Yoko Ono	The One-to-One Concert	Soundtrack / Live Album
Finnigan & Wood	Crazed Hipsters	Album

BUMS IN BAGS

"Where's John and Yoko?"

During the summer of 1972, the music industry "It Couple" was both *everywhere* and *nowhere* at the same time.

Everywhere: They were in the middle of a media blitz to promote John's new album, *Some Time in New York City*, which was released in June. They were also in a very public custody battle with Yoko's ex. And with George Harrison's movie for the *Concert for Bangladesh* in theaters that summer, John was working on a high-profile benefit movie of his own—the One-to-One concert from Madison Square Garden.

Nowhere: Behind the soundproof doors of Record Plant on Forty-Fourth Street, the real work was taking place. John and Yoko were putting the finishing touches on the Elephant's Memory release for Apple Records, while belaboring the mix on their concert film for Ann Arbor activist John Sinclair, who was imprisoned on a marijuana charge. At the same time, Yoko was ready to start recording her new album. And the FBI was keeping close tabs on their whereabouts.

John and Yoko traveled to San Francisco mid-summer for business meetings and a *Rolling Stone* magazine interview, and, once Kellgren found out they were in town, he begged Tom Donahue to help set up a lunch with them at the Trident. Since Gary had just stolen Roy Cicala's best engineer, it was time for him to also steal Record Plant

SECOND HOME

NY's best customer. Though few outside of the organization knew the difference, John and Yoko were at Roy Cicala's Record Plant NY, which was now a very different company than Record Plant LA.

The meeting never happened and Gary became obsessed with attracting the couple to his Sausalito studio. He was following their every move in the media. He was checking in on them regularly with the staff in New York. His obsession only deepened after the accident. So, with his partner in pain and under pressure, Stone offered to help get John and Yoko to the late-October studio opening.

The party was to be a Masquerade Ball. And in keeping with Gary's concept of "big" Record Plant party invitations, this one was a half yin-yang slab of carved redwood decorated with silk-screened bats and pumpkins, and the psychedelic Record Plant logo, reading:

HALLOWEEN MASQUERADE BALL
STUDIO OPENING
MUSIC, DRINK, DANCING, B.Y.O.D. (Bring Your Own Drugs)
OCT. 29 6 P.M. TO 2 A.M.

Gary sent one of the invitations to John and Yoko at the studio in New York but received no response; the pressure was on Stone to deliver them for Gary's grand soirée.

First, Stone tried Tom Donahue who had produced the Beatles' last public concert in San Francisco's Candlestick Park in 1966. Donahue said he made a few calls but never received a response.

Beatles roadie Mal Evans had been hanging around the LA studio but couldn't get an answer, either.

Phil Spector, as usual, was MIA.

Finally, as a last resort, Stone tried Roy Cicala in New York, who laughed in his face.

Less than three weeks before the party, Stone knew he had to break the bad news to Gary. He flew up north to tell him that he had struck out with John and Yoko, arriving at the site that was, even at this late date, still in a state of chaos.

Tom Scott was overseeing the studio construction. After months of little progress, he whipped his crew into action, commissioning the studio's (rented) API console and wiring the Record Plant's first pair

of 3M sixteen-track tape machines. It was the same technical setup they had just used to upgrade Studio B in LA for Stevie Wonder.

Trident designer Dave Mitchell and his team of redwood artisans worked seventy-two hours straight on an enormous multitone marquetry of a sunburst that covered the entire wall of Studio A. Velvet-covered plywood clouds hung from the ceiling. Mitchell had already crafted a floor inlay of a redwood tree in reception, room-size murals, and an amalgam of other ornate wood designs in the bathrooms and halls. The conference room was a wall-to-wall waterbed. His work, which would define the opulence of the space, was either going to be Chris and Gary's greatest achievement or their ultimate creative folly. As things turned out, it would be both.

Tom Hidley was spending most of his time out of the country, "overseeing" the Sausalito studio's new control room construction via staticky overseas phone calls. The room was a now standard Kellgren/Hidley control-room design anyway, with its compression ceiling, masonry walls, and large soffit-mounted monkey-lip monitors. But this time Kellgren and his artisans added a large-stained glass arch overhead. Several former World War II boatwrights were hired out of retirement to help finish the build with a unique nautical feel. It all looked cool—very Marin County—and that was Gary's original vision.

The October 29, 1972, opening of Record Plant Sausalito was supposed to be a rock-star extravaganza. Tom Donahue called every musician and producer in town to stop by, and Gary scrambled around the clock for weeks with a team of coked-out carpenters to complete the job on time.

Gary had already selected a bright-purple Napoleon costume for his Bay Area debut; the outfit let him support his ailing arm like the famous French general posed with his hand in his coat. Like Napoleon, Kellgren acted invincible, having built three major studio complexes, in three major markets, in just over four-and-a-half years. Record Plant Sausalito was Gary Kellgren's Fontainebleau.

Opposite: Invitation to the Masquerade Ball opening party (above) for the Sausalito Record Plant on October 29, 1972. Photographs from the party (below) show Fran Hughes in feathers, Buddy Miles on the drums, Chris Stone dressed as a riverboat gambler, and Gary Kellgren as Napoleon.

CHAPTER THREE

After surveying the construction, Kellgren and Stone had a driver take them for a ride in GREED through nearby Mill Valley. If Record Plant Sausalito was going to be a destination studio, there had to be residences, and Kellgren had found a section of town with a series of houses tucked into the mountains.

On the way down the hill, Kellgren broke the news to Stone that the studio wasn't going to be operational for the opening. By now, Stone was accustomed to the drill. The party was still on.

"And what about John and Yoko?" Kellgren then asked.

Stone flashed back to that first party in March 1968 when he arrived late from a business appointment, still dressed in his Revlon uniform of black suit and black tie and had to tell his partner that Jimi Hendrix had a gig up in Canada and wasn't showing up.

Kellgren didn't say anything at first. He had his driver drop Stone off at his hotel. Before Chris closed the door, and said goodnight, Kellgren remarked, "Don't worry about it Stone . . . I'll get John and Yoko . . . without me, you'd still be hawking nail polish at Macy's."

Stone cut his trip short and went home to LA the very first thing the next morning; he had learned that, when it came to managing talent, sometimes it made sense to shut up and take the money.

The partners didn't talk again for three weeks and when Stone returned the weekend of the opening, Gary acted as if nothing had happened. Stone played along too, but he would always remember that trip as a turning point in their relationship. He had never thought Gary considered him expendable—until that night when he told him straight to his face how he felt. The truth was that Gary had considered ending their business relationship even before leaving New York.

In keeping with his Masquerade Ball persona of a Mississippi riverboat gambler, Stone would play his cards close to his chest on their biggest opening night of all.

Besides, Kellgren was on edge. A tremendous quantity of coke was being consumed to get the studio done on time. For that final week, it was back-to-back all-nighters for Kellgren, Tom Scott, Dave Mitchell, and their crews. Just as Stone had grown to expect through the years, it all magically came together at the end. While surveying the final studio design, Kellgren said something to his partner that must have been bothering him for years:

SECOND HOME

"This place puts Electric Lady to shame."

The night of the opening, *Los Angeles Herald Examiner* sent a journalist to report on the party and interview its star attractions, John and Yoko:

> They came from all over—the beautiful people of the inner jet set of the music industry, surrendering their silk-screened wooden invitations at the door to enter the costume ball, heralding the formal opening of Record Plant in Sausalito. All evening, there were rumors that Yoko and John were flying out from New York to attend. Suddenly, two costumed partygoers entered, covered from head-to-toe in black-vinyl bags. They walked in the front door, through the party, and out the back door never again to be seen. Yes, everyone agreed certainly that Yoko and John had flown 3000 miles to have this moment of anonymous sport.

Were those two bagged partiers really John and Yoko?

The writer from the *Herald-Examiner* implied that it was a long way to fly for a five-minute party drive-by. However, other news outlets helped spread the rumor:

> *MELODY MAKER* REPORTED: Record Plant is opening studios in Sausalito (right across the Bay from SF). To celebrate they are giving a party—confirmed to attend are John and Yoko, Don McLean, Neil Young and America.

> *ROLLING STONE* MAGAZINE CLAIMED: Record Plant Studios opened a new branch in Sausalito, California, today, and celebrated with a big opening party. John and Yoko were reportedly in attendance—in the Halloween spirit of things, dressed as trees (record plants?)

Engineer Lee Kiefer was there: "John and Yoko supposedly came dressed in two, big, old, huge trash bags. No one ever knew whether it was John and Yoko or not. No one ever saw them."

Apple Records exec Allen Steckler, who received one of the redwood invitations and was working on Yoko's new album in New

CHAPTER THREE

York in late October 1972, said, "To the best of my knowledge they did not leave New York during that time. I would have remembered that."

An authority on the couple's day-by-day activities, "Lennonologist" Chip Madinger, concluded that, if they had gone at all, it would have been a very quick day trip, since Yoko performed one of her art pieces in Lower Manhattan on the night of October 28 and then re-tracked two songs for her solo album at Record Plant on Forty-Fourth Street the night of October 30.

With or without the couple in attendance, the party raged on until 3 a.m. Buddy Miles played drums. Ronnie Montrose worked out some riffs behind a tie-dyed gobo wall in the hall. Tom Hidley's monitors were demoed with Stevie Wonder's *Talking Book* album, which Motown had just released the day before.

"Big success . . ." Stone declared, as the partners surveyed the party damage, including a slow leak in the conference-room waterbed. A young blonde woman was bathing alone in the outdoor redwood Jacuzzi. After airing the place out, Stone welcomed in the local cops who had monitored the crowd from their squad car for some leftover sandwiches and beer.

As was their tradition, the partners ended the night alone, this time seated in a pair of commercial airline-pilot seats that had been installed for producers in the back of the Studio A control room. Stone mixed himself a martini, while Kellgren cracked open a beer and lit up a cigarette.

"Well, I got a Beatle," Kellgren said, in a "told you so" tone of voice.

"You're telling me those bums in bags were John and Yoko?"

For the remaining five years of their partnership, Gary remained adamant that John and Yoko were there—that he never hired standins to propagate the myth that rock royalty traveled cross-country for the opening of Gary Kellgren's new studio.

Studio A (above, left) combined redwood with Tom Hidley's trademark stonework. The lobby (center) was decorated with opening-party invitations and the front door of the studio building (below) also featured fun designs. The control room (above, right) featured a Tiffany-glass ceiling.

TAPE 20

STUDIO	ELECTRIC LADY STUDIOS, NY / RECORD PLANT LA	
ARTIST	**TITLE**	**FORMAT**
Stevie Wonder	*Talking Book*	Album
Stevie Wonder	"Superstition"	Single
Stevie Wonder	"You Are the Sunshine of My Life"	Single

SUPERSTITION

Kellgren was looking for the wrong star to shine on his new Sausalito studio.

Instead of courting ex-Beatle John Lennon at a New York studio he no longer owned, he should have been looking four-hundred miles south to his own Studio B in Los Angeles, where Stevie Wonder was creating the biggest hits of the generation. At the same time as Lennon's *Some Time in New York City* was named "most disappointing album of the year" by *Rolling Stone* magazine, Wonder's back-to-back albums *Talking Book* and *Innervisions* were taking his career and the studio where they were recorded to new heights.

The magic that Stevie was creating on Third Street caught the attention of the other top talent at Motown. Frequent customers, Michael Jackson and his brothers were always around soaking up studio savvy. Diana Ross worked on her *Greatest Hits* album at Record Plant LA. Berry Gordy discovered the Johnson Brothers while they were there backing up Quincy Jones. Kellgren taught his engineers how to get the short, punchy delay sound that made a Motown record sound like a Motown record.

One of Gordy's assistants once asked Chris Stone if the label could have a "second key" to Stevie's vault at the studio, a request that he said was never accommodated. Cecil and Margouleff were directly his customers and, thus, only they had access to Stevie's Record Plant master-tape reels, even though their business relationship with Stevie had never been clearly defined.

Malcolm had left it up to Bob to negotiate their "Stevie deal," which was a handshake-only agreement for 1 percent of record sales.

Malcolm, Bob, and TONTO contributed to the whole new Stevie Wonder package—even the photo of Stevie with cornrows and a dashiki gown that graced the *Talking Book* album cover was shot by Margouleff, who sold it to Motown for $300.

"We lived a good life. My dog Taco was at my side. I had a Jaguar XKE that I would park in the Record Plant parking lot. It was a dark chocolate color, as was my dog. I would walk out of Record Plant at five in the morning, a joint planted firmly in my face and my hair down to my elbows, my dog sitting at my side, as I drove out to my pad in Malibu doing 100 mph on the Santa Monica Freeway, listening to "Superstition" on the radio," Margouleff remembered.

"Superstition" was the hit of the 1972 holiday season. Stevie's summer 1972 tour with the Rolling Stones field-tested the song before a crossover audience, earning it a spot atop both the *Billboard Hot 100* and R&B charts. The making of "Superstition" was a harbinger of things to come in Stevie's relationship with his musical team. Stevie had first promised the song to Jeff Beck and then told the guitarist and his producers that Motown wouldn't let him do it. "It was the first inkling I had that he was not being entirely truthful . . . that, in fact, the label still had control," Malcolm later declared.

> ## "I would walk out of Record Plant at five in the morning, a joint planted firmly in my face . . ."
>
> Robert Margouleff, engineer

In December 1972, Stevie finalized "You Are the Sunshine of My Life" in Studio B. His *Innervisions* masterpiece, "Living for the City" was finished there, too; every instrument was played by either Stevie or TONTO—and a cast of Record Plant employees spoke the parts in the song's famous arrest vignette. The song was originally recorded in just two days, though it required an additional six months of editing.

Stevie and Sly never collaborated or socialized, even though they were often working at Record Plant LA at the same time. There was a distinct similarity to the way the bass and drums in both of their recordings from this period were the lead instruments in the

Stevie Wonder performing "Living for the City" with TONTO—The Original New Timbral Orchestra—and its creators Malcolm Cecil and Robert Margouleff at Record Plant LA in 1973. A cast of Record Plant employees contributed to the voices in the song's arrest vignette.

SECOND HOME

mix, something made possible by the sonic depth of the studio's API consoles. At the same time, and quite coincidentally, both artists started recording in their control rooms, taking the room acoustics out of the equation by plugging electronic instruments directly into the console, and manipulating the faders, dials, and knobs themselves to investigate new sounds.

Because of his success, Gary courted Margouleff to bring in more business and even printed him up "Chief Engineer, Record Plant" business cards. Gary's master plan was to hire him for Sausalito so that Stevie would relocate up north, thus freeing up LA Studio B for a long list of customers, who were eager to tap into the room's hit-making magic. To initiate his scheme, Gary invited Margouleff over to his house for some B&B (business & blow). They retired to the backyard pool where Margouleff remembered waking up the next morning:

It was 6 a.m. We had been partying all night. There I was laying behind the swimming pool, looking out over the whole city and the sunrise. I was really fucked up, half-asleep, with my eyes half-closed, and I heard this tinkling noise. So, I opened my eyes all the way and there was Gary Kellgren with his blue fedora on his head and a cigar sticking out the side of his face, standing there bare-assed naked, and taking a leak into the pool. I couldn't believe it and just shook my head. I said to myself, "Margouleff, you have finally arrived. Hooray for Hollywood!"

TAPE 21

STUDIO RECORD PLANT SAUSALITO / RECORD PLANT NY

ARTIST	TITLE	FORMAT
Sly and the Family Stone	Fresh	Album
Gregg Allman	Laid Back	Album
Various	Live at the Record Plant: 72-Hour Concert	Broadcast
Grateful Dead	Wake of the Flood	Album
New Riders of the Purple Sage	Adventures of Panama Red	Album / Single
Bob Marley and the Wailers	Live at the Record Plant	Broadcast
Linda Ronstadt	Live at the Record Plant	Broadcast

SUPER FLYE

Kellgren left the running of the new Sausalito studio up to Stone. It was Stone who made sure the front office was staffed by smart, young, attractive women. He also met a drug dealer who connected him with the pot growers north of the city in Humboldt County.

Before long, bricks of sensimilla were being packed in road cases that shuttled back and forth between the two studios in LA and Sausalito. Everyone thought Stone was simply saving money by sharing microphones, outboard gear, and tape-recorder heads, while, in fact, the flow of gear was a clandestine way to transport weed.

"Record Plant was always about the best . . . the best engineers, best equipment, best maintenance, best vibe, and best drugs," Stone stated.

Record Plant Sausalito was in good hands. Tom Flye, the engineer who salvaged the original Woodstock tapes, whose audio fingerprints were all over the *Concert for Bangladesh*, and who made the already-classic "American Pie" possible, was the engineering anchor of the new venture. His very first Record Plant Sausalito session in early 1973, the New Riders of the Purple Sage's fourth album, *Adventures of Panama Red,* became a surprise radio hit and went gold.

Reports that John and Yoko had been at the opening-night party immediately built the studio's cachet. Tom Flye and Tom Scott both brought along their own followings. Additionally, Tom Donahue's involvement promised KSAN airplay for every Record Plant Sausalito release. The studio was cash positive within six months. There was lots of money, which brought along lots of coke.

Coke was a recreational drug in those days, long before everyone realized that it could drive you nuts. Chris Stone often started his days with a line of blow, but always made sure to end up back home in the evening with Gloria, the kids, and a martini.

On one of his weekly business trips up north, Stone found Donahue chopping a mound of cocaine on the polished metal surface of one of the studio's new 3M sixteen-track tape machines.

"Can you move that stuff over to the console," Stone barked, pointing at a mirror that had been embedded on top of the new API console for such purposes.

Stone led Donahue on a stoned tour of the new Studio B construction. Flye and Tom Scott were there hanging a set of floating plywood clouds that Dave Mitchell had just designed for the live room's ceiling. They all chatted briefly about plans to build Record Plant's first West Coast mobile truck, which everyone agreed was going to piss Wally Heider off.

Donahue had something else on his mind. "You ever worked with Sly?" he asked Flye.

"Back during *Woodstock*," Flye replied, adding, "Does he still have that dog?" (Back in New York, Sly's pit bull, Gun, had trapped him behind the console.)

"Want to work with him again?"

Later that day, the front desk called Stone to the front, advising him that a large Toyota station wagon had just pulled up and a group of roadies were unloading boxes of master tapes in the lobby. An energized Sly Stone hopped out of the back seat and greeted Donahue with a bear hug around his huge frame.

CHAPTER THREE

Without a booking, Sly had made the six-hour drive up from Los Angeles with his own engineer hauling all his tapes in the station wagon, and fortunately the studio happened to be available. Sly's Toyota was more than a mode of transportation, it was his vault. His tapes had been confiscated so many times due to unpaid studio bills that the station wagon now followed him everywhere he went, and his drivers were always armed.

The outrageous success of Stevie Wonder's "Superstition" had inspired Sly to go back to work. The sounds emanating from his Record Plant LA studio neighbor were all too familiar, and the album *Fresh* was going to be his response. Tom Flye described what happened in Sausalito Studio B next:

> Sly's engineer was sitting in the back of the control room in one of the airplane seats that Gary had installed. The entire control room was designed like an airplane cockpit with everything, even the light switches, mounted in the ceiling. I was sitting on a step, listening to what Sly was doing. It all sounded good to me. Then Sly asked, "Somebody get up here and help me." I didn't know what to do because he had his own engineer and the guy wasn't moving. So, I got up and pulled one of the tapes off a stack, put it up on a machine, and started going through it with Sly. At one point, Sly goes, "Somebody needs to start engineering." So, I brought up the faders and made sure we were getting everything on tape. Finally, the engineer that Sly brought in with him walked out. We never saw him again.

Within a week, Sly and Flye had re-recorded the entire *Fresh* album track by track. Sly played all the instruments besides drums and horns himself, and he never once used the live room to record, preferring to play and sing at the console. He rolled a large wooden Hammond B-3 organ into the control room to serve as his desk.

Much of the time was spent searching for takes. All the track sheets and engineering notes were lost and many of the tapes were stored in the wrong boxes. So, Flye did random playbacks for Sly just to see what stuck. Sly would give each tape a listen and, if he liked what he heard, he'd grab an instrument to add an overdub. And if not, he'd simply instruct his new engineer to move on to another tape.

Ultimately, *Fresh* was a patchwork of tape fragments that Sly and Flye pieced together. While working on the tune "Babies Making Babies," Sly fell in love with a four-bar progression and asked Flye if he could repeat it for the whole track. In those pre-digital days, Flye spent an entire day making a hundred copies of the two-inch tape and meticulously assembling the four bars into a sound bed for the three-and-a-half-minute song. Flye barely finished the job by the time Sly returned to the studio. He played it back for his new client who remarked with extra emphasis, "Now that's FUNKY! The whole thing is FUNKY!" He even gave the engineer his new nickname— "Super Flye" quickly became "Supe" for short.

Ken Roberts was so impressed, he asked Chris Stone how much it would take to buy Tom Flye out of his Record Plant contract.

Stone told him, "You can have him anytime he likes . . . just let me build Sly his own room."

> ## "You can have him anytime he likes ... just let me build Sly his own room."
>
> Chris Stone,
> studio co-owner

Roberts had one condition: "Build him whatever he wants, just make sure that engineer doesn't go anywhere near Stevie Wonder."

The album Sly had been struggling with for over two years was "finished" in less than a week with Tom Flye by his side at the new Record Plant Sausalito. However, no Sly Stone album was ever really "finished" until the masters were ripped out of his hands; so, for another month, Flye followed the artist and his tapes around the country for minor and often undecipherable touch-ups. They flew to Los Angeles just so Sly could use one of his favorite Les Paul guitars to overdub a single note. They hopped a Lear Jet to New York and spent their time eating barbecue instead of recording. Flye finally joined Sly in his mother's basement studio in San Francisco to finalize the mix, while, at the same time, he was called to engineer a marathon edition of KSAN's *Live at the Record Plant*, bouncing back and forth between live sessions in Studios A and B for three straight days.

CBS Records President Clive Davis scheduled *Fresh* for a June 1973 release; he even hired fashion photographer Robert Avedon to shoot the cover. Little did he know that, if it hadn't been for a gutsy studio manager, *Fresh* might have "spoiled" before it hit the record racks.

Michelle Zarin, studio manager, Record Plant Sausalito recalled:

> Sly called one Sunday morning and said, "I want to come down [to the studio] and get my tapes".
>
> See, Sly originally had permission to take his tapes whenever he wanted. Then the label called me and said, "Don't give him his tapes anymore." They didn't have the guts to tell him themselves.
>
> When Sly walked in, I was sitting at the desk in the tape library smoking a cigarette, drinking a cup of coffee. He told me he wanted his multitrack tapes and I told him "No".
>
> Then, suddenly, this guy who was with Sly took out a gun. So, I turned to them both and said, "You want to shoot me? Go ahead and shoot me. Go ahead, shoot me, and take your fucking tapes, go ahead. These tapes belong to Epic Records, and you're getting them over my dead body."
>
> I told him. "You have nothing to do with these tapes. Go home and go to sleep."
>
> Sly then turned to the guy and told him, "Come on, let's go." And they left and we held on to the tapes.

Above: Studio B in Record Plant Sausalito. It became Sly Stone's favorite room to work in with engineer Tom Flye. Below: Jerry Martini, Sly Stone, Cynthia Robinson, and Rustee Allen of Sly Stone and the Family Stone rehearse on April 3, 1973.

TAPE 22

STUDIO RECORD PLANT NY / REMOTE

ARTIST	TITLE	FORMAT
Rolling Stones	Stones Touring Party (STP)	Unreleased Live Album
Bruce Springsteen, Aerosmith, Blood, Sweat & Tears, John McLaughlin	King Biscuit Flower Hour	Broadcast
Lou Reed	Rock 'n' Roll Animal	Album
David Bowie	David Live	Album

WHERE ARE THE KEYS?

The reels and wheels were constantly rolling back in 1973.

Following Record Plant Remote's maiden voyage on the *Concert for Bangladesh*, the leased Wally Heider truck in New York was on the road constantly for an assortment of jazz, classical, and rock dates. The White Truck, as it was eventually christened, featured a small but reliable DeMedio console that had been kludged together to handle sixteen tracks even though it was built for half that amount; originally used on the Johnny Cash TV Show on ABC, the console featured analog components that gearheads now covet. The truck's electrical system needed significant upgrades to prevent meltdowns when plugged into the venue supply. Still, it was the only truck on the East Coast worth renting, and it came with its own Grammy after the *Concert for Bangladesh* won Album of the Year in March, 1973.

The White Truck would go anywhere and for any length of time. Just off their hit album *School's Out* in late 1972, Alice Cooper and Bob Ezrin hired the truck and parked it up at the Galesi Estate mansion in Greenwich, Connecticut, where the band was living, writing, and rehearsing. There was a guillotine in the ballroom and Alice's boa constrictor roamed freely around the building. The truck was parked outside in the driveway and the crew monitored the performances and parties via closed-circuit TV.

Much of Alice Cooper's *Billion Dollar Babies* was recorded by that truck at that location. The mansion gave the album both its unique mojo and sound. Shelly Yakus and his assistants recorded everywhere in the house, exploring the ballroom, bedrooms, and greenhouse for the right acoustics. Yakus explained: "Houses always sound better than studios. Think about this for a minute . . . groups usually come into the studio from a rehearsal hall, or from their basement or garage, and suddenly they're thrust into this 'dry' environment that's almost shocking in some ways, because when they touch their instruments in the studio the sound just doesn't respond like they're used to."

Ordinarily, A-team engineers like Yakus did not do remotes. Concert recording didn't require their type of expertise. Remotes needed engineers who enjoyed the unpredictable adrenaline rush of live entertainment—and someone drawn to life on the road. The studio's brilliant maintenance chief, Penn Stevens, was unable to take the pressure. And when Tom Flye left for Sausalito, his departure left a big hole in the White Truck's talent pool—until Jack Douglas found a friend from one of his old bands, named Frank Hubach, who just so happened to be an electrical engineer, loved audio, and needed work.

Hubach saw the job this way: "The key to live audio recording was making sure the red lights went on, the tape kept spinning, and the mics at least picked up the lead vocal, the lead guitar, and a drum sound, as well as some audience ambience. The job was more maintenance than creative engineering."

The White Truck took the Record Plant NY sitcom of fire extinguishers, pranks, and rowdiness out on the road. The truck's airtight interior made it a safe place for the managers and producers to get stoned while listening to the show. The crew was a ragtag bunch of kids, many away from home for the very first time. One of them once drove the truck under a low underpass in Central Park, peeling the roof and causing ongoing leaks whenever it rained.

Kooster McAllister, who started out working for free and ended up buying the truck at a bankruptcy auction in the eighties, remembered those early days on the road: "We didn't really answer to Roy. We were sort of like our own little renegade group and we didn't

CHAPTER THREE

have to live by anybody's rules but our own."

Frank Hubach recalled one memorable gig on the Rolling Stones STP tour: "We finished a show and then had a week hiatus before the next show, and we didn't want to drive the truck back and forth to New York. So, we got a garage and all flew back to New York. A week later, we flew back out, went to the truck and were standing there ready to open it up, when everyone asked the same question at one time, 'Who's got the keys?' None of us had the keys. The damn keys were sitting in the office back on Forty-Fourth Street."

Fortunately, plenty of money was being made in rock and roll touring in those days to support such bungling. When the White Truck's engine blew up in Texas, they hired a tow truck to drag it around the state from gig to gig. The truck carried so much two-inch tape that it was usually fined for excess cargo as it rolled through weigh stations. It would often sit cabled to the studio out on Forty-Fourth Street for weeks, adding a needed mix room to the complex, while collecting stacks of parking tickets on its windshield.

The 1973 record industry boom was being fueled by bands like Pink Floyd and Led Zeppelin on the road. But the grandest live music event in 1973 was a new series of Sunday-night rock concerts produced by DIR Broadcasting called the *King Biscuit Flower Hour*. Distributed to three hundred radio stations around the country, the weekly live show would run for the next fifteen years.

Someone had to record all those concerts, edit them down to one hour, and run two-track dubs for distribution. That someone was Record Plant NY, and Record Plant's someone was Frank Hubach. All the millions made from the records that were produced in that converted office space on Forty-Fourth Street was small change compared to the studio's real money maker in the seventies, the White Truck.

After a pilot project with Peter Frampton, the first *King Biscuit* program was produced in January 1973, and featured three separate concerts, from three sections of the country, all recorded within two weeks. The assignment fell to Frank Hubach, who was ready to go but needed someone who could drive a heavy and unwieldy rig in the snow.

Chris Stone knew just the right candidate and made the connection. A race car driver and former air force mechanic turned recording engineer named David Hewitt had just unsuccessfully applied for a job at Record Plant LA before returning back east. Hewitt walked in the door at Record Plant NY in January 1973 and virtually never left, even though he was rarely ever there, always on the road recording live shows.

Hewitt remembered how he got started at Record Plant NY: "Frank [Hubach] said, 'What are you doing?' I said, 'Looking for work as a recording engineer.' He literally grabbed me by the collar and asked, 'Can you drive a truck?' I replied, 'Yeah, I can drive anything.' So, we jumped into the White Truck and I didn't come back for ten years."

The debut broadcast of the *King Biscuit Flower Hour* aired on Sunday, February 18, 1973; it was the first live concert series of the rock era to reach a nationwide radio audience. The inaugural triple bill of Columbia Records artists featured Blood, Sweat & Tears, Mahavishnu Orchestra (with Aerosmith opening), and Bruce Springsteen. It would be the first time Record Plant NY recorded two of its biggest clients of that era, Aerosmith and Springsteen. The Springsteen show at Max's Kansas City is still considered an early Boss classic.

Record Plant Remote went on to record live *King Biscuit* concert broadcasts in 1973 for The J. Geils Band (New York), Ten Years After (Orlando), Joe Walsh (University of Texas), Poco (New Jersey), Seals and Crofts (New York), The Who (Philadelphia), and Mountain (New Jersey), among others.

Alice Cooper went out on its *Billion Dollar Babies* tour that same year. The Record Plant Remote was part of a caravan of semi-tractor trailer trucks carrying the largest inventory of tech, costumes, and props to ever hit the road in support of a rock band—26,000 pounds of gear lugged to sixty-four concerts, in fifty-nine cities in just ninety days. Alice, the band's frontman, only trusted the audio guys with his boa constrictor, which they toted around in the back of their air-conditioned van.

The White Truck also somehow squeezed two of the greatest rock concert albums of all time into that year's schedule: *David (Bowie) Live* (July, Philadelphia) and Lou Reed's *Rock 'n' Roll Animal* (December, New York).

Advertisement from 1976 for a fleet of Record Plant recording trucks that were available for rent from Los Angeles and Sausalito. The service offered "We Do It, Where You Do It" recording for music and television in the mid-seventies.

SECOND HOME

Soon, the White Truck was joined by a nationwide Record Plant fleet on both coasts, with Stone and Kellgren building three trucks and breaking their deal with Wally Heider to stay out of the West Coast circuit. Back in New York, in 1978 Hewitt would build the studio's state-of-the-art Black Truck, which would go on to record hundreds of live concerts before getting totaled in a black-ice crash in 1989.

The original White Truck, heavily modified but fixed to the same Heider chassis, kept rolling rubber and tape for the next forty-five years.

TAPE 23

STUDIO THE WICK, LONDON

ARTIST	TITLE	FORMAT
Ron Wood	*I've Got My Own Album to Do*	Album
George Harrison, Ron Wood	"Far East Man"	Single

BIG FAN

The Beatles were an obsession for Gary. He even kept a mental checklist:

> He recorded *Bangladesh* with George – *check*.
> Ringo played alongside Jim Keltner onstage at *Bangladesh*, too – *check*.
> John and Yoko were at the Sausalito opening – *check*.
> Paul was still MIA.

CHAPTER THREE

That was one of the reasons that Gary and Chris went to London in spring 1973. Mal Evans, the Beatles' roadie, was spending time at Record Plant LA and dating studio manager Fran Hughes; he promised them a meeting with Paul, but the introduction never took place.

On that overseas trip, Gary worked at guitarist Ronnie Wood's townhouse studio in London, which would result a year later in Wood's first solo album release, *I've Got My Own Album to Do*. As the credited producer, Gary recorded an early take of George Harrison and Wood's song "Far East Man," with Mick Jagger and David Bowie contributing backup vocals.

While recording in the UK, Harrison invited Gary over to his mansion to help tune his new sixteen-track home studio. He sent his white Mercedes-Benz limousine to pick him and Chris up at their hotel, and when they arrived at the Beatle's castle on the Thames, a small party was underway on the front lawn.

George spotted Gary and immediately led him inside to check out the room. Chris followed, but someone handed him a drink that he reflexively swallowed. And within minutes, he was feeling tipsy. He never made it to the house and, instead, wandered off into a maze of gardens. At one point some joker led him to a rowboat, and he floated into a moat under Harrison's house. By the time the boat emerged from total darkness, Stone was seriously tripping. He was greeted by the laughter and hoots of other guests.

Stone slept most of the way back to London. But he wasn't too stoned to miss the news that his partner was staying in England for a few more weeks to help George straighten out his studio, and, in exchange, Harrison had agreed to mix his new album in Sausalito. Having his second Beatle at the new studio was a very big deal for Gary, though George made him swear to keep it a secret.

A few weeks later, Harrison was in LA with Lennon to contribute to Ringo's new solo album over at Sunset Sound. Harrison brought along his masters for the album that would become *Living in the Material World*, and Kellgren and he agreed to take a road trip up to Sausalito.

Kellgren and Harrison sat together in the back seat of GREED listening to records as they wound their way north up US 101.

SECOND HOME

The "Jim Keltner Fan Club" button (above, left) was modeled by Ringo Starr (above, right) in 1974. Ringo Starr and George Harrison announced the formation of the fan club in the liner notes of their 1973 albums to honor their session drummer, Jim Keltner (below), in 1985.

Before they left, Gary had sent an assistant to raid Tower Records on Sunset for some new LPs to play on a portable turntable that was wired into the car. One of the albums was Paul McCartney and Wings' just-released *Red Rose Speedway*, which Harrison listened to with particular interest. Studying the album credits, he pointed out the kitschy callout for a new "Wings Fun Club" on the bottom of the album's back cover. Harrison would later poke fun at Paul by starting his own "Club," which he dubbed "The Jim Keltner Fan Club" on the liner notes of the *Material World* album cover. Ringo published a similar "Jim Keltner Fan Club" note on his own solo album, *Ringo*.

> ## "And we'll call it the Jim Keltner Fan Club Hour."
>
> Gary Kellgren,
> studio co-owner

In keeping with Record Plant tradition, the Jim Keltner Fan Club soon morphed in Gary's mind into a weekly jam session that would help him introduce Keltner's new house band (Danny Kortchmar, Paul Stallworth, and David Foster) to LA's most influential musicians. He ran the idea by George Harrison with Marta up at the house and he gave his okay. Gary brought it up over dinner with Jim Keltner and their wives; the couples were close and often socialized together, sometimes going for bike rides together in Griffith Park.

Kellgren said, "We ought to do some jam sessions in the studio on Sunday nights."

"Yeah, that would be cool," Keltner replied.

"We'll open the room up. You'll invite friends down. And we'll call it the Jim Keltner Fan Club Hour."

Keltner was uncomfortable with the brand. But it stuck.

TAPE 24

STUDIO RECORD PLANT NY / REMOTE

ARTIST	TITLE	FORMAT
Alice Cooper	*Billion Dollar Babies*	Album / Tour
Yoko Ono	*Approximately Infinite Universe*	Album
New York Dolls	*New York Dolls*	Album
John Lennon	*Mind Games*	Album
Kansas	*Kansas*	Album

ABE & EDDIE

Abe Silverstein was sitting in the executive dining room, high atop the Warner Communications building in Manhattan's Rockefeller Center. It was an opulent canteen for the lieutenants of Steve Ross's media army. Silverstein had recently left the corporation and was looking for something else to do.

Silverstein was having lunch with Albert Sarnoff, chief financial officer of the corporation, who was explaining that they were having trouble disposing of a small asset that came along with the TVC cable acquisition, Record Plant NY. The prospective buyer, the studio's chief engineer Roy Cicala, had signed a letter of intent but was struggling to put the money together. The studio was a cash cow for Warner, Sarnoff said, but it posed too many potential risks with the unions and the law to be worth the effort. Besides, with every record label ridding itself of its studios, now wasn't the time for the Warner Music Division to get into the business.

"Cicala has no concept of money, but there's plenty of money to be made," Sarnoff advised.

Silverstein remembered the studio from the meeting several years back with the original owners (Chris and Gary) and one of their eccentric engineers (Jack Adams). He also remembered how Steve Ross said he wanted out of the studio business. Now,

CHAPTER THREE

Silverstein was looking for something new to sink his teeth into. He told Sarnoff to arrange a meeting with Roy.

Silverstein wrote about visiting Record Plant for the first time: "The well-known musical artists and recording engineers were like a fraternity. The record companies were the customers, but it was the musical artists who we had to keep happy. And keeping rock stars happy is a very interesting business."

Silverstein agreed to fund the buyout, supplementing the cash that Cicala had already pieced together from a network of seventeen investors and key employees.

One of those small-time investors was RCA Records producer Eddie Germano, a chain-smoking, former cement-truck driver from Queens, who worked the nightclub circuit as lounge-singer Eddie Jason. Germano often took Roy up on his offer for free recording time if a room was open. The Record Plant NY engineers didn't like his music ("He sang flat," Jack Douglas recalled) but he was the boss's friend.

Once the deal with Warner was completed, Germano moved into the tenth-floor office as studio manager. He was the perfect fit for Roy. Germano was all business; Roy was not. They shared a passion for motorboats and expensive cars. And Eddie had no problem being the bad guy in their "good guy–bad guy" routine. With Silverstein handling the books and Germano managing the bookings, Roy could do what he loved most—recording.

There were rumors that mob money backed the studio's Warner buyout. The claim was never substantiated, although the vowels at the end of all the names at Record Plant NY contributed to the stereotype—as did the wiseguys from Teamsters Union Local 966 who shared the tenth floor with the studio staff. The union officials mingled freely with the rockers, sometimes wandering in on sessions and ordering Roy's assistants to "play some of that new John Lennon stuff," as if they owned the place.

Lennon's residence at Record Plant NY during the spring of 1973 marked a low point for the artist. The shellacking he had taken from the critics for *Some Time in New York City* sent him into a deep depression, the drugs he was taking were getting heavier, and, to top things off, US immigration authorities had just given him sixty days to leave the country.

SECOND HOME

John and Yoko weren't usually together at Record Plant in those days. There were rumors of an imminent split. Yoko was on a creative tear with Jack Douglas in the studio on her album *Feeling the Space*. John wasn't recording; when he was around the studio he usually hung out with Eddie and Roy in the office where he read, doodled, and played with Roy's son, Jade. At Record Plant, he was home and part of a family.

Abe Silverstein ran into Lennon on one of those occasions. He wrote in his memoir: "Upon my arrival on one of my first days at the studio, I noticed a funny-looking guy with granny glasses sitting in the reception area with his coat on. He sat there all day, for about eight hours. When I was leaving, I couldn't resist asking the receptionist 'Who is that guy?' She looked at me incredulously and said, 'That's John Lennon.'"

Keeping Lennon happy was Eddie Germano's job. When John mentioned he wanted to study his mixes at home, a new high-end system appeared at his doorstep. The studio was well stocked with John's secret stash of Hershey bars—always kept well hidden from Yoko. When some demo tapes and rough mixes from the *Some Time in New York City* sessions went missing, Germano knew where to go to get them back.

Eddie Germano took a big load off Roy's shoulders, especially at a time when Roy and his wife, Lori, were having their own personal problems back at home in Montclair, New Jersey. The new studio manager, however, never developed the same rapport with the Record Plant NY staff as the chief engineer had. And his arrival signaled a core change in the Record Plant culture.

Night maintenance tech, Paul Prestopino, remembered: "I was the night guy. I had keys to every door in that studio. There was not a room in that place that I could not get into. The minute Eddie walked in the door, I could no longer get into the office. He was a secretive guy. I owned 1 percent of the studio, but he let me know that I was the help."

Staffers faulted Roy for being too trusting of his friend. But Eddie was a natural with the clients. Besides John Lennon, he befriended producer Bob Ezrin who also lived in the same apartment building on East Fifty-Second Street. The following year, Germano would

CHAPTER THREE

arrange a penthouse rental there for John and his then girlfriend, May Pang, too.

TRIAL BY EZRIN

While Lennon was the ideal client, usually on time and always easy to work with, Ezrin was a terror in the studio. The twenty-two-year-old Canadian wunderkind instigated many of the studio hijinks, once tossing a live guitar amplifier down the elevator shaft just so he could record its fall.

Ezrin recalled: "I was very young, I was completely indefatigable and bulletproof at that age, so I let off steam at the end of the night by goofing around, by playing pranks and running around like a crazy person. For me this was the equivalent of throwing the television sets out of the hotel rooms at the Hyatt. There were a lot of pies in the face and fire-extinguisher blasts in the groin. There was one famous all-night battle that left the studio in such bad shape that I paid Roy $1,000 for cleaning costs."

Ezrin more than covered the damage with all the studio time and concert remotes he booked for Alice Cooper during 1972 and 1973. Ezrin was Alice Cooper's partner in the sessions that produced two rock-theater masterpieces, *School's Out* and *Billion Dollar Babies,* in the space of nine months. He became a fixture in the Forty-Fourth Street studios for eight years before leaving for England to work on *The Wall* with Pink Floyd. And like a generation of New York artists, producers, and engineers in the seventies, Roy mentored him the hard way in the studio. Ezrin explained:

> I was warned that Roy had a habit of saying that he needed to go to the bathroom and then never returned to the session. And sure enough, most nights, Roy would just slip away. No fanfare, no announcement, I'd just look up and Roy would be gone. And there I would be in the middle of a session with an assistant who had never operated the console. I had to sit at the console and push buttons and turn knobs and do stuff, and not be afraid. Roy taught me not to be afraid in the studio. Sometimes it would be horrible and sometimes it would absolutely be brilliant. But I was this punky kid and I already

had hit records and I was being chased for projects. For a kid of my age, it was heady stuff, and it was ego-filling. Roy made me feel like I could do anything, like I was the king of the world.

Roy used me to train his new assistants. He'd throw them in the room with me for a week and if they survived, then he would consider taking them on. I'd terrorize the kids. But part of the terror was getting them to listen and pay attention. That ability to pay attention, to listen, to attend to detail, and to find a way to be selfless in a session, is how to cut it in a recording studio. You realize none of this is about you. It is about the work and it's about the art.

Ezrin was the first to recognize that Jack Douglas could be a record producer after watching him turn studio bedlam into the first New York Dolls album for its actual producer, Todd Rundgren.

And during the Alice Cooper *Billion Dollar Babies* sessions at Record Plant NY, Ezrin told Roy that a young, cocky reject from A&R Recording was cut out to be his next assistant. "This kid Jimmy Shoes has a future," Ezrin told Cicala, nicknaming him after his flashy stack-heeled boots.

Nobody could possibly predict how bright the future would be for nineteen-year-old Jimmy "Shoes" Iovine.

JIMMY SHOES

Little Jimmy Iovine wanted to be Phil Spector. It was his look. It was his money. It was his women. It was his sound. But the famed producer and this nobody from Red Hook, Brooklyn, shared one thing in common: their personalities were much larger than their five-foot-five-inch frames.

Jimmy had personality, which was the only way a kid his size could survive by the docks in Brooklyn. Cool clothes helped; he worked in a local clothing store where he sold white polyester suits before *Saturday Night Fever* made them trendy. He played bass–badly–in a band called Phantasy, and this led him across the East River to Manhattan, where he was introduced by a cousin to songwriter Ellie Greenwich, who was famed for her hits, "Be My Baby" and "Leader of the Pack." Like most people, Greenwich immediately took a liking to the kid. She got him his first job sweeping floors for a small midtown New York City recording studio. And after being fired, she sent him over to A&R Recording where owner Phil Ramone offered him a ninety-day tryout. It was there that Jimmy saw something that changed his life:

"I'm in the studio one night and this pretty girl came in with the engineer, Elliot Scheiner [owner Phil Ramone's assistant turned independent engineer]. He had a great leather jacket and a leather bag. I said, 'Fucking leather, wow!' It blew my mind. I'd never seen a guy with a leather bag before. He was an engineer, so that's what I wanted to be," he told *Rolling Stone* magazine.

Unfortunately, Iovine didn't cut it. He was let go on the ninetieth day of his trial period. Engineer Shelly Yakus at Record Plant NY got a call from a friend at A&R who asked him if they needed a runner.

"He's a wise-guy, but I think he could do really well. He just seems like a wild card. Wanna give him a shot?"

Jimmy put on his favorite pair of side-zipper boots and stood a few inches taller as he walked west through Times Square over to Record Plant for his job interview; he introduced himself to Shelly Yakus with an outstretched hand.

"Hi, I'm Jimmy Iovine," he said.

"So, what," Yakus snapped back before sending him upstairs to meet Roy.

Roy Cicala and Eddie Germano were reading boat manuals with their feet up on their desks when Iovine arrived. The studio owner and his manager ignored the newbie as they gossiped about what they were going to buy, acting like they had all the money in the world but nothing to share with this unproven kid.

Little Jimmy had been around his father's social club enough to recognize an initiation.

"What's your name?" Germano finally asked.

"Iovine," he answered with respect.

Jimmy had everything he needed to get his foot in the door at Record Plant NY—an Italian last name.

"Iovine . . ." Germano repeated while lighting up a cigarette, "You're hired."

Roy immediately put him to the "Ezrin test." Ezrin was recording

Alice Cooper's *Billion Dollar Babies* LP and the producer recalled: "So, they gave me Jimmy Shoes. I don't even know why. But I do remember that we had him so on edge within the first week that just out of fun, I kept calling him by other names to see if he'd respond. I had him so wired to respond to a bark, to a command, that if I yelled out, 'Fred,' he'd go, 'What?'"

Years later, after he had worked in the studio with Bruce Springsteen, Patti Smith, Tom Petty, U2, and Stevie Nicks, and had co-founded Interscope Records and Beats headphones, the music mogul described how much this early job experience meant to his career:

> Record Plant formed 100 percent who I am. I wasn't anybody when I walked in there. Those first five years at Record Plant taught me everything. It taught me about life, it taught me how to behave and what to do. It was my entire education. I never thought I knew how to do anything. But I did—I knew how to make people like me.

Roy liked him. An almost paternal relationship developed between the thirty-four-year-old studio owner and the twenty-year-old recruit. While staffers warned that the kid was a slacker, who would hide out on the tenth-floor roof to take in some sun when he should have been working, Roy overlooked the comments. He assigned the newcomer to assist Shelly Yakus, and Iovine quickly learned that he didn't have the chops to be an engineer. Besides, he really wanted to be Phil Spector and, as a result, paid more attention to the producers and the engineers like Jack Douglas who were on their way to becoming one.

Jimmy watched Jack Douglas and Bob Ezrin tag team the mix during the Alice Cooper sessions, six hours on and six hours off. He watched Douglas bail out Todd Rundgren during the raucous New York Dolls sessions for their debut LP. And he also watched Douglas, who was then making big money behind the board, take Ezrin's advice to go out on his own to produce. Jimmy Shoes learned that the producers made a whole lot more money than even the best engineers and didn't work nearly as hard.

CHAPTER THREE

"I was from Brooklyn," Iovine told *Rolling Stone.* "Money enticed me. I was willing to do anything to be one of those guys."

So, when Cicala called Jimmy at home on Labor Day 1973, Iovine jumped from his seat at the family dinner table and eagerly took his boss's call.

"Hey Jimmy . . . I need you to come up to the studio . . . we need somebody to answer the phones."

Without questioning, Iovine grabbed his new leather coat and headed uptown.

As he walked into the tenth-floor studio office, he greeted Cicala who was there smiling smugly, before doing a double take to make sure it was really John Lennon who was sitting by his side. Roy didn't need anybody to answer the phones. He needed an assistant who was willing to drop everything and come to work just because he asked him to.

"Go set up a couple of mics in the studio," Roy instructed. "John wants to work."

Iovine had seen John and Yoko around the studio but knew that the generals were expected to keep their distance from the stars. But on Labor Day 1973, he was seated beside his mentor and John Lennon who was working on songs for his new album, *Mind Games.* With Roy teaching Jimmy how to get Lennon the vocal sound he liked, this nobody from Brooklyn, at least for a few precious moments, imagined that he was producing a Beatle and that he was the one in charge.

One evening, Cicala, Ezrin, and a group of engineers and musicians were heading over to have a steak dinner at Downey's. Roy and Bob were bringing up the rear, with Jimmy Shoes entertaining a group up front. Roy turned to Bob as they walked towards Eighth Avenue; pointing at the back of Iovine's head, and with a proud-smile he remarked: "See that kid up there? We made him."

TAPE 25

STUDIO RECORD PLANT LA / RECORD PLANT NY

ARTIST	TITLE	FORMAT
Stevie Wonder	*Innervisions*	Album
Stevie Wonder	"Living for the City"	Single
Isley Brothers	*3+3*	Album
REO Speedwagon	*Ridin' The Storm Out*	Single / Album
John Lennon	*Rock 'N' Roll*	Album

INNERVISIONS

Album credits were a must-read at Record Plant LA. Even before listening to the vinyl, the studio staff would scrutinize the small print on the sleeve to see how the artist had treated those who had toiled over their work. It was usually in very tiny type but it was a very big deal to engineers and assistants for whom this was the only recognition they would ever get for long hours, tireless patience, and very little compensation.

It was also good for business.

"Motown booked some time with us the other day and we asked them how they heard about us. They said they picked up fifty albums and our name was on the back of more of them than any other, so they thought we must be the best," Gary Kellgren told an interviewer.

So, when *Innervisions* was released on August 3, 1973, Kellgren handed one of the assistants some cash and the keys to GREED to drive up the hill to Tower Records on Sunset Boulevard to buy a few copies of the new album to pass around. He was thrilled that Record Plant LA was credited right at the top and marched with the album under his good arm into Chris Stone's corner office. He leaned over his partner's desk and pointed out the studio's top billing on the record that would win the industry's Album of the Year.

"Stone, remember when Jimi first released *Electric Ladyland*?"

CHAPTER THREE

"Of course," Stone replied, giving his partner room to answer his own question.

"We were totally booked for months . . . we were running 24/7 . . . and that's when we started talking about building Studio B," he said.

Stone knew what Kellgren was up to. He had seen it before. His latest project, Sausalito, was already operating on autopilot. The two Toms (Flye and Scott) had Sausalito Studio B up and running and were nearing completion of the West Coast's first truck. They had leased two properties up in the hills to house the out-of-town clients who were drawn there by all the publicity being generated by the *Live at the Record Plant* radio concerts on KSAN. Kellgren was bored.

Gary reached into his Igloo cooler and pulled out a baggie of coke, which he poured into the *Innervisions* album cover crease. He again pointed at the album cover and remarked, "It's time to start talking Studio C here in LA. C . . . as in cocaine."

The partners had been talking about building a third room on Third Street for a while; they needed a big studio to compete for the orchestral dates and film scores. Kellgren had already drawn up preliminary plans to convert the warehouse in the back into the largest ever Record Plant recording studio. The space had originally been the site of a swimming tank where Tarzan movies were filmed in the 1930s and '40s. A producer of a Saturday-morning kids' show sublet the space to cage his "talking" chimpanzees, branding the space "The Monkey House" for years to come. The building almost burned down in its early days when a motorcycle parked by a band member burst into flames.

Studio C was going to be the studio's first post-Hidley room. The Record Plant's all-star audio tech had moved on to sell his own design services and pricey, prized monitors around the globe. The Record Plant clientele was getting tired of his "dead" studio design anyway; in NY, the staff was constantly tearing up the rugs and arranging plywood sheets in Hidley's Studios A and B to liven up the sound. Ever-attentive to what his customers were hearing, Kellgren now wanted his new LA studio to sound big and loud.

Just around the corner and down the hall in Studio B, Cecil and Margouleff were also reviewing the *Innervisions* album cover, and both were upset by their credits. They knew the album would be a leading contender for multiple Grammy Awards and seeing their names buried at the bottom of Stevie's credit list, below the assistant engineers, coordinators, and tape operator, they believed, was an intentional slight.

Malcolm had been pushing Stevie hard in the studio, especially while putting the finishing touches on "Living for the City." Stevie played every instrument on the song and sang all the backup vocals. It was a masterpiece. But Malcolm felt that the fourth verse desperately needed an angry edge.

Malcolm tried to coax more emotion out of Stevie's voice but nothing he tried worked. In the past, he would have "nursed" the artist along. But that day he tried a different technique: in the middle of one of Stevie's takes he had the operator abruptly stop the tape, something he knew would drive Stevie nuts. After the third interruption, Stevie was visibly pissed. On the next take, Malcolm let the tape run.

Malcolm finally got the vocal he was looking for. But at a cost.

Cecil told *WaxPoetics* magazine, "I was seeking too much perfection, and I overstepped the bounds as Stevie saw them. Up until then, we had been producing everything as a team. I started to get pushy, much like one of his old Motown producers had done to him. I realized after the fact that it wasn't smart, because that's what Stevie was getting away from."

Bob and Malcolm made another false move. Right in the middle of finishing *Innervisions*, they cut a deal with CBS Records' president, Clive Davis, to produce the Isley Brothers' first Epic Records release, *3+3*. The album was recorded at the same time as *Innervisions*, right down the hall at Record Plant in Studio A, and it was scheduled to hit the street a few days after *Innervisions*. Worst of all, it contained the Isleys' biggest hit—"That Lady."

There was only so much airtime for an R&B single, so working with the Isleys at the same time as they were working on Stevie Wonder's new record didn't endear Bob and Malcolm to the Motown management team. The Motown brass knew that the Isleys were always looking for the hot new sound, and Motown didn't appreciate CBS stealing Stevie Wonder's.

CHAPTER THREE

And *3+3* had Stevie's sonic stamp all over it. During the Isley sessions that summer, Bob and Malcolm schooled the band on the use of electronic instruments for the first time. They introduced their keyboardist, Chris Jasper, to the ARP 2600 synthesizer that Stevie was then using. They even let him sit in on a Stevie session while he was recording "Don't You Worry 'bout a Thing" to see how it was played.

Ironically, that same ARP synthesizer helped distance Stevie from his associate producers. The instrument was the first reliable synthesizer for working musicians; it stayed in tune and was easy to use. With the ARP, Stevie didn't need anybody's help creating his sounds and, to some extent, the new instrument made TONTO seem antiquated in comparison.

So, for all these reasons, Malcolm wasn't surprised to see how Stevie buried their credits on the *Innervision* liner notes. But to make matters worse, rumors were spreading that their assistant engineer was taking credit for their work. Malcolm had Chris Stone pull him from any future Stevie Wonder sessions. And that's when their new assistant Gary Olazabal stepped in.

The tape operator on *Innervisions*, Gary Olazabal began working with Stevie as his assistant engineer after the album's release and Wonder's near-fatal car crash in August 1973, and he continued to work with him for decades. Stone gave the trusted assistant access to Stevie's vault and, with renewed vigor, the artist and his new engineering partner went back to work on his next album.

Stevie enjoyed working with young assistants who were more his age. Olazabal said: "Stevie moved quickly and didn't really have an agenda. He went from writing songs to overdubbing and it would switch on a dime. He needed someone who could keep up with him."

With Stevie Wonder back in business in Studio B, and Studio A booked around the clock by the Bee Gees, REO Speedwagon, Billy Joel, The J. Geils Band, and America, Kellgren began construction of Studio C in Los Angeles. C's control room was going to feature the largest console ever built. The studio walls were outfitted with reflective surfaces to create brighter and bigger sounds. The vocal booth had mirrors on the ceiling. The centerpiece was a marble stage surrounded by a large velvet curtain. The room featured theatrical stage-lighting designed by Woodstock's Chip Monck. A secret hideaway over the control room ceiling gave the studio owner a place to spy on the sessions. C was directly connected by a hallway to the studio's back hotel rooms.

Kellgren began working on Lennon to work in his big new room. He socialized with the ex-Beatle and his girlfriend at the Roxy and other local clubs. He gave them rides around town in GREED and hosted them at parties on Miller Drive. Gary took John on a tour of the Studio C construction site, sharing his dream for insider-only jam sessions every Sunday night.

Kellgren and Lennon never hit it off. Gary blamed Cicala for trash-talking him with his prized client. Stone believed that Lennon was upset over the way Kellgren used him and Yoko to hype the Sausalito studio opening. But most of all, Lennon was EMI-trained; to him a recording studio was a serious place to do serious business and Record Plant LA simply had too many distractions.

Lennon occasionally stopped by Record Plant LA at the beginning of his Lost Weekend in October 1973 to continue partying after the clubs had closed for the night. Lennon also knew it was where he would run into Stevie Wonder.

In the Studio A control room one night, Lennon asked Kellgren if Wonder was around. Kellgren got word into the Studio B control room where Wonder was working, and several minutes later Olazabal walked in, guiding Stevie by the arm.

Olazabal remembered: "It was one of those moments when you have a spotlight on you. It's one of those moments when the music stops. John got up from his chair, walked right up to Stevie, stared him right in the face, and planted the biggest kiss squarely on his lips."

LOST WEEKEND

The phone rang on Roy's desk in New York. It was John's girlfriend/ assistant, May Pang, from LA, asking if Roy could have someone go uptown to John's apartment at the Dakota to gather up his guitars and send them out to him on the West Coast.

Pang explained that Lennon was going back into the studio with Phil Spector in the middle of October to work on a project of rock and roll classics (*Rock 'N' Roll*). Three of the songs were included

John Lennon with his drinking buddies Harry Nilsson, Alice Cooper, and Micky Dolenz. Known as "The Hollywood Vampires," the gang was pictured here on November 21, 1973, at the Troubadour in Los Angeles, California. Record Plant on Third Street was the after-hours stop.

SECOND HOME

in the album to settle a lawsuit with mobster label executive Morris Levy who was suing Lennon for copyright infringement. Spector had already lined up his session players and had booked time at A&M Studios, where he had an outstanding obligation.

Then Pang told Cicala: "John said to Phil, 'You can have everything else. You can pick your studio, you can do whatever, but I've got to have my engineer.'"

Roy was that engineer. It wasn't the best of times for him to leave the studio and his family for an indeterminate period of time. Besides, it had been a pleasure working with John on *Mind Games* without having Phil Spector around.

Roy told an interviewer that "[Spector] and John would get at it and then we'd always have to break it up." In truth, Phil was intimidated by the strong-willed Italian studio owner from New York. John once told him that Roy was "connected," which may also explain why Spector agreed to let him engineer the *Rock 'N' Roll* sessions.

Around that time, Spector was increasingly showing dark and erratic behavior. During the "Happy Xmas" recording sessions in New York, he frequently passed out drunk on cherry brandy under the console. But more recently his drunkenness was accompanied by threats of violence. Spector strung barbed wire around his Los Angeles mansion and had guard dogs roaming the property. One Spector biographer described: "When you see Phil screaming with bulging red eyes, it's like seeing Satan."

John was willing to put up with anything, so long as Spector would produce the new album; he appealed to Spector who enjoyed being solicited by an ex-Beatle. "It took me three weeks to convince him [Spector] that I wasn't going to co-produce with him, and I wasn't going to go in the control room. I said, 'I just want to be the singer, just treat me like Ronnie [Spector]. I just want to sing. I don't want anything to do with production or writing or creation. I just want to sing,'" Lennon was quoted as saying on the *Lennon Tapes*.

Torn between serving his best client and running his business in New York, Roy had another issue to contend with—problems at home.

Lori Burton recalled: "At least for the time being, Roy and I somehow worked our problems out. But the next thing you know, I got pregnant again—just when John first told Roy that he was going out to California and he wanted him to go out there with him to record. That's when Roy got this idea for me to go out there with him. He told me he'd even bring his mother, Molly, to babysit. So, I agreed to go."

Cicala added: "I really didn't want to go, because I knew it was going to be chaos and I might end up never going back home to New York. So, I told John that and he said, 'Well, bring your family.' I said, 'I'm not going to charge you for bringing my family,' and he said, 'No, I don't pay for it. EMI does.' That's how it was with the biggest artists, and so EMI rented me a bungalow at the Beverly Hills Hotel with four or five bedrooms."

For this important road trip, Roy picked Jimmy Shoes to assist. Lennon was comfortable with the personable, young engineer-in-training, and Roy thought he might even be able to charm Spector. The kid had never been on a plane before and had never stayed in a hotel. He was excited to learn he was going to work with his idol—Phil, not John. He ran home to Brooklyn to pack and the next morning was on a flight to LA.

Iovine said: "Traveling blew my mind . . . seeing the hotel we were staying in blew my mind . . . but what happened afterwards really blew my mind. Being in the middle of the whole John Lennon, Phil Spector thing. The Lost Weekend. It was totally nuts."

LOUSY DRUNK

The *Rock 'N' Roll* sessions began October 22, 1973, at A&M Studios on the old Charlie Chaplin lot on La Brea near the corner of Sunset Boulevard. Patterned after Phil Spector's original LA base of operations, Gold Star Studios, A&M and its hard walls were perfectly suited to recording live reverberant sound. The Carpenters tracked in there a lot. It was at A&M that Carole King and her producer Lou Adler recorded *Tapestry*.

Their first night there, John, Roy, Jimmy, and a roomful of highly paid session musicians waited three hours for Phil Spector to arrive. Fortunately, Jimmy and Roy needed the extra time; thirty-five musicians were in the room, half of whom were part of the rhythm section. Jimmy hadn't ever set up mics for an ensemble that large, and the console was too small for so many instruments. Everyone, including John, was drinking heavily, leaving it up to the two engineers, working in a new room and with an unfamiliar console, to make sure that when the producer arrived, they were ready—even if nobody else was—to record.

"I was working my ass off," Iovine recalled. "It was all hands on deck. And everybody was drunk as hell by the time Phil Spector arrived. Bad, bad, bad drunk—cocaine, everything."

Spector's entrance shattered the mental image that Little Jimmy Shoes had of his boyhood idol. The producer was stinking drunk, sipping a bottle of Manischewitz wine through a straw. He was dressed like a surgeon and madly waved a wand while barking incoherently at the band. That first night they worked on the song "Bony Moronie," but when it was finally time for John's vocals, he was too drunk to sing.

"The drinking started right away, or at least an hour into it," Cicala confirmed in an interview, "I myself took it a little bit easy sometimes, because I was the designated driver. But then again if you didn't indulge, you couldn't get with it in that company. So, I would partake, too. It was pretty crazy. [John] was drinking Dewar's White Label. I went through a bottle a day, and I don't know how we didn't all die."

Lennon was a lousy drunk. His mood swings while liquored up were notorious. And he was hanging out in bad company, carousing on the Sunset Strip with other famous rock and roll boozers like Harry Nilsson and Keith Moon. One night, John was so unruly after a session at A&M that his engineers had to tie him to a chair in the parking lot until he calmed down.

Cicala described another memorable night:

> It was four in the morning. We were leaving A&M Studios.
> John wanted to go for a walk and [guitarist] Jesse Ed Davis was
> with him. They headed up La Brea. So, I took Jim Keltner and
> Jimmy Iovine home in this big-ass Lincoln rental.
>
> We were driving home and we saw these two guys dancing
> right in the middle of the street. And who was it? It was John
> and Jesse Davis. I said to the guys, "The cops are going to see
> them." I knew if we left him in the street, we would have been
> back at the Beverly Hills Hotel, getting a phone call from him

CHAPTER THREE

from jail. So, we pulled over, and pulled them into the car. And we started driving back to [producer] Lou Adler's place [where he was staying].

We were so drunk. And I was the one driving. And then John started kicking everyone in the back seat. There must've been some other stuff involved because this wasn't just drunkenness [John had lost his glasses and couldn't see without them]. Oh God, he went ballistic. He just kicked the hell out of Jimmy and whoever else was in the back seat—and then he started kicking the back window. He didn't break it but he was kicking like crazy.

I just kept driving. I wanted to get off the streets as soon as I could.

The engineers had to restrain Lennon again, once they arrived at Lou Adler's house on Stone Canyon Road. And after he finally calmed down, Cicala and Iovine drove back to the bungalow at the Beverly Hills Hotel, where they sat shell-shocked around the kitchen table with Roy's wife, Lori, who was answering phone calls from May Pang. After they left, Lennon had vandalized the place, including its expensive antiques; May was desperate for Roy and Jimmy to return to the house and help.

Roy wasn't going anywhere but to bed. Lori suggested that he get some sleep and call Yoko first thing in the morning. Roy didn't want to make the call. He told her: "You don't know what's going on here. It's insane. Yoko keeps calling me up in the studio and begging, 'How am I going to get John back?' I can't deal with it. What am I supposed to do? I'm in the middle of a session. Lori, why don't you call her? Please, Lori, I need a break."

Lori refused. And the next morning, with only a few hours of sleep, with his son, Jade, bouncing on the bed and his mother, Molly, screaming at the Watergate hearings on the TV in the other room, Roy called Yoko.

He laid it out straight for her. May Pang had no control over John. When John drank, he was like Jekyll turning into Hyde. Spector was crazy—dangerously so—and Roy was suspicious that he was stealing the tapes. Then Roy outright begged:

SECOND HOME

"Yoko, you have to come out here. John needs you. You're the only one who can help."

Something Roy said must have registered, since Yoko flew out to LA to see John for a few days in late 1973. Roy remembered her staying in a bungalow right next to his. However, there was no apparent reconciliation. John went back to work at A&M, and Yoko headed back east after less than a week in town. Lori, Roy's mom, and their son packed their bags and followed suit several weeks later.

Then came the guns. Spector's moods were constantly changing, along with his costumes, and a gun was always within reach. So many stories about Phil Spector and guns in the recording studio have surfaced over the years that his conviction for murder in 2009 should have come as no surprise.

Spector's bringing a gun into the studio went against standard practice. Drummer Jim Keltner recalled: "In the very early days, I would do projects with artists who would come into the studio, pull their gun out of their overcoat, and then hand it to the secretary who'd put it in the drawer at the bottom of the desk until we were done for the night."

One night, Spector learned that Quincy Jones was over at Record Plant working on a film soundtrack project from which Spector had just been fired. Spector and his bodyguards left Lennon at A&M, and paid an unannounced visit to Jones at Record Plant LA.

Quincy's engineer, Phil Schier said: "I'm guessing it's Saturday night at ten or eleven o'clock, and, all of a sudden, in through the door comes Phil Spector with two of the biggest, hugest guys you ever saw on the planet. He's packing two silver guns, shoulder-holster kind of things. And he is rip-snorting mad. I'm standing by the tape machines just listening to this rant go on, when Phil comes up to me, and I swear to God his nose is five inches from my nose, and I'm feeling those pistols pressed against my chest, and he said to me, 'If you roll this tape one more time, it'll be the last time you roll tape in this town ever again.'"

Spector would come every night to the session dressed in a different costume. One night he arrived wearing a butcher's coat with blood on it. Jim Keltner recalled: "At the beginning of each night the band would play really well, and then as the night wore on everybody, not just Phil, but everybody in the band was getting completely effed up on the drug of your choice."

During those sessions at A&M, Spector reportedly fired a few rounds into the studio's ceiling in a scene that was dramatized by Al Pacino in an HBO biopic. Arlene Reckson was with Joni Mitchell in the studio when Spector threatened them both at gunpoint not to leave the room. Jimmy Iovine heard Spector's gun go off in the A&M Studios' bathroom. Everyone thought Spector was doing it for show and only shooting blanks. Still, the staff engineers reported his gunplay to the front office, which caused him and Lennon to be thrown out of A&M on December 3, 1973—right in the middle of recording "Here We Go Again." Or not.

That popular story was amended by the discovery, forty years later, of a letter from Lennon to Spector from the period. Written in red ink on lined paper, and entitled "A Matter of Pee," it read:

> Phil — See ya around 12:30! Should you not yet know, it was Harry [Nilsson] and Keith [Moon] who pissed on the console! We left at 11:30 . . . [A&M owner] Jerry [Moss] now wants to evict us or that's what Capitol tells us. Anyway, tell him to bill Capitol for the damage if any. I can't be expected to mind adult rock stars nor can May [Pang], besides, she works for me, not A+M! I'm about to piss-off to Record Plant because of this crap!
> — John

This sheet of rare rock memorabilia was auctioned off in London in 2014. And the winning $69,000 bid came from someone for whom it had special meaning—Jimmy Iovine, who had just sold his Beats headphone company to Apple (Computers not Records) for three billion dollars.

EAR WITNESSES

Almost seven years to the day before he was killed, John Lennon had a close call with a shooting at Record Plant LA. There are multiple "ear witnesses" who remember the night of December 11, 1973, when Phil Spector fired his gun at the Third Street studio. Most of the stories have become mythically mixed up over the years in the fog of

SECOND HOME

memory and the debauchery of the times. Like the plotline in Akira Kurosawa's film *Rashomon*, each witness seems to remember the incident in a different way.

CHRIS STONE, CO-FOUNDER, RECORD PLANT: Roy [Cicala] was planning to head back to New York. John was so out of control that Roy knew the album wasn't going anywhere. So, the three of us were sitting in my office, me, Gary, and Roy. Probably the first time we were together for years. And Gary was like, "Wow! I finally am getting a chance to record John Lennon."

Roy told Gary how to mic John's voice. And he told him how to set up the tape machines so it would get that slapback echo sound that John liked. And he warned us of a few things. One . . . to keep an eye on the tapes . . . he didn't trust Spector. And two . . . if we saw Spector walk in with a manila envelope . . . that meant he had a gun.

LEE KIEFER, ENGINEER, RECORD PLANT: Gary [Kellgren] didn't like guns. And Gary said to me, "If Phil brings a manila envelope in the studio with him, if it's heavy, it's probably a weapon and I'm not going to be in the room." Sure enough, Phil comes in, throws a manila envelope on the engineer's chair. It's heavy. It spins the chair around and falls on the floor under the console. So, Gary looks at me, pats me on the back and says, "You're on."

DAVE THOMPSON, SPECTOR'S BIOGRAPHER: Every moment that [John and Phil] spent in Record Plant, another temper would fray, another slight would be thrown, another instrument would be broken. During one particularly fraught take of "Angel Baby," Spector admonished John for continuing his count after the band started playing, and Lennon muttered, "No wonder Ronnie [Spector] left you."

Finally, Spector had had enough. He drew his gun, raised it above his head and fired.

The sound was deafening, shocked the room to silence, and left Lennon clutching his ears in pain. It was minutes before the singer was finally able to speak, and tried to defuse the situation with at least a flash of wit: "Listen Phil, if you're going to kill me, kill me. But don't fuck with me ears. I need 'em."

CHAPTER THREE

MAY PANG, LENNON'S GIRLFRIEND AND ASSISTANT: John and Phil were in the Record Plant LA lounge, along with [former Beatles road manager] Mal Evans. Everyone else, including me, was in the control room, listening to a mix.

That's when we all heard a gun go off out in the hall, and everybody in the studio ducked, including Phil's mother, Bertha. She was there, too. But being the girl from New York City, I ran toward the danger.

When I got to the lounge, there was Phil with a gun in his hand. Mal was trying to grab the gun from Phil. And there was John, grimacing with his finger in his ear.

I screamed, "What the hell just happened?"

That's when John yelled at Phil, "If you're going to shoot, shoot me. But don't fuck with my ears, man. I need them!"

I asked Mal what had happened and he explained, "We were all clowning around, and Phil kept hitting me. I told him to stop because it hurt. Phil didn't like it, and said, 'You can't tell me what to do.' He backed up, pulled the gun out and it went off."

At the time, we thought that there were no real bullets in the gun. Just blanks. However, the next day, Mal pried one out of the ceiling and handed it to John. That's when we realized how close it had been; that's when John and I really freaked out.

JIM KELTNER, DRUMMER: I came right in behind the whole thing. Phil had shot the floor and the bullet ricocheted up into the ceiling, up into the side of the wood canteen where there were the Coke machines and the coffee and everything. And, when I walked in, Mal Evans had already gone up there with a butter knife. He was up on the counter and stretching up to get the slug out of the top of the wall there. And that's when he told me what had happened. Phil shot at the floor and it ricocheted up.

ED FREEMAN, RECORD PRODUCER: Gary [Kellgren] invited me into the studio one night and it was just jammed. It was a typical Phil Spector, mass-musician session. I looked up to Spector. He was one of my gods. And the thing I remember most clearly is Gary introducing me to him and saying, "This is Ed Freeman, he produced *American Pie*." Spector's reaction was to pull a gun out of his pocket, put it to my temple, and say, "You steal any of my secrets and I'll blow your fucking brains out." And I laughed. I thought it was a cap pistol, it's funny, it's a strange joke. But later on, he and Lennon went into the bathroom to take a leak and somebody walked in. And apparently, Spector was piss shy, and he whipped around and fired a gun at the door.

CHRIS STONE: Kellgren told me that Spector pulled out a gun, aimed it at John and pulled the trigger. Click. Everyone assumed there were blanks in the gun. Phil then went into the toilet and sat down on the bowl, and apparently then accidentally pulled the trigger. This time the gun went off with a loud bang, though nobody could ever find the bullet.

BOB MERRITT, ENGINEER, RECORD PLANT LA: Lennon and Spector walked down a long hallway, past the canteen and Jacuzzi, towards Chris Stone's office. Suddenly, we heard, bang, bang! Nobody moved. A couple of minutes later the two of them walked back in with their arms around each other, and they're laughing, and we continue with the session.

So, after the session, a few of us tried to find bullet holes somewhere. From the echo sound of it, we thought the gunshots happened in the canteen, but we couldn't find any bullet holes anywhere. We looked in the Jacuzzi too, but we didn't find any holes in there, either.

Years later, when Record Plant moved from Third Street, we took down the gorgeous walnut paneling from Chris Stone's office and stored it in the shop until we used it for another studio project. I was running one of the panels through a planer when it grabbed and wouldn't go through, and son of bitch don't you know, there were two bullets lodged right in the tongue and groove?

The Jacuzzi was right next door to Chris Stone's office. So that's where the shooting must have taken place. The bullets went through the wall into Chris' office, where they got lodged, hidden in the paneling for must be twenty years.

MAL EVANS, ROADIE, PRODUCER (as told in the book *Living the Beatles Legend*): Phil [often] goes a little too far. [That night] he

CHAPTER THREE

karate-chopped me on the nose, my spectacles went flying, and I got tears in my eyes I can tell you. I turned around with a real temper and told Phil, "Don't ever lay another finger on me, man." [And that's when Phil,] maybe to reestablish himself in his own eyes [pulled out a handgun and] fired it off under our noses, deafening us both, the bullet ricocheting around the room and landing between my feet.

John Lennon interview with Pete Hamill, *Rolling Stone*, June 1975:

HAMILL: What about the stories that Spector's working habits are a little odd? For example, that he either showed off or shot off guns in the studios?
LENNON: I don't like to tell tales out of school, y' know. But I do know there was an awful loud noise in the toilet of the Record Plant [LA] West.

YELLOW PAGES

Guns were everywhere in the LA music scene in 1973 . . . like the night the police raided Sly Stone's house.

Sly had just returned home to Los Angeles from a tour supporting *Fresh* and its hit single "If You Want Me to Stay." He planned to spend a few days working with engineer Tom Flye in his LA home studio. It was the usual madhouse at Sly's mansion when he arrived.

Flye was already busy being the chief engineer up in Sausalito. That first year of operation included sessions with the New Riders of the Purple Sage, Ronnie Montrose, Jerry Garcia, Stephen Stills, America, Commander Cody, Joe Walsh, Three Dog Night, Yes, Marvin Gaye, and Tower of Power—plus the live KSAN radio concerts. But Kellgren made it clear that Sly was always Supe's top priority.

Flye was up in Sly's soundproof hideaway studio, getting ready for the sessions by studying the notebooks and tapes. He heard the studio's hidden doorway slide open, and loud party music rushed in. He saw Sly running up the stairs with a posse from behind. Someone breathlessly told him that the house was surrounded by the police.

The neighbors were always calling the cops on Sly's parties. The resident of the mansion across the street—a house used as the set for the *Beverly Hillbillies* TV show—had called in a complaint, saying that Sly was holding teenage girls hostage. The police went to investigate en masse, since it was no secret that Sly had an arsenal of weapons and a pack of vicious dogs roaming his property. They pounded on the front door and nobody answered, while inside the partiers were frantically stashing the guns, flushing the drugs, piling out of windows or doors, or finding a place to hide.

Up in the studio, Sly started dialing the phone.

"Who are you calling Sly?" someone asked.

"I'm calling a cab," he replied.

Sly wasn't calling just one cab. He was calling every cab and limousine company in the *Yellow Pages*, and within ten minutes the cars started showing up, one after the next, surrounding the squad cars with blinding bright headlights. Soon, Sly's driveway was a parking lot of cops and cabbies and, surveying the confusion below, Sly planned his escape. He removed his wig, motioned for Flye to follow, and said:

"Grab the tapes and your notebook, Supe . . ."

Together they snuck downstairs, through a back hallway and out by the pool. They zigzagged through the shadows and grabbed the last black Town Car to arrive. Turning to look out the back window as the car sped off, they watched the partiers filing out of the front door with their hands raised above their heads.

"It tells you something about Sly . . ." Flye recalled. "With all the women, bodyguards, family, and friends in the house during the bust . . . the one person he picked to save was his engineer."

TAPE 26

STUDIO RECORD PLANT NY

ARTIST	TITLE	FORMAT
Aerosmith	Get Your Wings	Album
The J. Geils Band	Nightmares . . . and Other Tales from the Vinyl Jungle	Album

THE MINNESOTA STRIP

Boston may have been where Aerosmith took flight, but Times Square, New York, was where they "got their wings."

In 1974, there were 2,000 prostitution arrests, 245 peep and porn shops, and over 200,000 heroin addicts on the streets around the Port Authority Terminal on Eighth Avenue where Record Plant NY was located. During the next four years, Aerosmith successfully synthesized the chatter, rhythm, and noise of the Times Square neighborhood into songs that sold millions of records worldwide. The name of the band's second album, *Get Your Wings*, was itself street slang for getting hooked on drugs.

> "There's a band up in Boston I want you to hear."
>
> Bob Ezrin, record producer

Aerosmith managers Steve Leber and David Krebs first approached Bob Ezrin to produce that second Aerosmith album but, as he explained, he was "in the middle of a fight with my own demons" and, instead, recommended Jack Douglas. Leber and Krebs also managed the New York Dolls, so they knew how much Douglas had done to get a credible album out of their other client.

Ezrin and his protégé took a ride in the back seat of his Lincoln Town Car in Central Park late one night. It was in the same back seat that Ezrin had originally convinced Douglas to leave Record Plant NY for a career as a producer.

"There's a band up in Boston I want you to hear. They're yours if you want them," Ezrin said.

Douglas first met Aerosmith in the back room of a North End, Boston, mob restaurant where they were rehearsing: "They were raw and lean and hard. I just loved it. They didn't really like anybody. They were tough kids, especially Joe [Perry]. They were like, 'Yeah, fucking record companies, fucking managers, fucking producers. They all want to fuck us over, but who the fuck are you?'"

Douglas had something to prove with this new band from Boston after working on the Alice Cooper band's disappointing last album. He had learned a thing or two from the *Muscle of Love* sessions, though: the right session musicians could make any band "sound better" in the studio, and New York City was his true, creative home.

With new songs to be written and a make-or-break album to be made, Douglas brought Aerosmith down to Record Plant NY to record. All the kids who made it, like Jack, went back to "Roy's studio" to spend their record-label budgets. They knew the studio, the gear, the staff and, most of all, the engineers. And they owed it to Roy who, everyone knew, was always having trouble paying his bills—even when business was booming.

Aerosmith's first album had been a disappointment for both the band and Columbia Records. In his autobiography, Joe Perry recalled: "When I heard the playback, I kept thinking, 'We're better than this. We should sound better than this. We're being recorded wrong. We sound fuckin' flat.' But I lacked the studio chops to prescribe a remedy."

While Perry blamed their first producer, other band members admitted that they were all just doing too much blow. Either way, everybody agreed that the fundamental problem was that nobody was in charge.

"Columbia (Records) was going to dump us after the first record," Perry said. "Jack Douglas really pulled our nuts out of the fire. We got to use Record Plant and Jack was there to help us, to kind of guide us through the recording process."

Douglas had learned from Ezrin how to be the boss in the recording studio. Perry recalled an early clash with their new producer:

> We're out in the studio, getting the headsets adjusted, and all
> of a sudden this earsplitting feedback shoots through and just

CHAPTER THREE

about bounces the headphones off my head. And I just let loose a stream of "Fuck, oh, fucking, fucking motherfucking, and what the fuck, you guys fucking can't do anything right," and suddenly it's dead quiet, there's dead silence.

Jack walks into the studio and walks up to me, squats down, pulls the headphones off my ears, and he goes, "If you want to talk to me, let's go in the other room, but if you talk to me like that again in public, I'm going to have to bust you in the jaw." That's when I got my first lesson in studio etiquette. He let me know who was in charge and we were ready for that.

Jack could afford to risk a fight in the studio because he had Jay Messina behind the board. *Get Your Wings* initiated a creative codependency between Jack and Jay that would last decades.

Like other Record Plant NY engineers, Messina was an alumnus of A&R Recording who would arrive promptly at nine o'clock in the morning for a major advertising client (e.g., Ford Motor Company, United Airlines) and record a forty-piece session that would be in the can by noon. Messina knew how to work fast and smart; while some engineers would take a full day to get a drum sound, Messina had it ready to go in less than an hour. He also worked around the clock, aided by a pocketful of Black Beauties. After the ad guys left for lunch, he would usually stick around to do a few jazz dates, followed by long nights with rock and rollers, whose ambition usually outweighed their abilities.

Aerosmith included. The big challenge for the band was that Joe Perry and Brad Whitford were not the guitar players they thought they were; they wanted to play solos like Jeff Beck and Eric Clapton, but, at least at that point in their careers, they didn't have the chops. Having successfully worked with several great session guitarists on Alice Cooper's recent album, *Muscle of Love*, Douglas suggested that they bring in others to play the guitar leads. Perry and Whitford went ballistic at first.

"But no one will ever know," Douglas replied.

Steven Tyler supported Douglas, but the lead singer had issues of his own. Douglas insisted that Steven change his vocal style for this album, telling him:

SECOND HOME

"You gotta be kidding me. With those pipes, there's no way you are going to sing that way. Let's get back to your real voice."

"I haven't used that voice in a while," Tyler said.

Douglas insisted, "Let's use it on this record, now."

Get Your Wings was the first time the band had to write songs on the clock in the studio. Tyler labored over his lyrics at the keys of the John Lennon Piano that Douglas rolled into Studio A; he was a brilliant yet tormented lyricist who drew his inspiration from late-night strolls around the neighborhood.

It was a scary time of day to be roaming the streets of Times Square. The band members were in the habit of walking home to the Ramada Inn on Eighth Avenue after a night in the studio, huddled up in a group, while walking down the middle of the street instead of the sidewalk. They were afraid that someone would jump out of a dark alley and mug them for their instruments. Like many Record Plant NY staffers in those rough times, Douglas carried a concealed weapon for protection.

> ## "It was bad … I mean it was dangerous, but we loved it. It was reflected in the music …"
>
> Jack Douglas,
> record producer

"It was really bad," Douglas remembered. "I mean it was dangerous, but we loved it. It was reflected in the music, really. Steven would go for walks and listen to the sounds of the street to get lyrics. You'd hear these amazing phrases, whether it was a hooker, or a pimp, or a drug dealer, they had these phrases that you'd never heard before, and they ended up on Aerosmith records because Steven had an ear for a strange but useful phrase."

Times Square in the winter of 1974 inspired the album's Steven Tyler-penned "Lord of the Thighs," a paean to the plight of a hooker and her pimp that remained a concert mainstay for the band for years. Its opening beat and lyrical theme set the stage for the band's next best-selling tune "Walk This Way," written and recorded at Record Plant NY the following year.

Steven Tyler stands on plywood planks in Record Plant NY during a 1974 recording session for *Get Your Wings*. Jack Douglas and Jay Messina went to great lengths to get a live sound out of the out-of-vogue Hidley studio acoustics, laying down sheets of plywood.

Above: Steven Tyler brought a mop into the control room at Record Plant NY—maybe to remind Jack Douglas that he started out there as a janitor. Below: Jay Messina flanked by Jack Douglas and Joe Perry at AIR Studios in London, August, 1977.

CHAPTER THREE

Jack and Jay worked through Christmas and New Year's in Record Plant Studio A to finish the album. At one point, for the cover of the Yardbirds' hit "The Train Kept a-Rollin'," they raided the Record Plant NY vault for some crowd noise outtakes from the *Concert for Bangladesh* recordings that George Harrison had left there for safekeeping. Energized by speed and impatience, the pair worked fast—recording and mixing the entire album in less than one month. They spent long nights working alone on the final mix—and wreaking havoc whenever they needed a break.

Shelly Yakus was working with Johnny Winter across the hall in Studio B one night, when suddenly the lights went out and the machines groaned to a halt. It was pitch black in the studio; someone had covered the EXIT signs with cardboard. Yakus felt his way to the door and it wouldn't open; it had been duct-taped shut from the outside. He kept banging for help and finally pushed his way out. Exiting into the blinding hallway light, he was greeted by Douglas and Messina who blasted him with fire extinguishers.

Whatever occurred that night worked. The final mix that Jack Douglas played for Columbia Records chief, Clive Davis, the following day validated the label's faith in this "baby band" and gained Douglas a production deal for their next album. Jack Douglas, Jay Messina, and Aerosmith recorded their greatest hits together at Record Plant NY. After *Get Your Wings* (1973–74), they returned from the road to record *Toys in the Attic* (1975), followed by back-to-back, mega-platinum sellers *Rocks* (1976) and *Draw the Line* (1977).

Only at Record Plant could a janitor go platinum.

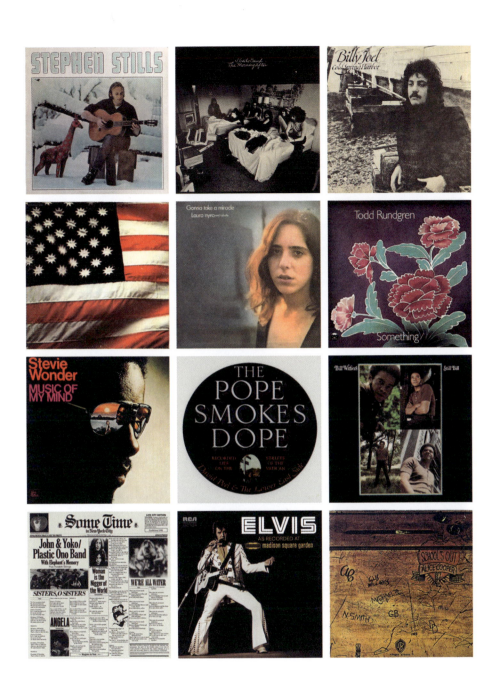

From top left: *Stephen Stills*, Stephen Stills, 1970; *The Morning After*, The J. Geils band, 1971; *Cold Spring Harbor*, Billy Joel, 1971; *There's a Riot Going On*, Sly and the Family Stone, 1971; *Gonna Take a Miracle*, Laura Nyro & Patti LaBelle, 1971; *Something/Anything?*, Todd Rundgren, 1972; *Music of My Mind*, Stevie Wonder, 1972; *The Pope Smokes Dope*, David Peel & The Lower East Side, 1972; *Still Bill*, Bill Withers, 1972; *Some Time in New York City*, John Lennon & Yoko Ono, 1972; *Elvis as Recorded at Madison Square Garden*, Elvis Presley, 1972; *School's Out*, Alice Cooper, 1972.

From top left: *Vol. 4*, Black Sabbath, 1972; *Talking Book*, Stevie Wonder, 1972; *Homecoming*, America, 1972; *Elephant's Memory*, Elephant's Memory, 1972; *Crazed Hipsters*, Finnigan & Wood, 1972; *Approximately Infinite Universe*, Yoko Ono, 1973; *Life in a Tin Can*, Bee Gees, 1973; *Billion Dollar Babies*, Alice Cooper, 1973; *Fresh*, Sly and the Family Stone, 1973; *New York Dolls*, New York Dolls, 1973; *Innervisions*, Stevie Wonder, 1973; *3 + 3*, Isley Brothers, 1973.

From top left: *Mind Games*, John Lennon, 1973; *Laid Back*, Gregg Allman, 1973; *Wake of the Flood*, Grateful Dead, 1973; *Adventures of Panama Red*, New Riders of the Purple Sage, 1973; *Ridin' The Storm Out*, REO Speedwagon, 1973; *Rock 'n' Roll Animal*, Lou Reed, 1974; *Kansas*, Kansas, 1974; *Get Your Wings*, Aerosmith, 1974; *I've Got My Own Album to Do*, Ron Wood, 1974; *Nightmares . . . and Other Tales*, The J. Geils Band, 1974; *David Live*, David Bowie, 1974; *Rock 'N' Roll*, John Lennon, 1975.

4

VIP CLUBHOUSE
1974–1975

"Record Plant was literally like ancient Rome in its heyday."

AL KOOPER
musician, producer

TAPE 27

STUDIO RECORD PLANT LA

ARTIST	TITLE	FORMAT
The Eagles	*On the Border*	Album
Lynyrd Skynyrd	*Second Helping*	Album
Mick Jagger	"Too Many Cooks"	Single
John Lennon & Paul McCartney	*A Toot and Snore in '74*	Bootleg Album

BUZZ ME IN, GATELY

It was Kellgren's job to go out and find business. And there was no better place in the early seventies for a recording studio owner to find business than the Rainbow Bar & Grill on Sunset Boulevard.

Alice Cooper started his LA drinking club, the Hollywood Vampires, there in the summer of 1973, bringing along fellow Vampires including Keith Moon, Harry Nilsson, Ringo Starr, and Micky Dolenz. When John Lennon came to town in October, he also became a de facto founding father. Soon every rocker in town wanted to be there.

All Kellgren had to do was be upstairs in the VIP Lounge at 2 a.m. when the Rainbow closed for the night so he could invite everyone (who mattered) over for the exclusive "after-party" on Third Street.

Kellgren had an instinct for studio marketing. His hallways, bedrooms, and studios soon became the true rock-insider scene every night when only the real Hollywood Vampires were still awake, wanting to party, screw, and make music.

To handle the mob scene, Kellgren and Stone hired an imposing gentle giant named Michael Gately to guard the night desk. Gately was a red-headed singer-songwriter in the Harry Nilsson ilk, who ultimately became famous as the night-guardian of the gate at Record Plant LA. He knew which musician could help on a session, and those who might cause a fight, beat up a groupie, or bring in bad drugs. Young ladies would flash him their breasts to get into the exclusive party within.

VIP CLUBHOUSE

Above: Michael Gately pictured in the office at Record Plant LA. The good-natured gatekeeper decided who to "buzz in" to the studio. Below: Motown artist Mandre, the Eagles, and Lynyrd Skynyrd would convene in the studio canteen to play pinball in 1975.

CHAPTER FOUR

"Buzz me in Gately" became the catch-all code for LA rock and roll all-access in the seventies. Gately himself was believed to be the inspiration for the "night man" who the Eagles wrote about in "Hotel California" as in that line:

"'Relax,' said the night man, 'We are programmed to receive. You can check out any time you like, but you can never leave.'"

FIREBALL

With all the advanced audio equipment at Record Plant LA, the only machine to get credited on the liner notes of two records at once was Fireball, a pinball machine that Kellgren installed in the Record Plant LA canteen.

"It was probably our most profitable piece of gear," Stone laughed, "and it was free!"

Nothing was free at Record Plant. Kellgren and Stone were selling time; the time that the bands spent in the canteen playing pinball was every bit as billable as their time in the studios. And the pinball machines were a whole lot cheaper to own and maintain than the studio's finicky tape machines and consoles.

Fireball was a last-generation, analog pinball machine that "caught fire" in arcades in the early seventies because of its flashy, sci-fi paint job, concert-style sound, and extendable flippers. The game went wild when kick-out holes named after the "Fire Gods, Odin and Wotan," ejected three "bonus" balls into random play.

Along with the music and technical lineups, Odin and Wotan were credited on the liner notes of both *On the Border*, the Eagles' third album, and *Second Helping,* Lynyrd Skynyrd's second album—both recorded December 1973–January 1974, in Record Plant LA Studio A and Studio B respectively. In typical Record Plant style, the bands and their producers mingled frequently when they weren't locked in their rooms recording. Their producers were old friends. Bill Szymczyk (with the Eagles) and Al Kooper (with Lynyrd Skynyrd) were early members of the Record Plant NY family. Kooper wrote in his book that the pair met for dinner in Nashville years later and, over a few bottles of wine, agreed that "practically all of today's country music [was] founded on either one or both of those albums—they just imitate what we did [at Record Plant LA] twenty years ago."

Bill Szymczyk checked back into Record Plant LA in December 1973 and didn't check out until he completed four records with the Eagles. He had originally fled LA after the earthquake of 1971, vowing never to return, and ended up in a town outside of Boulder, Colorado, where he worked with Joe Walsh. There, they made two great rock and roll records together—*Barnstorm* and *The Smoker You Drink, the Player You Get*—and Walsh's solo career took off with the Szymczyk-recorded hit "Rocky Mountain Way."

Joe was at Record Plant LA in late 1973, preparing to work on a new album with Dan Fogelberg (*Souvenir*) for their mutual agent, Irving Azoff, who also handled the Eagles. Azoff was an important Record Plant LA client and all his dealings with Stone were on a handshake basis, with the session paperwork obliquely labeled, "Verbal Irving."

The next "Verbal Irving" was the Eagles' *On the Border*. The band had abandoned their recording sessions with the producer of their first two albums, Glyn Johns (Led Zeppelin, Rolling Stones, The Who), at Olympic Studios in London due to "creative differences." They toured Europe for eight weeks, and with the songs all written and recorded once already, they just needed a producer to bring the album home.

Walsh suggested that they talk to Szymczyk whose albums were defined by a fat lead-guitar sound. It was a boom period in guitar tech innovation, and Szymczyk and Walsh were on the cutting edge. The Eagles especially liked the tones they had captured on *Barnstorm* and decided it was exactly the right sound for *On the Border*.

Szymczyk wasn't sure it was the right fit at first. "I don't want to do a country band. I'm not country rock. I'm rock and roll," he told Walsh.

"Oh, no, no, no. They want to rock, too. Really, trust me on this," his friend replied.

Azoff arranged a meeting at Record Plant LA to interview Szymczyk for the job. Stone put in a good word for him with Azoff, telling the manager: "You know those big-ass speakers in the studio. We built them for Bill. He blew everything else up."

If Record Plant NY's steak joint was Downey's on Eighth Avenue, Record Plant LA's was Chuck's just two doors down the back alley. Record Plant had its own table in the back, so the stars could sneak

Above: Bill Szymczyk (far right) worked with the Eagles on their third album, *On the Border*, in his friend Gary Kellgren's LA studio in 1973. Below: Al Kooper (far right) moved Lynyrd Skynyrd from an Atlanta studio (pictured) to LA to finish their album *Second Helping*.

VIP CLUBHOUSE

in and out without causing much of a commotion. It was at that table that Szymczyk, Walsh, Azoff, and the Eagles met to determine the future of the third Eagles album. Szymczyk recalled:

> They were 'sussing' me out. . . They'd made two records
> with Glyn Johns in England and they'd gotten nine cuts into
> a third, and then went head-to-head. The band would say to
> Johns, "We want to rock out some more." And Johns would say,
> "You're not a rock band. The Rolling Stones are a rock band.
> You're a vocal band."
>
> When you want to rock, and this pompous English dude is
> telling you that you don't know how, that doesn't make for the
> best working conditions. So, they blew it off, hung it up, came
> back to the States, and started looking for another producer
> who would let them rock.

Szymczyk was friends with Glyn Johns. In fact, his own sound was a combination of the American R&B sensibilities of Tom Dowd at Atlantic Records and the bombast of Englishman Glyn Johns's rock and roll. The seventies' British rock guitar invasion was in full swing, and the Brit bands were recycling American blues and selling it back to American kids; Szymczyk and his incendiary guitar blues productions were on a mission to bring the music back to where it all began.

After several rounds of Tanqueray and tonics, Szymczyk and the band made a deal. "I'll do it," Szymczyk said, "but first I've got to get it cleared with Glyn Johns."

Szymczyk called Johns up the next morning: "Glyn, the Eagles want me to produce them."

"Better you than me, mate." Johns replied.

The band first wanted to give him an audition. Azoff booked a weekend in Record Plant Studio A and the Eagles and their pending producer went in to record. Two days later, they walked out with the final mix of "Already Gone."

"First track out of the box. Rocked out. Mission accomplished," Szymczyk said.

The rest of the album was recut in less than twenty days, with the band rerecording everything except two of the mellower cuts they'd

CHAPTER FOUR

done in England with Johns, "Best of My Love" and "You Never Cry Like a Lover."

Record Plant Studio A was booked for a minimum of twelve hours a day (usually from 2 p.m. to 2 a.m.), at a day-rate of $2,000. They'd start every session drinking beer. Then around 5 p.m., they'd start smoking dope (they had two gallon-sized baggies of marijuana—one was "working weed" and the other was "let's-get-stoned" weed). Then they'd go out to dinner, come back, and start doing coke until they were done at 2 a.m. Breaks and occasional overnights were spent in the Record Plant hotel rooms.

In his memoir, guitarist Don Felder recalled "one of these nights": "The first night I stayed, I can't even remember going to bed, but when I woke in the morning, I thought I'd died and gone to hell. The particular room I'd crashed in had an S&M theme, with a leather headboard, whips, chains, and a cage hanging from the ceiling. I stared up at it all, blinking hard. 'What on earth did I take last night?' I asked myself."

Studio B opened up at the same time, because Stevie Wonder was still recovering from a car accident that almost took his life. Al Kooper grabbed the opening and, five months after the release of their debut album, Lynyrd Skynyrd flew to Los Angeles to join their producer to record their second one. The songs were almost all recorded when they arrived, including the hit, "Sweet Home Alabama," which only required guitar and vocal overdubs. In between sessions, Kooper made good use of the Jacuzzi.

"The personnel that staffed the place were trained to accommodate every whim of every client. It was literally like ancient Rome in its heyday," Kooper wrote in his autobiography.

Assistant engineer Peter Chaikin was assigned to work with the Eagles when their assistant engineer, Gary Ladinsky, left for another gig.

He recalled: "There was so much you needed to learn to be successful in that environment. Even if you were the best in the world, you wouldn't last long in that environment if you didn't have the people chops, political chops, know your place, and get the sense of the rhythms."

Stone was fond of saying "We're not selling shoes here," whenever an assistant started to complain about the long hours.

VIP CLUBHOUSE

Engineer Phil Schier played a lot of Fireball with the Eagles: "Glenn Frey and I used to gamble on pinball and at one point he owed me $50,000. I'm saying to myself, 'This cannot be. I'm making $1.25 an hour and this rock star already owes me 50 grand.' I can remember fouling out every game just to get back to zero. I knew my place. I was not going to even take five cents from that guy."

TOO MANY COOKS

It was one of those nights when everyone was in town, everyone needed a place to go, and everyone somehow ended up at Record Plant LA to play.

The evening began at a party up the hill at Gary and Marta's pink mansion on Miller Drive. Mick Jagger was there and he wanted to jam. Drummer Jim Keltner was also there and witnessed a super-session in the making. He left messages on musicians' phone services around town to fill out the band.

Bassist Jack Bruce from Cream was in LA with his family for Christmas. Saxophonist Bobby Keys was celebrating his thirtieth birthday. Al Kooper was in town from Atlanta. Harry Nilsson was always around. Ike and Tina Turner's backup singers were already at Record Plant working with Stevie Wonder. Danny "Kootch" Kortchmar brought along a song for everyone to play.

Kortchmar and Kellgren hadn't seen one another since the days back in New York when Gary was recording demo discs for Carole King at Dick Charles Recording. He was awestruck by the size of the house and the other people in the room—the same engineer, who had been cutting songwriter acetates less than ten years earlier, was now royalty to rock royalty. Kootch brought a copy of the 1969 funk/soul single "Too Many Cooks (Spoil the Soup)" by the band 100 Proof (Aged in Soul) to the party and gave it a spin on Gary's turntable.

"They were groping around for a tune that was non-partisan, that wasn't going to be a song written by one of the people who was there. 'Too Many Cooks' is a rocking tune, and it was just an obvious thing to do," Kortchmar reminisced. Not to be confused with the song by Willie Dixon, this "Too Many Cooks (Spoil the Soup)" was by the writing team of Edith Wayne, Ronald Dunbar, and Angelo Bond, working for the Hot Wax label out of Detroit. The lyrics were

CHAPTER FOUR

licentious ("I know your love is boiling hot / Don't want another man putting his spoon in the pot") but the song's title spoke to the potential clash of egos in one recording session at one time.

Kortchmar watched the tune connect with the room and knew something was happening when he saw Jagger scribbling down the lyrics on a scrap of paper. They had the song. They had the band. And fortunately, Studio A on Third Street was open and on hold for John Lennon and Harry Nilsson.

Producer Richard Perry, Lennon, and his girlfriend, May Pang, were out for dinner when they heard that a super-session was about to get underway at Record Plant LA and they headed over to Third Street to join the fun. The last time Lennon and Jagger had jammed together was at Record Plant NY, playing with Elephant's Memory. Richard Perry was at the top of his game and already producing Lennon cohorts Ringo and Harry Nilsson.

Marta Kellgren recalled: "Word got around fast. I remember them all coming down. Jagger, Lennon, Ringo, Keltner, Kooper, Kortchmar, Nilsson, Keys, plus many other fabulous musicians, with Gary at the helm and totally in charge."

Popularly credited as the song's producer, Lennon really didn't have to do much to wrangle a classic live performance out of the musicians in Studio A that night. This was the next generation Wrecking Crew of LA studio talent, all of whom knew how to play—live. "We made a good track," Lennon mentioned to a New York radio DJ. "I was so-called 'producing' it, meaning sitting behind the desk."

"John and Richard Perry weren't exactly producing . . . they didn't have to produce anything . . . they were having fun and hanging out like everybody else," drummer Jim Keltner said.

"[John] was the producer because he was paying for the room," Chris Stone later made clear.

Either way, it was one of those rare musical moments where the song was right, the vibe was right, and they happened to be sitting in a world-class studio with Gary Kellgren, one of the greatest engineers of all time, behind the console. Jagger felt the moment, too.

"I think it's one of Mick Jagger's best performances outside of the Stones," Keltner commented.

VIP CLUBHOUSE

Kortchmar remembered: "We were all flipping out because [Mick Jagger's] performance was so brilliant, with a tune he had never heard before; he learned it and made it his own, bang, just like that. Great lead singers know how to lead a band. If they know how to sing rhythmically and really drive a tune forward, that's where you get your shit from right there. And that was the case here for sure. And Jimmy [Keltner], of course, fell right in, being the great drummer he is, and suddenly we were off and running."

Keltner added: "The whole thing was live. There were very few baffles, if any, in the room. And when you hear that recording from way back then, it still has that old analog sound, which is fantastic—one of my favorite sounds of all time. That little song is testament to Gary Kellgren's skill, his incredibly great skill as a recording engineer. This was not a situation where you came in and did overdubs. This was live on the floor recording with a live vocal. And Gary Kellgren captured all of that in a perfect way."

Though often mistaken for the first in a historic series of Sunday night Jim Keltner Fan Club Hours

> **"Normally these sessions [at Record Plant] were just blues jams. And they'd just go on, everyone would get very sort of stoned and they'd play on it, but nothing would really come out of it, you know."**
>
> Mick Jagger,
> musician

that would take place at Record Plant LA in the mid-seventies, this night they were making a record, not just fooling around. Super-sessions were a heralded Record Plant tradition. Jimi Hendrix's "Voodoo Chile" was the first Record Plant jam session to make it onto disk *(Electric Ladyland)*. "Too Many Cooks," which was left in the can for nearly twenty-five years until it was finally released in 2007 on Mick Jagger's greatest hits album *The Very Best of Mick Jagger*, was another.

CHAPTER FOUR

A TOOT AND A SNORE

There were no senior engineers working the night of the last ever recording session with both Paul McCartney and John Lennon at Record Plant LA on March 28, 1974.

Roy Cicala and Jimmy Iovine had left the building earlier that day after recording John and Harry Nilsson's version of Dylan's "Subterranean Homesick Blues."

Stevie Wonder's techs, Gary Olazabal and Austin Godsey, were alone in C's control room that night, scrambling to prepare for this historic, impromptu "Beatles Reunion." Ringo's drum set was even there, still set up from being used by the Beatles drummer on the *Pussy Cat* sessions that John Lennon was producing with Harry Nilsson earlier that day.

The only Lennon and McCartney in-studio "come together" since the Beatles' breakup in 1970 was part of Gary Kellgren's series of Jim Keltner Fan Club Hour jam sessions in Studio C. It was a private moment made public years later by an "audio verité" bootleg album named *A Toot and a Snore in '74*. And it didn't sound pretty. It was one of those nights with problems galore, particularly with the microphone and headphones levels. And considering *who* was playing, there simply were not enough experienced hands on deck. Since they weren't paying gigs, Stone and Kellgren rarely assigned a first engineer to the Keltner jam sessions.

"If you were a low man on the totem pole, you got stuck on the Keltner thing because it was on a Sunday and it wasn't a paying session and it went on all night," engineer Olazabal said.

Lennon was playing acoustic guitar in Studio C alongside Jesse Ed Davis on electric, while Paul was pounding away on Ringo's pearl-gray Ludwig set, with Jim Keltner backing him up. Linda McCartney was on the Hammond organ, May Pang and Mal Evans were playing tambourines, and Klaus Voormann was on bass. Harry Nilsson struggled to sing with a torn vocal cord.

McCartney and his wife, Linda, were in town to attend the Academy Awards where "Live and Let Die" was nominated for Best Original Song. "We were stoned," Paul told *Rolling Stone* magazine. "I don't think there was anyone in that room who wasn't stoned. For some ungodly reason, I decided to get on drums. It was just a party, you know."

In the middle of the mayhem, the control room phone rang. Olazabal answered. It was Stevie Wonder, calling from his nearby apartment.

"What's going on in the studio?" Stevie asked.

Olazabal told him that music history was being made, but left out the part about all the drugs, drink, and craziness.

"Come and get me . . . I want to be part of this," Stevie said.

Leaving the tech team further stressed, Olazabal went to pick up Record Plant LA's number one client. By the time he returned with Stevie, the session had spun out of control. None of the musicians seemed able to get past a lazy three-chord blues progression or even settle on a song. Olazabal led Stevie to the Rhodes electric piano in the studio, just as the rest of the room started to play "Stand by Me."

"Hey Steve!" McCartney yelled, welcoming the artist.

"Do you want a snort, Steve?" Lennon asked. "A toot? It's going round."

For a very short period, Lennon and McCartney harmonized together before John's mic was turned off, leaving Paul singing alone. Then, Lennon ordered the engineers to "Give Stevie a vocal mic . . ." before asking roadie Mal Evans, "Where's all that drink they always have in this place?"

> **"Do you want a snort, Steve . . . A toot? It's going round."**
>
> John Lennon,
> musician

Wonder got his mic and started harmonizing with McCartney on Sam Cooke's "Cupid." Nilsson joined in, but he was having mic problems too, as they moved on to a short medley of "Working on the Chain Gang" and "Take This Hammer," with Paul taking the lead vocal before fading out.

Stevie Wonder wasn't there very long. At one point, Olazabal saw him motioning for help. He ran into the studio and asked what was wrong.

"This is terrible," he whispered. "I've got to get out of here."

It was also an uncomfortable night for Jim Keltner. He knew that the "Fan Club" moniker was originally a jibe against the former

Beatle bassist who was now sitting next to him in the studio. Paul was the only Beatle he had never recorded with, and for that professional first, Paul oddly opted to play drums.

Keltner said: "Paul came in and he sat at Ringo's drum set right next to me, and we were jamming and playing like crazy, and I'm looking at him, you know, I'm looking over at Paul McCartney, saying, 'Wow, I'm playing with Paul on Ringo's drums, what a trip.' Then suddenly Paul's drumstick went right through the snare drum head. And I was flipping out. That was the drumhead that Ringo had played on the Ed Sullivan Show! To a drummer that's a real big deal. So, in horror, I straight away said to Paul, 'Wow, you just broke Ringo's Ed Sullivan head.' And he just replied nonchalantly, 'Oh, I'll get him a new one.'"

Later, Keltner realized his own incapacity after being dosed with angel dust clandestinely sprinkled in a joint. He remembered, "I was drumming like never before, totally in the pocket, when I realized I was lying on the floor with no drumsticks just miming my imaginary kit."

If the *Toot and a Snore* session at Record Plant Studio C had any other lasting legacy, it was that it convinced John to get back to serious recording.

"It got a little near the knuckle, that's when I straightened out . . . that's when I realized there's something wrong here, you know? This is crazy, man!" John told an interviewer. "So then, I suddenly was the straight one in the middle of all these mad, mad people."

Years later, Chris asked Gary why he didn't engineer that night. Recording all the Beatles had always been his dream, and like Keltner, Kellgren had never worked with Paul.

"Maybe John didn't want me?" Kellgren replied.

"Why wouldn't he want you?"

Gary only surmised: "To make sure they didn't end up with a song?"

PHIL'S PREMONITION

Then, Phil Spector disappeared and John Lennon's *Rock 'N' Roll* sessions at Record Plant LA ground to a halt. Lennon told what happened next in a 1980 BBC Radio interview:

One day when [Spector] didn't want to work, he called me . . .

[*imitating Spector*] John, you won't believe it, [Record Plant] just burned down.

[*as himself*] Oh . . . the studio has burned down, you say?

[*addressing the interviewer*] So, I got somebody to call the studio; it hadn't burned down.

The following Sunday, [Phil] called and said on the phone . . .

[*imitating Spector*] Hey Johnny . . .

[*as himself*] Oh, there you are Phil, what happened? We're supposed to be doing a session.

[*imitating Spector, whispering*] Johnny, I got the John Dean [Watergate] tapes.

[*as himself*] What?

[*imitating Spector*] I got the John Dean tapes . . .

[*addressing the interviewer*] What he was telling me, in his own sweet way, was he had my tapes, not the John Dean Watergate tapes; he had my tapes locked in the cellar behind the barbed wire and the Afghan dogs and the machine guns. So, there was no way you could get them. So, that album [*Rock 'N' Roll*] was stopped in the middle for a year, and we had to sue through Capitol to get them back.

After a few more *Pussy Cats* sessions with Harry Nilsson at Record Plant LA and a sound stage in Burbank in early April, Lennon left LA. He never worked at "Record Plant West," as he called it, ever again.

Phil Spector seemed to have had a premonition, though: Record Plant LA Studio C burned down several years later, in January 1978.

TAPE 28

STUDIO RECORD PLANT NY

ARTIST	TITLE	FORMAT
Harry Nilsson	*Pussy Cats*	Album
John Lennon	*Walls and Bridges*	Album
John Lennon	"Whatever Gets You Thru the Night"	Single
John Lennon	*Record Plant, July 13*	Bootleg Album
Johnny Winter	*John Dawson Winter III*	Album

LOCKER ROOM STINK

Lennon (aka Dr. Winston O'Boogie) returned to New York in April 1974 to work on the *Pussy Cats* album with Cicala (Nilsson came later) at his regular place of business, Record Plant NY. His *Rock 'N' Roll* tapes were still in Phil Spector's possession and Lennon didn't care.

While Capitol Records was negotiating with Spector for the Lost Weekend masters, John was trying to put LA behind him. Exhausted from a year and a half of debauchery and turned off by the party atmosphere at Record Plant LA, John returned to his adopted hometown ready to record and determined to clean up his act.

Roy Cicala had his own issues. His staff was warning him to keep an eye on studio manager Eddie Germano, but Cicala wanted to focus on the music, not the business. He was spending more time at home in order to work on his relationship with Lori. He told a TV reporter: "We went back [to New York] and we continued in the studio, and there was hardly any drinking going on. We realized that LA was just too dangerous for us. There was so much going on out there. It was just crazy."

Yoko had been consistently working on Forty-Fourth Street while John was "lost" in LA, but when he returned, Record Plant NY once again became John Lennon's studio. The pool table in the tenth-floor lobby was where John hustled anyone he could coax into a game of

Above: John Lennon with Harry Nilsson at Record Plant NY during a recording session for Nilsson's album *Pussy Cats* in May 1974. Lennon produced the album at both Record Plants in LA and NY. Below: Nilsson takes a cigarette break and poses in his "John & Yoko" T-shirt.

eight-ball. Working downstairs, Shelly Yakus asked John for a song for Johnny Winter's album *John Dawson Winter III*, and Lennon gave him the single, "Rock & Roll People." The J. Geils Band vocalist, Peter Wolf, remembered participating in a Record Plant NY jam with "Lennon, Nilsson, Remy Martin and Milk." Raspberries front man, Eric Carmen, wrote about literally running into the former Beatle for the first time:

> [Record Plant] had a tiny cubicle of a bathroom that was right off the front door as you walked into the recording studio; it was very tiny and you kind of had to squeeze in and squeeze out. So, as I was opening the door to leave the bathroom I heard a thump, and as I opened the door further, I saw John sitting on the floor. And I immediately wanted to kill myself, because this was not the way I envisioned meeting a Beatle for the first time, knocking him down with a bathroom door.

Assistant engineer Dennis Ferrante told a story about John pranking Paul Simon:

> John and Harry loved playing practical jokes—who's the most unlikely musician they should bring in to jam with? They got the idea to jam with Paul Simon. So, they got someone to call him, and he showed up with his guitar. Paul plugged in, John showed him the chords and told him to wait for his cue. Band started playing, Paul was waiting . . . and waiting . . . John said, "How come you didn't come in?" Paul asked to try again. Band started playing. Paul was waiting . . . and waiting . . . again, John said, "How come you didn't come in?" Meanwhile, Harry and I were rolling on the floor in the control room, laughing! Third time, Paul came in—John stopped everything, "I didn't cue you yet." Paul packed up his guitar and stormed out. "Fuck him!" he said, "I'm just as big as John Lennon!"

By early summer, the *Pussy Cats* tapes were mixed, mastered, and delivered to RCA. Working on his upright piano, Lennon had, meanwhile, been writing an album's worth of new songs to record

VIP CLUBHOUSE

himself. And then, at exactly the same time, Capitol Records' VP, Al Coury, bought the *Rock 'N' Roll* tapes back from Phil Spector.

Forty reels of two-inch Ampex tape arrived on Forty-Fourth Street from LA and were immediately taken in a handcart up to Lennon on the tenth floor where he was working. John liked the privacy of the upstairs studio that had originally been built for Jimi Hendrix; like Jimi, John liked riding the elevator up to work like it was an ordinary job.

Work on the Spector tapes and the song "You Can't Catch Me" resumed the next day. But it quickly became apparent that they were in worse shape than anyone remembered. The tracks, including all the studio chatter, were an agonizing reminder of the Lost Weekend. So, John chose to focus on his new album of original material, instead. He flew in his core crew of Jesse Ed Davis (guitar), Jim Keltner (drums), Ken Ascher (arranger/keyboards), and Klaus Voormann (bass) for rehearsals. They were joined by Bobby Keys on sax and Nicky Hopkins on piano.

A bootleg from the July 13 rehearsal sessions at Record Plant NY—cut from a compilation tape the studio had prepared for John's reference—offered an inside look at a disciplined band playing fully arranged *Walls and Bridges* songs. Lennon's vocals sounded raw and fresh without Roy's trademark slapback echo. The John Lennon Piano was both his composing and performing instrument on this date. Just two days after the studio musicians arrived in New York, it was obvious that Lennon and the band were ready to record.

> **"Elton arrives, and I'm praying he won't want to play the piano."**
>
> Jimmy Iovine,
> assistant engineer

"We started recording *Walls and Bridges*, and everything started going like clockwork," Cicala told *Studio Sound* magazine. "We'd do one track a day, one song a day. And the next day we would come in and listen to the song we recorded the day before. [If] we loved it, we went onto the next song. [We worked on] only one song a day. We finished the basic tracks with a band of the best musicians in the world."

Above: John Lennon with (left to right) Jesse Ed Davis, Eddie Mottau, Klaus Voormann, Jim Keltner, and Shelly Yakus at Record Plant NY during a 1974 recording session for *Walls and Bridges*. Below: Elton John stopped by the studio and ended up playing on John's single.

VIP CLUBHOUSE

Facing deportation, time in the studio was of the essence to John. Music journalist Al Aronowitz was in the tenth-floor studio covering for *Rolling Stone* magazine and he described a scene of Lennon in the control room acting like a "mad coachman who keeps whipping (his band) like horses," adding that they were still "one of the most dynamic bands ever to put locker-room stink into a studio."

One of the session highlights was the arrival of Elton John who stopped by to add some simple "ooh and aah" overdubs to "Whatever Gets You Thru the Night." Elton offered to play keyboards and sat down at the John Lennon Piano, catching Jimmy Iovine by surprise. Iovine told *Rolling Stone*:

> Elton arrives, and I'm praying he won't want to play piano. Every piano player who walked into a studio back then wanted Elton John's piano sound. I [have] no idea how to do it. I try to hide the piano. So, Elton sings. He plays the organ.
>
> Then he says: "John, give me a piano."
>
> I'm like, "Fuck."
>
> I take two vocal mics you shouldn't use for a piano and put them up. Then I learn my biggest recording lesson up to that point. As John McEnroe would say, "It's not the racket." When Elton started playing, he sounded like no one else on that piano. He sounded exactly like Elton John. I'd never seen anybody hit the piano harder.
>
> [Elton] comes back into the control room, listens, and says: "Great piano sound!"
>
> John turns to Elton, points at me and says, "That's one of the reasons I use him."

Then, just two days before the album was due at Capitol Records, the studio pranksters struck again; Roy was told that the final *Walls and Bridges* tapes were destroyed. The coda to this story has been told several ways, but here's the studio owner's version:

> I'm in Studio A working on *Walls and Bridges* and we send it upstairs to our mastering room to cut a lacquer. John calls down: "It's a mess, the machine broke!"

CHAPTER FOUR

I run upstairs to look and there's this pile of tape all over the machine. I turn to the mastering engineer [Greg Calbi] and say: "This didn't really happen, did it?"

They all look at me, serious as priests.

I don't know whether to cry or get angry. I go back downstairs in the elevator and into my car. I drive home to New Jersey . . . and I'm halfway there and I get a phone call. [I had one of those early radiophones in my car]. I pick it up and I can hear them back in the studio. John's just laughing like you wouldn't believe—like it was the funniest thing in the world.

"You son of a bitch, John!" I scream.

TAPE 29

STUDIO	RECORD PLANT, LA	
ARTIST	TITLE	FORMAT
Stevie Wonder	*Fulfillingness' First Finale*	Album
Stevie Wonder	"Creepin'"	Single
Stevie Wonder	"Boogie On Reggae Woman"	Single
Minnie Riperton	"Lovin' You"	Single
Peggy Lee & Paul McCartney	"Let's Love"	Single
Paul Williams	*Phantom of the Paradise*	Scene / Soundtrack

STEVIE TIME

There was this corridor outside Studio B. It was just about six-foot wide and you could just about touch both walls with your fingers if you really stretched out. Stevie would stand in the middle of the corridor and stretch out, and your job was to get back in the control room without him being able to know it. Nobody ever did it. Nobody ever got past Stevie. You'd think you got by him and then, all of the sudden, this hand would shoot out of nowhere and grab you. And I said to him some years later, "Stevie, how did you do that?" And he said, "You hear people's breathing, you feel their temperature, you can feel the air on your skin, you can smell their breath."

Robert Margouleff, producer, engineer

Stevie Wonder's behavior became increasingly erratic after his car accident in the summer of 1973. His engineers, assistants, handlers, and friends all learned to act as if nothing unusual was going on. One time he told a young assistant to work on a mix while he went out for dinner, and he didn't come back for five days. Arriving two hours late at the studio was a good night for Stevie.

They called it "Stevie Time."

After winning four Grammy Awards including Album of the Year for *Innervisions* in March 1974, Stevie went right back into Studio B on *Fulfillingness' First Finale*. Like Sly, Stevie was doing much of his work in the control room, with a Hammond B-3 organ and set of conga drums filling up the space. Lexicon delivered its first digital processor in a Samsonite suitcase to Margouleff who used its innovative sixty-millisecond delay all over Stevie's *Fulfillingness'* vocals.

However, you never knew what to expect when Stevie came into work.

In an interview, assistant engineer Peter Chaikin described the making of the song *"Creepin',"* which captured the process of an artist at his peak:

Bob [Margouleff] called me one day and said, "OK, set up for mixes." It was three o'clock and he was on his way. I figured they'd be in around five. And just after that, I got a call and they said, "Stevie wants to talk to you," and Stevie said, "Set up for tracks." I replied, "Stevie, Bob said, 'Set up for mixes.'" Stevie responded, "Peter, set up for tracks."

Stevie came in and played 130-something bars of drums that day. He did it part of the way through and then went back and did it all over again from the top. If you listen to "Creepin'," just imagine that there was nothing there but drums, and you will understand how amazing it was.

He then came into the control room to put down an ARP bass track. I remember Stevie putting his hands on the machine, the filters, and getting the sound of the bass just the way he wanted it. It was pretty amazing because he was unsighted. He could not read the labels on all those controls, but he instinctively knew where they were.

By the next morning, the track for "Creepin'" was done— including vocals. That happened all in one night, all from Stevie. I remember walking home and the sun was coming up. I didn't have a car. I was living within walking distance of Record Plant. While I was walking, I was saying to myself, "What was that? How did that just happen?" It was just the rhythm of everything that happened, every molecule of creativity coming from Stevie, and the whole rhythm of the session.

Bob [Margouleff] once said, "The control room is my instrument." Until then I had never thought of it that way. We were all living inside that instrument.

Stevie was generous with his instrument. He and his production team were simultaneously using Studio B to produce Minnie Riperton's *Perfect Angel* LP, which included her classic hit "Lovin' You." Stevie played uncredited piano on the song. And the famous bird chirps on the album were inspired by the team's success creating "sonic pictures" on "Living for the City." TONTO was featured in the cult-classic movie *Phantom of the Paradise*. Paul McCartney stopped by to test Stevie's studio out for a duet with Peggy Lee.

A fifteen-year-old Michael Jackson was around too, providing backup vocals with his brothers on his studio mentor's new album. He would spend late nights there doing homework with his tutor, but he was really going to school on how Stevie worked.

Fulfillingness' First Finale was the product of a creative team at its zenith. The album would win three Grammy Awards the next year, including Album of the Year. It included two major singles,

"You Haven't Done Nothin'" and "Boogie on Reggae Woman." But their fourth album together was, in fact, the "finale" for Stevie, Bob, and Malcolm.

Things changed once Malcolm and Bob started squawking about money. Stevie avoided the discussions. But his lawyers started spending a lot of time around the studio, often meeting behind closed doors in Chris Stone's corner office. Stone's door was rarely shut; so, everyone knew something important was going on.

"Let's just say we had a lot of conversations about who, exactly, owned the masters," Stone said.

Down the hall, tensions soon came to a boil in Studio B. Like Jimi Hendrix in Gary Kellgren's first living room studio back in New York, Studio B in LA had become a late-night party scene for Stevie and his friends. And the party ultimately led to a nasty breakup between the artist and his producers.

Margouleff recalled: "There were all these hangers-on in the studio. They were all voicing their opinions and stuff. There were all these guys smoking weed, and they would always bring weed into the control room and say, 'Oh here, have a joint. Can I sit in the back?'"

During one late-night session, things got so rowdy in the control room that Malcolm turned and snapped at the crowd, "Would you mind quieting down? I can't hear Stevie."

Stevie warned Malcolm: "Don't you speak to my friends like that!"

"Well, maybe they should make your record," Malcolm replied, abruptly leaving the control room.

The session may have been the breaking point, but what really brought things to a head was—of course—money. After spending $50,000 in legal fees, Bob and Malcolm had reached an impasse with Motown over getting production points on Stevie's records. There was nothing in writing between Stevie and his producers. So, Malcolm told Bob: "The only way we're going to do this is if we take the tapes and hold them hostage. It was the only way we were ever going to get this resolved. Take all the unreleased stuff and hold onto them until Stevie agrees that we get production points on anything that was released off this stock."

Unbeknownst to Malcolm, the tapes were already gone. Someone had gained access to the tape vault and had removed them from the

CHAPTER FOUR

premises. Malcolm knew only one other person who had the keys, and he knew exactly where to find him.

He ran down the hallway and right through the open door of Chris Stone's corner office, yelling, "After all I've done for you and after all the things . . . I brought you Stevie. It's got to be a couple of million dollars of business over the years. How could you do that to me?"

Stone told Malcolm, "Take it up with Stevie's lawyers."

The relationship between Malcolm and Bob unraveled around the same time.

"Margouleff and I had a deal," Malcolm explained. "We had what we called a veto clause. In other words, if one of us said, 'No, we're not going to do it,' then we didn't do it. Bob wouldn't agree, so I said, 'Well, it's the veto, I'm vetoing working with Stevie.' Bob said, 'F— you, I'm working with Stevie.'"

The denouement of their divorce took place during an ill-fated performance by TONTO and Billy Preston on the late-night variety show, *Midnight Special*. Everyone's nerves frayed when, minutes before airtime and while baking under the hot studio lights, TONTO went out of tune; the instrument and its makers never made it onto national TV.

TONTO's meltdown symbolized the end of one of the greatest creative partnerships in popular music history, one that resulted in ten Grammy Awards, including two Albums of the Year. Though the synthesizer appeared on occasional albums in future years, it eventually ended up with its connectors oxidizing in a barn at Malcolm's farmhouse in Saugerties, New York. In 2018, it was recommissioned for the electronic music collection of the National Music Centre in Calgary, Canada, nearly half a century after twenty-one-year-old Stevie Wonder first asked to "meet" TONTO on a sweltering Memorial Day weekend in an upstairs studio in New York City.

Above: TONTO was eventually sold to the National Music Centre in 2018, where it was carefully restored by the NMC's staff. Below: Stevie Wonder shows a young Michael Jackson the ropes at Record Plant LA in 1974, with Robert Margouleff in the shadows.

TAPE 30

STUDIO RECORD PLANT LA

ARTIST	TITLE	FORMAT
Steely Dan	Live at the Record Plant	Broadcast
Keith Moon	Two Sides of the Moon	Album
Chaka Khan & Rufus	Rufusized	Album

MOON LANDING

The action didn't stop at Record Plant LA once John Lennon left town for New York. Finishing off *Pussy Cats* and *Walls and Bridges* in less than four months, Lennon's backup band shuttled back and forth between Forty-Fourth Street and Third Street. Steely Dan debuted live on FM radio. Chaka Khan and Rufus recorded their gold album *Rufusized*. The Keltner Jam Sessions continued every Sunday night in Studio C. And Beatles roadie Mal Evans was producing The Who drummer Keith Moon's solo album in the big room.

The most expensive rock and roll vanity project of the era, Moon's *Two Sides of the Moon* was funded by MCA to keep The Who fans placated until the movie version of *Tommy* was released the following spring. Ringo's eponymous 1973 album had been a hit and featured an army of A-list musicians, and MCA was hoping to replicate the formula with the drummer from The Who.

A total of sixty musicians, including many Ringo had used, converged on Record Plant Studio C to contribute to Moon's recordings: Harry Nilsson, Ricky Nelson, Joe Walsh, Bobby Keys, Klaus Voormann, David Foster, Danny Kortchmar, Paul Stallworth, John Sebastian, and Flo & Eddie (Mark Volman and Howard Kaylan). Beach Boy Brian Wilson played an uncredited cameo performance on the new pipe organ the studio had just purchased. Lennon contributed a track, "Move Over Ms. L," to Moon's effort. Keith went through seven different staff engineers, including Kellgren.

VIP CLUBHOUSE

Roadie turned record producer Mal Evans remained a Record Plant LA regular even after Lennon left town, taking advantage of comp studio time courtesy of Kellgren and Stone, and falling in love with the studio manager, Fran Hughes. He was a sweet character who had been part of the Beatles inner circle since their Liverpool days (he rang the alarm clock on "A Day in the Life"). After separating from his wife and moving to LA, Evans joined Lennon's Lost Weekend entourage and, according to legend, played a number of roles in the Phil Spector shooting incident—depending on who told it. He discovered and produced Badfinger for Apple Records and penned a song, "You and Me (Babe)," with George Harrison that made its way onto Ringo's self-titled LP.

Mal Evans lived his adult life close to stardom but none of the Beatles' studio magic ever rubbed off. Kellgren had his best engineers on call, but Mal was hopelessly helpless with both the talent and the technology. When Evans submitted the original Moon tapes to MCA, the solo effort was rejected by the label. Deciding to double down on their investment with another round of recording sessions with another producer and engineer, the record label trashed the tapes and fired Evans. The final album was actually recorded twice, with two producers, and with Chris Stone billing MCA $200,000 extra for studio time.

In his biography, Howard Kaylan, Eddie of Flo & Eddie, recalled:

> Same songs. Same drugs. I couldn't tell the difference blindfolded. MCA, however, with their superior powers of perception, thought it was amazing and finally released the album in a beautiful die-cut foldout sleeve. It tanked. I loved that wacky Brit. And we did many mad things together. Record Plant will certainly never be the same. It was cocaine and caviar. First class, baby. Both times. Anywhere, anyhow, any way I choose.

Joe Walsh was next door recording his third studio album, *So What*, along with producer Bill Szymczyk. He was sharing engineer John Stronach with Keith Moon and he stepped into the sessions in Studio C one night to add guitar licks to The Who's classic, "The Kids Are Alright." Walsh later described the results as "semi-train wrecks." To

Keith Moon, musician and drummer for rock band The Who, is pictured playing the drums at Record Plant LA's Studio C in 1976. He first recorded his solo album, *Two Sides of the Moon*, at the studio in 1974.

Moon's biographer, he explained: "I'm amazed that it only took two sets of producers, because Keith would fry anyone he worked with."

Keith was Keith, and though many remember him as being clever and polite, he always left detritus in his wake. Blowing up or kicking his bass drum off the stage was part of The Who's concert routine. Leaving hotel rooms trashed or rental cars damaged were regular items on his expense accounts. At Record Plant LA he destroyed a vintage tambourine borrowed from the Eagles. He shut down Studio C by spilling a mimosa on the console. While struggling to record vocals in Studio B, he smashed a light bulb in the studio ceiling every time he missed a note, not stopping until the room was pitch dark.

"That's why we always had staff carpenters," Chris Stone told Keith Moon's biographer. "We wouldn't say anything; they would tear it up; we would put it back [together]; and they would pay for it."

Michael Braunstein was one of those carpenters who Stone paid to stand by for a quick fix or construction project. He had just started at the studio in July 1974 for finishing touches on the hotel rooms and remembered his first encounter with rock and roll recklessness:

> Keith Moon was staying at the Beverly Wilshire Hotel, I believe. We rented him a reel-to-reel recorder, so he could take rough mixes back to the hotel and listen to that day's recordings. One day, he came back to the studio with a packing blanket and dropped it on the floor and was laughing and cursing at the same time.
>
> We opened up the packing blanket and it was all in pieces. The wooden case was cracked and one of the motors was hanging out, and all the parts were loose. Apparently, in his Keith Moon-type way, he couldn't get it working right, so he lit it on fire and threw it out the window into the alley; and then he had somebody go down and pick it up, pack it up, and say that the equipment rental company should refund his money.
>
> Moon said, "This thing doesn't work. It runs slow."

Chris Stone had the rental company write Moon a letter of apology for the faulty machine. And Stone billed MCA an additional $8,000 in studio time to cover the bill.

CHAPTER FOUR

MIND FLYERS

The original Gary Kellgren East Coast posse converged on Record Plant LA in the fall of 1974:

Bill Szymczyk was in town from his new home in Miami, Florida, working with Joe Walsh on *So What*, while prepping for the new Eagles studio LP.

Frank Zappa was there too, cutting and pasting several in-concert and studio albums together at one time, including his most successful LP, *One Size Fits All*.

Buddy Miles usually came around at three in the morning, dosed and dusted and causing a commotion—Record Plant was the only studio in town that still let him in.

Al Kooper had just sold his label to MCA and kept active in the Jacuzzi while waiting for his next project with the Tubes to begin in Sausalito.

And then there was Tom Wilson. Wilson was now a stranger to the predominantly white clientele who frequented the studio. None of them knew that he was one of the studio's founders.

The original Record Plant partners rarely got together anymore, but on one occasion that fall they shared a meal at the Entourage French restaurant next door. Commonly called "Studio E" by Record Planters, this was Stone's "other office" where escargots and a martini were his go-to lunch. Stone ate there so often that he had a telephone wired to his table. And the partners used that phone that day to call Ancky Revson who was living in Palm Beach.

Wilson needed money.

Money had never been a prime motivator for him. In fact, Stone remembered that the producer let years' worth of checks pile up at home without being cashed. But Wilson hadn't had a hit in years. Moreover, he had cashed in all his Warner stock from the Record Plant NY sale the year before. And, though he was now a consultant to Motown, Wilson was having trouble finding talent, being typecast as too white for the Black artists, and too Black for the white artists. Now in his forties, Wilson had visibly aged. His tall frame now seemed more lanky than athletic. His hair and beard were turning gray and he breathed heavily when he spoke. He would have his first heart attack two years later and would die from a second heart attack two years after that.

Wilson had just flown in from London where he was working on a rhythm and blues opera. He was rebranding his career by delving into the musical roots of the Afro-American experience. He needed money for his dream project, though, and since Ancky had seeded both Record Plant and *Hair*, she was a logical investor.

Like the Harvard grad he was, Wilson told Ancky that the future of the music business was "multimedia." He quoted a speech he had given to an industry group in the late sixties where he stated presciently that "pictures, sounds, symbols will become fused into a freely associative entertainment form." He told her about this new technology called the "video cassette" that would bring movies and concerts into everyone's home. That's when Ancky told him to "send me what you have" and abruptly said goodbye.

Stone was interested in what Wilson had to say about the video cassette since he was already planning his own concert-video side deal with Ampex and Tom Donahue up north. The Record Plant partners had been talking about making music videos from the days of the original TVC acquisition five years earlier.

With Ancky gone, Wilson's attention turned from the telephone to a brunette sitting in the adjacent banquette with a group of other Record Plant customers, including David Bowie.

"Can you get us any of that video business?" Stone asked.

Wilson told them that Hugh Masekela was producing a concert film in Africa with James Brown and needed someone to make a record.

He only had one request: "Get me my commission on that one up front, will you?"

TAPE 31

STUDIO RECORD PLANT SAUSALITO / REMOTE

ARTIST	TITLE	FORMAT
Various	When We Were Kings	Soundtrack
Various	Soul Power	Soundtrack
Various	Zaire '74	Live Album

MUSIC AND FIGHTING

Stewart Levine had a secret and Gary Kellgren couldn't pry it loose.

They sat together on the chartered DC-8 flight out of Los Angeles, which was due to land for a stop in New York to pick up James Brown and his band before heading overseas. There was a second, scheduled stop in Madrid for refueling before they arrived at their final destination, Kinshasa, Zaire, for a three-day concert preceding the Rumble in the Jungle—the 1974 world heavyweight fight between George Foreman and Muhammad Ali.

The concert promoter Levine and South African trumpeter Hugh Masekela came up with the "crazy idea" to produce a concert of African and Afro-American artists to coincide with the much-publicized fight. "It was going to be an 'African Woodstock,' you know? Three days of love and whatever the fuck they called it. I wanted three days of music and fighting," Levine said.

Levine and Masekela sold the idea to the Liberian Minister of Finance for $1.5 million, and Levine went on a spending spree. He hired the best concert cinematographers, including Albert Maysles (*Gimme Shelter*). He contracted the best show producers: Chip Monck (Woodstock) and Bill McManus (Elton John, The Who). And thanks to Tom Wilson, Record Plant was his choice for remote recording.

"I didn't want to record it the way Woodstock had been recorded only five years earlier. Although it was massively successful, the music from Woodstock sounded like shit," Levine said.

Tom Scott out of Sausalito was Kellgren's go-to guy for the assignment. He had the best remote recording chops in the organization, dating back to the *Concert for Bangladesh*. This time there would be no truck, so Scott and his team packed all the gear into a mountain of road cases, including an API console and three sixteen-track 3M tape machines.

"Why three tape machines?" Kellgren asked.

"Where do you think we're going to find parts for a sixteen-track in Africa?" Tom Scott replied.

"Classic Wally Heider upsell," Stone said.

Leaving New York, Levine had just received word from fight promoter, Don King, that George Foreman had been cut sparring and the fight was being postponed. He had already advanced the artists and production crew half of their money and the rest was due upon landing in Zaire. The only question in his mind was, would there still be a concert?

At N'Djili Airport in Kinshasa, James Brown and his entourage deplaned like royalty. The artists and the rest of the crew were shuttled to the recently opened Inter-Continental Hotel where they could sign for anything—no matter how low or high they were on the pecking order. "I told two-hundred-and-seventy-five people to put everything on their bill, so everyone ate, drank, and bought clothes. We wiped the place out," Levine said.

If Stewart Levine was worried about money, he didn't show it at the time. Once Stone got word from his banker in LA that the promoter's check had cleared, he gave Tom Scott the go-ahead to start setting up the studio for the show.

Scott's decision to bring a third tape machine was prescient. As had happened at the Concert for Bangladesh at Madison Square Garden, one of the tape machines smashed to pieces on the tarmac while it was being unloaded. There would now only be one operable backup machine, plus several boxes full of spare parts that Scott salvaged from the wreckage.

With Record Plant paid and the stadium stage and studio ready, the production crew went on a guided tour of the bustling African capital. Kinshasa had a flourishing cultural scene. It also had a major sex trade and, in later years, would be pinpointed as ground zero of the AIDS epidemic. The city had a significant rock and roll lifestyle perk: it was the site of a Merck pharmaceutical cocaine factory.

CHAPTER FOUR

For Stone, the entire experience was one prolonged and frightening high. "Here we were drunk and coked-up in the middle of this politically charged, militarized city," Stone recalled. "Anything could have happened at any moment."

And it did. As the visitors wandered through the crowded streets of Kinshasa, an engineer discovered that his pocket had been picked. Their tour guide called some soldiers and within minutes they found "a culprit," tied him to a tree and viciously beat his back bloody. Stone made a mental note, which he later shared with every member of the Record Plant crew, "Better not fuck up!"

That first night of the concert, the recording team captured a tight and studio-quality sound using gear that had been set up in what would have been Muhammed Ali's locker room. There was no problem with crowd ambience since there wasn't much of a crowd— the ticket prices were too high for the locals, and without the fight, there were no tourists in town who could pay the price.

To get an audience for the cameras the next day, the army rounded up random citizens at gunpoint and brought them by bus into the stadium to watch the show. There was no food, water, or bathrooms. "The smell of the place was terrible," Tom Scott recalled. "Just as the final acts were going on, the stadium plumber went upstairs and discovered that the only bathroom up in the projection booth had overflowed, so he shut off the water to the entire building and locked the door."

The water was also being used to cool a pair of generators that had been brought in to power the show. Five minutes after the water was cut off, the generators exploded, bringing the lighting and sound and the whole concert to a halt. Then, as if on cue, it started to rain, and *Zaire '74* was over.

A total of sixty hours of music and concert footage were in the can. But getting all that recorded media out of the country required some maneuvering. Levine had run up a tab of $220,000 at the hotel, and the management wanted the bill paid before anybody or anything left the country.

Fearing the worst, Stone and his crew stored the tapes in the hotel suite of the Liberian ambassador to Zaire where they were protected by diplomatic immunity. By the time the concert was over, his room

Musician James Brown arriving in Kinshasa, Democratic Republic of Congo, in September, 1974, for *Zaire 74*. The three-day live music festival took place from September 22 to 23 with thirty-one performing groups and eighty thousand attendees.

CHAPTER FOUR

was piled high with hundreds of reels of film and two-inch audio tape. Stone had a Liberian fishing boat wait nearby on the Congo River and, in the middle of the night, a bucket brigade was formed to pass the recorded media down a staircase to the back of the hotel where a truck smuggled it all to safety.

Levine had a charter plane standing by at the airport to get everyone else out of Kinshasa. But by the time they arrived, soldiers were armed and waiting. Stone remembered the beating he had witnessed and kept boarding, leaving Levine to take the heat.

The commanding officer agreed to let everyone else go, as long as Levine and Masekela stayed behind and under house arrest. The plane took off and they returned to the Inter-Continental Hotel where they had the run of the place for another ten days before they could skip out on the bill and take a plane to Rome.

It took twenty years of legal wrangling for Levine to get access to the film footage and audio tapes. The boxes that were smuggled out of Zaire were the source of two film documentaries—*When We Were Kings* and *Soul Power*—and one concert album—*Zaire '74*. Levine maintained that it was the quality of those original recordings that made it possible to tell the true story of this historic cross-cultural event.

"They were hot! They were energized. We caught it on tape," Levine recalled. "It was the golden age of multitrack recording; it was sixteen-track recording, and the tapes held up. The artists came alive when you pressed play. It was all still there!"

TAPE 32

STUDIO RECORD PLANT SAUSALITO / RECORD PLANT LA

ARTIST	TITLE	FORMAT
Jimmy Buffet	Live at the Record Plant	Broadcast
Sly and the Family Stone	Small Talk	Album
Fleetwood Mac	Live at the Record Plant	Broadcast
Bill Wyman	Stone Alone	Album

HOLE IN THE GROUND

"Gary's dead!"

Chris Stone heard crying in the front office and bolted down the hallway to see what was going on. Someone at the desk said she had just gotten a call from up in Sausalito: there had been a shooting. Two guys with Uzis had broken into the studio and held Sly on the floor at gunpoint. She heard that Gary was with him and was shot and killed.

Stone grabbed the phone and called up north. He had been bracing himself for the worst in recent months, but nothing quite this bad. Kellgren had been spending a lot of time recording Sly's new album, *Small Talk*, at Record Plant LA. While he assured him it was all "just business," Kellgren was becoming part of the entourage that hung around Sly for his designer drugs.

Gary once told Chris, "The dope, the hanging out, it's all part of the sell." And he assured him that it would be worth the wear and tear: "Sly's our new Jimi."

He should have said that Sly was their "new Stevie." The recent break up between Stevie, Malcolm, and Bob meant that their classic period cash cow was coming to an end, and Record Plant always depended on at least one million-dollar client.

The drugs were making Gary do strange things, and the partners' moods and methods were often out of sync. They were fighting a lot, so much so that they worked hard to stay out of each other's way.

CHAPTER FOUR

So, Chris wasn't surprised to hear that Gary was dead. It wasn't the first time. A couple of months earlier the studio's speedboat had been found floating abandoned around the Sausalito marina after Gary had taken it out for a spin. He eventually turned up at one of the studio's houses on Bay Road up in Mill Valley, passed out on the couch with his pet raccoon, Rocky, wrapped around his neck.

Chris called Tom Flye, who confirmed that there had been an incident but assured him that Gary wasn't there. Flye explained:

> I was working with Sly and, for some reason, he sent his bodyguard up to 7-Eleven to get some stuff. We're working, and there's some deal going on that I don't want to know about. And all of a sudden, the door opens. There are five of the largest, meanest guys with Uzis and shotguns running in the door. They're there to rob Sly. You've got to realize, Sly always had $150,000 worth of jewelry and watches on him, you know.
>
> They've got everybody at gunpoint. They put Sly down on the floor and they're stripping him of his jewelry. They couldn't get one of his rings off and they were threatening to cut his finger off to get the ring. And Sly's going, "I'll get it off. I'll get it off," while I'm going, "Holy shit." Sly's spitting and sucking, and he finally got that ring off, and then they disappear. That's around when the bodyguard came back. Strange, huh? I don't know what was really going on. I don't know if it was real or not. I just know they took all the drugs and money and ran.

Kellgren showed up several days later on Third Street down in LA. Stone's spies alerted him, and he followed his partner into the Jacuzzi, where Kellgren explained he had finally sold Sly's manager Ken Roberts on building Sly his own studio up in Sausalito. Sly had been evicted from the mansion in Beverly Hills and was moving up to a ranch in Marin County, where he needed a local place to record. Especially after the recent studio shakedown, Sly wanted to find a very private, secure, and personal place to make records.

Tom Flye was there when Gary and Sly first came up with their unique studio design:

I remember [Sly] telling me, "All the studios I've been in, you're in the control room, and you're looking down into the studio. I want a studio where you look up." It's just the way he was. He had a hat one time with a lot of rhinestones on it. And when they designed it for him, they were putting rhinestones on the outer brim and he says, "No, put the rhinestones underneath the brim. I want to see the rhinestones. I don't care what anybody else sees. I want to see the rhinestones." That's the way he was. He always wanted a studio where he could look up at the musicians, and this was going to be that place.

Using Clive Davis's money, Kellgren built the Pit—a maroon, plush-carpeted, underground control room where Sly could live and work. It was a monument to the hole that Sly and Kellgren were both digging themselves into.

When consulted, Hidley told Stone it was a crazy idea. But with CBS's money in the bank, Stone chose to bet again on his partner. Jimi Hendrix made his best-selling album in the original Record Plant NY Studio A. Grammy lightning struck consistently for Stevie Wonder in Record Plant LA Studio B. The Pit in Record Plant Sausalito would extend Kellgren's winning streak of rooms that helped musicians make successful records.

The studio construction began by drilling through an eighteen-inch concrete slab that the navy had laid when the structure was originally built during World War II, causing a massive flood of sea water to rush into the building from the nearby harbor. Undeterred, Kellgren had the workers fight back against nature by building a big cement tub below sea level. He installed a Quad Eight console at the base of the room with the tape machines isolated behind glass sliding doors. The musicians performed on a shag-carpeted ledge up above in an acoustically deadened space, which was reached via a "trippy" curved wooden staircase. To the side, through a curtain decorated with what looked like the pair of lips in the Rolling Stones logo, was Sly's private living quarters upholstered in red and black velvet. In the center of his room was a round bed surrounded by soffit-mounted JBL loudspeakers and a patch bay so the artist could plug in and sing or play guitar while lying down flat on his back. The bed frame

CHAPTER FOUR

featured a trap door that led to a coffin-size compartment where Sly could hide if ever necessary. There was a bathroom with an oak toilet seat and a wraparound school-style desk with a small embedded mirror, so the occupant could chop and snort coke while doing their business. Sly could enter (or escape) the Pit via a trick bookcase that was connected by a hidden hallway to the lobby.

"It looked like something out of Thunderdome," producer Al Kooper wrote. It looked cool. It sounded lousy. And Tom Flye was always cleaning up the mess of Sly's vocals or Tower of Power's horns that resulted from trying to make music in an acoustically ill-conceived, subterranean control room. Unlike a typical Hidley room, with its carefully measured walls and tightly controlled audio, the Pit spit the sound out in waves from all angles.

"The Pit wasn't Gary's best room. We played off of Sly's ego and his paranoia too," Stone remarked. Stone and Kellgren agreed to build Sly whatever studio he wanted—and paid for—with the contingency that they could rent it out whenever he was away. And Sly was away a lot, either on tour or on a bender. Ken Roberts and Chris Stone continued fighting over Sly's bills. In Sly's oral biography, Roberts recalled, "I started to look into the studio charges and things like that. I saw that we were being charged for our studio time while we were on the road. I didn't make a friend of Chris Stone when I stopped that. Chris Stone, at that point, started telling Sly he should be getting rid of me, that I was a bad influence."

Stone denied ever overbilling a client. But in his later years he was candidly reflective about that period in his life where his ambitions knew no bounds. Up north in Sausalito, he did his own share of drugs, went to his share of parties and, without Kellgren around, felt like he alone owned the place.

"GREED probably should have been my license plate at that point," he said.

TAPE 33

STUDIO RECORD PLANT LA

ARTIST	TITLE	FORMAT
Dan Fogelberg	Souvenirs	Album
The Eagles	One of These Nights	Album
The Eagles	"Lyin' Eyes"	Single
Frank Zappa	One Size Fits All	Album
Frank Zappa	"Inca Roads"	Single
Barbra Streisand & Kris Kristofferson	A Star is Born / Evergreen	Scene / Soundtrack

SOUL POLE

The Soul Pole was back in Los Angeles. That was the Eagles' nickname for Bill Szymczyk, their six-foot-three-tall producer of Polish descent, who was looking to book a room at Record Plant LA for the band's fourth album. Unfortunately, Record Plant LA Studio A, his go-to studio since B. B. King's *Indianola Mississippi Seeds*, was already occupied. The new API console in Studio C had not yet been commissioned. That left Studio B.

Stevie Wonder and TONTO had moved out of Studio B after their three-year tsunami of hits. Joe Walsh and Dan Fogelberg had made a successful record in that room that summer (*Souvenirs*), and Walsh raved to Szymczyk about the API console's sound. The room was smaller than Szymczyk and the band were used to. Still, it had the right mojo, helping Stevie win one helluva lot of Grammys.

All the Eagles needed now were some songs.

"We entered the make-it-up-as-you-go-along phase. They had run out of tunes," Szymczyk remembered.

Szymczyk and the Eagles checked into Studio B in late 1974, and their nine-month stay extended the room's Grammy-winning streak for another year. *One of These Nights*, their first album entirely produced by Szymczyk, became the first Eagles album to hit number

CHAPTER FOUR

one on the *Billboard 200* chart, spawning three top-ten singles: "Take it to the Limit," "Lyin' Eyes," and "One of These Nights." "Lyin' Eyes" landed the group their first Grammy Award for Best Pop Vocal Performance.

But getting it made was a painful process.

"The spiraling use of cocaine caused us to waste incredible amounts of time obsessing over things we couldn't even really hear. We'd spend countless hours doing stupid stuff, overworking ourselves, and pushing already strained relationships still further," the band's new guitarist, Don Felder, wrote.

As the producer, it was up to Szymczyk to guide the band through the madness—and to the music. The Soul Pole loomed large in the small studio control room and he commanded the band's respect by managing their egos and making them sound better than they were. They played, wrote and recorded from two in the afternoon until two in the morning, with Szymczyk trying to eke out four good hours of work before the partying began.

Singer-songwriter Bernie Leadon had lost control of the band he had founded. The consummate country musician, Leadon didn't like their new sound. The more they rocked, the less he was into it. Furthermore, his social life was interfering with his relationship with the rest of the band, too.

Leadon was dating Patti Davis, daughter of Ronald Reagan, then the governor of California. She co-wrote one of the album's songs ("I Wish You Peace") and often stopped by the studio to see her boyfriend. Whenever she showed up at the front desk, Michael Gately had strict orders not to buzz her in without calling the control room first.

If a call came in announcing that "Patti is in the building," engineer Michael Braunstein wrote, "Joints were extinguished, mirrors were wiped clean, and a general cleanup ensued. You could tell that the other band members were getting a little stressed about the State Police escort car in the parking lot. Whether those tensions were part of Bernie's exit from the band or not, I don't know. I just know it was always 'different' when the governor's daughter showed up."

Another anecdote from Bill Szymczyk expressed the prevailing vibe inside Studio B:

We had finished some tracks the night before and we were listening to this rocker the next day around two in the afternoon. We listened to four or five takes. The band was behind the board with me, except for Bernie. He was on the couch in front of the console where I couldn't see him. I asked everybody, "What do you think?"

"I like Take Two."

"I like Take Three."

There was nothing from Bernie, so, I asked, "Bernie, what do you think?"

There was a long pause. Then Bernie got up, stretched, and said, "I think I'm going surfing," and he left.

With the drama and drugs getting out of hand, Szymczyk decided that the best way to finish the album was to move the band out of town. Record Plants had historically been the scene of several band breakups (e.g., Jimi Hendrix and the Experience) and producer firings (e.g., The Who) and Szymczyk's job was to make sure neither happened here. Szymczyk had a home in Miami and knew a local studio where he could finish the job.

Criteria Studios was where Eric Clapton recorded his hit album *461 Ocean Boulevard*, which was named after the house where the studio clients usually stayed while recording there. Stephen Stills, the Bee Gees, and other bands liked recording at Record Plant LA and then mixing down at Criteria (but not the other way around). Both studio designs were influenced by Tom Hidley, and Criteria was the testbed for the designer's work with local audio manufacturer MCI, which resulted in a breakthrough line of affordable recorders and consoles.

Criteria Studio C featured a one-of-a-kind MCI console with superfast, touch-sensitive controls that were perfect for compiling ("comping") multiple vocal takes into one seamless, performance. The Bee Gees, who would record *Saturday Night Fever* at Criteria several years later, were working next door to the Eagles at the time and perfected their falsettos on that board.

The final vocals on "Lyin' Eyes" were also made on that MCI console. According to Szymczyk, the song's opening line, "City girls just seem to find out early," was compiled ("comped") from six different takes from four different days. In fact, the two syllables "Ci" and "ty" were pulled from two different vocal-booth performances.

"That's the minutiae that we were going through," Szymczyk recalled. "We were now into our nitpick phase. We were striving for the perfection of perfection."

DEATH TO ANALOG!

Then, in 1975 everything went to "bits."

Altair assembled the first do-it-yourself computer kit, ushering in the PC revolution. Casio shipped the first LCD watch. And, using electronic components developed for the Vietnam War, Eventide introduced a digital sound processor that used RAM chips to produce the first smooth and musical studio delay in a box. Until then, engineers created the effect with purpose-built chambers, heavy metal plates, or bathrooms and stairwells. In comparison, the Eventide could dial in delay increments to the millisecond. You could hear the difference in the albums that came out in 1975; everything sounded a bit more precise from that point forward.

The engineers at Record Plant were excited about the creative possibilities. The artists were thrilled to discover new sounds. Stone was ecstatic about how much more time was being booked for experimentation. Gary knew that digital was a very big deal. Up in Sausalito, the studio owner hosted many local musicians who worked day jobs in Silicon Valley; nearby Ampex was at the forefront of developing computer storage; and the FBI hired Record Plant Sausalito engineers to analyze a garbled cassette from the Patty Hearst kidnappers with the first digital audio workstation.

After its introduction at the September 1974 Audio Engineering Society Convention in New York, the word quickly spread about the new Eventide digital delay. All three Record Plants got one early and had a jump on the competition for about six months. And it was around that time that Kellgren gave analog audio its fiery send-off.

Like many analog artists of the era, Kellgren wasn't so sure that digital was much of an improvement. One evening he was working on a mix in LA's Studio B when he heard the assistants buzzing about the studio's new Eventides. His reaction to the conversation was hard to read. Then he suddenly left the room and returned a few moments

VIP CLUBHOUSE

later with a blow torch, which he dramatically fired up with a pack of Record Plant matches. At just the point when the mix needed a crescendo, and as if he was foretelling the "death of analog recording," Kellgren turned the blow torch on the tape machine and melted the take-up reel into a molten blob.

In February, 1979, Record Plant LA made music history when it produced the first digital rock and roll record for Stephen Stills and CBS. The manufacturer 3M selected the studio as the site of its worldwide introduction of its new thirty-two-track digital recorder. Stills wrote a song for the occasion.

The digital audio revolution promised perfect sound reproduction and no audible tape degradation during mixdown. And much to the glee of studio owners like Chris Stone, it expanded the customers' track count from the standard twenty-four to thirty-two.

Engineer Michael Braunstein was behind the API board for the session. In contrast to the PR hype, and in reference to the legendary Record Plant NY Don McLean recording, "American Pie," Braunstein darkly called that digital date in 1979, "The night the music died." He explained:

> Digital audio changed everything. We knew it that night in Studio C. It not only changed the way we stored audio but, more importantly perhaps, the way we "made" music was mutated. The interpersonal collaborative method of musicians standing or sitting face-to-face and instantaneously being able to adapt to the nuances of their collaborators in the studio room was gone for good. Not to mention the fact that the early digital was obviously poorer quality sound.
>
> As we recorded that night, we compared the analog and the digital in A/B fashion and with the flip of a switch we heard the difference. At one point Stephen wrote on the back of a track sheet in Sharpie and held it aloft for everyone to read.
>
> "Scientists, you've failed!"

TAPE 34

STUDIO RECORD PLANT NY

ARTIST	TITLE	FORMAT
Aerosmith	*Toys in the Attic*	Album
Aerosmith	"Walk This Way"	Single
Bruce Springsteen	*Born to Run*	Album
Bruce Springsteen	"Jungleland"	Single
David Bowie	*Young Americans*	Album
John Lennon	*Salute to Sir Lew Grade*	Broadcast

BAND OF MOTHERFUCKERS

As digital-audio technology was making its early moves, Roy Cicala was all in on analog. He was full-force focused on capturing the rawest possible sound for John Lennon. And that meant using those skills that the first generation of rock audio engineers had perfected—capturing the feel, not just the signal.

Amidst deportation hearings, legal wrangling with the Beatles, and his lawsuit with music mobster Morris Levy, John Lennon finally faced the oldies album he had been avoiding. With Phil Spector out of the picture, John told Roy he wanted *Rock 'N' Roll* to have more of a Jerry Lee Lewis vibe than a Wall of Sound. "It wasn't a perfect record. It wasn't an audiophile-type record," Cicala said in a magazine article. "It was a live sound . . . very raw . . . very raw."

Lennon resumed work on the *Rock 'N' Roll* project only one month after the release of *Walls and Bridges* and it was rerecorded over a four-day period at the end of October, 1974, using the *Walls and Bridges* band (Ken Ascher, Jim Keltner, Klaus Voormann, Jesse Ed Davis, Arthur Jenkins). "There was no track that I didn't have to do something to, either resing it, overdub it, chop it up, eat it. I did everything but rerecord them. There was no track that was in my opinion good enough to be released in the form that Spector gave it to me," Lennon told an interviewer.

Roy used the sessions to groom his assistant engineers. Even John Lennon wasn't immune to Roy's disappearing act. One day, Jimmy Iovine was setting up the board for the song "Sweet Little Sixteen," while waiting for Roy to show up. Iovine told *Rolling Stone* magazine that Lennon and May Pang walked into the control room during a playback and John loved what he heard. When Pang asked Jimmy to go get them coffee, Lennon snapped at her. "You get the coffee, unless you can make it sound like that," he said. "Wow, that's exactly what I had in my head."

John sat next to Jimmy at the board and Iovine mixed his first ever record.

Recording vocals was a private affair between John and Roy. Though Record Plant NY owned every imaginable microphone, it was a cracked and commonplace Shure SM57 that John preferred; so much so, that when Iovine misplaced John's favorite, they bought another one and, fresh out of the box, cracked it in exactly the same place.

With the *Rock 'N' Roll* album almost finished, John began his final flurry of creative activity before his five-year retirement. "Lennonologist" Chip Madinger published this six-month timeline:

OCT. 30, '74 Photographer Bob Gruen takes the iconic photograph of Lennon flashing the peace sign in front of the Statue of Liberty. Overdubbing takes place that same night on the *Rock 'N' Roll* album from 4 p.m. to 12:30 a.m. up on the Record Plant tenth floor.

NOV. 12, '74 Lennon meets with mob record-label owner Morris Levy and a Record Plant engineer delivers a master of the finished *Rock 'N' Roll* album to him on ¼-inch tape. Levy uses that tape to press a mail-order version of the LP (which he called *Roots*) before Lennon and Capitol Records can release the official version.

CHAPTER FOUR

NOV. 26–28, '74 Elton John and his band rehearse with Lennon at Record Plant for Elton's Madison Square Garden show on Thanksgiving eve. "Whatever Gets You Thru The Night" and "Lucy in the Sky with Diamonds" are performed on stage as a thank you for Elton's help making "Whatever Gets You Thru the Night" a number-one hit.

JAN. 13, '75 Lennon co-produces several songs for Cicala's wife, Lori Burton, at Record Plant and co-writes material with Roy for an album project by Record Plant's house band.

FEB 5, '75 Lennon preps the *Rock 'N' Roll* masters at Record Plant for vinyl. That same night he joins David Bowie downtown at Electric Lady Studios where he co-writes and plays rhythm guitar on "Fame."

MARCH 10, '75 Lennon releases "Stand by Me" as the first single from the *Rock 'N' Roll* album the same day that David Bowie's album *Young Americans* is released—including two Lennon tracks, "Fame" and "Across the Universe."

March, 1975, was a critical month in the Roy Cicala/Record Plant continuum. Even with Jack Douglas and Aerosmith working downstairs on *Toys in the Attic,* and with Bruce Springsteen about to walk in the door, for many "Planters," that month marked the beginning of the ten-year slide towards bankruptcy for the iconic West Side studio.

Roy walked into the office one morning and his studio manager was waiting to speak to him. Boating magazines were piled on Eddie Germano's desk; he had just taken John and May out fishing. Roy expected the usual gossip about the studio's prized client; instead, Eddie said: "I'm leaving. I'm buying the Hit Factory."

Hit Factory was Record Plant NY's primary competitor. Owned by songwriter Jerry Ragovoy ("Time Is on My Side," the Rolling Stones; "Piece of My Heart," Janis Joplin), the two-room studio was located on Forty-Eighth Street, just north of Record Plant. Ragovoy was hoping to unload the operation for $30,000 down and assumption of the studio's debt.

Record Plant could handle the competition. "Record Plant was probably the busiest studio in the world at the time," Roy told an interviewer. But the recording scene was changing. Musicians were looking for a livelier sound than Record Plant's Hidley design could deliver. Less expensive tape machines and consoles from MCI were equipping new competitors with lower overheads and twenty-four-track capabilities. The mob, the union, and the landlords were all taking their cut of the action in the seventies New York music scene.

Meanwhile, Roy was never quite the same after he came back from LA. He was disappearing for hours at a time. He was tired of the crazy hours. He was under pressure at home. He was still drinking. "Roy would live, breathe those groups for days and weeks at a time, but I think, after *Rock 'N' Roll*, he started to back off even with Lennon," Lori Burton recalled. "Everybody wanted a piece of Roy's time."

Eddie had taken a load off Roy's back. And now he was loading it back on.

> # "Record Plant... that's where I make my records in New York."
>
> John Lennon to Howard Cosell, WABC Radio

Burton remembered: "From the start, Eddie was planning to compete with Roy; he wanted his own studio, he needed someplace to meet clients and learn. Roy was spending a lot of time with John Lennon, working all hours of the night. But he wasn't paying attention to what Eddie Germano had going on behind the scenes. Eddie used Record Plant as a launching pad for his buyout of the Hit Factory. And it really got bad—especially when he started lifting Record Plant clients. Roy was really upset, but there was not much he could do."

Bob Ezrin, Germano's and Lennon's neighbor at the Southgate Towers apartment building, saw Eddie's side of the story: "I said [to Eddie] 'If you don't do this you're out of your mind. Take the studio, bring your people, build something Eddie-style.' We encouraged him. He took the leap and he was really scared. For a while, if they couldn't get into the Plant, he was the next call. Then suddenly, after a certain amount of time, he became the first call. He did, as we all know, exceptionally well."

John Lennon performing "Stand by Me" and "Slippin' and Slidin'" from his album *Rock 'N' Roll* on The Old Grey Whistle Test on April 8, 1975. Lennon recorded and mixed the album at the studios he called Record Plant West and Record Plant East in 1974–75.

VIP CLUBHOUSE

Like Stone in LA, Germano saw his function as basically that of a hotelier, but instead of renting rooms to travelers, he rented space to record companies and producers. In an interview in *The New York Times*, Germano, explained that his main job was making people happy. "I entertain," was how he put it.

The Hit Factory's success in multiple locations over the next twenty-five years was based in large part on Germano's keen attention to customers' needs. This talent helped him get especially close to John Lennon.

May Pang wrote in her book *Instamatic Karma*: "One great advantage of living in that apartment building [Southgate Towers] was having a neighbor like Eddie [Germano]. He was the guy to go to if you needed anything and he would always oblige John. If John needed anything . . . he'd tell Eddie and it'd be ready when we got there."

For the time being, John remained fiercely loyal to Roy and Record Plant. "He became like a brother and a friend to me," Cicala told an interviewer. However, after the *Rock 'N' Roll* release, there wasn't much recording for them to do.

In April, 1975, the BBC filmed a live session in the studio, featuring John and a band of Record Plant house musicians managed by Roy named the Band of Motherfuckers (BOMF). This was followed several weeks later by Lennon's last live performance (with David Hewitt and the remote) for a televised tribute to his music publisher, Sir Lew Grade. Lennon and his band wore masks on the back of their heads to satirize Grade's two-faced business practices.

Meanwhile, John was ready to work on another album. He had hired a new band, including keyboardist Billy Preston, and told Roy he was planning to revive some older material. Roy remembered that John sounded upbeat about returning to Record Plant to record. But then, without warning or explanation, the session was canceled and John stopped returning Roy's calls. There were rumors that Eddie Germano had wooed Lennon away to work at the Hit Factory. Some said that Yoko felt that Roy was a bad influence on John.

Then one day, Lennon unexpectedly stopped by the Record Plant office with some news. Cicala told PBS: "[John] came into the office and he said to me, 'Listen, don't tell anybody, Yoko's pregnant.' He was jumping up and down in my little office, saying 'Please don't tell

CHAPTER FOUR

anybody.' Joy was on his face again. That probably made him the happiest person in the world. He said, 'I have to take care of the baby,' but he never said he was not coming back to the studio."

Roy and John talked on the phone throughout the rest of Yoko's pregnancy. Lennon stopped by Forty-Fourth Street a few times in September 1975 to finish work on *Shaved Fish,* his post-Beatles compilation album. Then their baby Sean was born (on John's birthday, October 9) and, according to Roy, "That's when there was silence."

Five years later in 1980, John and Yoko finally returned to the studio for their album, *Double Fantasy*—although that studio wasn't Record Plant. With Roy Cicala's protégé, Jack Douglas, producing, John and Yoko booked Eddie Germano's Hit Factory instead; later that year, though, they brought several unreleased singles from the *Double Fantasy* sessions back to Forty-Fourth Street to finish up on the tenth floor. They were working on "Walking on Thin Ice" on that fateful night of December 8, 1980, when John was assassinated within minutes of leaving Record Plant NY.

BRILLIANT IMPOSTER

Bruce Springsteen moved into Record Plant NY when John Lennon moved out in 1975. In fact, if Lennon hadn't canceled his sessions for a new studio album that spring, there may not have been a *Born to Run* as we know it.

In late March, 1975, the rocker from the Jersey Shore was shopping for a studio to finish his third album, which he had been working on for over a year. The word had spread throughout the New York City studio scene that Bruce was a high-maintenance, low-budget customer. Fortunately, Record Plant NY had an open room, since John was only rehearsing upstairs for his *Salute to Lew Grade* concert.

"I said to Bruce, 'You are a first-class artist, you belong in a first-class recording studio' . . . so we moved to a popular recording studio at the time—the Record Plant," Jon Landau said in a documentary.

They didn't have much of a choice: 914 Studios where Bruce was recording was about to implode. Named after its Westchester area code, the studio in Blauvelt, New York, was where Springsteen had made his first two albums, *Greetings from Asbury Park* and *The Wild,*

258

the Innocent & the E Street Shuffle. It was a suburban spin-off of Phil Ramone's A&R Recording in partnership with producer/engineer Brooks Arthur who had cut songwriter acetates alongside Gary Kellgren and Bill Szymczyk at Dick Charles Recording Studios in the sixties.

"We went in to cut the album and began to have problems; we were unable to get a satisfactory take of a single song. The piano was broken; it was making a weird sound. Things didn't sound right, and it became very frustrating," Springsteen said in the "making of" film.

Jon Landau panned Lennon's *Rock 'N' Roll* in a review in *Rolling Stone* magazine, but this didn't stop him from hiring Lennon's engineer Roy Cicala to rerecord what would turn out to be Bruce's magnum opus. But unbeknownst to Landau, the studio booking didn't include Roy. The studio owner/engineer was burned out and not up to spending months in the studio with an artist who didn't know how to say "Enough!"

Lori Burton recalled: "Roy was originally offered Bruce Springsteen. He wanted the business for the studio but didn't want to do the sessions himself. He was tired of all those crazy hours with Lennon. He heard that Bruce Springsteen was a perfectionist, that he would be up all kind of hours and days or whatever. Roy didn't want to deal with it, and he knew that Jimmy [Iovine] was hot to trot. So, Roy pulled the 'old Chris Stone bait-and-switch.' He brought Jimmy in as his assistant and then disappeared."

In his book, Springsteen remembered meeting Jimmy Shoes for the first time: "On our first evening there, a skinny Italian kid was operating the tape machine. His job was to change the tape reels and turn the player off and on upon the engineer's command. He was a classic New York character, quirky, funny, with attitude to spare. When I came in the next night, he was sitting at the center of the long recording board . . . I asked Jon [Landau] if he thought this kid could pull it off. He said, 'I think he can.'"

The fact that Iovine already had an album credit with John Lennon on *Walls and Bridges* and had built a Wall of Sound for Phil Spector was street cred enough for Landau; but Iovine's technical reputation far exceeded his actual expertise. Iovine could be a slacker. If he was supposed to be painting the tape library, he'd pay another guy a dollar

CHAPTER FOUR

and a quarter an hour so he could go up on the roof with a reflector and take in some sun. It was up on that roof that Iovine and Lennon once posed together in matching Brooklyn T-shirts, rolled up jeans, and buckled boots—and it was John who was dressing up as Jimmy.

John liked Jimmy. So did everybody else.

After Lennon retired from recording, Iovine had virtually nothing to do until Roy called him into his office and offered him *Born to Run*. "I'm twenty-one and I have my second client. I'm spoiled," he told *Rolling Stone* magazine. "So, I go in, and [Bruce is there] playing piano—'Thunder Road.' I heard this guy sing—and those lyrics. I said, 'Oh, my God.' Then they played me the track that they already had recorded for 'Born to Run.' Landau looked at me and said, 'Hey I-veen, can you do this?' 'Absolutely,' I said."

Recording John Lennon was no preparation for working with Bruce. They were from a different generation of rockers who viewed the studio in different ways. Lennon cranked out a song a day. Springsteen perseverated on every sound, every note, every take.

> ## "I run all my companies like an assistant engineer."
>
> Jimmy Iovine,
> record producer

Iovine recalled in his *Rolling Stone* magazine profile, "Springsteen was a fascinating contradiction. He knew exactly what he wanted on his records yet took forever in the studio to articulate and achieve it . . . We were creating everything from the ground floor on *Born to Run*. His first two albums were just songs with some electric guitar. *Born to Run* was 'No, I'm tired of that. No more compromise.' The guitar parts on 'Thunder Road' were thirteen hours in the studio. All that he said for thirteen hours was 'Again. Again. Again.'"

While recording the lead vocal on "Jungleland" one night, Iovine dozed off with his feet up on the console just as Bruce was ready to sing. Landau turned to assistant engineer Dave Thoener and asked if he could pick up where Jimmy left off. When Thoener said, *"Sure,"* they lifted Jimmy's legs and slid him to the end of the board. Iovine didn't wake up and Thoener recorded Bruce's vocals without missing a beat.

260

VIP CLUBHOUSE

"The assistants were all very close, and we were happy when one of us got a break. Soon Jimmy started giving me gigs—sometimes recording and sometimes overdubs. Not long after that, Jimmy started producing with Shelly [Yakus] engineering, and the rest is music-biz history," Thoener told *Mix* magazine.

The *Born to Run* Record Plant sessions lasted from late March until mid-July, 1975, at which time Bruce and his band were scheduled to go out on tour in support of an album that still didn't exist. At the end, they worked seventy-two hours straight and, on the night of July 19, just one day before they were due to open their tour, Bruce and his horn player Clarence Clemons pieced together the famed "Jungleland" sax solo phrase by phrase in one room, while they gang-mixed "Thunder Road" in another, and did the final vocals on "Backstreets" in a third Record Plant room. Meanwhile, the rest of the band, including new members Roy Bittan on piano, Max Weinberg on drums, and Steve Van Zandt on guitar, held a marathon rehearsal in the abandoned former Vitagraph screening room down the hall from the tenth-floor studios.

And still the album almost didn't happen.

With Bruce out on the road, Iovine worked with the studio's mastering engineer, Greg Calbi, to ready an acetate for manufacturing. But first Bruce needed to give it a listen, and Iovine went down to Baltimore to play it for him.

Iovine said: "Jon and Bruce were at a motel where you sleep around the swimming pool. I go into Bruce's room, and he goes, 'Okay, I-veen, put it on.' We're listening to it on a stereo he'd just bought with two speakers and a turntable. When the album is over, he gets up, takes it off, walks outside—and throws it in the pool."

Iovine was crushed. Bruce was talking crazily about rerecording the entire album live on stage. "I couldn't deal with it. I went back to New York on the train. I must have taken ten Valiums on the way home," Iovine said.

Landau then made his biggest contribution to the project. He convinced Springsteen to let go. The finally finished album put Springsteen's face on both *Time* and *Newsweek* the same week. Its success assured Iovine a seat at the console when Springsteen returned to Forty-Fourth Street to record his next album, *Darkness on the Edge of Town*.

CHAPTER FOUR

"Jimmy Iovine, brilliant imposter, young studio dog with the fastest learning curve I've ever seen . . . became the engineer on the most important record of my life," Springsteen wrote in his book.

WALK THIS WAY

After recording *Get Your Wings*, Aerosmith hammered the road for a year while the record company was calling for another record. They were playing their hearts out every night, and when the band came off the road, not only were they better musicians, but they also had tons of great riffs to turn into songs.

Aerosmith returned to Record Plant NY during the winter of 1975 to write and record their seminal album, *Toys in the Attic*. Years later, guitarist Joe Perry and producer Jack Douglas reminisced about the birth of their monster hit, "Walk This Way."

JOE PERRY: One night Jack said, "I think we need one more up-tempo song," so I sat down and wrote "Walk This Way."

JACK DOUGLAS: It was the only track that didn't have the lyric . . . and we almost lost it.

JOE PERRY: Yeah, [Record Plant] was in a funky part of town. We loved it that way because we were seedy kind of people. We wrote seedy music. We recorded seedy music. It was the perfect environment for us to write and record.

JACK DOUGLAS: We just couldn't come up with a lyric or a rhyme or a rhythm for a vocal for "Walk This Way." It was a Sunday afternoon and we decided to take a break from the studio, since we were banging our heads against the wall. We walked down Broadway to Forty-Second Street where all the movie theaters were. And we went in to see [Mel Brooks' movie] *Young Frankenstein*.

JOE PERRY: Actually, I didn't go to the movie because I was frustrated at that point; I had written the music, and I was sitting there thinking, "It's going to end up on the fucking

262

VIP CLUBHOUSE

B-side of whatever."

JACK DOUGLAS: There's a scene in *Young Frankenstein* where [comedian] Marty Feldman says "Walk this way" to the people who come to the castle, and they all start walking like hunchbacks. It killed us. We were all dying laughing, and we couldn't get it out of our heads. We went back to the studio and started walking around like hunchbacks; we put the track up and "do-do-do-do do-do-do-do-do," seemed like hunchback-walking music. Then Steven [Tyler] says, "I'll be right back." He goes into the studio stairwell, disappears, and jots it all down. About forty-five minutes later, there it was. Steven came back with the whole thing. He started with the chorus, "Walk this way," and then he came up with the most off-the-wall verse, which was early rap. When the single was released, I remember somebody calling me up in Los Angeles, and saying, "Congratulations." I was like, "For what?" "It's a big hit." I couldn't believe it.

JOE PERRY: I remember getting a call from David Johansen from the [New York] Dolls with the biggest compliment of all. He said, "That's the filthiest song I ever heard on the radio."

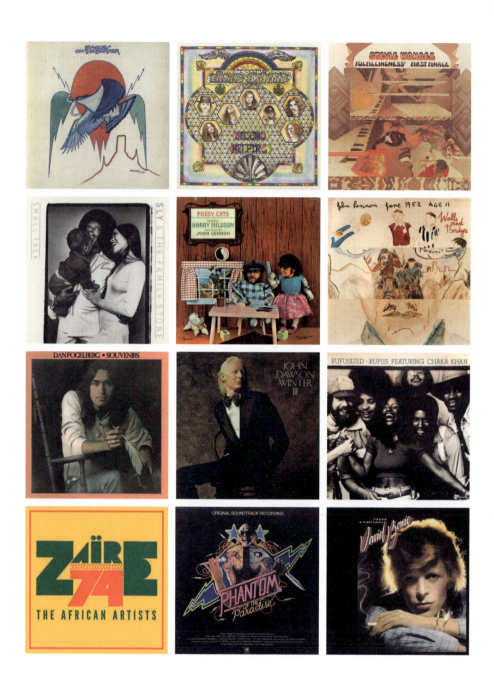

From top left: *On the Border*, the Eagles, 1974; *Second Helping*, Lynyrd Skynyrd, 1974; *Fulfillingness' First Finale*, Stevie Wonder, 1974; *Small Talk*, Sly and the Family Stone, 1974; *Pussy Cats*, Harry Nilsson, 1974; *Walls and Bridges*, John Lennon, 1974; *Souvenirs*, Dan Fogelberg, 1974; *John Dawson Winter III*, Johnny Winter, 1974; *Rufusized*, Chaka Khan & Rufus, 1974; *Zaire '74*, 2017; *Phantom of the Paradise*, Paul Williams, 1974; *Young Americans*, David Bowie, 1975.

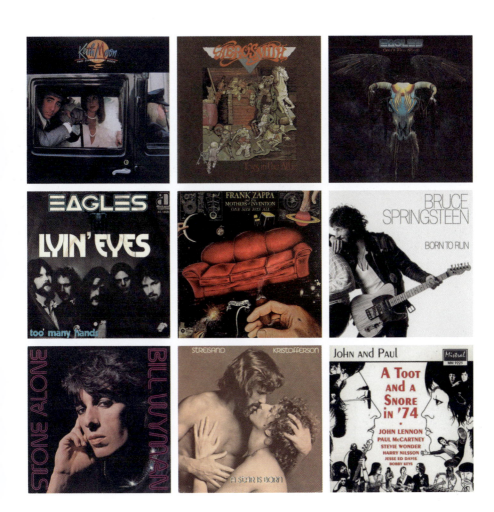

From top left: *Two Sides of the Moon*, Keith Moon, 1975; *Toys in the Attic*, Aerosmith, 1975; *One of These Nights*, the Eagles, 1975; "Lyin' Eyes," the Eagles, 1975; *One Size Fits All*, Frank Zappa, 1975; *Born to Run*, Bruce Springsteen, 1975; *Stone Alone*, Bill Wyman, 1976; *A Star is Born*, Barbra Streisand & Kris Kristofferson, 1976; *A Toot and a Snore in '74*, John Lennon & Paul McCartney 1992.

5

HOTEL CALIFORNIA

1975–1977

" The studio was designed to fulfill the expectations of a music industry at the height of excess."

MICK FLEETWOOD
musician

TAPE 35

STUDIO RECORD PLANT SAUSALITO

ARTIST	TITLE	FORMAT
Joe Cocker	"You Are So Beautiful"	Single
Sly Stone	High on You	Album
America	Hearts	Album
Peter Frampton	Live at the Record Plant	Broadcast
Pablo Cruise	Pablo Cruise	Album
Paris	Paris	Album

ROOMS FOR ROCKERS

As a destination studio, when bands came to record in Sausalito they needed a place to stay. Local hotel rooms were scarce, so Kellgren explored nearby Mill Valley, just five minutes northwest of the studio, where music celebs like Tom and Raechel Donahue and Jerry Garcia lived. He rented a place for Sly on Bay Road, a winding street near Mount Tamalpais. Maintenance engineer Tom Scott bought a house at the beginning of the same street. Tom Flye also purchased a house there. Then, when another Bay Road house came on the market, Record Plant bought it, too. The seven-hundred-block of Bay Road became known by the locals as "Record Plant Lane."

After the studio carpenters finished Sly's Pit, Gary took them up to the new residence and directed them to, "Make it fabulous." So, they did. The carpenters installed a hot tub, built a succession of stacked decks, and turned the garage into a separate apartment for the studio's night manager, Cathy Callon, who looked after the property. Its cedar paneling and shag rugs resembled the studio's interior. Kellgren recessed a TV in the wall adjacent to the fireplace. And an upright piano was placed in the L-shaped living room.

Kellgren or Stone would occupy the Bay Road houses whenever they were available. Staffers who ran equipment back and forth between the LA and Sausalito studios would stay there.

George Harrison liked Bay Road so much that he never made it to the studio. A neighbor once walked out to the mailbox to find Rastafarians with Bob Marley's band playing soccer in the middle of the street with members of the Rolling Stones. Two in-house organic cooks could satisfy any craving at any time of the day.

It was all part of the Record Plant business plan—to rent rooms of all types to rockers.

"Artists live a sort of double life," studio manager Michelle Zarin explained to *Billboard* magazine. "First, they spend all that time on the road, then they suddenly make the switch into the studio to create a record they will be known by . . . our job is to make it as easy a transition as possible . . . to help inspire them."

Studio staffer Cathy Callon was Joe Cocker's inspiration for at least one take of "You're So Beautiful [to Me]." Joe was holed up in Sausalito Studio B for several weeks, tripping on LSD virtually every night, and he was having a hard time with his vocals. Callon remembered: "They go, 'Cathy, come in here. We need you to sit in here so Joe can sing this song to you.' He actually sang that song to me . . . yes, to me! At Record Plant, you loved what you did, even if it meant cleaning the toilets."

HOBO KEN

Then Tom Donahue died.

Nobody was shocked that "Big Daddy" passed from a heart attack at the age of forty-six. He weighed 350 pounds, and had a raging coke habit. He was always retrieving small foil envelopes filled with powder from his pockets, supplied by the label promotion guys to gain airplay for their acts. Cocaine had replaced cash in the pay-for-play radio game of seventies FM radio. Fittingly, Donahue's ashes were mixed with the Hawaiian weed everyone was smoking at his Irish wake, which was attended by over five-hundred family, friends, and fans, and featured performances by Van Morrison and Boz Scaggs.

Donahue's death in April 1975 put an end to a concert-video side-venture that he was starting with Chris Stone that would have predated MTV by five years. Chris was trying to get Steve Ross at Warner interested in a pop-music cable channel by reminding him that this had been the plan for the TVC/Record Plant NY acquisition.

CHAPTER FIVE

Donahue's demise temporarily pressed pause on the series of *Live at the Record Plant* concerts. It also exposed Chris Stone to the wrath of Ken Roberts, or "Hobo Ken" as Sly nicknamed the promoter from Hoboken, New Jersey, in a song.

Roberts blamed Chris for ending his management contract with Sly. The manager and artist had a blowup after Sly failed to appear at a concert in Maryland and Roberts believed that Chris Stone had somehow been involved. He told the author of the Sly Stone oral biography that, "Sly would get easily swayed with whoever he was standing with at that minute. Maybe Chris Stone gave him money, I don't know what he did. I have no idea. I wasn't there . . . He just needed money . . . There was no Kapralik. There was no Ken Roberts. It was only Chris Stone."

Chris Stone only managed Sly Stone for several months in early 1975. Sly was then paying almost half of all the studio's monthly bills and Chris wanted to keep him there recording, so he could pay the bills.

Stone booked a concert for Sly at Radio City Music Hall in New York and scored him a $25,000 advance. He remembered bringing a brown paper bag filled with cash up to Sly's Novato ranch only to find everyone else dawdling in the living room, waiting for Sly to arrive. When Sly finally walked in, he led Chris into his bedroom where he asked, "So where's the money?"

Stone poured the cash onto Sly's bed and he dutifully started counting it for his client. Sly told him not to bother. He grabbed a fistful of money and stashed it in a dresser drawer. Then he took the bag out into the living room, where he turned it upside down on the rug. The members of his band started fighting over the money. Sly sat down in a corner chair, laughing at the mêlée he had started.

Sly never showed up for the concert at Radio City, either, creating another mess for Chris to clean up. Meanwhile, Sausalito's prized client was causing problems back at the studio, too. Sly once was invited into an REO Speedwagon session to play piano and ended up performing all the parts. For a time, he took up residence in Studio B and wouldn't leave—even Sly would take any opportunity *not* to record in his Pit.

The Pit became a bone of contention between the Record Plant partners. They fought about this "white elephant" one night up in one of the houses on Bay Road. Kellgren was in his usual position to alleviate the pain in his arm, flat on his back on the couch in the living room. The television was blaring. A stack of books was by his side on the floor. He was drinking rum and smoking menthols, while petting his pet raccoon.

"Let's just fill in the hole and build another room," Stone said.

"The Pit is a Ferrari; all it needs is someone who knows how to drive it," Kellgren replied.

Kellgren's assistant and close friend, Jimmy Robinson, was his next call. Robinson was working with Bob Welch who had just left Fleetwood Mac and had secured a contract with Capitol for his new band, Paris. They had already completed most of the tracks at Record Plant LA, but Robinson was still eager to please his boss by seeing if he could get a decent mix out of the strange hole-in-the-ground in Sausalito.

"Not many people believed in the Pit," Robinson related. "That was why Gary was like, 'Look, I need you to do an album in there because you're a leader. People see you do that and then they'll do it too.'"

The Bob Welch album was not the big break that Kellgren was hoping for. The Pit was more suited to partying than to recording. Welch wrote: "Once I woke up in there and the clock said 'two.' I thought, 'Oh, I'm late, it's 2 p.m. and we better get started.' I peeked outside for a minute and realized it was 2 a.m., not 2 p.m. I had been asleep for twenty-four hours. Yes, there were lots of drugs at those sessions. I especially remember a Bayer aspirin bottle full of coke that was constantly replenished [from the album budget]!"

Kellgren also tried to make the Pit work with his friend Rolling Stones bass-player Bill Wyman, whose second solo album, *Stone Alone,* Kellgren was producing. "[Kellgren] was constantly kicking me up the backside, saying; 'C'mon, let's do another track,'" Wyman recalled in his autobiography.

The Stones had jammed earlier that year at both Record Plant NY and LA in preparation for their 1975 Tour of the Americas. Wyman's solo album sessions in Sausalito began with informal jams in Sly's Sausalito Pit, where Welch and others improvised with Wyman

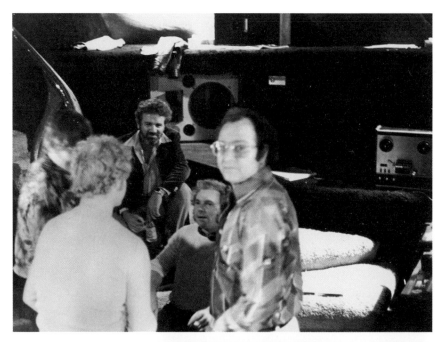

Above: Musician Van Morrison (seated) with Chris Stone (center) in the Pit at Record Plant Sausalito. Gary Kellgren built the Pit as a hideaway for Sly Stone to live and work in. Below: Rolling Stones' bass guitarist Bill Wyman and Sly perform together during a recording session in 1975.

while sitting on the plush, purple studio ledge along with Dr. John, Van Morrison, Stephen Stills, Tower of Power, Ron Wood, Leon Russell, and Joe Walsh. Sly Stone sat in at his Hammond organ and contributed vocals to the sessions. "It was totally out of control," recalled Welch. "Bill Wyman was very straight. He didn't touch any drugs, but everybody [else] was stoned out of their brains. I remember Stephen Stills taking an hour and a half to tune a guitar, while sitting under the piano."

Once again, the Pit proved to be more suited to partying than serious recording. The final album was actually recorded several weeks later at Record Plant LA and eventually was mixed in Miami's Criteria Studios.

The Pit was the least of Chris Stone's problems. Ken Roberts was out to get him; he should have been scared but he wasn't. "Ken got all excited and threatened to kill me once and I told him to go fuck himself."

Roberts had a different plan to get even. If Chris Stone was going to steal Sly, he was going to steal Gary.

Roberts had just come into money. KROQ, the radio station he owned in LA, was generating plenty of cash, enough for him to buy the famed, 112-acre Robert Taylor Ranch in Brentwood. Once he learned there was friction between the Record Plant partners, he went in for a different type of "kill." Roberts told Kellgren about Chris Stone's concert-video side deal with Tom Donahue. He told him how "brilliant" the Pit really was. He also promised to fund Kellgren's new project—a resort studio in an old-Hollywood mansion called "The Castle" on Sweetzer Avenue, off Sunset Boulevard.

Gary had big plans that would take big money. With Roberts pushing him to sign a deal, Kellgren was finally ready to change partners.

TAPE 36

STUDIO RECORD PLANT LA

ARTIST	TITLE	FORMAT
Barbra Streisand	Lazy Afternoon	Album
Rufus & Chaka Khan	Rufus featuring Chaka Khan	Album
Tom Waits	Nighthawks at the Diner	Album
Attitudes	Attitudes	Album

THE CASTLE

Restaurants, nightclubs, and bars were key settings in the history of the Record Plants NY, LA, and Sausalito. The Scene nightclub on New York's West Side was where it all began: it inspired Kellgren to build a living room studio for Jimi. The penthouse décor of the Playboy Club on Sunset shaped Record Plant LA. The Hellfire Club's kinky basement alcoves in New York's Meatpacking District begat LA's hotel rooms. The Trident in Sausalito was the style-guide for Kellgren's getaway studio by the Bay. Chuck's, Entourage, and Gottfried's Deli were the go-to restaurants in LA. Downey's and Smith's were the favorite house watering holes in Times Square.

Then in late 1975, Kellgren began frequenting The Source, a vegetarian restaurant on Sunset and Sweetzer Avenue in West Hollywood. The Source was up for sale as part of a larger real-estate parcel that a group of lawyers was trying to sell, including the Gold Crest Retirement Home across the street, a large dirt parking lot out back, and a classic Sunset Boulevard mansion on the side of the hill.

Mount Kalmia, the house in question, was set on four acres that ran in a narrow rectangle up the hill above Sunset Boulevard. It was one of the last great Hollywood mansions and one of the largest pieces of real estate then available in the Hollywood Hills. The lawyers assured Chris and Gary that they could get the mansion rezoned for commercial use.

Stone tagged along on an hour-long showing of the premises. And while walking through the terra-cotta halls, he could tell that Kellgren already had his next big idea. As always, Kellgren first found the building, and then the business model followed.

The 7,500-square-foot three-story mansion was designed in a Normandy style, with turrets, towers, and battlements. It had one-hundred-and-twenty-five stained glass windows, hand-painted wallpaper, an underground conveyor belt from the street to the kitchen for deliveries, and a bathtub shaped like a canoe. There was a music room, solarium, library, reading room, coffee room, nursery, billiard room, an original Louis XVI drawing room, a forty-foot-long dining hall, and maids' and chauffeur's quarters. Previous owners included Buster Keaton and Howard Hughes' business manager, Noah Dietrich. In the early seventies, Berry Gordy held lavish Motown parties there. Future occupants would include celebrity attorney Marvin Mitchelson and actor Johnny Depp.

Kellgren told the lawyers and Stone that he was interested in the entire parcel of land—the Castle, the retirement home, and The Source. All of it. They all shook hands and the partners returned to Record Plant separately in GREED and DEDUCT where they debriefed in Stone's corner office.

"No fucking way. We're not putting our money into that place," Stone told his partner.

Kellgren pushed back. He explained that he was going to convert the Castle into a compound of recording studios, luxury suites, dining rooms, rehearsal, and performance centers for A-list rock stars only—and that the Gold Crest Retirement Home across Sunset would be rehabbed into a rock and roll hotel where the road crews and bands would all stay. A Disneyland-like tram would connect the front entrance of the Castle to the rooftop of the hotel on the Boulevard down below.

It was the part about the tram that put Stone over the edge. "You're paying for everything out of your own pocket, Gary," Stone said.

"You know Chris, you're supposed to be there so I can do my thing and be creative and drive Record Plant to be the greatest recording studio in the world. This is big. This is going to make us millions. The Castle is going to save the music industry!"

A photograph of Mount Kalmia Castle taken in 1945. The three-story mansion sits above Sunset Boulevard in Hollywood and has been home to numerous tenants, including Berry Gordy and, more recently, Johnny Depp, who purchased the castle in 1995.

CHAPTER FIVE

THE BIG C

No finished albums ever came out of the Jim Keltner Fan Club Hour jamborees in Studio C, though assistant engineers always rolled two-track tape just in case magic happened. Built in the empty garage that had once housed the pool where the Tarzan movies were filmed, the room could handle bands, film dates, or loud, expensive rock and roll jams.

Studio C was all marble, mirrors, stone, and glass, with twenty-five-foot-high ceilings and reflective, shiny black floors. The lighting was designed by Woodstock's Chip Monck and, in keeping with tradition, the gobos were distinctively purple-hued tie-dyed walls. The studio was conveniently connected by a small hallway with the studio bedrooms. "C" was Gary Kellgren's rock and roll interpretation of the great record label studios of a bygone era—Capitol Records' Studio A and Columbia Records' Church.

"It was a magical room," engineer Michael Braunstein recalled, "I mean, man, you had no musical muse if you didn't want to record in that room. It absorbed the artistry of anyone who recorded there."

One of "C's" early clients was Barbra Streisand, who used it for her *Lazy Afternoon* sessions and for the recording studio scene in *A Star is Born*. This booking was especially important to Stone who had his eye on the film sound business and he was hoping her name would attract the high-priced scoring sessions to Studio C. In later years "C" would produce soundtracks for movies including *The Blues Brothers*, *Yentl*, and *Best Little Whorehouse in Texas*; *Spinal Tap* was filmed and recorded there for a year in the early eighties.

More immediately, though, the Streisand sessions gave Record Plant the imprimatur that C could handle larger dates, which led Tom Waits and producer Bones Howe to book it for two nights in mid-summer 1975 to record a live in-the-studio concert (replete with a burlesque stripper) that became Waits's classic *Nighthawks at the Diner*.

Three songs on *Lazy Afternoon* were recorded in "C" by Kellgren and Record Plant's rare female engineer, Deni King, along with an unknown Record Plant LA regular David Foster on keyboards.

Just in from Canada, Foster became a fixture in the studio's house band that included Keltner on drums, Paul Stallworth on bass, and

278

Danny Kortchmar on guitar. The group eventually formed a band of "musicians' musicians" called the Attitudes.

In Foster's biography, the future mega-producer wrote about a typical Keltner Sunday-night jam where he would customarily play with his back to the other musicians to separate the sound of his piano:

> "I'd put on my headphones and we'd start jamming. And as time passed, the music would sound lighter. Suddenly, there would be no bass. And then the guitars would fade out. And then there wouldn't be any drums. And before long, I'd be sitting there playing by myself and I just kept going. Eventually I figured out that, one by one, the guys were going into the back rooms to do drugs. But I didn't go back there, I kept playing. I was just happy to be there. And eventually the bass would come back in, followed by the drums and the guitars, and then I'd hear the sax and we were jamming together once again."

KICKS ON ROUTE 66

Word started to spread that Tom Donahue's death had been a mob hit. Supposedly, a major-label executive with underworld ties had sent a message to DJs around the country that either they played his artists—or faced the same consequences. But just as quickly as it spread, the story vaporized from the rock and roll rumor mill. Like everyone else familiar with Big Daddy's health and habits, Kellgren and Stone were sure he was a "victim of his own devices."

The mob had moved up the corporate ladder in the music business in the mid-seventies. The Feds were investigating the record labels for using drugs in their dealings with DJs and musicians. The mob was buying recording-studio receivables at usurious rates. A grand jury was looking into corporate expense accounts, too, which concerned Stone, whose record-label invoices usually contained plenty of padding for parties and payoffs.

Concurrently, record revenues were slowing down and radio stations were gaining absolute control over what the record-buying public was getting to hear. To drive revenues and break new artists, A&M, Warner, and CBS all diversified into touring in the summer

CHAPTER FIVE

of 1975, handling some of their artists' concerts from transport to lodging, and not surprisingly the Record Plant mobiles were busier than ever.

Kellgren and Stone started talking about ways to capitalize on this trend by taking the Record Plant experience out on the road. Kellgren went back to the original Steve Ross/Warner playbook and started talking about a chain of luxury-suite rock and roll hotels in major concert cities around the country. Stone always liked this idea. At the brink of the dissolution of their business relationship, Kellgren and Stone were talking again. And, though they were individually scheming to push one another out, right now the partners agreed to give it one more try.

But first they needed money. Ken Roberts's name came up in a conversation, but both nixed the idea, since Chris Stone and Roberts hated each other, and Kellgren was keeping that relationship in his back pocket.

They decided to go to the press, which was a huge deal for a business built on privacy. Stories about a recent Rod Stewart sex romp in the Record Plant LA Jacuzzi had spread to the local press and Stone had worked diligently to keep a lid on the details about Rod drawing phalluses in black marker on all the white keys of the Studio C piano.

An article about Record Plant LA ultimately ran in the August 11, 1975, edition of *People* magazine, "buzzing" millions of readers through the door of a secret place that nobody but rock stars had ever seen. Headlined "A Curious L.A. Hostelry Caters to The Music and The Macho in Rock Stars," the magazine showcased the studio's sex but none of its sound. Not a single control room was shown; the photo editor lensed women on beds in the sexy Sissy and Rack Rooms instead.

The writer pounded a licentious drum roll from the lead on:

> "You can't always get what you want," wails Mick Jagger in one of the Rolling Stones' best-known hits, "but if you try some time, you just might find you get what you need." The philosophy is enough to make a hedonist blush, but it sums up the business success of Gary Kellgren, a 36-year-old music entrepreneur in Los Angeles, and his slightly kinky Record Plant.

HOTEL CALIFORNIA

In retrospect, Kellgren and Stone were amazingly transparent about what they were selling:

"Rock stars get sick of the Howard Johnson motif," Kellgren says. An obvious advantage to his emporium is that it keeps the musicians on the premises—and not getting into trouble— during costly and protracted recording sessions. The Plant has everything they need—food, liquor, relaxation. Some of the artists who have laid down both album tracks and their sleepy heads at the Record Plant include the Eagles [whose *One of These Nights* is now at the top of the album charts], drummer Buddy Miles, and Sly and the Family Stone. Harry Nilsson, John Lennon, and Mick Jagger have recorded there at a price of $140 per hour. All the activity keeps Kellgren's gross humming at $2 million a year.

And like his role model Hugh Hefner, Kellgren was just a wholesome, Midwestern family man who lived and sold a fantasy.

"What I sell is a life-style, a consciousness," insists Kellgren, a native of Shenandoah, Iowa, who wandered into the record business in New York 10 years ago on his way to the Sorbonne. Kellgren and business partner Chris Stone, 40, built a recording studio with the best mixers, microphones, solo chambers, and other equipment available. Then Kellgren came up with a special touch: lavish, if bizarre, suites in which rock musicians could live while taping. For $50 a night the artist [and friends, groupies, even wives] can try out the $30,000 "Boat Room," for example, which features a bed surrounded by fish tanks. Aspiring de Sades can wind down in the "S-and-M [Rack] Room," a comfy dungeon whose bed is a rack and whose bathroom has bars on the door. For those with more delicate tastes, Kellgren offers what he calls the "Sissy Room," a confection of canopy bed, flowing chiffon draperies and exotic flora. He also provides a Jacuzzi, sauna, and game room for more conventional fun.

Kellgren's wife, Marta, a self-styled "Latin from

Manhattan," [they have one boy, Mark, 8, and a girl, Devon, 5] tries to minimize the Plant's prurient appeal. "After all, sex is a private thing," she says, and professes to be oblivious to what goes on behind the closed doors.

The short, five-hundred-word article ended with a classic Kellgren close:

Kellgren . . . envisions a nationwide chain of hotels modeled on the Record Plant . . . for touring rock musicians and others wanting special kicks on Route 66.

Copies of the magazine, with Sonny Bono on the cover, were strewn throughout the LA studios for everyone to read. The press didn't generate the business activity that Stone and Kellgren had hoped for. Rather, it increased label scrutiny of their billing practices from then on.

The record-label presidents' families read *People* magazine; they didn't read *Billboard* or *Rolling Stone*.

THE BOOK
Fran Hughes was the first in a succession of women who ran "The Book" at Record Plant. She was the studio manager in New York, which turned into a powerful job that made careers, made hits, and made the studios a lot of money.

The Book was the studio calendar. It charted what artists were working in what studio at what time, and with what engineer and assistants. Managing the Book required juggling multiple calendars for multiple rooms. It involved buying an artist out of their time or convincing them that they'd be better off working in another room. The studio manager who ran the Book had to know the temperaments of the engineers, so they could match them up with the right producer or artist. The job sometimes required saying, "Sorry, we're booked," to A-list rockers, who were never told "No."

Opposite: Staged photographs from the August 1975 *People* magazine article show Gary Kellgren in the Jacuzzi (above), while staffers lounged in the Sissy Room and Marta Kellgren in the "S&M Room" (center). Kellgren also posed with his prized client, Stevie Wonder.

CHAPTER FIVE

New York engineer Shelly Yakus remembered, "The Book controlled your life. It could make or break your career. The producers would call and ask them to recommend the right guy. Making producers happy was their job."

Fran Hughes set the standard for generations of future studio managers at all three Record Plant studios. At the Record Plant front desk, she invented the art of "creative booking," which like a Rubik's Cube moved artists and sessions around the clock and calendar to maximize capacity and billings.

When Kellgren and Stone moved out west, Fran and her husband engineer Bobby Hughes followed, with Fran managing the Book on Third Street and Bobby working with studio-tenant Artie Ripp and his artist Billy Joel. The couple lived in the Hollywood Hills with engineer Jack Adams, whose drinking had already ended his career. Fran became pregnant, and she and Bobby had a daughter. With Jack Adams as his docent, Bobby Hughes delved into the early-seventies Hollywood gay party scene, which soon ended his marriage to Fran.

Now a single mom, Fran ran the front office and hired and trained a team of young women to fill out the LA staff. Deni King became an engineer, building an A-list clientele that included Barbra Streisand, Nils Lofgren, Barry Manilow, and Boston. Rose Mann, a former-booking agent from Chicago, ended up running the place for thirty-five years. All of "the girls" worked alongside the Wall of Fame built from the brick invitations from the studios' opening night party in 1969. The front-office bench became a popular hangout for off-duty artists and engineers. It was in that front office that Mal Evans first saw Fran Hughes, and George Harrison asked Kellgren to introduce them.

Still aching from having been fired from the Keith Moon job, Mal Evans soon moved in with Fran and her three-year-old daughter at her Fourth Street duplex apartment around the corner from Record Plant. Fran took some time off from the studio to care for her child and Mal. She helped negotiate a book contract for his memoirs about the early days of the Beatles, which he wrote while listening to Elvis records and playing with a collection of real and toy cowboy guns and western paraphernalia in an upstairs bedroom. Mal's depression deepened and he became dependent on a concoction of cocaine and Valium that exacerbated his funk. The couple once fought so loudly in the Record Plant LA front office that Stevie Wonder recorded their screaming to use on a future production.

At Fran's urging, Mal co-produced a "Beatle-esque" band of LA rich kids called Silverspoon. However, his engineer Bob Merritt recalled: "Mal was the best, but he was not a producer; I'll just leave it at that. Franny tried to push him into producing, and that wasn't the chair for him to sit in."

Silverspoon band member J.W. Haymer added in his blog: "Behind the big, gentle teddy bear of a façade, Mal had another, much darker side that he tried to keep hidden."

Here's how the story ended, according to Haymer: "On the fifth of January [1976] Mal's depression had hit its pinnacle. Mal had ingested a large amount of Valium and was upstairs in his office [and memorabilia room]. I don't know what prompted those unfortunate series of events that led to his final episode, his last stand, on that horrible Monday evening."

Mal became destructive and he was brandishing a weapon. Unsettled, Fran called the police.

Haymer wrote:"[Mal] was at the top of the stairs [with] a weapon in his drug-induced stupor when [three LAPD policemen] told him to drop the gun. He said, and I vividly remember these words as they were told to me on the next day, 'You'll have to blow me away.'"

They did. The police fired six shots, four hitting Evans, killing him.

"Suicide by cop," was how Merritt referred to the incident.

Fran Hughes never returned to the music business. She built a career in celebrity real estate and managed her own Book of agents. Decades later, ironically, she worked at a desk in a Sunset Boulevard office tower that overlooked the twin palm trees of Gary Kellgren's mansion on Miller Drive across the street.

"Gary knew how to bring in the right people and how to treat people. It was a party. It was always a party," she said. "Unfortunately, there were a lot of people who didn't survive."

TAPE 37

STUDIO RECORD PLANT NY

ARTIST	TITLE	FORMAT
Kiss	*Destroyer*	Album
Blue Öyster Cult	"Don't Fear the Reaper"	Single
Meat Loaf	*Bat Out of Hell*	Album
Aerosmith	*Rocks*	Album
Patti Smith	*Radio Ethiopia*	Album
Cheap Trick	*Cheap Trick*	Album

DON'T YOU EVER

Two a.m. Record Plant NY, Studio A. Producer Bob Ezrin was in session with Kiss, working on their fourth studio album, *Destroyer*. A mound of cocaine was openly sitting on the mirror that was custom-embedded next to the faders on the control room's Spectra Sonics console.

Out of nowhere, two New York City policemen barged in. The unmasked members of Kiss stopped playing. Somebody blurted out, "What the fuck!" Ezrin turned to the door, wondering how two policemen got into the studio in the first place. Eyeing the coke on the console, he slowly rolled his chair to obscure it from view.

"We're looking for Bob Ezrin," one of the cops barked.

Ezrin identified himself to the police.

"You're under arrest, Mr. Ezrin," the other cop said.

Nobody moved. Time stood still in the studio, until someone demanded to know, "What is he being arrested for?"

"Possession of narcotics," one of the cops replied before handcuffing Ezrin and informing him that, "We're taking you in."

Strangely, the men in blue did not confiscate the drugs as evidence. Ezrin did a "perp walk" through the studio and into the front lobby where he asked to use a pay phone to call his lawyer. One of the cops gave him a coin and watched the producer frantically leaf through a tattered *Yellow Pages*. Ezrin couldn't find the number and subsequently lost the coin in the phone.

That's when the stoic policemen started to laugh and a stunned Ezrin spotted a group of Record Planters standing in the studio doorway, enjoying the practical joke. The police had been hired as retribution by a session musician who Ezrin had previously gaffer-taped like a mummy and dumped in a garbage bin for early morning pickup.

Everyone expected things like this to happen when Bob Ezrin booked Kiss in the New York studio in January 1976. The boy-wonder producer from Toronto had laid waste to both the studio and the assistant engineers when he last blew through Forty-Fourth Street several years earlier with back-to-back hit albums for Alice Cooper. Those two albums, *School's Out* and *Billion Dollar Babies*, cemented Ezrin's public reputation as a rock-theater impresario. Among the Record Plant NY insiders, he would always be known as the king of chaos.

> **"Record Plant was where great adventures happened and lots of magic took place."**
>
> Bob Ezrin,
> record producer

Record Plant was Ezrin's favorite rock and roll studio. The attraction was as much the neighborhood as the studio itself. It was the nearby Great White Way that brought out the theater in his music. The twenty-six-year-old producer started working with Kiss at the same time as *Chorus Line*, ultimately one of Broadway's longest-running musicals, opened down the block at the Shubert Theatre. The making of *Destroyer* was its own backstage revue. The band chose Ezrin to produce their next studio album because he convinced them there was more art to their act. He saw them as characters in a rock drama. "All of us were theatrical," Ezrin told Bob Lefsetz in a podcast interview, adding that they all wanted more than the "cock-and-balls approach of early Kiss."

Like any stage director, Ezrin was a taskmaster during the *Destroyer* sessions; he dressed in a "Time Is Money" T-shirt and

CHAPTER FIVE

shouted commands with a counselor's whistle slung around his neck. He taught them how to tune their instruments with harmonics and offered a crash course in music theory; he had all four band members intimidated from the start. Guitarist Paul Stanley called it "a boot-camp of sorts."

After months of writing, arranging, rehearsing, and pre-production, the band, Ezrin, and his attitude took up residence in Record Plant Studio A right after New Year's Eve. Engineer Jay Messina remembered: "Kiss was playing at one point and somebody messed up so they stopped. Ezrin gets on the talkback and says, 'Don't you ever . . .' Like he was talking to little kids . . . 'Don't you ever stop a take unless I stop you.' And Gene and Paul were looking at each other like 'Wow, I think we're getting yelled at here.' So that became the joke of the album. 'Don't you ever . . .'"

Ezrin explained the method to his madness in the studio: "One of the things that I learned in terms of getting performances out of the bands was that I had to entertain them. And that if I put on a good enough show and entertained them well enough, their reaction would be one of energy and excitement and they'd roll with the flow that I created."

> ## "Don't you ever stop a take unless I stop you."
>
> Bob Ezrin,
> record producer

He needed the perfect stage for hisperformance and he found it at this Times Square studio. "The studio inspires the band," Ezrin acknowledged, explaining that he also needed somebody who knew how to get a hard-rock sound out of a dead-as-a-doornail Studio A.

Jay Messina knew Studio A. The engineer's stock at the Record Plant operation had just gone up with his work alongside Jack Douglas with Aerosmith, and successful follow-up sessions with Supertramp, Peter Frampton, and Three Dog Night. Assisting him was a young up-and-comer, Corky Stasiak. Stasiak worked alongside Jay and Jack on *Toys in the Attic*, was part of the engineering crew on *Born to Run*, and had just received his first engineering credit on Alice Cooper's *Welcome to My Nightmare*.

321 West Forty-Fourth Street was a player in the band, too. Roy gave Ezrin the run of the property and he made use of it all. The

Above: Gene Simmons, Peter Criss, Paul Stanley, and Ace Frehley of KISS pose with a choir at Record Plant NY while recording their album, *Destroyer,* in 1976. Below: In full costume, Bob Ezrin (center) and KISS celebrate Ezrin's magic at A&R Recording studios, New York.

CHAPTER FIVE

band played upstairs in an abandoned screening room on the tenth floor. Stasiak took a microphone out onto Forty-Fourth Street to get authentic car horn and dashboard radio sounds. Ezrin washed the dishes in the downstairs bathroom while wearing a microphone. The back hallway behind Studio A was where he recorded the drums.

Drugs fueled the chaos. An engineer could pick up the phone at two in the morning at Record Plant in those days and half an ounce of blow would appear on the board in less than an hour. Lead singer, Gene Simmons, was surprisingly innocent when it came to the drugs; at first, he wondered why they had a mirror on a mixing console.

Sex was Simmon's drug of choice at the time. It was Times Square in the seventies: sex workers and porn were everywhere. Stasiak told an author about one evening when they were about to do a take:

> Gene said, "Listen, I can't do this. I need a hooker first."
>
> And Bob [Ezrin] said, "What do you mean you need a hooker?"
>
> Simmons explained, "I just gotta get a blowjob."
>
> Everyone looked at Stasiak who said, "I'm sorry man that's not in my job description."
>
> So, then they all looked at Bob who told Gene, "If you need this to make it happen, go ahead. I'll give you the money but I'm not gonna help you out."
>
> Gene left the studio and within twenty minutes was back at the front door with three hookers; he brought them into the studio and asked everyone politely to leave until he was finished. To his amazement everyone left the room.
>
> And you know, he finished, and then we did the take.

The band spent a month cutting an album that was characterized by massive drum sounds, an orchestra, a kids' choir, calliope, backup studio musicians, backwards tracking, and a sound-effects radio play. Not everybody loved what they heard. In fact, panicked by early reviews in the long-lead press that said Ezrin had destroyed the band's hard-rock sound, the band members and their management considered remixing the entire album. Ezrin's production of the 1976 Kiss "Broadway Musical" was ultimately vindicated when *Destroyer* went platinum and broke the top ten on the *Billboard* album chart. Today, it is generally regarded as the band's masterpiece. And Kiss remained a faithful fixture on Forty-Fourth Street (and, when in LA, Third Street) for ten more albums.

TAPE 38

STUDIO RECORD PLANT SAUSALITO

ARTIST	TITLE	FORMAT
The Tubes	*The Tubes*	Album
Nils Lofgren	*Cry Tough*	Album

TANKS A LOT

There is a time for all high-functioning drug users when, sooner or later, their high stops functioning. Stone worked for decades on a regular bump of cocaine from his nasal inhaler, and a steady diet of gin and tonics. Kellgren kept the party going for a decade himself before delving deeper into designer drugs.

For the studio's business, however, having access to a stock of narcotics was as important as having an open purchase order with Ampex; both coke and tape were the raw materials of running a studio in the mid-seventies.

Producer Ed Freeman remembered how drugs were dispensed at Record Plant Sausalito back in those days:

> I would get there at eleven o'clock in the morning and at twelve o'clock this guy would walk into the studio with an attaché case and say, "Hi. What do you want?" I would say, "What do you have?" He would say, "What do you want?" We did this

CHAPTER FIVE

every day. It was sort of like a ritual. Then he would open his attaché case and there was like six different kinds of pot and different kinds of cocaine and God knows whatever other pills and everything else. I just picked my drugs for the day from him. He was there every morning.

Kellgren and Stone looked at drugs like any other Record Plant service. They had to be the best. And just like technology, their studio had to have them before anyone else.

This search for unique highs that could accelerate the creative process for their clients led Gary to experiment with Green, the Vietnam field hospital anesthetic, ketamine, that looked like coke but carried a mightier punch. For a while, Gary also made nitrous oxide a part of the Sausalito studio's regular amenities by convincing a local supplier of "laughing gas" that the studio engineers needed it for record mastering. This industrial-grade version of nitrous wasn't cut with oxygen like the kind you'd get at the dentist; it was serious stuff and potentially lethal.

"... and there was like six different kinds of pot and different kinds of cocaine ..."

Ed Freeman,
record producer

At one point, a nitrous tank was plugged into the patch bay of the Studio A console so an engineer could take a hit between takes. Gas masks were hung from the control room ceiling for a session with the Grateful Dead. Sly had a tank installed in his bedroom in the Pit, so he could take a puff without leaving the comfort of his bed.

Longtime client Al Kooper befriended "the tank" when he was hired by A&M to record the second Nils Lofgren album, *Cry Tough*, and was convinced by Chris Stone to try out the Pit. Kooper spent several days with a guitar in his lap on an upper level of the Pit with his legs dangling down below, comatose, with the trusty tank by his side, and inhaling between takes. He wrote in his memoir about a friend of Kellgren's who died while on the tank: "While in a dream world, the tank toppled over on him, the tube remained in his mouth, and his lungs froze, killing him instantly. And that was certainly the end of *that*."

That wasn't the whole story.

Chris was at home in LA one night, just getting out of bed, when he got a frantic call from Gary at the studio up north. He and his friend had been wandering the studio all night long with a nitrous tank and two helmet-like gas masks. At one point, Kellgren had enough and left the friend there fast asleep but still attached to the tank. The friend died from lack of oxygen sometime that morning, and Gary didn't know what to do.

"Here's what you're going to do Gary," Stone said, methodically. "Get a driver and get in the back seat of GREED and get back here to LA."

Somehow, the friend was found later that day in bed at home with the nitrous tank by his side, the gas mask still on his face. His were the only fingerprints on the tank. The friend was a known Sausalito drug dealer, so the cops ruled it an accidental overdose.

Stone and Kellgren never talked about the incident again. And like so many other moments in their relationship over those ten years, it almost brought things to an end. Gary was spending less time around the studio and more time up at the Castle, with an increasingly sketchy group of friends.

But then, once again, just as their partnership was about to unravel, magic happened, money flowed, and the studio and its clients turned magnetic tape into platinum for the very first time.

TAPE 39

STUDIO RECORD PLANT LA / RECORD PLANT SAUSALITO

ARTIST	TITLE	FORMAT
Stevie Wonder	*Songs in the Key of Life*	Album
Fleetwood Mac	*Rumours*	Album
The Eagles	*Hotel California*	Album / Single

THREE ALBUMS

While Gary Kellgren was offering a reward for a missing gold record wall plaque that he was given for engineering *Electric Ladyland*, record sales had already moved on to the next level of precious metals.

The record industry went platinum that year. It took *Their Greatest Hits (1971–75)* album by the Eagles for the industry to create a new category for a record that shipped a million copies to record stores. Vinyl sales were at a record high during that winter of 1976 and over the next year another fifty albums would go platinum in the United States.

Three of those platinum albums owned the top slot on the *Billboard 200* album charts for a full fifty-two weeks from the end of 1976 through much of 1977. All three were made and/or mixed at one or both of the Record Plant West Coast locations.

First there was Stevie Wonder's *Songs in the Key of Life* (LA and Sausalito). Then came the Eagles' *Hotel California* (LA). Then, Fleetwood Mac followed with *Rumours* (Sausalito and LA). Released between September 28, 1976, and February 4, 1977, these three albums would each garner either a Grammy for Album of the Year or Record of the Year. Over time, they would collectively rack up one-hundred-million unit sales (one-hundred-times platinum).

All three albums reflected a changing record-business model in the mid-seventies where a tremendous amount of money was being made and spent. In 1976, the industry topped $3 billion for the first time. Stevie Wonder had just inked a record-breaking contract with

Motown. *Their Greatest Hits* gave the Eagles financial breathing room to work on their next album for as long as they liked. And right as the *Rumours* sessions started up in Sausalito, Fleetwood Mac's single "Rhiannon" raced up the singles charts, more than justifying their exorbitant studio spend. The success of these three albums was proof positive of Gary Kellgren's original vision of a studio that was more a living room than a lab.

Though they never sounded as good as sixteen-track, the studio's new twenty-four-track machines (which could run sixteen-or twenty-four-track depending on the heads) extended session times. Rather than getting it right in record, clients were now filling the tracks and saving decisions (and indecisions) until the final mix. Twenty-four-track on two-inch magnetic tape became the industry standard and this new recorder format was Record Plant's new cash cow.

None of those three albums was exclusively recorded at Record Plant, however. Those days were gone. Even A-list artists would often have to take what they could get in an overbooked LA studio market that now housed over fifty twenty-four-track rooms. Sometimes they made their own move in search of a different sound, fewer distractions, or a change of scenery.

Still, they usually returned to one of the studios that Gary Kellgren built. In the superstitious minds of insecure artists, hit studios begat hits. Just like the fictional *Hotel California* that Don Henley and Glenn Frey wrote about in one of the Record Plant hotel rooms, customers could check out any time they liked, but they could never leave.

STUDIO IN THE KEY OF LIFE

Stevie needed to get out of Los Angeles in the spring of 1976. Motown was on his back to finish *Songs in the Key of Life*. And he needed to put some distance between the product and the production.

The final *Songs in the Key of Life* sessions coincided with Stevie's new $37 million contract with Motown. Still, the Motown offices on Sunset Boulevard were too close for comfort for Stevie. The label was notoriously intolerant of an artist being late with their album, and Stevie did not want executives stopping by the studio to "just listen." *Songs in the Key of Life* was every record label's nightmare and every studio owner's dream.

CHAPTER FIVE

Kellgren did not have to sell Stevie on using his Sausalito studio getaway. An API console and Kellgren/Hidley control room four-hundred miles away from Motown were just what he needed. Kellgren hoped he'd check out Sly's Pit while he was there. Sly wasn't using it; nobody else seemed interested, and Kellgren hoped that someone with Stevie's studio skills could validate his hole-in-the-ground control room design.

Stevie's longtime engineer Gary Olazabal remembered the night when he and Stevie first arrived in Sausalito to record. Jimi Hendrix was playing over the speakers. Kellgren was in the Pit, waiting for them to arrive. Partiers were sitting on the carpeted ledges and lounging in Sly's bedroom. A nitrous tank was in the middle of the studio floor.

Stevie never recorded in the Pit. He preferred the Kellgren/Hidley control rooms, where he and his engineers spent weeks working on "I Can't Help It," a new song that Wonder ultimately gave to Michael Jackson. They spent hours perfecting the sound of a gong (and reverse gong) to start (and end) "Pastime Paradise."

Record Plant Sausalito was a relatively short stopover during the long twenty-four-plus months that Stevie Wonder worked on *Songs in the Key of Life*. The project started in New York at Eddie Germano's Hit Factory, moved out west to Crystal Recording Studios in Hollywood and made use of all three Record Plant studios on Third Street.

Returning to Record Plant was a big deal for Stevie since his block-booking of Studio B had ended in 1974. The release of *Fulfillingness' First Finale* marked the finale of his historic, four-record run with Margouleff, Cecil, and TONTO. To break from his disgruntled production partners and their obsolescent synthesizer, Stevie moved to New York, where he block-booked nights at the Hit Factory while Steely Dan recorded there during the days. The mid-town-Manhattan studio wasn't working for him, though; only one take from the Hit Factory sessions ended up on the final record.

The project moved back to LA where Stevie booked time at Crystal where he, Bob, and Malcolm originally started out on the West Coast. Stevie liked the open space at Crystal, and he was fond of the young co-owner and engineer, John Fischbach, who he teamed with Olazabal. Crystal had become a popular Motown spot, and it was also credited with a range of mid-seventies pop hits from REO Speedwagon, Jackson Browne, and James Taylor.

There were nights when even Stevie Wonder couldn't get into Crystal, though. On other nights Stevie missed the API console and facilities at Record Plant LA. Olazabal still hung out there with the engineers in the Record Plant canteen, drinking twenty-five-cent beers and playing Fireball. And Stone was eager to let Wonder try out Studio C, even though the room was too busy for an extended stay.

"Stevie liked to move around studios because he's a person who loves to capture magic. He obviously captured the most magic at Record Plant Studio B. He felt comfortable there. He got inspired there. He knew a lot of great stuff happened for him there. Record Plant not only got him the sounds, but it contributed to the energy of his performance," Olazabal said.

By then, Cecil had moved TONTO out of Studio B and up to his new studio in Malibu, since Wonder had moved on from that first-generation electronic instrument. The three-keyboard Yamaha GX-1 synthesizer that he nicknamed the "Dream Machine" was his new creative instrument of choice for this latest production. Its strings sounded so real that some producers believed Stevie when he fibbed that they were the London Philharmonic.

> **"Stevie liked to move around studios ... he's a person who loves to capture magic."**
>
> Gary Olazabal, engineer

Wonder tried out Studio C and liked it. The big room was where he recorded "Saturn" and "Ebony Eyes." He liked playing drums up on the big studio's marble stage. He also enjoyed a Brunswick air-hockey table that the studio installed in the outside hall. Stevie was eating up $175 an hour for Studio C while he was just playing air hockey and he still needed to scrape together a quarter to play the machine.

"Chris made a lot of money on air hockey," Olazabal remarked.

Stevie was so good at the game that the studio manager, Rose Mann, thought he was lying about being blind. Engineer Bruce Hensel and others griped that he hustled them for money at the table. He

CHAPTER FIVE

could track the puck movement by the sound of it careening against the table walls. Stevie's ear in the studio was legendary for more than just air hockey, though.

Hensel remembered creating some new material with just Stevie and a keyboard in Studio C one night. He rolled the twenty-four-track machine while Stevie pumped, jammed and vocally scatted nonstop for twenty-five minutes, filling up a reel of tape with his improvisations. When he was done, Stevie instructed the engineer to roll back the tape just short of ten-minutes. Hensel rewound and pressed play. And somehow, even amid a creative trance, Stevie remembered exactly where the magic had happened. Hensel spliced a tape leader to that spot and that's how a new Stevie Wonder song was born.

Stevie delayed delivery of the final masters to Motown several times that spring; he repeatedly changed his mind about the album sequence and right at the end decided to rework the entire thing. Some songs were mixed thirty times.

It was worth the money and well worth the wait. When it was released in the fall of 1976, *Songs in the Key of Life* debuted at number one where it remained for fourteen weeks. Stevie took home four Grammys the following year, including one for Producer of the Year. But, despite it being his greatest creative and commercial achievement, *Songs in the Key of Life* was Stevie Wonder's last Record Plant album.

Wonder ended his classic period by checking out of Third Street, but he never truly left.

One-time Record Plant assistant engineer, Olazabal, remained Stevie's trusted production partner for decades. And at one point, Stevie rented the Record Plant mobile truck to park outside of his own studio, Wonderland, trying to replicate the sound of the API from Studio B.

"You have to remember Stevie's history at Record Plant LA," Olazabal added. "We spent a zillion hours working there. He learned a lot of his production techniques there. Maybe that's why Stevie leased the truck and its equipment from Record Plant for so long. He could have bought it many times over for what he spent."

The Record Plant truck remained parked outside of Stevie Wonder's Wonderland studio for over forty years.

RUMOURS MILL

Somebody finally figured out how to get a hit out of the Pit.

Stevie Nicks wrote Fleetwood Mac's first number one single in Sly Stone's Pit at Record Plant Sausalito during the winter of 1976. Taking a break from the main studio one day, she discovered the strange sunken studio and wandered into Sly's adjacent black-and-red bedroom. She sat down with her legs crossed on his big, black velvet bedspread and, with a Fender Rhodes keyboard in front of her, found a drum pattern, switched on her cassette recorder and wrote "Dreams" about her broken love affair with Lindsey Buckingham in less than ten minutes.

Fleetwood Mac had been up there once before in December, 1974, on a Sunday-night KSAN *Live at the Record Plant* radio broadcast, but that was before Nicks and Buckingham joined the band. The reconstituted group was now riding high on *Fleetwood Mac*—its first album together, with its three hit singles "Over My Head," "Rhiannon," and "Say You Love Me"—and Mick Fleetwood chose to escape all of the media attention in LA and hide out in Sausalito to start their next album.

"The studio was designed to fulfill the expectations of a music industry at the height of excess," Mick Fleetwood wrote in his autobiography.

Richard Dashut, who co-produced the album with Wally Heider Studios engineer Ken Caillat, told an interviewer that "Mick [Fleetwood] thought that if he took us out of our homes, we'd all have to hang out together with very few distractions."

Those distractions traveled with them up north. The recording of *Rumours,* beginning in February, 1976, at Record Plant Sausalito, took place amidst the meltdown of the respective relationships of band members John and Christine McVie, and Stevie Nicks and Lindsey Buckingham. Yet, their personal feuds only fueled their music.

"We'd grown obsessive about the album, perhaps because it had become a diary of our pain," Mick Fleetwood also said in his book.

Caring for that pain and keeping the band creative and comfortable in Sausalito for an extended period of time required a heightened level of service and extra TLC from the studio staff. As evidenced by

CHAPTER FIVE

a photograph of the band and the Record Planters from that short period, they were one big, incestuous, Mormon-size family.

"We were beginning to become rock stars and we had to get another album together. Sausalito was as romantic as you could possibly imagine. It was gorgeous up there, right by the ocean, in this fabulous studio with Indian drapes, little hippie girls making hash cookies, and everybody having dinner round a big kitchen table," Nicks told *Blender* magazine.

In his memoir, Ken Caillat reported stumbling back into the Bay Road house one night after a fifteen-hour day of recording only to find two naked groupies waiting in his bed. Even though he was being paid by the band, a staff-engineer paycheck of $1,500 per week was handed to him every Friday by the studio manager, under instructions from Chris Stone.

The dealers of Sausalito had carte blanche to wander the halls on Bridgeway. And the band quickly made plenty of their own connections at Agatha's Pub in town. A three-ounce baggie of coke was always in plain view on the console during the sessions. Caillat once pranked the band by spilling a bag of flour (instead of coke) on the control room floor, and everyone got on their hands and knees to snort it all up. At one point the band considered thanking their coke dealer on the album credits.

The drugs were slowing down the band's progress and the abundance of cocaine, in particular, was causing them to second guess every take. Assistant engineer Cris Morris remembered spending ten hours just to get a kick-drum sound. Lindsey Buckingham had his guitar restrung every twenty minutes.

"Eventually the amount of cocaine began to do damage," Morris said in an interview. "You'd do what you thought was your best work, and then come back the next day and it would sound terrible, so you'd rip it all apart and start over again."

To make matters worse, the *Rumours* sessions were famously wracked by technical malfunctions. Christine McVie incessantly complained that the Record Plant piano was out of tune, regardless of how many different tuners they hired. Mick Fleetwood remembered a tape machine nicknamed "Jaws" that had an appetite for destroying fresh reels of tape. And down deep, Caillat was never a Record Plant

Above: Fleetwood Mac's Stevie Nicks finds her voice in Studio A at the Sausalito Record Plant studio. Below: The console that was used to record the eleventh studio album by Fleetwood Mac, *Rumours*. Strips of tape were used to make the console "off limits" to others.

CHAPTER FIVE

acoustics devotee: "It was a Tom Hidley room, a very dead room, and I didn't like the sound in there. You'd walk into the control room and it was so still that you'd almost hurt your ears."

As Chris Stone had expected, Fleetwood Mac returned to LA that summer. They had made a lot of progress up north but opted to finish the album at home where they could also rebuild their lives. Caillat and the band tried out every available studio in town but eventually settled back home at Wally Heider's studio, where Caillat thought the Sausalito tracks sounded the best.

Until they all fell apart—literally. As the LA sessions progressed, the *Rumours* engineering team noticed that something was off with the tapes. Caillat remembered asking himself, "Are my ears going or does this sound duller than usual?"

He wasn't hearing things. The thousands of hours spent overdubbing the recordings wore out the original twenty-four-track masters, literally shedding the oxide and sound off the tape, and damaging the high-end frequencies. For a short period in the final months of recording *Rumours,* the engineers believed all was lost.

Fortunately, the Record Plant Sausalito team had run a twenty-four-track backup of all their sessions. This common Chris Stone upsell, which ironically, he had learned from Wally Heider, padded the tape budget, but this time it actually saved the day. The engineering team hired a technician to transfer the tracks meticulously and manually onto the backup reels. "Without him, *Rumours* would have been dead," Caillat wrote.

Caillat may have preferred the sound of its rooms, but Heider's was no Record Plant. One day, his assistant called down to the front office to ask for a refrigerator and was told that they were going to be charged and that they would also have to come down to the office to pick it up themselves.

"Record Plant didn't charge us for a refrigerator," Caillat told the Heider studio manager.

She snapped back, "Well then, why don't you go back to the Record Plant!"

Which they then gladly did.

"We wanted to be pampered the way we had been in Sausalito," Caillat remembered. "We had started *Rumours* at the Record Plant, so it was fitting that we finish it at the Record Plant."

Three thousand hours in the studio and one year later, *Rumours* became the best-selling Record Plant-recorded album of all time, ultimately shipping over forty-five million copies. When it entered the *Billboard* charts in the spring of 1977, *Rumours* bounced *Hotel California* from the top slot for twenty-seven weeks.

Fleetwood Mac and the Eagles crossed paths at Record Plant LA and Criteria in Miami, while they were recording their best-selling albums. Caillat recalled that both bands were having their own "Hotel California" moments:

> The title song [of *Hotel California*], with its sense of lost, hopeless decadence, and eerie, druggy, claustrophobia, was written about being trapped in the studio, panicked and sweaty and unable to get out. The Record Plant LA was their Hotel California . . . Our Record Plant stay in Sausalito was something different from the Eagles' experience, unique to us. Yet our recording sessions certainly shared a lot in common with their experiences; they were druggy, claustrophobic, and there were days where I felt that I could never leave.

CHECK OUT TIME

Was Record Plant LA the Real Hotel California?

One night Jimmy Robinson began copying the lyrics from the new Eagles song "Hotel California" into Gary's Book. At the time, it was just an absent-minded scribble. But the more words he transcribed off the cassette copy from the studio, the more he realized that this was something he had to show his boss right away.

Kellgren had started filling a diary with miscellaneous notes and doodles. Among other things, Gary's Book, as it was called, was the studio owner's compendium of plans for his new rock and roll resort, and trusted friends like Jimmy could contribute to it anytime they liked.

By 1976, Robinson had become Kellgren's closest confidant. The Record Plant staff was starting to split into two camps, those who were with Chris and those who were with Gary. Jimmy Robinson was Club Gary all the way. He kept an eye on Stone for his mentor. He

CHAPTER FIVE

clued Gary in on all the studio gossip. He looked in on the VIP clients and made sure they were satisfied.

Robinson remembered what happened when his boss read the lyrics to "Hotel California" for the first time. Gary was at the Castle and working with an architect on a scale model of the studio resort property. Robinson waited for an opening and then handed him the Book.

"Where did you get this from?" Kellgren asked.

Robinson replied, "It's a new song the Eagles are working on at the studio."

"My God, they're writing about Record Plant!"

For anyone who worked at Record Plant LA in the mid-seventies, the parallels were just too obvious to ignore. The studio at 8456 West Third Street was a Mexican-style stucco building with a confusing maze of passages, including a long open-air hallway that served as the main artery into the complex. There were mirrors on the ceiling of the Studio C vocal booth and Lexan plastic mirrors over every bed in the back hotel rooms. The Boat Room, with its extra-long ceiling mirror over the bed, was frequented by the Eagles band members for writing sessions and breaks from recording.

And what about pink champagne on ice? Gary Kellgren was more of a Korbel Brut guy (though Korbel sold a bubbling rosé).

Further down the stoned rabbit hole of rock lyrics analysis, staffers have also pointed out that his "master's chambers" refers to the echo chambers down the hall from Studio C. The studio's walled-in parking lot was the "courtyard" where staffers partied and hung out. Michael Gately, the "night man" knew who "to receive." Rose Mann, the Latin-looking studio manager, was the "lovely face" who greeted the Eagles on her first day at work, as they arrived to record their new album. And, of course, the LA studio opened with all the "spirit" of the times back in "1969." The only line that didn't fit was that there wasn't "plenty of room" at Gary and Chris's "Hotel California": the three studios were booked solid all the time.

Don Henley dismissed the comparison. He told *Rolling Stone* magazine that the song originally clicked in his mind while he was playing a cassette of Don Felder's original twelve-string guitar riff while driving past the Beverly Hills Hotel, which ultimately appeared on the album cover.

"The song has absolutely nothing to do with the Record Plant, except that portions of it were recorded there," he said.

In a lawsuit with a Mexican hotel that claimed to be the "Real Hotel California," Henley testified that the song is not about a real place at all; it's a metaphor for "the dark underbelly of the American Dream and about excess in America."

Most Record Planters remain unconvinced. During the Eagles' residence, both *People* magazine and the *LA Times* published popular articles about this "rock and roll mini-hotel." They remember Henley and Frey writing lyrics in those bedrooms, while the rest of the band was playing ping-pong in the adjacent Studio C.

Engineer Michael Braunstein recalled: "The lyrics for 'Hotel California' were written during the period of time that they were ensconced in Studio C. Frey and Henley wrote those lyrics under duress."

For inspiration, the band roadie went out to the drugstore to buy every magazine he could get his hands on. They would cut out pictures and tape them to the control-room wall with funny captions underneath. Record Plant's *People* magazine feature was one of those articles. Another was a photo of two men on a tightrope walking toward each other over a giant chasm; the caption read: "Henley and Frey working on the final lyrics of 'Mexican Reggae' [the working title of 'Hotel California']."

Many years later, Kellgren's daughter, Devon, was introduced to Glenn Frey at a Hollywood party and asked the musician if "Record Plant was the real Hotel California?" Frey replied, "Yes!"

Jimmy Robinson agreed: "I'm sure that Don Henley doesn't want to cop to it, but he wrote a song about a place where he and the rest of the Eagles worked on that album for nine months. They were writing in the studio. They were under pressure and looking for ideas. For God's sake . . . 'You can check in but never check out' . . . that's how Kellgren and Stone built the place . . . so the musicians wouldn't leave."

"You can never leave." That was also the line that resonated with Chris Stone after hearing the song for the first time. Finding customers to block-book extended stays was part of the original pitch to Ancky Revson. "The longer we kept them there the more

CHAPTER FIVE

money we made. That's why we built the Jacuzzi, the hotel rooms, the cheap beer, and pinball machines. The customer service. The gear and maintenance. The dope. Sure, everyone worked in other studios. But they always came back to Record Plant. It was all about repeat business," he said.

Only 50 percent of the new Eagles album was actually recorded at Record Plant, with the other half happening at Bill Szymczyk's home base in Miami, Criteria Studios (also, Studio C). The first two attempts at recording the song "Hotel California" took place at Record Plant LA, though the first was in the wrong key and the second was too fast. Szymczyk assembled the third and final cut from thirty-three separate tape edits from five different takes the band recorded at Criteria. The control room of Studio C in Miami was also where the famous guitar duel between Joe Walsh and Don Felder took shape over two days of trial and error.

Ever the marketer, Stone still appropriated "Hotel California" as his LA studio's unofficial theme song. Years later when he and Gary were inducted into the recording industry's TEC Hall of Fame, the tune blared over the PA, and Eagles band member Joe Walsh and album producer Bill Szymczyk were guest presenters. *Hotel California* was one of the few albums Stone ever played at home; the RIAA platinum album plaque hung over his desk long after he retired.

"Was the Record Plant the Real Hotel California?" Chris Stone was once asked.

"We were anything our customers wanted us to be," he replied.

The "Hotel California is Record Plant" legend can be traced back to the Rainbow nightclub around the time the album started charting number one in early January, 1977. Kellgren spread the rumor himself. At the Rainbow Bar & Grill one night, the editor of *New Times* magazine overheard a conversation about a "Real Hotel California" and, sensing a scoop, assigned investigative reporter Lucian K. Truscott IV to dig into the story.

Around that time, Robinson was up at the Castle and remembered watching Kellgren descend the staircase in the middle of the night. The studio magnate stepped down the stairs deliberately with a cigarette between his fingers and a bullwhip in his hand. Gary circled the architect's model like the former pilot he was and studied the flow of the property from high above. Then, cracking the whip like gunfire over the scale model of his next empire, Kellgren's words echoed throughout the large, empty hall: "Maybe I'll fuck 'em and start all over again. Hell, I'll call this place Hotel California."

IS IT SIX YET?

Everybody focused on the wrong Eagles song from *Hotel California*. The one that Gary and the rest of the Record Plant LA crew should have been analyzing was "Life in the Fast Lane." Like the song's protagonist, the studio owner's behavior was starting to unwind.

There were rumors around town about strange things going on at the Castle. Chris once sent a runner up the hill on an errand and he didn't return for three days. Visitors spread stories about orgies, S&M, and condoms filled with cocaine. Gary was desperately looking for a band who would rent the place to help him pay the bills.

While Kellgren was up there partying and plotting his next move, Bill Szymczyk was down the hill on Third Street making a record about the recklessness of such a hedonistic lifestyle. Still friends, they had taken different paths since they started in the business ten years earlier at the same songwriter's demo studio on Seventh Avenue. While Gary was going full throttle in the fast lane, Bill couldn't get on the off-ramp fast enough. Kellgren was building a studio empire. Szymczyk was content just making hits.

He was making plenty of hits. Besides Joe Walsh and the Eagles, Szymczyk's guitar army from the period included Elvin Bishop, Wishbone Ash, Michael Stanley Band, REO Speedwagon, Edgar Winter, Rick Derringer, Bob Seger, and the Outlaws. And though The J. Geils Band desperately wanted him to work on their new record at Record Plant NY, the Eagles beckoned and Bill knew his priorities.

"Coach," as the Eagles called Szymczyk, again joined the band there in April, 1976, to begin their yet-to-be-named fifth album (*Hotel California*). He hesitantly agreed to return to the craziness of Record Plant LA when, this time, Chris Stone promised him Studio C. To show how much he valued their business, Stone installed a refrigerator in the control room and a ping-pong table in the back of the studio where they also had carte blanche access to the hotel rooms for writing and/or recreation.

CHAPTER FIVE

"We were drooling to get into the big room," Szymczyk recalled, though admittedly he hated working in LA. He also knew the town and its temptations weren't right for Don Henley and Glenn Frey, either, or for his good friend Joe.

When they started recording for *Hotel California*, Joe Walsh had just officially joined the Eagles and was trying to learn Bernie Leadon's licks and find his place in the band. Record Plant LA was the worst possible studio for a rock guitarist with a raging cocaine habit to be working at—especially as the new guy in a reconstituted band that had a high-pressure album to make.

To make matters worse, that band didn't have any finished material, though they did have plenty of song fragments, licks, and phrases. "We really didn't know how to start. We had no name. We had no concept. What we did have was some pretty cool stuff. We took all of that and put it on a table and we said, 'Okay, let's pretend this is a jigsaw puzzle' and we started piecing things together," Walsh explained.

Henley and Frey were inspired by random riffs, so the pressure was on the band's new guitarists to find ones that could be turned into songs. Don Felder's descending twelve-string guitar line gave birth to "Hotel California." And Joe Walsh's backstage guitar drill became "Life in the Fast Lane."

Walsh explained: "That was a coordination exercise I would do in the dressing room before we played live. It's crosspicking and other stuff. Don and Glenn came in and said, 'What the hell is that?' And I said, 'It's just my warm-up exercise.' They said, 'No, it isn't.' They put it in the jigsaw puzzle and it became one of the things Don Henley wanted to write about—Los Angeles at the time, life in the fast lane. We knew it was going to be the most rock and roll thing that the Eagles had attempted, so far. They turned me loose on that one."

"Life in the Fast Lane" would become the album's standout track. It was written after a crazy car ride Glenn Frey had on Interstate 405 with his coke dealer. In the studio, the song hit too close to home for Don Henley; just listening to it during playbacks made him sick. The coke and booze were also keeping the band from getting anything done. Coach needed to get the sessions under control and here's one of the ways he did it.

On the run-off, inner groove of the first three-hundred-thousand copies of *Hotel California* released at the end of 1976, Szymczyk had the question "Is it six yet?" inscribed in tiny letters. Szymczyk always had his mastering engineers etch such "vinyl graffiti" on his records, and this one memorialized how Szymczyk tried to manage the Eagles during those early months of writing and recording and drinking and doping in Studio C.

Szymczyk said: "I made a rule after it got a little unruly at first. I said, 'All right, guys, we have to get in here at two o'clock in the afternoon and we've got to get work done until six o'clock so I don't want any ingestion of anything other than coffee. At six o'clock you can get your beer, get your this or that, go to whatever you like. That worked for a few weeks but then, in the middle of doing takes, they're all out in the studio and I'm changing reels or something like that in the control room, and I started to hear them muttering things like, 'Is it six yet?' Followed by, 'It had better be.'"

Once the band started ignoring his "six-o'-clock" rule, Szymczyk knew it was time to get everyone out of the "fast lane" and back down to Miami. "Every time we were at Criteria (in Miami), the guys were actually quite happy to be out of LA and away from all the partying and the hangers-on," Szymczyk told an interviewer.

Despite the success of the album's title cut, "Life in the Fast Lane" always held a special meaning for Szymczyk. The sixties-retro whooshing sound before the fade became one of the album's sonic trademarks. And those who knew its roots with Kellgren heard a metaphor for musicians like Hendrix who flamed out too fast. Or maybe, as Szymczyk said, he just wanted the listeners to feel the rush of wind in their hair?

One thing was sure—to get the phasing effect, Szymczyk used a full-on *"Electric Ladyland* two-track flange" technique, which he originally learned how to do from Kellgren. By 1976 there were plenty of digital boxes that could make the effect, but Szymczyk remembered the artistry of the way Kellgren sculpted the sounds with his hands and chose the old-school analog way instead.

"When I suggested phasing at the end of the song, Henley and Frey were a little skeptical," Szymczyk recalled.

One of the band members said, "Oh, don't do that, it might sound

CHAPTER FIVE

like 'Itchycoo Park,' [the Small Faces song from the sixties]."
To which Szymczyk replied, "Well, that's the idea!"
Szymczyk phased the ending anyway and it worked.

TAPE 40

STUDIO	RECORD PLANT SAUSALITO	
ARTIST	**TITLE**	**FORMAT**
New Riders of the Purple Sage	*New Riders*	Album
Joe Cocker	*I Can Stand a Little Rain*	Album
Van Morrison	*Period of Transition*	Album

WHERE'S SLY?

Sooner or later, somebody was going to get busted for drugs at a Record Plant. And, of course, when it finally happened, Sly Stone was the one responsible.

ROB FRABONI, PRODUCER FOR JOE COCKER: There was a chase over the Golden Gate Bridge. Sly Stone's coke dealer was being chased by the DEA. The van ended up in front of the studio and there were bullet holes in the back; they were shooting at it. Oh, it was crazy.

CATHY CALLON, STAFF, RECORD PLANT SAUSALITO: They'd been in the city and were in the process of getting busted and they sped a getaway across the Golden Gate Bridge over to Record Plant. They parked outside and knocked on the door. They were Sly's people; I let two of them in. One was a "Kellgrenite," one of Gary's friends, too. They said they wanted to make a quick phone call. So, a few minutes later, I was in the shop and this guy came in with a shotgun and told me to put the phone down. I'm like, "Excuse me. Who the hell are you?" He said, "Put the phone down . . . This is a bust," and he raised the gun at me and showed me his badge. He took me out into the hall and there were people on the floor and others standing with their hands up against the wall.

TOM FLYE, CHIEF ENGINEER, RECORD PLANT SAUSALITO: I was in the control room of Studio A doing the New Riders [of the Purple Sage]. I sent my assistant out to get some tape. He didn't come back. The band was ready to go. I needed tape. So, I went out of the control room into the lobby and all of a sudden, I was hoisted up against the wall with a shotgun at my back. There were police everywhere.

CATHY CALLON: I got on the phone to call [Chris] Stone; they said, "Put the phone down." For the first few hours they wouldn't let me even answer the phone or go to the bathroom. Joe Cocker was in Studio A and his engineer was one of the ones detained because he had fourteen grams of hash on him. The other guy from the New Riders had some pot. Sly's coke dealer and the guy she was with were being detained in the game room. Finally, I snuck away and got to a phone, and called Chris Stone. I went, "We're being busted." He said, "What do you mean?" I told him. Chris said, "Don't let them search the place. I'm calling the lawyer."

PHIL RYAN, ATTORNEY, RECORD PLANT SAUSALITO AND LA: I got a phone call late one night. It was Chris Stone calling from LA. He said, "I need your help. Sly Stone is under suspicion of having made a dope deal in San Francisco, and he is trying to hide in the Record Plant. There's a whole bunch of sheriffs out front, wanting to arrest him and search the place."

CHRIS STONE, CO-FOUNDER, RECORD PLANT SAUSALITO: I'm pretty sure Sly was there. There was always some question about that, though. If he was there; somehow, he disappeared.

PETE SLAUSON, PRODUCER: In the lobby area [of the studio] there was a door-wide bookcase built into the wall in the lobby. If you pushed on the right book the whole wall moved and opened an entrance to Sly's Pit. You could get in and out without being seen. Sly also had a secret hiding space built in his bedroom, maybe four-feet-by-six-feet big. If you pushed on the secret panel, it would open, and someone could easily crawl in there and hide.

PHIL RYAN: When I got there, the sheriffs were milling around. I introduced myself to the top sheriff and said, "I received a phone call from the owner of the Record Plant and he was absolutely outraged at the notion that anybody could be using illegal substances in his world-class recording studio. He insisted that he wants you to search this place thoroughly, and any rascals who are involved in this should face the full force of the law."

CATHY CALLON: When the lawyer arrived, I said [to the police], "Look, all these other people need to go back to work, because you're costing me a minimum of 120 bucks an hour per room. Is the State of California going to pay for that?" They held Sly's guys and the others they'd busted and let everyone else go back to work.

TOM FLYE: They finally said, "You guys can go back to work. Just stay in the studio and keep the door closed." Of course, the New Riders had a bunch of pot with them. They were all saying, "Lock the door. We're smoking all this shit before they come in." I'm going, "Wait a minute." And I grab all the pot and start hiding it inside the equipment.

CATHY CALLON: Then I remembered the (nitrous) tank. I hadn't seen it all night. I'm like, "Where the hell is the tank? We're getting busted."

TOM FLYE: I'm back in the studio hiding all the stuff, working as fast as I can. Then I find that Gary [Kellgren] had left a couple of nitrous tanks in the back. I pulled up the carpet and hid them under the console.

PHIL RYAN: They wanted to search the place. So, I recommended that they start with the electronics shop, because the staff had told me they needed some more time to do their cleanup work in the studios.

The shop was filled with all these little electronic gadgets, and little boxes that would take forever to look through, and the sheriff took one look at that, and he looked at his string of deputies, and he said, "All right, start the search there."

CATHY CALLON: They had me go through all these rolls of tape in the tape library. When they finally finished, they took me into the kitchen where we stored herb spices in bulk. Half of them looked like pot.

PHIL RYAN: They were ready to search the studios. This poor deputy, this young guy who had to do this search, said, "Couldn't we like . . . if just one of us goes in there, just listen to them play for a little bit?" I said, "Well, I'll have to ask them; they're very touchy about that." So, I went in there first, made sure the room was clean, and said, "Give this guy a couple of chords." And they did.

TOM FLYE: Then one of the cops said, "Joe Cocker, where's Joe Cocker? I hear Joe Cocker's here." We told him he was in Studio B. So, they knocked on the door. Out came Joe. The guy said to Joe, "Man I've always wanted to meet you. You're my favorite singer." Joe was drunk. There were cops with shotguns everywhere. There were cops praising him. He was just freaking out.

CATHY CALLON: They finally left about four thirty in the morning. As soon as they'd gone, someone asked for some coke. It was all gone. Really! There was not even a line left in this place.

ROB FRABONI: Chris Stone begged me to keep quiet about what happened that night. "Please, don't ever tell this story to anybody."

TAPE 41

STUDIO	RECORD PLANT NY / REMOTE	
ARTIST	**TITLE**	**FORMAT**
Kiss	*Kiss Alive!*	Album
Frank Zappa	*Bongo Fury*	Album
Bruce Springsteen & the E Street Band	*Bruce Springsteen & the E Street Band Live 1975–1985*	Live Album
Jackson Browne	*Running on Empty*	Album

THE "LONG" RANGER

In 1976, the original Record Plant NY White Truck recorded eighty-eight concert dates in over fifty different cities at the same time as Record Plant LA and Sausalito were now rolling trucks of their own. With the success of *Frampton Comes Alive* that year, suddenly more labels than ever were hot to record and release live albums. The White Truck and Eddie Kramer produced *Kiss Alive!*, the band's biggest album to date. Elsewhere, remote trucks were recording *Bob Marley Live*, *Lou Reed Live*, *Stephen Stills Live*, King Crimson's *USA*, Frank Zappa's *Bongo Fury*, which ended up being big sellers that year.

Live albums made money.

"Remote recording has several key advantages to studio recording. It is really not as expensive as studio time. It is usually easier on the musician who gets paid for the concert and gets his next LP done at the same time," Chris Stone wrote.

Those live albums were rarely all live, though. Like *Woodstock* and *Bangladesh*, concert tapes always required weeks and sometimes months of post-production work in the studio. In Frank Zappa's case, live recordings were core elements in all his studio albums. Frampton and Kiss thoroughly overdubbed their concert performances back home. Either way, "live albums" all required running tape in concert—and plenty of it.

Engineer David Hewitt's personal 1976 gig sheet offered a snapshot of the live-album business model in action. It was a solid one-hundred-thousand-plus-miles-per-year perpetual road trip, with occasional pit stops at the Forty-Fourth Street facility for billing and tech maintenance, all run by a crew of stage vets, David "DB" Brown and Phil Gitomer, who were relative unknowns back at the studio.

The White Truck that debuted with *Concert for Bangladesh* just five years earlier had become a music money machine, constantly recording a variety of music genres from rock and roll to television, to jazz and classical. But it was rock that fueled Hewitt and his crew. During those twelve months, they followed on tour and archived for posterity concerts by Aerosmith, David Bowie, the Allman Brothers, Judy Collins, Corky Laing Band, YES, Steve Miller Band, The Band, Foghat, Crosby & Nash, Graham Central Station, Jimmy Cliff, Kiss, Frank Zappa, Hall & Oates, Neil Young, and KC & the Sunshine Band.

Hewitt reminisced:

> "From the studio's standpoint, that truck was kind of invisible: I don't know if 'poor stepchild' is the right word, but from the studio's standpoint, it wasn't Studio A, B, or C. It was outside the building, outside the purview of almost everything else. Jimmy Iovine once called me the 'Long Ranger,' because I was always gone. Come to think of it, I was always gone, my entire life; I was always the outsider on the road. But Roy still made me part of that Record Plant family back at the studio. And driving up to the building after every gig, it was like coming home."

TAPE 42

STUDIO RECORD PLANT LA

ARTIST	TITLE	FORMAT
Frank Zappa	Studio Tan	Album
Frank Zappa	Hot Rats III / Street Dirt	Album
Frank Zappa	Orchestral Favorites	Album
Crosby, Stills & Nash	CSN	Album
Grand Funk Railroad	Good Singin' Good Playin'	Album
Frank Zappa	Live in New York	Album
Angel	On Earth as it is in Heaven	Album
Dave Mason	Let it Flow	Album
Monti Rock III	A Piece of the Rock	Album
Bette Midler	Broken Blossom	Album

STUDIO TAN

Frank Zappa was there at the beginning and there at the end.

Everyone usually associates the original Record Plant with Jimi Hendrix. However, the Record Plant was always, and significantly, a product of Frank Zappa's design.

In 1967, Zappa introduced Kellgren to the coolest room in New York, Apostolic, which had a hippie vibe, the precursor to the API console, and the town's only twelve-track Scully tape recorder. The twelve-track would become the new Record Plant's main technical attraction. APIs became the secret sauce of the Record Plant sound.

Even before Jimi raved about his mind-blowing speakers, Zappa discovered Tom Hidley at TTG Studios in Hollywood, where he recorded his first two albums (*Freak Out* and *Absolutely Free*) with a prototype sixteen-track tape machine.

Zappa never recorded at Kellgren's original Record Plant NY. What's more, Record Plant LA was never his exclusive Los Angeles creative space—Whitney Studios out in Glendale was Frank's favorite option. However, his friend Gary's studio became the site of several of his greatest studio achievements, including *One Size Fits All* and its live studio masterpiece "Inca Roads." In one of the oddest rock and roll pairings, Zappa produced Grand Funk Railroad's final album (*Good Singin', Good Playin'*) there in 1976. For seven years, Frank consistently worked on Third Street between tours (which were also all recorded).

"He liked the sound of the stuff that was coming out of there. And the staff was always very good to Frank. They knew he was tight with Gary," the Zappa "Vaultmeister," Joe Travers, recalled.

By the mid-seventies, Zappa regularly booked nights in Stevie Wonder's Studio B; he liked its API console and Bösendorfer grand piano. Frank spent much of his studio time trying to induce unconventional sounds out of that black beauty.

It was in the control room of Studio B that Record Plant engineer Michael Braunstein named one of Frank's albums and coined a term that defined the common condition of all overworked engineers.

Braunstein was working around the clock. By day he was in session with Stephen Stills, the reconstituted Crosby, Stills & Nash, and Dave Mason—and Zappa owned his time at night. He had a habit of listening to playbacks in Studio B by closing his eyes and tilting his head back as if sunbathing. The monitors were closer together in this room, making this a better listening position.

In the midst of one of those private moments, Frank walked into the room.

"What are you doing?" he asked.

"I'm working on my 'studio tan,'" Braunstein deadpanned.

"Be careful not to get a monitor burn," Frank warned.

Soon, engineers around the country were comparing who was busiest by the paleness of their skin. "The paler you were, the better your studio tan," was the word on the street.

Zappa and Braunstein whitened their studio tans during marathon editing sessions that winter and early spring, compiling an assortment of studio recordings, overdubs, and live-concert takes into *Studio*

CHAPTER FIVE

Tan, *Hot Rats III / Street Dirt*, *Orchestral Favorites* and *Live in New York*. With these four albums, Frank fulfilled his contract and ended his relationship with Warner Bros. Records.

Warner responded to this snub by putting a freeze on Frank's access to his master tapes in the Record Plant vault. They withheld payment on the four albums, too, putting Frank under tremendous financial pressure. At one point, it was questionable if Zappa could even pay his band, and he was already way behind on his studio bills.

"1977 was a tough year for Frank," Joe Travers volunteered.

Frank dealt directly with Gary Kellgren when it came to business, and Gary usually gave his old friend the best engineers and best possible deals. There were a lot of similarities between the two men: they first met as young fathers in the middle of the lust fair of the Summer of Love. They both owed their careers to the same man, Tom Wilson. They both owned Rolls-Royces that they rarely drove. They both were chain smokers, though the only other drug or drink that Zappa ever touched was high-octane Turkish coffee.

Gary straightened out whenever he was around Frank. "Party Gary" instantly became "Engineer Gary" whenever they were in the same room. Gary knew that Zappa had no patience for druggies. The word on tour was if you were "wired you got fired." And Zappa expected no less of the staff who served up his tech.

"Frank wasn't going to say, 'Hey, Gary, come in and work on my sessions,' because he knew that he was pretty heavy into partying at the time. But as long as Gary kept it out of his face, Frank wouldn't blow up a friendship over something like that," assistant engineer Davey Moire recalled.

There was one thing that Frank couldn't talk to his good friend Gary about, which was why Frank's wife, Gail, uncharacteristically invited Chris Stone up to their house in Laurel Canyon for a visit. Stone knew exactly where they lived, since early Record Planters crashed and partied across the street in a house rented by engineer Jack Adams.

Frank was waiting outside in the driveway when Stone pulled up in DEDUCT. He led him downstairs, along a long hallway stacked with tape boxes and reels of film, to a small production studio that he kept in the basement.

"You should let us build you a room at Record Plant," was how Stone opened their conversation.

"I'd rather have a home studio," Zappa replied, making it the first time Stone ever heard the term for the future tech trend that would eventually turn big studios like Record Plant into record-making rarities. Two years later, Zappa would build the home studio he'd use for the rest of his life, which cost a then unprecedented $1.5 million.

Zappa asked if Stone could get him a tape out of the studio vault; he said that he only needed a short guitar solo from a particular live show, on a specifically dated tape, which he'd dub before returning the otherwise unused master.

Stone explained that the only way he could release them was to have Frank's manager Herb Cohen indemnify Record Plant first.

Unfortunately, not only was Zappa leaving Warner at the time but he was suing his manager, too. He said that he was making a clean sweep of his business dealings and that his ten-year relationship with Cohen was also coming to an end.

Stone locked onto that one comment. "Ten years . . ." he muttered to himself, ". . . like me and Gary."

THE WIZ

Gary was the Wizard of Ears.

Originally nicknamed "the Wiz" by Tom Wilson in the sixties, Gary Kellgren was now acclaimed as the "Man behind the Curtain" on the 1977 hits by the Eagles, Fleetwood Mac, and Stevie Wonder. The common thread of all their music was Kellgren's Record Plant magic mojo.

Kellgren cultivated his image as the Wiz, appropriately, at the VIP-only Over the Rainbow room at the Rainbow Bar & Grill, where even the biggest rock stars sought him out to listen to their tapes. He circulated stories that his Castle was the original movie set for the Emerald City, and that Debbie Reynolds wanted to house her Hollywood memorabilia collection, including her prized pair of Dorothy's ruby slippers, in his new space. The studio owner's Technicolor reputation was further enhanced by insider reports about his tech ("he invents his own"), his ears ("he hears in colors"), and his parties ("they're experiences").

(MORE COMPRESSION ON THE CYMBALS)

Late May 1976, Grand Funk

HOTEL CALIFORNIA

One particular Kellgren story made the rounds for years at the Rainbow. As engineer Lee Kiefer remembered it, John Lennon and Phil Spector were recording at Record Plant LA Studio A. Although he was supposedly the session engineer, Kellgren showed up only once, when the artist and his producer were out on a break. He listened to what they had been working on, an early take of the song "You Can't Catch Me," and took a razor to the tape to make a quick edit. Kellgren eyeballed his slice and splice and, without even a playback or waiting for his clients to return, he turned and left the room. Lennon and Phil were both shocked to learn that the studio owner had made an edit without their permission. But it was Kellgren, so they listened.

"Spector must have played that thing thirty times," Kiefer recalled. "And he finally says, 'I like it. I like it.' Everyone agreed that Kellgren's cut made the song."

Producer Ed Freeman had his own favorite Gary Kellgren story:

I once asked Kellgren, "Gary, how do you stand these speakers? They're awful. You sit down and there's no bottom end. And you stand up and there's no top end."

And then Gary said something that changed my life forever: "Hey, man, don't listen to the speakers. Listen to the music."

Up until that point, I had been one of these speaker freaks who had to move the speakers two inches to the left and take one dB out at 20K, or something crazy like that. I never had a problem with speakers after Gary's comment. Something just switched and changed me forever.

Another testimonial to Kellgren's artistry would soon appear in *New Times* magazine:

Producer Margouleff brought two tapes into the studio to play for Kellgren. The first was a soul/disco group, pumped up with strings, synthesizers and electronic effects that pushed disco

Opposite: The signed photograph (above) that Frank Zappa gave to Michael Braunstein (below) shows them both at the console during a Grand Funk Railroad recording session that took place in Studio A in May, 1976. Braunstein is proudly wearing the satin tour jacket that was gifted to him by Gary Kellgren.

321

into a kind of modern Young Rascals sound. Kellgren closed his eyes and nodded his head. After two cuts, he raised his hand. That was enough.

"This music isn't saying anything to me," he said.

The tape rewound with a soft whisper. Margouleff had a look of resignation on his face. He claimed not to be surprised by Gary's blunt comment. "That's why I came over to play the songs for him," he explained. "One listen from Gary can save you thousands and thousands in studio time."

ZONED OUT

In the spring of 1977, the Wiz was worried. Everything was changing, all at once.

The music was changing. Despite the unprecedented sales success of the Big Three Record Plant albums of 1977, consumer musical taste was undergoing a seismic shift, which was impacting the way the music was being produced. Punk was quick in-and-out, cheapo recording. Disco was a throwback to single-only sessions, at a time when the studio business model was built on cutting albums.

The technology was changing. The analog wizards of Kellgren's generation were losing their magical edge to the machines. Anybody with a $4,000 box could replace analog tape jockeying with a twist of a dial. At that spring's Audio Engineering Society convention in LA, Mitsubishi and Soundstream both introduced the first digital tape recorders.

The record business was changing. At a time of great excess, the corporate CFOs were taking control of the artists' expenditures and, as a result, studio rates and extras were under more scrutiny than ever. Gloria Stone hired a second bookkeeper just to keep up with increasing inquiries from record label accountants. Chris exercised more "discretion" in his billing practices.

His personal life was changing. Gary had a new girlfriend and secretary, Kristianne Gaines, a tall Black woman who handled all the paperwork for his endless dealmaking. Gary spent time at the house on Miller Drive primarily to be around the children, since he and Marta each had their own separate love lives. Kellgren was building a very public life up at the Castle where every night was another party, another group of musicians, dope dealers, models, and movie celebrities, fueled by constant deliveries of champagne and condoms filled with cocaine. Gary was starting to show the wear and tear—his hair was turning grayer, his bright green eyes were ringed with dark circles, and he had developed a painful urinary infection that needed immediate attention.

Like Frank Zappa, he was cleaning house, too. That meant finally getting rid of Chris Stone. He had numerous suitors, all of whom sooner or later backed away from making a deal. A gang of custom boat builders down in Miami were interested, but after several trips down to Florida, Gary wound up with two racing boats he was unable to pay for, but no bona-fide offer. This left Ken Roberts, who still wanted to buy the studio just to rankle Chris Stone. But Roberts's terms had changed since he originally started courting Gary; despite his early enthusiasm, he had cooled on the Castle and just wanted the studios—plus majority control.

All this was coming down at the same time as the Wiz was being evicted from his Castle. Kellgren couldn't get the Hollywood zoning board's approval to run a recording studio in a historic residential district. And he had thirty days to come up with a deal.

Then Eddie Kramer showed up in LA to record the band Angel.

The first of hundreds of engineers hired by Record Plant and now an A-list producer, Kramer was looking for a mansion to record in. Gary and Chris had given Eddie his big break in the United States, before he built Jimi his own studio. Kramer went independent after leaving Electric Lady in 1974, and he recorded, mixed and produced an unprecedented series of rock and roll hits in the mid-seventies: the Rolling Stones' *Love You Live*, Led Zeppelin's *Physical Graffiti* and *The Song Remains the Same*, Peter Frampton's *Frampton Comes Alive!*, *Kiss Alive!*, and Bad Company's *Run with the Pack*. He was a frequent customer of the Record Plant NY White Truck and a regular resident of Record Plant NY Studio A.

Eddie Kramer had discovered an old rectory near his home in Armonk, NY, called the Cenacle, where he recorded the band Brownsville Station. He mistakenly mentioned it to Jack Douglas and Jay Messina, who booked it out from under him for Aerosmith's *Draw the Line*. So, this left Eddie Kramer looking for another mansion,

CHAPTER FIVE

which brought him back in touch with his old boss, Gary Kellgren. Kramer offered this peek behind the curtain during the final days at the Wizard's Castle.

> It was an adventure, in the true Hollywood sense of the word . . . We heard through the grapevine that Gary Kellgren had a mansion off Sunset Boulevard, and I called him up, and he said, "Why don't you come by and check it out, you know?"
>
> On the appointed day, I showed up at the mansion, and there was Gary's purple Rolls-Royce parked outside in the courtyard. I remember looking at it and saying, "My God, this thing's in terrible shape!" It had scratches and dings and dents all over it. Anyway, we opened the front door and walked in, and the place was pretty much empty; there was no furniture. It was absolutely, from what we could tell, deserted. I yelled, "Gary!" You could just hear this long reverb, floating through the ether.
>
> We trudged up the stairs, a massive semi-circular staircase, going up to the next floor. "Gary!"
>
> Then, all of a sudden, I heard this creaking, groaning, mumbling sound emanating from one of the bedrooms. I knocked on the door and opened it a little bit. There was Gary in bed with his secretary, with bottles of champagne on both bedside tables. It was noon, and they were just getting up.
>
> "Hey, Gary, listen, you know, you told me to come by . . . we want to rent this place, we want to record here."
>
> "Yeah, yeah, no problem, man," Gary replied without moving, "Come by Record Plant and we'll put this together."
>
> "Cut to maybe a week or so later. I brought in carpenters with huge piles of soundproofing material and sheets of plywood for all the windows and screwed it all into the walls. I didn't give a crap, I just said, "That's it, we're going to soundproof the whole bloody place," because in the middle of Hollywood, if you're recording a band, it is not a good idea to disturb the neighbors.
>
> We managed to get things together and Record Plant sent a truck over. We managed to track everything. We had to stop

recording at about eight o'clock every night because the cops came over a couple of times. But we managed to get the shit done and I remember it sounding great. Great drum sound.

Then Kellgren's Castle got shut down by the police.

You needed the right neighbors to play loud music in the Hollywood Hills. And the Castle didn't have the right neighbors. Kellgren's lawyers were in the middle of a last-ditch negotiation with the zoning board, but this bust put an end to Gary's dream of a rock and roll resort in the middle of Hollywood—and after just this one session.

That's when Kellgren decided to finally give Ken Roberts a call. Record Plant was his. He could have it all.

G-L-O-R-I-A

The sound of vacuum cleaners in the morning was the wake-up call that the studio now belonged to the Family Stone. Not Sly's band. Chris Stone's family.

Behind the rock and roll façade, Record Plant was very much a family business, with Chris running the operation and his wife Gloria collecting the money, paying the bills, and keeping her husband's ego in check. Like a Record Plant version of Eloise at the Plaza, their young daughter Samantha roamed the halls, where she learned how to blow dry her hair from Rod Stewart and how to sing harmonies with Joe Walsh.

At a time when the studio billings were at a record high, and all five studios in LA and Sausalito were running twenty-four seven, Stone was becoming increasingly unsure about how long it would all last. Instead of the Castle, Stone felt they needed to diversify into TV and movie sound but knew it would require a massive investment. His moods and ambitions swung wildly between "Fuck Gary" to "I'm fucked without Gary." Gloria pushed him to call Ancky for advice. But for some reason he wouldn't, so she did it herself.

"Remind Chris that it may be his business but it's not his brand," Ancky advised.

Record Plant was unequivocally Gary Kellgren's brand, but those in the know recognized the qualities that Chris Stone brought to the business:

CHAPTER FIVE

"Record Plant's success was all about the marketing. It was Chris's marketing magic that made it work," Al Kooper said.

"He played by the rules, but they were his own rules. And I always liked his rules," Bill Szymczyk added.

"Chris was every bit as creative as Gary, but in a different way. You couldn't create an empire like Chris Stone did without having creativity," Michael Braunstein concluded.

If Chris gave Gary the chance to be Gary, Gloria gave Chris the chance to be Chris. She mentored several generations of young women in the front office who she scolded for doing too much coke, sleeping with the clients, and not dressing modestly enough. Quietly, in the office directly across the hall from Chris, Gloria meticulously managed the money, as well as the moods of her mercurial husband who was battling his inclination to be the one to buy out his partner.

Chris called Gloria into his office one morning that spring and showed her a gift-wrapped package the size of a brick that had been left on his desk from the night before. It was indeed a brick, a left-over invitation from the opening night party for the LA studio in 1969 that had been inscribed with the name of a new guest: "Ken Roberts."

"I guess Gary is telling you something," she pointed out.

"Ken Roberts?"

"It's over Chris, it's time for us to go."

Already sounding lost, Chris asked, "Now what'll I do?"

"You'll rent an RV and take your family on a summer vacation . . ."

THE LAST PARTY

Gary figured fame out. To him, fame was a series of boxes, one within the other. The biggest box was the fans. They were constantly trying to get inside the next smallest box, which contained the rock stars. But there was another box, inside the box containing the rock stars. It was a box the fans didn't even know about. The box contained Gary Kellgren. The box was the Record Plant.

Lucian Truscott IV, "Inside the Real Hotel California,"
New Times magazine

At the worst possible time, a journalist called Gary for an interview. An investigative reporter with war-zone experience, Lucian Truscott IV was assigned by *New Times* to take readers inside the "Real Hotel California." Chris, Gary, and Ken Roberts were finalizing their deal and the last thing they needed now was an article in a national magazine known for its hard-hitting reporting. *New Times* was no *People* magazine.

Gary wanted the article. Before the deal with Ken Roberts was over, he wanted recognition for having created the sound of seventies rock and roll; he wanted to finally come out from behind the curtain and take a bow. Besides, he was certain that Record Plant was the real Hotel California and he was pleased someone else wanted to tell the story.

"Inside the Real Hotel California" may have been the headline but the real angle of the article was much deeper than the reporter originally professed. Truscott's editor saw Kellgren as the symbol of the corporatization of seventies rock and roll. Hell, the guy had a purple Rolls-Royce named GREED.

Stone finally agreed to give Truscott the run of the studio for two nights. Bette Midler was in Studio B and Frank Zappa was set up in Studio C. The reporter interviewed Jimmy Robinson and Bob Margouleff, among others. Kellgren was friendly but he wasn't talking; he let Truscott join a party in the Rack Room, where a tray of cocaine was laid out on the bed for everyone's consumption. The reporter saw that the studio owner was in pain, especially when he went to the bathroom. At one point, Truscott called his editor to confirm, "Fuck, you were right, this guy's dying in front of my eyes."

His editor replied, "Just write it down."

So, he did. Truscott watched Kellgren in the Rack Room stumble from bed to bathroom where he was pissing blood. Nobody said anything. His staff were obsequious to an extreme. Truscott wrote:

> Gary Kellgren seems to have taken upon his shoulders the entire weight of the old rock and roll ethic, the sensibility which once demanded that one live life right out to the edge, take every chance, do every drug, experience every high, dig every low, keep oneself awake every possible moment until finally one crashes and reaches the state of new bliss . . .

New Times magazine photographer David Strick took one of the last pictures of Record Plant co-founder Gary Kellgren (above) in June, 1977, showing off a scale model of his next project (below)—a recording studio compound with residences in a Hollywood mansion.

On the third night, Gary finally granted Truscott an interview, inviting him up to the Castle to talk. When he arrived with photographer David Strick at the big Normandy mansion off Sunset, it was as if Gary was staging a rock and roll version of the movie *Sunset Boulevard*.

> Upstairs, there were noises, a blaring stereo, a television turned up to compete with the music, the last party at the Castle. And now Gary and a group of his friends descended a winding grand staircase. He had gotten himself up as a jester . . . or was he a wizard? A long piece of white silk was wrapped around his head like a turban, and another piece formed a sash about his waist. Hanging from the front of the sash was a condom filled with two ounces of cocaine. In his right hand was a wooden pointer, and in his left, a bottle of Coors.

At the bottom of the stairs, Gary approached the detailed scale model of his Record Plant dream village, illuminated by four architect's lamps. His voice echoed eerily through the dirty terra-cotta floors of the empty ballroom, as he took the pointer and cracked it loudly against the plywood base of the model. Truscott recorded Gary's rant:

> "This is my Emerald City [CRACK], Oz [CRACK]. All I'm trying to do [CRACK] is preserve this place [CRACK], preserve a little of the old Hollywood [CRACK]. But I'm gonna lose it [CRACK]. And then it's up for grabs [CRACK]. They'll build some kind of tinsel tower [CRACK] where I wanted to build my vision of the Record Plant [CRACK], turn it into everything it should be [CRACK]. Now it's just going to be pissed away [CRACK], because we can't get a fucking [CRACK] zoning [CRACK] ordinance [CRACK] changed [CRACK]. It's sick, man [CRACK]. Sick [CRACK]."

The article's photographs of a studio tycoon in a decaying Sunset Boulevard mansion from 1977 would come up in Google searches for Kellgren's name decades later. Jimmy Robinson and his model girlfriend, Angeline, showed up and Gary started using her as a "prop"

CHAPTER FIVE

in his performance. Kellgren posed alone for a featured series of portraits in an arched doorway, with an acoustic guitar (that he couldn't play) strapped across his back. The most famous picture from the photo shoot was of Kellgren with a condom filled with coke stuck up his nose.

In the early morning, Kellgren got a call that Frank Zappa was asking for him, so he and Robinson jumped in the backseat of GREED for the short ride down the hill to the studio. That's when Kellgren confessed to him that the Castle project was "going down the tubes," and that he was weeks away from a deal to "get rid of Stone." Robinson described his friend as acting like a "broken man" that night and remembered Kellgren saying, "This is the end."

Truscott and his photographer followed GREED to the studio in a rented Ford Pinto. They were buzzed inside and found Kellgren nearly passed out in a swivel chair with his feet up on the console in Studio C. When Frank Zappa arrived, Strick watched Kellgren's demeanor change: "Once he was in the room with Zappa, he was solicitous. He was still fucked up but he was almost physically deferential to Zappa that night."

Kellgren listened to a playback of something Frank was working on but had to excuse himself several times for trips to the bathroom. Finally taking him aside, Truscott suggested that Kellgren should see a doctor and offered to take him to the emergency room; surprisingly, Kellgren agreed to go but told Truscott to pick him up at the Castle around noon the next day.

When Kellgren and Robinson returned to the mansion, the party was still going on. Before he left and before Gary headed upstairs to rejoin the revelers, Robinson watched his friend circle the scale model. Kellgren lit a cigarette, struck his characteristic pose with his bad arm propped behind his neck, and studied the replica of what could have been his most spectacular Record Plant of all. Gary then picked up the pointer he had used earlier that evening, kept circling, and then started smashing the toy village into a cloud of dust.

Opposite: A contact sheet of photographs from June, 1977, taken by David Strick at "The Last Party" at Gary Kellgren's Mount Kalmia mansion on Sunset Boulevard. The photographs of Kellgren taking cocaine would troll the studio owner's memory for decades on the Internet.

CHAPTER FIVE

Truscott surveyed the mess when he picked Gary up the next day. Here's what he said happened next:

> Since nobody else would, I took Kellgren to the emergency room at Cedars Sinai. When he emerged a few hours later, I drove him back to the Record Plant, and there, sitting on the bed in the Sissy Room in the company of two rather brutal looking guys from East L.A. who had come bearing condoms filled with cocaine, Gary described his visit to Cedars. "Turns out I've got a kidney stone, man. I should have figured what it was, with all the blood I've been pissing. I already had the doctor book the surgery. I'm gonna have him open me up and cut the little fucker out. I'm gonna have him cut it out and then I'm gonna have a ring made, so when I walk into a room and somebody asks what kind of stone it is, I can hold it up to the light and say, 'kidney, man, kidney.'"

Truscott returned to New York to write. When his article hit the newsstands six weeks later, Gary was already dead.

K-HOLE

NIH NATIONAL LIBRARY OF MEDICINE WEBSITE:
Ketamine hydrochloride, also known as Special K, Kit-Kat, K, or Green, can cause severe dissociation known by recreational users as a 'K-hole'—where a person feels completely divorced from reality and their body.

On July 20, 1977, Gary Kellgren died with his girlfriend in a rare double drowning in the pool at his home on Miller Drive in Hollywood. Though he had just received word from the LA Planning Department that the Castle's rezoning had been approved, he had already vacated the space and was spending more time at the family house with Marta and the kids.

Kellgren had always been drawn to the water. He had planned to build a pool at the studio on Third Street, until Stone convinced him to go with a Jacuzzi instead. The Boat Room in LA and the portholes in the Sausalito studio lobby were signature Kellgren designs.

He leased a 110-foot yacht and held recording sessions at sea with Jimmy Webb, Art Garfunkel, and Sly Stone. Kellgren was considering adding underwater speakers to the pool at his Miller Drive house.

The final days of Gary Kellgren's life and the cause of his death have become mixed up in the fog of memory of the witnesses who were there, each with their own theories about what happened:

JIM KELTNER, SESSION MUSICIAN, FRIEND: I saw him right after he had his horrible kidney-stone operation. My friend Paul Stallworth—the bass player—and I decided to go see him while he was recuperating. We said, "Okay, so what we're going to do tonight is we're going to encourage Gary to get sober and we're going to show him that we can have a good time being sober." But it didn't work out like that. Gary answered the door. He pulled his robe back and showed us his scar, and that scar was from his navel to the back of his spine. Gary, he just was superhuman, you know. Here he was answering the door instead of being in bed and he's cut halfway around his body. He soon got us all drinking and smoking and everything.

CHRIS STONE, CO-FOUNDER, RECORD PLANT: After his surgery, Gary was ready to make changes. He was buying me out. He was ending our marriage. He was even done with GREED.

MONTI ROCK III, PERFORMER, RECORDING ARTIST, ACTOR: Gary couldn't drive because he could barely use his arm. If he couldn't drive with one arm, how could he swim?

MICHAEL BRAUNSTEIN, ENGINEER, RECORD PLANT: Then, all of a sudden out of nowhere, I heard that I'm supposed to be second engineer on Gary's album that he was doing with Wes Farrell, his old friend, for a disco act named Monti Rock III. It was a step back but there was no getting out of it. It was a real paradox, because you could love Gary, but in some ways, he was kind of scary. You didn't want to get trapped having to go back into one of the bedrooms and partying with him till dawn. But when we started doing the album, it was like a cloud came into the control room. We had eighteen musicians in there and Gary just sat down behind the console and within minutes, literally

CHAPTER FIVE

minutes, we were able to record. I took over the sessions when Gary went to his twentieth high school reunion in Shenandoah and finished it after he died.

LOREANA WRENCH, KELLGREN'S DAUGHTER: I heard from my grandma that Gary was at his high-school reunion right before he died and he was jumping at every sound that night. He was nervous as all to get out. He was saying that the mob was trying to get into his business. She said that he called her from LA the day that he died and made financial arrangements for Marta and the kids. He wanted to make sure that my grandma took care of the finances. To her dying day, she said he was murdered; she was adamant that his death was not an accident.

JIMMY ROBINSON, MUSICIAN, ENGINEER, PRODUCER, FRIEND: Everyone, everyone, everyone thought that Stone had something to do with Gary's death. They didn't know about the deal that was about to go down behind the scenes, which was about to make Stone very rich.

CHRIS STONE: We had a done deal with Ken Roberts, everything but the signing. Then I heard that Gary was working on another way to buy me out. There was some sketchy guy from the Starwood nightclub, and there were some drug runners from Miami. I didn't care who I sold to, as long as I got my money.

NEIL HAUSMAN, FINANCIAL ADVISOR, MARTA'S BOYFRIEND: Gary decided to sell out to Ken Roberts, too, because he had enough of the aggravation. He was still going to manage the studio, and everything else, and at the time, we were still discussing his management contract. One of the things that irritated everybody at the table, just two days before he passed away, was when I asked, "What happens if he dies? What happens to the money and the management contract?" That caused an argument. "What do you mean he's going to die?" somebody asked.

JIMMY ROBINSON: The day he died, Gary was in the backyard of his house on Miller Drive shooting the shit out of a tree with a BB gun. He and Marta were fighting like cats and dogs. I could hear him on the phone with his mother, going, "Listen! Listen, they're going to kill me, Mom! They're going to kill me! I don't know. This is crazy, but I'm telling you right now, somebody is going to have to step in and help Marta and the kids." He knew something was up, man. He knew something was going down.

NEIL HAUSMAN: I was actually the one who found them in the pool. I'm the "business associate" the police referred to in their report who was there that evening. I pulled them both out and I tried to give them CPR. [His girlfriend Kris] was the same size and healthier and probably weighed as much as Gary. When I found them at the bottom of the swimming pool, she was behind him with her arms wrapped around his arms.

MICHAEL BRAUNSTEIN: I was with Stephen Stills and engineer Bill Halverson in Studio B. It was about ten o'clock at night. We were working on vocals and the phone rang. Someone was calling from the house and the news was that Gary had died. Gary had "died" before, but this time it was confirmed. Stephen was out at the vocal mic, and I just stopped everything, and he came in and asked, "What's wrong?," and I told him that Gary died. He asked me if I wanted to stop the session, and I just laid down on the floor for a while, and I didn't know what to do. Everybody in the studio was in a state of shock, and we just continued to work, and waited for the news to come in. It was like a pall had been cast.

RAY COREY, GOFER: When I came in the next morning, Gary's father-in-law was in the driveway sitting in his favorite chair, and he was crying. Neil [Hausman] filled me in. The speculation was that Gary's secretary, Kris Gaines, was floating around in a rubber raft in the pool and Gary was lounging in a chair on the side of the pool. Kris stood up in the rubber raft, fell out, and couldn't swim. Even though it was just like two arms' length to the side of the pool, she was going into a panic. So, Gary jumped in to get her to the side of the pool. She grabbed hold of Gary where he had his stitches and dragged him underwater.

CHAPTER FIVE

RON WOOD, ROLLING STONES GUITARIST: His wife Marta found him drowned in his swimming pool with one of his girlfriends. He had been trying to fix his underwater speakers. His girlfriend was trying to help him but she couldn't swim properly either, so they both drowned.

CHRIS STONE: Somebody found a half-smoked joint with Green [ketamine] in it on the side of the pool. You feel no pain on that shit, until you die. The next day Gary's sister (Aleda Michelle) came into my office screaming, "You killed my brother!"

LAPD INVESTIGATOR STATEMENT TO THE *LA TIMES*: Nothing we have found at this point indicates there was any foul play.

JIMMY ROBINSON: I never was satisfied with the investigation. I don't even think it was an investigation. I never saw two people whisked away so fast. No funeral, no service, no memorial, no anything. It was just like he was gone and that was it. There's not a minute in my life, every day, that I don't ask myself, like "What the fuck happened here?" You know what I mean? I'm at a loss. This thing, it's not just some fucking story, it's a story that fucked up my life.

> *SAN DIEGO READER*: What ended Monti Rock's career . . . was a dead guy in a swimming pool. Gary Kellgren owned the Record Plant recording studios, and Rock was staying with him in Hollywood at the time. Everybody said Monti murdered him, and even though he didn't . . . the accusation stuck and it killed his career.

CHRIS STONE: I got on the phone with Ken Roberts who still wanted to go ahead with the deal. Now, he wanted to give me a management contract, but this time he said he was adding a "death clause," which really pissed me off. Right then, I made up my mind to walk on the deal. I said, "Go fuck yourself. I'm keeping my studio."

From top left: *I Can Stand a Little Rain*, Joe Cocker, 1974; "You Are So Beautiful," Joe Cocker, 1974; *Hearts*, America, 1975; *The Tubes*, The Tubes, 1975; *Destroyer*, KISS, 1975; "Don't Fear the Reaper," Blue Öyster Cult, 1975; *Bongo Fury*, Frank Zappa, 1975; *Lazy Afternoon*, Barbra Streisand, 1975; *Nighthawks at the Diner*, Tom Waits, 1975; *High on You*, Sly Stone, 1975; *Rufus featuring Chaka Khan*, Rufus & Chaka Khan, 1975; *Pablo Cruise*, Pablo Cruise, 1975.

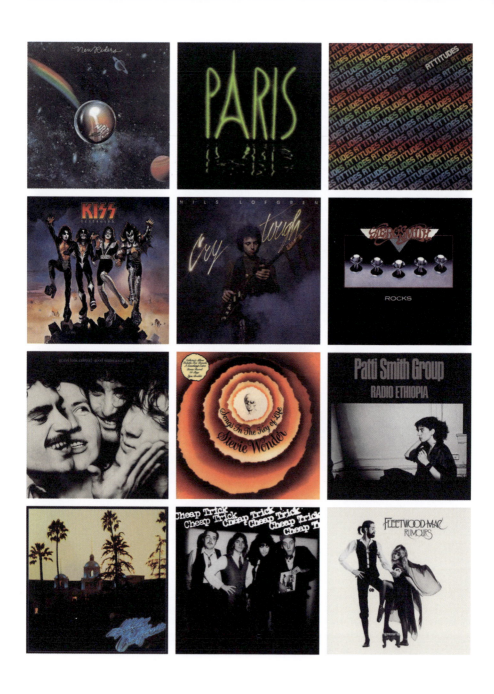

From top left: *New Riders*, New Riders of the Purple Sage, 1976; *Paris*, Paris, 1976; *Attitudes*, Attitudes, 1976; *KISS Alive!*, KISS, 1976; *Cry Tough*, Nils Lofgren, 1976; *Rocks*, Aerosmith, 1976; *Good Singin' Good Playin'*, Grand Funk Railroad, 1976; *Songs in the Key of Life*, Stevie Wonder, 1976; *Radio Ethiopia*, Patti Smith, 1976; *Hotel California*, the Eagles, 1976; *Cheap Trick*, Cheap Trick, 1977; *Rumours*, Fleetwood Mac, 1977.

From top left: *On Earth as it is in Heaven*, Angel, 1977; *Period of Transition*, Van Morrison, 1977; *CSN*, Crosby, Stills & Nash, 1977; *A Piece of the Rock*, Sir Monti Rock III, 1977; *Bat Out of Hell*, Meat Loaf, 1977; *Broken Blossom*, Bette Midler, 1977; *Running on Empty*, Jackson Browne, 1977; *Live in New York*, Frank Zappa, 1978; *Studio Tan*, Frank Zappa, 1978; *Hot Rats III/Street Dirt*, Frank Zappa, 1979; *Orchestral Favorites*, Frank Zappa, 1979; *Bruce Springsteen & the E Street Band Live 1975–1985*, Bruce Springsteen & the E Street Band, 1986.

6

SANCTUARY OF SOUND

1977–1980

"We're here to stay."

YOKO ONO
artist, musician

TAPE 43

STUDIO RECORD PLANT LA

ARTIST	TITLE	FORMAT
Eddie Money	*Eddie Money*	Album
Cheap Trick	*Heaven Tonight*	Album
Stephen Stills	*Thoroughfare Gap*	Album
Marshall Chapman	*Jaded Virgin*	Album

GARY'S CHURCH

Then, even stranger things began to happen.

The week after Gary's death in July 1977 there were major technical glitches in all the rooms, in all the Record Plant studios, in all three cities. It was such an unprecedented series of malfunctions that the maintenance staffs all started attributing them to "Gary's Ghost."

Accordingly, many of Gary's friends sought preternatural answers to the questions about his passing.

Jimmy Robinson tried to solve the mystery by arranging a late-night vigil with horror-TV hostess Elvira to conjure up clues. "We were trying to figure out if there was anything that Gary was trying to come back and tell us from the dark."

Jim Keltner recalled that Kellgren had been reading a book about angels right before he died. "I remember distinctly when I got the news, I remembered that little book and I remembered thinking, 'He's good. He's good now.'"

Back on Third Street, the lights began to inexplicably flicker in the tiny, hideaway above Studio C called "Gary's Church." The room featured a very small, stained glass panel window overlooking the studio, which Gary would use to spy on the sessions below. Someone suggested there may have been a short in the electrical system. Everyone began to refer to those phantom happenings as "visitations" from Gary.

Reality sank in once the *New Times* article hit the newsstands later that week. Lucian Truscott's editorial takedown of the studio owner made it abundantly clear that Kellgren was an accident just waiting to happen and even prophesied his imminent demise.

Truscott's story didn't stay current among the rock and roll cognoscenti for long. Three weeks later, talk about the drowning of this rock and roll kingmaker was eclipsed by the death of the King of rock and roll. Elvis Presley's overdose on August 16 that summer made the death of this secretive studio millionaire a mere footnote in the directory of dead rock stars from the era.

> ## "We were trying to figure out if there was anything Gary was trying to come back and tell us."
>
> Jimmy Robinson, musician and engineer

FIRE & RAIN

GLORIA STONE, LETTER TO HER MOTHER: Sunday, January 8, [1978]. I went to the Record Plant and Chris took the kids to the desert to visit a friend. At 11 a.m. someone came into my office and said, "Don't get excited, but I think there's a small electrical fire in the hallway." I ran to get a fire extinguisher and by the time we got to where the fire was, there was so much smoke we couldn't even go inside. The area above Studio C was storage for all our old files and paperwork back to 1970. It went up like a tinderbox.

AL KOOPER, MUSICIAN, PRODUCER, AUTHOR: We were working in Studio A with [singer/songwriter] Marshall Chapman. If we hadn't hit the fire alarm instantly, the entire complex might have burned completely to the ground.

CHRIS STONE: I was out in the desert with our two kids riding motorcycles. Gloria somehow found me having lunch in a restaurant and told me that we were on fire. She said that one of our maintenance guys was running around the place, yelling, "Save your tapes, save your tapes, we're on fire, go save your tapes."

The fire that destroyed LA's Studio C in January, 1978 (above) started in a hideaway above the control room. Producer Andy Johns posed in front of the ruins (below left), while fast thinking by producer Al Kooper saved priceless master tapes from destruction (below right).

ROSE MANN, STUDIO MANAGER, MIX MAGAZINE: Those were in the days when we had a lot of velvet and cushy stuff in the studio. Sparks flew and it just went "poof."

GLORIA STONE, LETTER. Fortunately, we got a lot of equipment out but the fire ran across the roof of Studio C and blazed for about five hours. We had at least ten fire trucks fighting the fire. Because of our crazy quilt layout, they had to bring hoses in through the offices. It didn't take long for our employees to hear about the fire. They all came down immediately and, while the firemen were fighting the blaze on the roof, they carried out important things from other parts of the building. We saved every single tape. We had no damage of any kind to any tape—and in our business the tapes are the most important thing.

MARSHALL CHAPMAN. MUSICIAN, SONGWRITER, AUTHOR: A bunch of us formed a line to salvage the master tapes from the Record Plant archives. We might as well have been rescuing Rembrandts from the Louvre. Boxes containing master tapes of some of the best-known names in rock passed through our hands. Every now and then I would glance down and see one marked "Linda Ronstadt" or "Sly and the Family Stone." I remember seeing "Hotel California" on one, and "John Lennon" on another. I nearly fainted when I realized I was holding a box containing a master tape from Stevie Wonder's *Songs in the Key of Life*.

ROSE MANN: The first thing we did was to pull tapes from the library. Three artists had just finished their projects that weekend and there were masters everywhere. Steve Stills was there—in fact, he was the first person to work in Studio C when it opened and he was the last.

GLORIA STONE, LETTER: When the roof caved in, we lost "C," which was our largest room, and nearly all the equipment in it, including a pipe organ, Hammond organ and grand piano. A quick estimate right now is about $500,000 in equipment because our shop, with all of its expensive test gear, was also lost. Stephen Stills lost $16,000 in equipment, drums, guitars, etc.

CHAPTER SIX

GLORIA STONE, LETTER: Then on Monday it started to rain. Not a drizzle—a downpour! We had to buy everyone boots and slickers so we could get the mess cleaned out. Telephone repair didn't want to come out in the rain; the Department of Water & Power didn't want to work in the rain. We had to get the rest of the equipment out from under the rubble in "C," but it wasn't safe to go in because part of the roof was still hanging down and the experts we hired to make it safe didn't or couldn't work in the rain.

ROSE MANN: A few weeks later, Chris Stone called a meeting and said he couldn't afford to pay anybody. We all worked together for three or four weeks without paychecks.

AL KOOPER: As it was, we could no longer continue to work there with Marshall Chapman. The studio assigned me its remote truck and crew, and we finished the album at my house with a remote truck parked in the driveway.

BOB EDWARDS, ENGINEER: We turned the music room in Al [Kooper]'s house into a studio and the Record Plant gear was outside in the truck. I remember Al didn't want any of the backup singers to know where he lived. He rented them a limo and blindfolded them and he took them all the way up to his house in Coldwater Canyon so they wouldn't know how to find his house.

CHRIS STONE: A $50,000 advance from CBS saved us. So, the music never really stopped. The place still smelled, but by February Cheap Trick was in with [producer] Tom Werman in Studio B recording "Surrender."

TAPE 44

STUDIO RECORD PLANT NY / REMOTE

ARTIST	TITLE	FORMAT
Bruce Springsteen and the E Street Band	*Palace Theatre, Albany, 1977*	Live Album
Lou Reed	*Street Hassle*	Album
Bruce Springsteen	*Darkness on the Edge of Town*	Album
Patti Smith	*Easter*	Album
Dictators	*Bloodbrothers*	Album
Blondie	*Parallel Lines*	Album
Tom Petty and the Heartbreakers	*Damn the Torpedoes*	Album

WHERE'S JIMMY?

In the music business, there was always another new kid in town.

Elvis was dead. Kellgren was forgotten. Punk was rising. Fleetwood Mac was number one. At Record Plant Sausalito, Prince was recording his first album, *For You*. And out of nowhere, Jimmy "Shoes" Iovine was running back and forth between Bruce Springsteen and Patti Smith sessions on Forty-Fourth Street. With *Saturday Night Fever* still in production in Brooklyn, this twenty-four-year-old from Red Hook had already crossed the East River to work with two of the hottest artists of the era, both at the same time.

It was the standard Record Plant hustle that Gary Kellgren invented and Roy passed on to the next generation of engineers—how to juggle two sessions, two egos, two studio setups at once, while making both artists think they were your only priority. Kellgren first pulled it off with Frank Zappa and Lou Reed at Mayfair in 1967. Cicala mastered the act, too, with Shelly Yakus always around to back him up. Now, Iovine was running the racket with two giant, demanding talents who were recording the greatest albums of their careers

CHAPTER SIX

(*Darkness on the Edge of Town* and *Easter*) simultaneously during the summer of 1977.

Engineer Thom Panunzio recalled: "Neither Patti nor Bruce ever knew that Jimmy was working both their two sessions at the same time. Roy taught us how to juggle *not* being in sessions. At Record Plant, you were always covering for somebody."

As important as Roy Cicala was to getting Jimmy Iovine started, Springsteen producer Jon Landau was his mentor for the next stage of his career. Iovine would take everything he learned in the studio with Jon and Bruce and walk it across the hall to try out on Patti Smith. "The combination of all these people, and especially Jon [Landau], gave me the line: 'This is not about you.' That was the biggest lesson that I ever learned in music. This is about the artist. And it's about the music. It's not about you," Iovine added.

Iovine had spent the past year sitting in the box of David Hewitt's White Truck, taping the one-hundred-and-forty live shows that Springsteen played in 1976–77, while waiting out Springsteen's legal battle with his first manager, Mike Appel. Bruce couldn't set foot in a studio, but he could record live. Those concerts gave Jimmy plenty of time to think and realize that this *wasn't* what he wanted to do with the rest of his life. Those live tapes also piqued Bruce's interest in trading out *Born to Run's* Wall of Sound for the more freewheeling, contemporary sonics he was hearing on stage, and which he believed Iovine's young ears could help him reproduce on disc.

As soon as the lawsuit was settled, Bruce started *Darkness* at Atlantic Studios, splitting the days with the Rolling Stones. The room wasn't working for him, so he returned to the familiar halls of the Forty-Fourth-Street office building where he felt he could make a better recording.

"In the seventies somebody decided that all ambient sound was bad . . . And if you listen to a lot of records from the seventies, the deadness on them, I find it makes my skin crawl," Springsteen said in a documentary.

Unbeknownst to the Boss, that enemy of "ambient sound" was Record Plant's own Tom Hidley and the very studio where he was now working was responsible for some of those "skin-crawling" seventies recordings. Kellgren and Hidley's once breakthrough "dead" room treatment was now out of vogue. New York City's Power Station on West Fifty-Third Street, owned by former Record Plant engineer Tony Bongiovi, with its vaulted ceilings and reverberant wood paneling, had become the hot new studio in town.

Record Plant's engineers tried everything to compensate. "We ripped the felt off the wall and pulled up the rugs but Record Plant still didn't have the high ceilings and, no matter what, you were not going to get that sound," engineer Thom Panunzio said.

To Jon Landau's credit, Bruce stayed put and persevered. Through endless trial and error, countless playbacks and overdubs, he and his team recorded and mixed for the next eight months, sometimes spending weeks just to get the right drum sound. Taking a cue from Bob Ezrin and Kiss, Iovine once positioned drummer Max Weinberg in the building's elevator shaft to record the right whacks. Ironically, Springsteen was overdubbing *Darkness* when the New York City 1977 blackout hit, with Bruce at first blaming Jimmy when the tape machines stopped and the studio turned pitch-dark.

The technical side was never Jimmy's strong suit. For him, it was all about the feel. So, to back up Iovine at the board, Landau and Springsteen brought in engineer Chuck Plotkin who would continue to work with them for the next forty-plus years. Plotkin mixed, while Bruce changed his mind, until the album was eventually finished in April, 1978.

Bruce had more music than he could fit onto his own album. Several Record Plant artists scored his help just by being at the right studio at the right time. The Dictators were recording their third album, *Bloodbrothers*, at Record Plant NY and ended up benefiting from an uncredited guest appearance by the Boss. Lou Reed was around too, and he coaxed Bruce to sing the line "Tramps like us, we were born to pay" on the title cut of his *Street Hassle* LP. Iovine convinced Springsteen to offer Patti Smith some songs for her third album; she picked "Because the Night," and it became her only hit single. Bruce wrote it the same night as "Fire," which he handed over to Robert Gordon.

"I'm in Bruce's hotel room, and he said, 'What's going on with Patti?' I said, 'We're making a great album, but I don't have that big introduction song, the single. You know that song you don't think

Above: Bruce Springsteen with the E Street Band during the day on the tenth-floor roof of Record Plant NY for the promotion of their 1978 album *Darkness on the Edge of Town*. Below: Bruce and the band returned to the roof after dinner for a photoshoot in the dark.

Above: Patti Smith with Jimmy Iovine at Record Plant NY during a recording session for her album, *Easter*, in the summer of 1977. Below: (l–r) Engineer Chuck Plotkin, Springsteen, producer John Landau, and engineer Iovine worked together on Springsteen's album.

CHAPTER SIX

fits your album?' He said, 'You think that would be good for Patti'"
I said, 'I'm positive,'" Iovine said.

Thom Panunzio engineered *Easter* with Jimmy. But, significantly, Shelly Yakus mixed "Because the Night."

"Jimmy said, 'Listen, I've got to be done with this mix by nine o'clock in the morning because I've got to bring it over to Clive [Davis]'s. Can you stay in a hotel tonight near the studio, and I'll call you when we're ready to mix?' I go to this hotel, and I go to sleep, and then he calls me an hour before he needs me. We started mixing at three o'clock in the morning and I remember the sweat marks on the board. It was like a hurricane; we were moving stuff and riding stuff. Jimmy took some faders; I took some faders; and we totally rocked it out," Shelly recalled.

Until "Because the Night," Iovine had always been Yakus's assistant. But, just as Jack (Douglas) had *his* engineer Jay (Messina), Iovine needed *his* engineer, too. And he unabashedly believed *his* engineer should be *his* boss, Shelly Yakus.

Yakus was the studio's "golden ears." Whenever a session needed a touch of magic or audio triage, he was the one everyone called. *Imagine* belonged as much to Shelly as it did to Roy Cicala. He created the Alice Cooper sound. His work with the Raspberries, Meat Loaf, and Blue Öyster Cult broke new ground for rock recordings. Yakus was the Cicala student who actually ran the school.

"I remember when [Jimmy] first came to Record Plant, I looked him straight in the eye and said, 'Listen kid, you're walking into a different world here and we're going to be depending on you.' I'm not sure he ever forgave me for treating him like that," Yakus recalled.

This runner turned assistant engineer turned producer already had big plans. And those sessions with Patti Smith and Bruce Springsteen only emboldened them.

"'Listen, when we have success, we should go out on our own, together. How about we join forces? I'll produce and you'll engineer,'" Iovine suggested to his superior.

It was a presumptuous idea, but it came at the right time for Yakus. Cicala was traveling to Brazil and was away from the studio for weeks at a time. Things at the studio were just never the same, again.

Lori Burton recalled:

Not surprisingly, the Record Plant started looking really shabby around that time. Nothing was going back into the studio. Roy was in another world. The studio was losing a tremendous amount of money; and the more it lost, the more Roy lost interest. There was nothing left for him to do. He was disgusted, and Roy just wanted to go on to something else.

All the engineers felt Roy's absence. But nobody felt it as much as Shelly, who began to explore his options.

Iovine made a deal with Tom Petty to produce his third album and asked Yakus to join him on the gig out in California. Petty's 1979 breakthrough album *Damn the Torpedo*es became a Record Plant production even though it was mostly recorded at the most un-Record Plant like studio, Sound City in LA; the studio lineup was entirely Record Plant-trained talent, including its producer, Iovine, his engineers, Yakus and Panunzio, their assistant, Gray Russell, and mastering engineer, Greg Calbi, and the album's final mixes were made "back home" at Record Plant NY.

Shelly sat elbow-to-elbow at the console alongside the future label executive and headphone billionaire during the liftoff of his production career. Following *Torpedoes* and over the next few years, together they recorded Stevie Nicks's *Bella Donna*, Dire Straits' *Making Movies,* and U2's *Under a Blood Red Sky*, beginning a ten-year run as a hit-making duo. Yakus and Panunzio would make sure a little bit of Record Plant was in every Jimmy Iovine production over at Interscope and A&M Records for the next twenty years. A&M Studios, where Jimmy Shoes first worked with Phil Spector and John Lennon, became their West Coast studio home.

"Jimmy was seven years younger than me," Yakus told a blogger. "Back at Record Plant, when he first talked to me about going out and doing stuff, I was thinking, 'Hey, I get a paycheck here every week. I'm supposed to leave here and take a chance with this kid?' And I did!"

UP ON THE ROOF

Recording studios were all air-locked, pressure-cooker chambers where the sound was deafening and the outside world didn't exist. At Record Plant NY, at least there was the roof.

CHAPTER SIX

The tenth-floor roof was first discovered by Jimi Hendrix when he moved upstairs to work in a private room Kellgren built exclusively for him. This maze of tar overlooking Times Square quickly became a popular destination for artists in search of fresh air and a view, and for photographers looking for light.

John Lennon goofed around for the camera up there, dressing like Jimmy Iovine and sticking his tongue out for May Pang. Musician Joan Jett tossed fire bombs into the alleys below.

Bruce Springsteen and the E Street Band's 1978 promo photos for *Darkness on the Edge of Town* were all taken with the Record Plant NY roof as their backdrop. Photographer Frank Stefanko recalled: "I had the boys assemble in every part of the roof, looking for the perfect shot. We worked for hours until it became dusk. I thought we were done, but Bruce said, 'Let's return in an hour when it gets dark.' The roof of the Record Plant took on a strange appearance at night. With the brick structures up there, the images looked like they were made in a city street, rather than this lofty perch overlooking Manhattan."

Blondie followed Bruce into the Forty-Fourth Street studio and onto that roof during the summer of 1978 for sessions that would become their mega-hit *Parallel Lines*.

For six weeks of intense recording, producer Mike Chapman pushed pop out of a band of punks. To Chapman's liking, the Westlake monitors in upstairs Studio C were unnervingly loud. He told an interviewer: "Having grown up listening to everything on "11", I'd turn things up as loud as they could go, thinking that if it felt good and sounded good at 4000 watts, then you knew you'd got it right."

Fortunately, the roof was down the hall and it was there that the band cleared their heads and posed for one of the most famous portraits in the history of rock photography—Blondie standing precipitously on the ledge of the Record Plant NY roof (or so it appeared).

Photographer Martyn Goddard was responsible for the in-camera trickery. He said: "I arrived at the recording studio and . . . I could sense a tense atmosphere. It was soon evident that Blondie, and Debbie Harry in particular, were having issues with record producer Mike Chapman. Two conflicting forces were in play: the group's New

Blondie band members Clem Burke, Chris Stein, Debbie Harry, Jimmy Destri, Frank Infante, and Nigel Harrison stand on a bench on the NY studio roof in 1978 to give the illusion of standing on the edge of the roof for the album cover of *Parallel Lines*.

CHAPTER SIX

York punk heritage (and their one take and done attitude) and Mike Chapman's quest for West Coast perfection."

With tapes and photos in the can, Chapman cut his six-month studio booking short to hide out with his engineer in the hills of Kentucky where they mixed the album that ultimately broke Blondie's first number-one hit "Heart of Glass" and turned a group of New York punks into global superstars.

TAPE 45

STUDIO	RECORD PLANT SAUSALITO / RECORD PLANT NY	
ARTIST	**TITLE**	**FORMAT**
Prince	*For You*	Album
Neil Sedaka	*A Song*	Album
Aerosmith	"Come Together"	Single

NANOSECOND IN TIME

It was rare for any celebrity to turn heads at Record Plant. The staff was trained to treat everyone the same. If any single music industry notable received special treatment, though, it wasn't a musician—it was the Beatles' producer, George Martin.

Martin invented the role of the rock and roll record producer. He opened the ears of a generation to how the imaginative use of audio technology could serve the artist and their music. A young Gary Kellgren transferred *Sgt. Pepper's Lonely Hearts Club Band* from vinyl to reel-to-reel tape so he and Frank Zappa could dissect it during the summer of 1967.

Guitarist Dan Peek of the band America with Beatles engineer Geoff Emerick (above) in Studio A at Record Plant Sausalito. For their fifth studio album, *Hearts*, the band and Beatles producer George Martin moved into the studio for three weeks in January, 1975.

CHAPTER SIX

When John Lennon first arrived at Record Plant NY to finish *Imagine* in 1970, his presence roused the nerves of the Record Plant NY staff; however, it wasn't Lennon alone who was breathing down the necks of the young engineers (at least in their heads). Shelly Yakus told an interviewer what he was thinking when he sat at the console with John for the first time: "I'm hoping that I can give him what he needs. He's used to working with George Martin, for God's sake!"

Martin knew recording studios. He built and owned AIR Studios in London and on the island of Montserrat, and years later, in 1989, as part of Chrysalis Records, he bought Record Plant LA from Chris Stone (while he turned down Record Plant NY).

Martin was no stranger to the Record Plant sound, either. By the time of his arrival on Forty-Fourth Street in 1978, he had quad mixed Paul McCartney's *Band on the Run* at Record Plant LA, had recorded two America albums (*Hearts* and *Harbor)* at Record Plant Sausalito, and had worked at Record Plant NY with Neil Sedaka on his comeback album, *A Song.*

Martin's return to Record Plant NY in 1978 was to rerecord his audio masterpiece, *Sgt. Pepper's,* for the soundtrack of the Robert Stigwood film adaptation of the legendary album. He and Jack Douglas had booked Studio A for Aerosmith's cover version of Lennon's song, "Come Together," though, by that time, John had been MIA from "his New York studio" for over three years

In his autobiography, Aerosmith guitarist Joe Perry wrote that working with George Martin was the "hook" that convinced the band to get involved in the "cheesy" movie in the first place. And in his own memoir, Aerosmith's lead singer, Steve Tyler, elaborated:

"The movie was a Hindenburg at the box office, but the dream come true is I got to meet George Martin . . . And I must admit that when I was singing the first verse of "Come Together" and looked through the glass at Studio A, Record Plant [NY], it was like, for that one nanosecond in time . . . I was John."

TAPE 46

STUDIO RECORD PLANT NY / REMOTE

ARTIST	TITLE	FORMAT
John Lennon & Yoko Ono	*Double Fantasy*	Album
John Lennon & Yoko Ono	"Walking on Thin Ice"	Single
John Lennon & Yoko Ono	"Watching the Wheels"	Single
Willie Nile	*Willie Nile*	Album
Leonard Bernstein	*Kennedy Center Honors*	Broadcast

... BUT YOU CAN NEVER LEAVE

When John Lennon returned from retirement in 1980 to record his *Double Fantasy* album with Yoko, he was ready for a change—as the song title said, he was "starting over." Though Record Plant NY regular Jack Douglas was picked to produce and Record Plant LA staffer Lee DeCarlo was his engineer, John and Yoko abandoned Roy for Eddie; they booked time at the Hit Factory instead of at their usual Forty-Fourth Street haunts.

"Everyone was sworn to secrecy. For about a month and a half . . . I had to warn everyone, 'If the word gets out that this record is being made, it'll stop.' Had we worked at the Record Plant on Forty-Fourth Street, there were always photographers outside waiting to see who came in, and he would have gotten busted. But over at Hit Factory on Forty-Eighth Street we could go in and out without being noticed," Douglas explained.

The sessions weren't really much of a secret, though. When Douglas's arranger accidentally went to Record Plant for the first date, the receptionist told him, "I think you want the Hit Factory."

Roy Cicala was openly hurt that John had chosen his arch-competitor to host his big return, especially now, when Record Plant needed to brush up its image with his business. "I guess people had told [John] that I retired and I'd left the country or something, which wasn't true, I was right there," he told an interviewer.

Jack was aware of the politics involved. "I had to explain to Roy, 'I have to do this. I have to be [at Hit Factory] now, and you just have to be okay with it.' It was difficult," he said.

As producer, it usually would have been Jack Douglas's decision where to record. However, some historians say that Yoko gave Douglas an ultimatum that he could record wherever he wanted "except for Record Plant NY and no California." According to Lennon biographer Ken Womack, "Yoko had come to resent Cicala's palpable deference to John's creative perspectives over her own."

Meanwhile, Yoko's West Coast embargo was easy to understand given its obvious roots in John's Lost Weekend. Unlike Lennon, who stopped drinking when he returned from LA, Roy was still on a bottle a day. And unlike John and Yoko's relationship, which had grown closer over the past five years, Roy and Lori were now angrily divorced. Roy's alpha male behavior was always a big problem for Yoko; he was the "male-chauvinist-pig engineer" she had referred to in the song "Sisters O Sisters" on *Some Time in New York City*.

"Sometimes, Yoko would say something, and Roy wouldn't even acknowledge her words," studio manager Arlene Reckson recalled.

Roy's birth date may have had something to do with it, too, since Yoko had her astrologist review the birthdays of all the musicians and production staff before they were accepted as members of the *Double Fantasy* team.

For a short time, the *Double Fantasy* team moved back to Forty-Fourth Street from Hit Factory to finish the album; but after completing mixes on "Starting Over," "Woman," "Watching the Wheels," "Kiss, Kiss, Kiss," and (possibly) "Beautiful Boy," John and Yoko disappeared. Without warning, one of their assistants called the studio and asked for the tapes to be returned to the Hit Factory where the couple wanted to continue their work. At first Roy was enraged and said, "Don't give them the tapes." One hour later he relented, and the tapes were released.

Then, following *Double Fantasy*'s successful release in mid-November, Jack, John, and Yoko again returned to Roy's Mixroom to finish a few new singles, including "Walking on Thin Ice." *Rolling Stone* had just named the album one of the top ten albums of 1980 and they were eager to get another single out before the end of the year.

When they arrived at Record Plant NY, Yoko informed the receptionist, "We're here to stay."

Roy's new tenth-floor Mixroom may have helped change John and Yoko's (or Jack's) mind. It was a large, comfortable, perfectly tuned control room with a small recording booth and, most importantly, a pyramid-skylight ceiling with a crystal chandelier. During his visits to Brazil, Roy had become convinced that the pyramid had special musical powers.

On December 1, 1980, John and Yoko settled back into the familiar Record Plant tenth floor, which still showcased their wall-sized acoustic "Baby Grand Guitar" from Yoko's 1971 solo art show at Syracuse University, which had been hanging there throughout their absence. Their photographer Bob Gruen had them pose in front of this unplayable musical oddity to document the return to their studio home.

John asked for the John Lennon Piano and had it installed in Roy's Mixroom so he could bang on it between mixes. "He loved it so much, he had it moved to every studio he worked in at the complex," Jack Douglas said.

John's return after his five-year hiatus thrilled the Record Plant staff. Night maintenance engineer Paul Prestopino said, "We were all excited. For one thing, if he came back, it might help us save the studio, because we were in that mode at that point. Anything to save the studio."

Coming off the *Blues Brothers* soundtrack sessions, assistant engineer Steve Marcantonio was assigned to back up Douglas on the new Lennon/Ono project. Marcantonio recalled John laying down a killer guitar solo one night, and every time they played it back, John and he would simulate the performance on dueling air guitars ("It was so surreal," Marcantonio remarked). John wanted to try out a Clap Trap, a new gadget that simulated the sound of claps, and he gave Marcantonio $200 to buy him one. The assistant engineer fantasized about going to his apartment at the Dakota to deliver the device in person.

Thom Panunzio was one of the last people at Record Plant to see

Above: John Lennon and Tom Jones at Lennon's last public concert at the Hilton Hotel in New York City on April 18, 1975. The Record Plant studios logo on Lennon's T-shirt was designed by Gary Kellgren. Below: Lennon with Yoko Ono and Roy Cicala in front of their "Baby Grand Guitar" in December, 1980.

John alive. He was producing Willie Nile's debut album downstairs, when he received a call from John asking if he had an extra pack of strings for a guitar overdub he was doing on Yoko's new song. Lennon insisted on paying for them, but Panunzio asked him to reimburse him with an autograph for a friend, instead.

The Record Plant NY remote crew had just returned to home base from a gig recording at The Kennedy Center in Washington, DC, and remote engineer DB Brown wrote in David Hewitt's memoir: "We were unloading the remote truck when we heard there was a party up in [Roy's] Mixroom for the couple who had been working there and over at the Hit Factory on a double album. Phil and I decided to go up and say 'Hi' and grab a couple of free beers; John Lennon [with his cowboy hat on] was sitting in the corner by the upright piano and Yoko Ono was sitting on his lap."

Douglas was scheduled to join John and Yoko for the limo ride back home but that night he had to stick around for another recording date. Marcantonio remembered what happened next: "I was scurrying around the studio getting ready for [Jack Douglas's next] session while John and Yoko were getting ready to leave. In my mind I had all these things I wanted to say to them, you know, 'Thanks a lot, it was great working with you. I'll see you with the Clap Trap . . . this and that.' As I'm walking back to the studio where John and Yoko were, they were already in the elevator. There was just barely enough time to say goodbye. So, they were nice and receptive and said, 'Take care, Steve.'"

Lennon's last autograph was made out to the Record Plant receptionist on his way out the door.

Panunzio was standing in the reception area with his own autographed Record Plant track sheet still in his hand, when the news broke on the room's large, wall-mounted TV. "We weren't there more than fifteen minutes when the announcer interrupted the show, saying 'John Lennon has been shot and he's dead.' We all looked at each other and joked . . . 'Yeah, Paul's dead, too' . . . because we didn't believe it . . . he had just been there minutes before. And then somebody mentioned on the news that John Lennon had just left the Record Plant and it finally sunk in. And soon the whole street was full of people."

CHAPTER SIX

Willie Nile was listening to a playback when Panunzio rushed in and exclaimed, "'Somebody just shot John!' I asked, 'John who?' It didn't make sense. He said, 'John Lennon.' I go, 'What?' Then you figure, 'shot,' what does that mean? Maybe in the hand, maybe in the foot?' Sadly, that wasn't the case," Nile said. "The phone started ringing off the hook. [Record-label owner] David Geffen called, the secretary answered, and he said, 'John's there, right? Yoko's friend just said he's on the way to the hospital and he's been shot! But he's there recording right?' And [the secretary] replied, 'Well, no, he left about fifteen minutes ago.' We were all crying. We watched it all on TV like everybody else."

The sessions in all four studios came to a halt. "I had to get the tapes and put them into the vault on the roof. For some reason I was scared—I don't know why—to take those tapes up to the vault," Marcantonio said.

One week later Yoko arrived at the studio for the last time wearing big black sunglasses and with several bodyguards by her side to work on a montage of John's dialogue that had been recorded during the *Double Fantasy* sessions. For some unknown reason, she took Jack Douglas's co-producer title off the album credits.

Roy Cicala never talked about that last day at Record Plant NY with John. One thing was certain, though—he was never the same. He increasingly lost interest in the studio and started spending more time in Brazil. Though he lived over thirty more years, some said Roy died with John that night. After years of working so close to stardom, it was as if the lights in the studio suddenly went out. And Roy was left alone in a very dark soundproof room.

Epilogue

CHAPTER 11

RECORD PLANT NY declined throughout the eighties, though the studio still recorded hits including Cyndi Lauper's *She's So Unusual*, and Prince's "Purple Rain." The original Record Plant closed in 1987, but Roy's Mixroom on the tenth floor is still being operated by Sony Music. Until his death in 2014, Roy Cicala worked in Brazil and built a studio there, Record Plant SA. The Forty-Fourth Street office building has been branded "The Plant" by its owners.

After the 1978 fire, RECORD PLANT LA was rebuilt, and the facility diversified into film and television recording with a studio on the Paramount lot, and then moved to its second location in Hollywood in 1986. Chris Stone sold the studio to Beatles producer George Martin and Chrysalis Records in 1989, and it has since had several owners, including entrepreneur Rick Stevens and performer Bruno Mars. During the Rick Stevens/Rose Mann era, Record Plant LA recorded artists including David Foster, Celine Dion, Mariah Carey, Red Hot Chili Peppers, Prince, Michael Jackson, Def Leppard, Beyoncé, Kanye West, Nine Inch Nails, and Lady Gaga. Chris Stone died in 2016. Record Plant LA closed in 2024.

As of 2024, RECORD PLANT SAUSALITO has reopened as 2200 Studios at its original location, with many of its original design details still intact. The studio was acquired in 1981 by a wealthy music fan, who in turn sold it to a drug trafficker, who was busted for amphetamine manufacturing in 1986. The government seized the studio while Heart, Journey, Starship, and Huey Lewis were in session. Rick James replaced Sly as the studio's primary artist-in-residence ("Super Freak"). Metallica had the Studio A roof raised to get a bigger drum sound. Huey Lewis and the News' hit-album *Sports* and Santana's comeback album *Supernatural* were both recorded there.

The music made at all three locations lives on . . .

From top left: *Eddie Money*, Eddie Money, 1977; *A Song*, Neil Sedaka, 1977; *Street Hassle*, Lou Reed, 1978; *Easter*, Patti Smith, 1978; *For You*, Prince, 1978; *Heaven Tonight*, Cheap Trick, 1978; *Darkness on the Edge of Town*, Bruce Springsteen, 1978; *Parallel Lines*, Blondie, 1978; *Thoroughfare Gap*, Stephen Stills, 1978; *Jaded Virgin*, Marshall Chapman, 1978; *Bloodbrothers*, Dictators, 1978; "Come Together," Aerosmith, 1978.

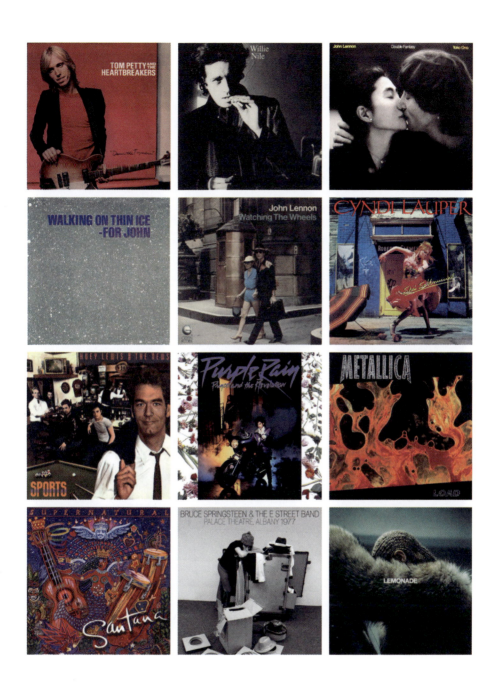

From top left: *Damn the Torpedoes*, Tom Petty and the Heartbreakers, 1979; *Willie Nile*, Willie Nile, 1980; *Double Fantasy*, John Lennon & Yoko Ono, 1980; "Walking on Thin Ice," John Lennon & Yoko Ono, 1980; "Watching the Wheels," John Lennon & Yoko Ono, 1980; *She's So Unusual*, Cyndi Lauper, 1983; *Sports*, Huey Lewis and the News, 1983; "Purple Rain," Prince, 1984; *Load*, Metallica, 1996; *Supernatural*, Santana, 1999; *Palace Theatre, Albany, 1977*, Bruce Springsteen and the E Street Band, 2017; *Lemonade*, Beyoncé, 2016.

Text Sources

PROLOGUE
Electra Glide Nails
Interviews: Chris Stone, Lucian K. Truscott IV

"Inside the Hotel California," Lucian K. Truscott IV, *New Times*, Aug. 5, 1977, editor, John Lombardi

LA Times, Southland Crime Report, July 22, 1977

TAPE 1
Nail Polish
Interviews: Lou Lindauer, Chris Stone, Gloria Stone, Marta Kellgren, John Townley

"Long Sessions Required for Serious Pop," Claude Hill, *Billboard*, Sept. 2, 1967

"The Hippies," *Time*, July 7, 1967

"Brief History of Scully Tape Recorders," Museum of Magnetic Sound Recording website

The Real Frank Zappa Book, Frank Zappa with Peter Ochiogrosso, Poseidon, 1989

Zappa, A Biography, Barry Miles, Grove, 2004

The Countess
Interviews: Chris Stone, Gloria Stone

Fire And Ice: The Story of Charles Revson, the Man Who Built the Revlon Empire, Andrew Tobias, William Morrow, 1976

Wilson
Interviews: Al Kooper, Chris Stone, Susan Schmidt Horning, John Richo

White Light/White Heat: The Velvet Underground Day-by-Day, Richie Unterberger, Jawbone, 2009

What's Welsh for Zen: The Autobiography of John Cale, Victor Bockris & John Cale, Bloomsbury, 1999

Chasing Sound: Technology, Culture, and the Art of Studio Recording from Edison to the LP, Susan Schmidt Horning, Johns Hopkins University Press, 2015

Tom Wilson, "A Record Producer is a Psychoanalyst with Rhythm," Ann Geracimos, *New York Times Magazine*, Sept. 29, 1968

"The Greatest Music Producer You've Never Heard of Is . . ." Michael Hall, *Texas Monthly*, Jan. 6, 2014

Words and Guitar: A History of Lou Reed's Music, Bill Brown, Colossal Books, 2013

ProducerTomWilson.com

Money
Interviews: John Richo, Chris Stone

"Absolutely Frank," *EQ Magazine*, Mar. 1994

"Youth cultural revolt of the 1960s," *Chasing Sound*, Susan Schmidt Horning, Johns Hopkins University Press, 2015

No Commercial Potential: The Saga of Frank Zappa, David Walley, Da Capo, 1996

"We are the Mothers . . . and This Is What We Sound Like!" Chris Michie, *Mix*, Jan. 1, 2003

Lumpy Money, liner notes, Zappa Records, 2008

TAPE 2
The Scene
Interviews: John McDermott, Al Kooper, Marta Kellgren, Chris Stone, Mayor Dick Hunt, Tom Flye

Clair Krepps, unpublished interview, Mar. 1999, courtesy of Susan Schmidt Horning

"Burning the Midnight Lamp," July 6, 1967, *Ultimate Hendrix: An Illustrated Encyclopedia of Live Concerts and Sessions*, John McDermott, Eddie Kramer, Billy Cox, Hal Leonard Corp., 2009

"Steve Paul, Owner of former Scene Nightclub Dies," *New York Times*, Oct. 24, 2012

JimiHendrix-Lifelines.net

Jimi Hendrix, Live at the Scene Club, N.Y., N.Y. Featuring: Jim Morrison, Johnny Winter, Buddy Miles (album bootleg), 1997

"The Greatest Music Producer You've Never Heard of Is . . ." Michael Hall, *Texas Monthly*, Jan. 6, 2014

Forty-Fourth Street
Interview: Chris Stone

Starting at Zero, ed. Peter Neal, Bloomsbury, 2013

Becoming Jimi Hendrix, Steven Roby & Brad Schreiber, Da Capo, 2010

Cinemontage, Journal of Motion Pictures Editors Guild, May 1, 2006

Where's Jimi?
Interviews: Chris Stone, Gloria Stone, Marta Kellgren, Lillian Davis Douma

"The House That Hendrix Built: Inside the Birth of the Record Plant," Martin Porter & David Goggin, *Rolling Stone*, Mar. 19, 2018

Fire And Ice: The Story of Charles Revson, the Man Who Built the Revlon Empire, Andrew Tobias, William Morrow, 1976

Just a Phase
Interviews: Bill Szymczyk, Vic Briggs, Marta Kellgren, Brooks Arthur

"Was Jimi Hendrix Out of Control During His Final Days in the Studio? Evidence Emerges on 'People, Hell and Angels,'" *Guitar World*, Alan DiPerna, Sept. 18, 2013

"What's the Difference between Phasing and Flanging?" Steve Howell, *Sound on Sound*, Mar. 2006

"Phasing," *Chasing Sound*, Susan Schmidt Horning, Johns Hopkins University Press, 2015

First Jam
Interviews: Eddie Kramer, Chris Stone, Roger Mayer, Jack Casady, Todd Rundgren, Jimmy Robinson, John McDermott, Lillian Davis Douma, Chris Morris

Electric Ladyland, liner notes, 50th Anniversary Reissue, 2018

"A Jimi Hendrix Doubleheader," Tony Glover, *Hullabaloo*, Feb. 1969

"Production Legend Jack Douglas on 18 Career-Defining Records," Joe Bosso, *Music Radar*, Dec. 19, 2012

"Classic Tracks: Jimi Hendrix 'All Along the Watchtower,'" Richard Buskin, *Sound on Sound* Dec. 2005

Ultimate Hendrix: An Illustrated Encyclopedia of Live Concerts and Sessions, John McDermott, Eddie Kramer, Billy Cox, Hal Leonard Corp., 2009

Jimi Hendrix: Electric Gypsy, Harry Shapiro & Caesar Glebbeek, Heineman, 1991

Foxy Ladies
'Scuse Me While I Kiss the Sky, David Henderson, Simon & Schuster, 2003

Zygote, Dan Storch, Apr. 7, 1969

Music Television
Interviews: Chris Stone, Eddie Kramer, John Storyk

Clair Krepps, unpub. interview, Mar. 1999, courtesy of Susan Schmidt Horning

Jimi Hendrix, "I Don't Want to be a Clown Any More," *Rolling Stone*, Nov. 15, 1969

368

TEXT SOURCES

Jimi Hendrix: Electric Gypsy, Harry Shapiro and Caesar Glebbeek, Heineman, 1991

"Local TV Cable Company Acquires 8 New Holdings," *Pittsfield Berkshire Eagle*, Oct. 18, 1969

TAPE 3

Go West

Interviews: Chris Stone, Tom Hidley, Mike D. Stone

"Redesign for the Record Plant," *Cashbox*, Feb. 1, 1986

"Tom Hidley, Right Between the Ears," Lunching with Bonzai, David Goggin, *Mix*, Aug. 1986

"Peter Tork's Infamous House," Psycho-Jello.com

"Tom Hidley: A Career Built on Breakthroughs," Paul Verna, *Billboard*, July 1, 1995

Hippie Hef

Interviews: Tom Hidley, Lee Kiefer, Mike D. Stone, Phil Schier, Chris Stone

Playboy and the Making of the Good Life in America, Elizabeth Fraterrigo, Oxford University Press, 2011

Third Street

Interviews, Mike D. Stone, Chris Stone, Phil Schier

"Recording Studio Presses Money," *LA Free Press*, Dec. 22, 1972

Always Under Construction

Interviews: Chris Stone, Lee Kiefer

"LA Studio Scene," *1971 Billboard International Directory of Recording Studios*

TAPE 4

Gi-normous

Interviews, Joe Walsh, Bill Szymczyk, Chris Stone

"How the James Gang Brought Rides Again Out of Chaos," Jeff Giles & Matt Wardlaw, UltimateClassicRock.com, Aug. 28, 2015

James Gang Rides Again, liner notes, 2000 reissue

Behind the Boards II: The Making of Rock 'n' Roll's Greatest Records Revealed, Jake Brown, Hal Leonard Corp., 2014

"Tom Hidley, Right Between the Ears," David Goggin, *Mix*, Aug. 1986

TAPE 5

Sex, Drugs & Rock and Roll

Interviews: Chris Stone, Jimmy Robinson, Jack Douglas, Rob Fraboni, Chris Morris

When Two Cents Was Money: A Memoir, Abe Silverstein,

iUniverse, 2013

Steve Ross, *Master of the Game*, Connie Bruck, Simon & Schuster, 1995

Roy

Interviews: Lori Burton, Chris Stone, Shelly Yakus, Jack Douglas, Arlene Reckson, Craig Alberino, Jade Cicala

Imagine John Yoko, curated Yoko Ono, Grand Central, 2020

Paper Airplanes

Interviews: Chris Stone, Chris Morris

"N.Y. Recording Scene Seethes, Sits, Checks Its Books," Chris Hodenfield, *Rolling Stone*, Mar. 2, 1972

Ultimate Hendrix: An Illustrated Encyclopedia of Live Concerts and Sessions, John McDermott, Eddie Kramer, Billy Cox, Hal Leonard Corp., 2009

Star-Spangled Banner

Interviews: Chris Stone, Jack Douglas, Eddie Kramer, Chris Morris

Forever Changes: Arthur Lee and the Book of Love, John Einarson, Jawbone, 2010

TAPE 6

Four Dead

Interviews: Bill Halverson, Mike D. Stone, Chris Stone, Bill Szymczyk

Graham Nash, Wild Tales: A Rock & Roll Life, Graham Nash, Penguin Random House, 2013

"Classic Tracks: LA Edition, 'Help Me,' Joni Mitchell," Barbara Schultz, *Mix*, Oct. 1, 2014

TAPE 7

Greed and Deduct

Interviews: Marta Kellgren, Grange Rutan, Gloria Stone, Chris Stone, Tom Hidley, Phil Ryan

TAPE 8

Ten Weeks

Interviews: Chris Stone, Marshall Chapman, Lillian Davis Douma, Tom Flye, Roger Mayer, John McDermott, Eddie Kramer

The Jimi Hendrix Experience, Jerry Hopkins, Arcade, 2014

Lipstick Alley, post by Positive Vibe

Just Kids, Patti Smith, Harper Collins, 2010

TAPE 9

Another Hendrix

Interviews: Chris Stone, Tom Flye, Marshall Crenshaw, Todd Rundgren

Hal Blaine and the Wrecking Crew, Hal Blaine with David Goggin, Rebeat Books, 1990

"David Kapralik, Influential Barbra Streisand, Sly Stone Music Exec, Dies at 91," Mike Barnes, *Hollywood Reporter*, July 1, 2017

There's a Riot Goin' On, reissue liner notes, essay by A. Scott Galloway, Epic Records, 2021

Sly and the Family Stone: An Oral History, Joel Selvin, Simon & Schuster, 2007

There's a Riot Goin' On, Miles Marshall Lewis, 33⅓ series, Continuum, 2006

"Sly and angel dust in LA," *I Want to Take You Higher: The Life and Times of Sly and the Family Stone*, Jeff Kaliss, Backbeat Books, 1994

ProducerTomWilson.com

TAPE 10

Naked Drum Booth

Interviews: Jack Douglas, Lori Burton, Andy Neill

The John Lennon Piano, *Sotheby's Auction Catalog*, June 24, 2014

Won't Get Fooled Again: The Who from Lifehouse to Quadrophenia, Richie Unterberger, Jawbone, 2011

The Day the Music Died

Interviews, Ed Freeman, Tom Flye, Robert Margouleff

"Classic Tracks: Don McLean's 'American Pie'," Blair Jackson, *Mix*, Jan. 1, 2005

"Classic Tracks: Don McLean 'American Pie,'" Richard Buskin, *Sound on Sound*, Mar. 2012

TONTO

Interviews: Malcolm Cecil, Robert Margouleff, Roger Mayer, Chris Stone

"TONTO: The 50-Year Saga of the Synth Heard on Stevie Wonder Classics," Martin Porter & David Goggin, *Rolling Stone*, Nov. 13, 2018

"Review: Tonto's Expanding Head Band, 'Zero Time," Timothy Crouse, *Rolling Stone*, Aug. 5, 1971

"The 40th Anniversary of the Stevie Wonder Classic, *Innervisions*," *WaxPoetics*, Chris Williams, Aug. 7, 2013

"Stevie Wonder," *Biography*, A&E Network, 2008

TAPE 11

Call Wally

Interviews: Tom Scott, Chris Stone, Allen Steckler, Lillian Davis Douma

TEXT SOURCES

George Harrison: Behind the Locked Door, Graeme Thomson, Omnibus, 2013
Phil Spector: Out of My Head, Richard Williams, Omnibus, 1972
Wally Heider, *Mix*, Nov. 2007

TAPE 12
Crazy Yank
Interview: Jack Douglas
"Production Legend Jack Douglas on 18 Career-Defining Records," Joe Bosso, *Music Radar*, Dec. 19, 2012
"Classic Tracks: John Lennon 'Whatever Gets You Thru the Night'," Richard Buskin, *Sound on Sound*, June 2009

Imagine
Interviews: Allen Steckler, Paul Prestopino, Shelly Yakus, Arlene Reckson, Jack Douglas, Lillian Davis Douma
Imagine John Yoko, curated Yoko Ono, Grand Central, 2020
The John Lennon Piano, *Sotheby's Auction Catalog*, June 24, 2014
Phil Spector: Out of My Head, Richard Williams, Omnibus,1972
Dennis Ferrante interview with Steve Trevelise, New Jersey 101.5, Dec. 10, 2018

The Garden
Interviews: Gloria Stone, Chris Stone, Allen Steckler, Lillian Davis Douma, Tom Flye, Tom Scott, Jonathan Taplin
"The Coming of Age of George Harrison," Graeme Thomson, *GQ* (UK), Nov. 18, 2013
George Harrison: Behind the Locked Door, Graeme Thomson, Omnibus, 2016
Stephen Stills, Change Partners: The Definitive Biography, David Roberts, This Day in Music Books, 2016

Ripp-Off
Interviews: Chris Stone, Lee Kiefer, Mike D. Stone
Billy Joel: The Definitive Biography, Fred Schruers, Crown, 2014
Always Magic in the Air, Ken Emerson, Penguin, 2005
Varispeed, HistoryofRecording.com

TAPE 13
The Accommodations
Interviews: Lee Kiefer, Michael Braunstein, Fran Hughes, Scott Stogel, Al Kooper, Mark Mothersbaugh, Marta Kellgren, Devon Kellgren
Shell Shocked: My Life with the Turtles, Flo & Eddie, and Frank Zappa, Howard Kaylan & Jeff Tamarkin, Hal Leonard Corp., 2013

Big Daddy
Interviews: Raechel Donahue, Chris Stone, Lee Kiefer, Rick Sanchez
Radio Waves, Life and Revolution on the FM Dial, Jim Ladd, St. Martin's Press, 1991
"History of the Trident Restaurant," Larry Clinton, Sausalito Historical Society
www.thetridentrestaurant.com
The Mix, KQED Arts website, Richie Unterberger, Feb. 4, 2017

TAPE 14
Gimme Some Truth
Interviews: Gary Van Scyoc, Bob Gruen, Arlene Reckson, Jack Douglas
"LennoNYC," *American Masters Podcast*, Episode 5, Oct. 8, 2010
Allen Ginsberg: The Last Word on First Blues, liner notes, Omnivore Recordings, 2016
"Yogi Bare," The Record Rack Column, *Albuquerque Tribune*, Mike Shearer, Mar. 23, 1972
Phil Spector: Out of My Head, Richard Williams, Omnibus Press,1972
"Unguarded Moments," *The New York Times*, Dec. 8, 2010

Tapped!
Interview: Chris Stone

TAPE 15
Electric Lady West!
Interviews: Phil Schier, Malcolm Cecil, Robert Margouleff, Chris Stone, John Storyk, Austin Godsey, Gary Olazabal
VMan, as reported in *Beatles News*, Feb. 28, 2011
Stevie Wonder and America, An American Band, Dan Peek, Xulon Press, 2004
"Making Stevie Wonder's Talking Book," *The Atlantic*, Chris Williams, Oct. 29, 2012
"Rufus—A Band into Everything," Doris G. Worsham, *Oakland Tribune*, Dec. 23, 1976

TAPE 16
Damn Dolby
Interviews: Chris Stone, Bob Ezrin
"N.Y. Recording Scene Seethes, Sits, Checks Its Books," Chris Hodenfield, *Rolling Stone*, Mar. 2, 1972

TAPE 17
Psychedelic Studio
Interview: Chris Stone
What the Dormouse Said: How the Sixties Counterculture Shaped the Personal Computer Industry, John Markoff, Penguin, 2005

"Silicon Valley's Long Obsession with LSD," *Big Think*, Derek Beres, Apr. 27, 2018
Sasaki, Walker and Associates (SWA), www.swagroup.com

TAPE 18
Twin Palms
Interviews: Chris Stone, Lee Kiefer, Marta Kellgren, Tom Scott, Raechel Donahue
Steve Ross: Master of the Game, Connie Bruck, Simon & Schuster, 1995
"41 Years Ago: Black Sabbath Release Vol. 4," UltimateClassicRock.com, Sterling Whitaker, Sept. 24, 2013
I Want to Take You Higher, Jeff Kalis, Backbeat Books, 2008

Lower Drawer
Interview: Chris Stone
Sly and the Family Stone: An Oral History, Joel Selvin, Simon & Schuster, 2007

TAPE 19
Bums in Bags
Interviews: Chris Stone, Tom Scott, Katherine Weiss, Tom Hidley, Raechel Donahue, Lee Kiefer, Chip Madinger, Allen Steckler
Los Angeles Herald-Examiner, California Living Section, Mar. 18, 1974
Lennonology: Strange Days Indeed, a Scrapbook of Madness, Chip Madinger, Scott Raile, Open Your Books, 2015
Melody Maker, Nov. 4, 1972
Rolling Stone, Random Notes, Oct. 31, 1972

TAPE 20
Superstition
Interviews: Robert Margouleff, Malcolm Cecil, Chris Stone, Mike D. Stone, Phil Schier, Gary Olazabal, Austin Godsey
SoulMusic.com, Sept. 20, 2012
"Some Time in New York City" Review, *Rolling Stone*, Stephen Holden, July 20, 1972

TAPE 21
Super Flye
Interviews: Chris Stone, Tom Flye, Raechel Donahue, Michelle Zarin
I Want to Take You Higher, The Life and Times of Sly and the Family Stone, Jeff Kaliss, Backbeat Books, 1994
"Recording Sly and the Family Stone's 'If You Want Me to Stay,'" Blair Jackson, *Mix*, Nov. 18, 2003
Sly and the Family Stone: An Oral History, Joel Selvin, Simon &

TEXT SOURCES

Schuster, 2007
"Sly Stone's Heart of Darkness,"
  Edward Kiersh, *Spin*, Dec. 1985

TAPE 22
Where Are the Keys?
Interviews: Frank Hubach, David
  Hewitt, Kooster McAllister, DB
  Brown
Welcome to My Nightmare, Dave
  Thompson, Omnibus, 2012
"Why 1973 was the Greatest Year in
  Rock History," *Louder*,
  July 8, 2022

TAPE 23
Big Fan
Interviews: Chris Stone, Ron
  Nevison, Jim Keltner
"Ron Wood: Not Just Another Pretty
  Face," *Rolling Stone*, Judith Sims,
  Oct. 24, 1974
*George Harrison: Behind the
  Locked Door*, Graeme Thomson,
  Omnibus Press, 2016

TAPE 24
Abe & Eddie
Interviews: Jack Douglas, Arlene
  Reckson, Lori Burton, Jade
  Cicala, Bob Ezrin, May Pang,
  Paul Prestopino
*When Two Cents Was Money:
  A Memoir*, Abe Silverstein,
  iUniverse, 2013
Cornflakes with John Lennon, Robert
  Hilburn, Rodale Books, 2010
Trial By Ezrin
Interview: Bob Ezrin
*What You Want Is in the Limo:
  On the Road with Led Zeppelin,
  Alice Cooper, and The Who in
  1973, the Year the Sixties Died
  and the Modern Rock Star Was
  Born*, Michael Walker, Random
  House, 2013
Jimmy Shoes
Interviews: Shelly Yakus, Bob
  Ezrin, Jack Douglas, Jimmy
  Iovine
"Jimmy Iovine: The Man with the
  Magic Ears," David Fricke,
  Rolling Stone, Apr. 12, 2012
"LennoNYC," *American Masters
  Podcast*, Episode 5, Oct. 8, 2010

TAPE 25
Innervisions
Interviews: Malcolm Cecil, Robert
  Margouleff, Austin Godsey, Gary
  Olazabal, Phil Schier, Peter
  Chaikin, Chris Stone
"Recording Studio Opens in
  Sausalito," Kathie Staska &
  George Mangrun, *Hayward
  Daily Review*, Jan. 26, 1973
"The 40th Anniversary of the Stevie

Wonder Classic, *Innervisions*,"
  Chris Williams, *WaxPoetics*,
  Aug. 7, 2013
"Classic Tracks: Isley Brothers'
  'That Lady,'" Blair Jackson,
  Mix, Nov. 1, 2003
"Six Degrees of The Isley Brothers'
  3 + 3," Dave Epstein, Wondering
  Sound.com, Sept. 29, 2011
ARP 2600, VintageSynthExplorer.
  com
Lost Weekend
Interviews: May Pang, Lori Burton,
  Jimmy Iovine
"LennoNYC," *American Masters
  Podcast*, Episode 5, Oct. 8, 2010
Tear Down the Wall of Sound, Mick
  Brown, Alfred A. Knopf, 2007
"Jimmy Iovine: The Man with the
  Magic Ears," David Fricke,
  Rolling Stone, Apr. 12, 2012
John Lennon, *The Lost Lennon
  Tapes*, Elliot Mintz, Westwood
  One Radio, 1988
*Waiting for the Sun: A Rock 'n' Roll
  History of Los Angeles*, Barney
  Hoskyns, Hal Leonard Corp.,
  2009
"Classic Tracks: John Lennon
  'Whatever Gets You Thru The
  Night'," Richard Buskin, *Sound
  on Sound*, June 2009
Lousy Drunk
Interviews: Jimmy Iovine, Lori
  Burton, Jim Keltner, Phil Schier,
  Arlene Reckson
*Wall of Pain: The Biography of
  Phil Spector*, Dave Thompson,
  Omnibus, 2009
"John Lennon Letter to Phil
  Spector Going up for Auction,"
  UltimateClassicRock.com,
  Mar. 20, 2014
"Classic Tracks: John Lennon
  'Whatever Gets You Thru the
  Night'," Richard Buskin, *Sound
  on Sound*, June 2009
"LennoNYC," *American Masters
  Podcast*, Episode 5, Oct. 8, 2010
"Jimmy Iovine: The Man with the
  Magic Ears," David Fricke,
  Rolling Stone, Apr. 12, 2012
Ear Witnesses
Interviews: Chris Stone, Lee Kiefer,
  May Pang, Ed Freeman, Bob
  Merritt, Jim Keltner, Tom Flye
Wall of Pain, Dave Thompson,
  Omnibus, 2009
"John Lennon: Long Night's Journey
  Into Day," Pete Hamill, *Rolling
  Stone*, June 5, 1975
*Living the Beatles Legend: The
  Untold Story of Mal Evans*,
  Ken Womack, Dey Street Books,
  2023
Yellow Pages
Interviews: Tom Flye, Chris Stone

TAPE 26
The Minnesota Strip
Interviews: Joe Perry, Bob Ezrin,
  Jack Douglas, Jay Messina, Shelly
  Yakus
"Muscle of Love, a Shocking Course
  in Pop Sex," *Circus*, Jan. 1974,
  Steven Gaines
Welcome to My Nightmare, Dave
  Thompson, Omnibus, 2012
*Rocks: My Life in and out of
  Aerosmith*, Joe Perry, Simon &
  Schuster, 2014
*Times Square Law Enforcement
  Council 1974 Report*

TAPE 27
Buzz Me In, Gately
Interviews: Jack Douglas, Bob
  Ezrin, Al Kooper
"Hotel California," lyrics by Don
  Henley, Glenn Frey
Fireball
Interviews: Bill Szymczyk, Al
  Kooper, Joe Walsh, Peter Chaikin,
  Phil Schier, Chris Stone
"Birth of a Record: *Hotel California*,"
  with David Goggin,
  NAMM Convention, Jan. 21, 2016
*Backstage Passes & Backstabbing
  Bastards*, Al Kooper, Hal
  Leonard Corp., 1998
*Lynyrd Skynyrd: Remembering
  the Free Birds of Southern Rock*,
  Gene Odom, Crown, 2002
Fireball, VintageArcade.net
*Heaven and Hell: My Life in the
  Eagles*, Don Felder, John Wiley &
  Sons, 2008
Too Many Cooks
Interviews, Jim Keltner, Al Kooper,
  Danny Kortchmar, Chris Stone,
  Marta Kellgren
Lennon interviewed by Dennis
  Elsas, WNEW, Sept. 28, 1974
The Very Best of Mick Jagger, liner
  notes, WEA/Rhino, 2007
Jack Bruce: Composing Himself,
  Harry Shapiro, Jawbone Press,
  2009
A Toot and a Snore
Interviews: Jim Keltner, Gary
  Olazabal, Austin Godsey, Lee
  Kiefer, May Pang, Chris Stone
A Toot and a Snore in '74 (album
  bootleg), Mistral Music
Paul McCartney Cover Story, Brian
  Hiatt, *Rolling Stone*, Mar. 12, 2012
"Would You Like to Record It?" self-
  published by Michael Verdick
"Four Beatles Town," *Disc News*,
  Apr. 13, 1974
Loving John: The Untold Story, May
  Pang & Henry Edwards, 1983
"The last known recording of Lennon
  & McCartney: 'A Toot and a Snore
  in '74'," dangerousminds.net,

TEXT SOURCES

Feb. 13, 2014
Phil's Premonition
"John Lennon, The Final Interview,"
  BBC Radio 1, Dec. 6, 1980

TAPE 28
Locker Room Stink
Interviews: Shelly Yakus, Jack
  Douglas, Jimmy Iovine, David
  Thoener, Jim Keltner
"LennoNYC," *American Masters
  Podcast*, Episode 5, Oct. 8, 2010
"Classic Tracks: John Lennon
  'Whatever Gets You Thru the
  Night'," Richard Buskin, *Sound
  on Sound*, June 2009
"Jimmy Iovine: The Man with the
  Magic Ears," David Fricke,
  Rolling Stone, Apr. 12, 2012
"Two Questions About Lennon,"
  Al Aronowitz, *Rolling Stone*, Aug.
  29, 1974
"On the Road with Ringo," Ken
  Sharp, EricCarmen.com, 2001
"From J. Geils Band to Midnight
  Souvenirs," Terry Gross, *NPR
  Music Interview*, Apr. 12, 2010
Dennis Ferrante, Interviewed by
  John Seetoo, PSAudio.com
*John Lennon Live at the Record
  Plant*, July 13, 1974
"John Lennon, The Final Interview,"
  BBC Radio 1, Dec. 6, 1980
"David Thoener, Memoirs of a
  Family Man," Maureen Droney,
  Mix, Jan. 1, 2001

TAPE 29
Stevie Time
Interviews: Robert Margouleff,
  Malcolm Cecil, Chris Stone,
  Gary Olazabal
"How Stevie Wonder Overcame a
  Near Death Experience to Make
  Fulfillingness' First Finale,"
  Okay Player, Chris Williams,
  2020
"Classic Tracks, Minnie Riperton's
  'Lovin' You'," Gary Eskow, *Mix*,
  Feb. 1, 2008
"TONTO: The 50-Year Saga of the
  Synth Heard on Stevie Wonder
  Classics," Martin Porter & David
  Goggin, *Rolling Stone*, Nov. 13,
  2018

TAPE 30
Moon Landing
Interviews: Chris Stone, Michael
  Braunstein, Fran Hughes, Ken
  Womack
Dear Boy: The Life of Keith Moon,
  Tony Fletcher, Omnibus, 2010.
*Nilsson: The Life of a Singer-
  Songwriter*, Alyn Shipton,
  Oxford University Press, 2013
Shell Shocked: My Life with the

*Turtles, Flo and Eddie, and
  Frank Zappa, etc.*, Howard
  Kaylan & Jeff Tamarkin, Hal
  Leonard Corp., 2013
Mind Flyers
Interview: Chris Stone
"Tom Wilson: The Man Who Put
  Electricity into Bob Dylan,"
  Michael Watts, *Melody Maker*,
  Jan. 31, 1976
"Remembering Bob Dylan and
  Velvet Underground's Pioneering
  Producer," David Browne,
  Rolling Stone, Nov. 4, 2015
Tom Wilson speech,
  www.ProducerTomWilson.com

TAPE 31
Music and Fighting
Interviews: Stewart Levine,
  Chris Stone, Tom Scott, David
  Sonenberg
"B. B. King and Celia Cruz at the
  Zaire '74 music festival, seen in
  the documentary 'Soul Power'",
  New York Times, July 5, 2009
When We Were Kings, directed by
  Leon Gast, Polygram Filmed
  Entertainment, 1996
Soul Power, directed by Jeff Levy-
  Hinte, Sony Pictures Classics,
  2008
"The Pre-Rumble in the Jungle,"
  Jesse Drucker, *Wall Street
  Journal*, Sept. 3, 2008

TAPE 32
Hole in the Ground
Interviews: Chris Stone, Tom Flye,
  Tom Hidley
*Sly and the Family Stone: An Oral
  History*, Joel Selvin, Simon &
  Schuster, 2007
*Backstage Passes & Backstabbing
  Bastards*, Al Kooper, Hal
  Leonard Corp., 1998

TAPE 33
Interviews: Bill Szymczyk, Michael
  Braunstein
"The Eagles: One of These Nights,"
  michaelbraunstein.com
*Heaven and Hell: My Life in the
  Eagles*, Don Felder, John Wiley &
  Sons, 2008
Death to Analog
Interviews: Chris Stone, Bruce
  Hensel, Michael Braunstein, Tom
  Scott
"A Brief History of Eventide, (Pt. 1):
  Trailblazing Audio Effects of
  the 1970s and 1980s," T. Eldar,
  PerfectCircuit.com. Jan. 2022
"CBS-Stills in 1st Rock Digital Date,"
  Jim McCullaugh, *Billboard*, Feb.
  17, 1979
AES Convention Archive, AES

49th Convention, New York,
  NY, USA, Sept. 9-12, 1974

TAPE 34
Band of Motherfuckers
Interviews: Lori Burton, Bob Ezrin,
  John Hanti, May Pang, David
  Hewitt
Howard Cosell, "Speaking of
  Everything," *WABC Radio*,
  Oct. 6, 1974
LennoNYC *American Masters
  Podcast*, Episode 5, Oct. 8, 2010
"The Man with the Magic Ears,"
  David Fricke, *Rolling Stone*,
  Apr. 12, 2012
*Lennonology: Strange Days Indeed,
  a Scrapbook of Madness*, Chip
  Madinger, Scott Raile, Open
  Your Books, 2015
"Classic Tracks: John Lennon
  'Whatever Gets You Thru the
  Night'," Richard Buskin, *Sound
  on Sound*, June 2009
Instamatic Karma, May Pang, St.
  Martin's Press, 2008
Brilliant Imposter
Interviews: Jimmy Iovine, Brooks
  Arthur, Lori Burton, Dave Thoener
*Wings for Wheels: The Making of
  "Born to Run,"* 2005
Born to Run, Bruce Springsteen,
  Simon & Schuster, 2017
"Jimmy Iovine: The Man with the
  Magic Ears," David Fricke,
  Rolling Stone, Apr. 12, 2012
Born to Run studio sessions, Bruce
  Base Wiki, Nov. 20, 2010
"40 Years Ago: John Lennon Makes
  His Last Live Appearance," Nick
  DeRiso, UltimateClassicrock.com,
  Apr. 18, 2015
"David Thoener, Memoirs of a
  Family Man," Maureen Droney,
  Mix, Jan. 1, 2001
Walk This Way
Joe Perry, Jack Douglas, "Birth
  of a Record: *Toys in the Attic*,"
  interviewed by David Goggin at
  NAMM, June 2017

TAPE 35
Rooms for Rockers
Interviews: Cathy Callon, Tom
  Scott, Tom Flye, Chris Stone,
  Raechel Donahue
"Artists Lead Double Life," Michelle
  Zarin, *Billboard*, Sept. 26, 1981
Hobo Ken
Interviews: Chris Stone, Jimmy
  Robinson, Raechel Donahue
*Radio Waves, Life and Revolution
  on the FM Dial*, Jim Ladd, St.
  Martin's Press, 1991
Ken Roberts, *Sly and the Family
  Stone: An Oral History*, Joel
  Selvin, Simon & Schuster, 2007

TEXT SOURCES

"R.E.O. Speedwagon: The Band That Flies Together," Steven Rosen, *Circus*, Nov. 1974

"Bill Wyman Solo: Happier in The Stones Because I Have This Outside Freedom," Lita Eliscu, *Phonograph Record*, Mar. 1976

"About Paris," Bob Welch, bobwelch.com, June 8, 2011

TAPE 36
The Castle
Interviews: Chris Stone, Lee Kiefer, Jimmy Robinson

"The Source: The Untold Story of Father Yod and The Source Family," *Isis Aquarian*, Oct. 1, 2007

"Fairy Lady's Medieval Castle Still Turns Heads," *LA Times*, Cecilia Rasmussen, Apr. 2, 2006

The Big C
Interviews: Michael Braunstein, Ron Nevison, Jim Keltner, Chris Stone, Peter Chaikin, Jim Keltner

Hitman: Forty Years Making Music, Topping the Charts, and Winning Grammys, David Foster, Simon and Schuster, 2009

Kicks on Route 66
Interview: Chris Stone

"A Curious L.A. Hostelry Caters to the Music and the Macho in Rock Stars," Laura Stevenson, *People*, Aug. 11, 1975

The Book
Interviews Fran Hughes, Shelly Yakus, Ken Womack, Bob Merritt, Jimmy Robinson

J.W. Haymer, "Silverspoon the Greatest Band Nobody Heard," blog memoir

Living the Beatles Legend: The Untold Story of Mal Evans, Ken Womack, Dey Street Books, 2023

TAPE 37
Don't You Ever
Interviews: Bob Ezrin, Jay Messina

"The Oral History of Kiss' 'Destroyer': 'It's a Miracle We're Alive'," *Rolling Stone*, Kory Grow, Mar. 15, 2016

"Bob Ezrin Pts 1 & 2, Bob Lefsetz Podcast, June 2020

Shout it Out Loud; The Story of Kiss's Destroyer, the Making of an American Icon, James Campion, Backbeat Books, 2015

KISS: Behind the Mask, David Leaf & Ken Sharp, Grand Central Publishing, 2008

Face the Music: A Life Exposed, Paul Stanley, HarperCollins, 2014

TAPE 38
Tanks A Lot
Interviews: Chris Stone, Ed

Freeman, Al Kooper, Peter Slauson

Backstage Passes & Backstabbing Bastards, Al Kooper, Hal Leonard Corp., 1998

TAPE 39
Three Albums
Billboard, "Inside Track," Dec. 4, 1976

"Classic Tracks: Stevie Wonder 'Pastime Paradise'," Richard Buskin, *Sound on Sound*, Dec. 2007

"The Eagles' 'Hotel California': 10 Things You Didn't Know," Jordan Runtagh, *Rolling Stone*, Dec. 8, 2016

"Classic Tracks: The Eagles 'Hotel California'," Richard Buskin, *Sound on Sound*, Sept. 2010

"Fleetwood Mac's 'Rumours': 10 Things You Didn't Know," Jordan Runtagh, *Rolling Stone*, Feb. 3, 2017

"Fleetwood Mac, Rumours and Beyond," Larry Crane, *Tape Op*, July/Aug. 2013

"Stevie Wonder: The Greatest Creative Run in the History of Popular Music," Jack Hamilton, *Slate*, Dec. 19, 2016

Billboard 200 Number One Albums Chart History, 1976–77, Billboard.com

RIAA U.S. Sales Database, 1973–2021

Studio in the Key of Life
Interviews: Gary Olazabal, Robert Margouleff, Malcolm Cecil, Bruce Hensel, Peter Chaikin

"Rose of the Record Plant," Mr. Bonzai, *Mix*, Feb. 1985

"John Fischbach: Recording Stevie Wonder's *Songs in the Key of Life*," Larry Crane, Luther Russell, *TapeOp*, Jan./Feb. 2001

"Inside Stevie Wonder's Epic Magnum Opus *Songs in the Key of Life*," Jordan Runtagh, *Rolling Stone*, Sept. 28, 2016

Yamaha GX-1, *SynthMuseum.com*

"Classic Tracks: Stevie Wonder 'Pastime Paradise'," Richard Buskin, *Sound on Sound*, Dec. 2007

Rumours Mill
Interviews: Chris Stone, Ken Caillat, Cris Morris, Cathy Callon,

"Fleetwood Mac: 'Dreams'," Johnny Black, *Blender*, May 2005

"Are my ears going . . ." "Classic Tracks: Fleetwood Mac 'Go Your Own Way'," Richard Buskin, *Sound on Sound*, Aug. 2007

"Fleetwood Mac at the Record

Plant," compiled by Barbara Schultz, *Mix*, Oct. 1, 2007

Making Rumours: The Inside Story of the Classic Fleetwood Mac Album, Ken Caillat with Steven Stiefel, Wiley & Sons, 2012

Play On: Now, Then, and Fleetwood Mac: The Autobiography, Mick Fleetwood & Anthony Bozza, Little, Brown, 2014

"Eyewitness, the Recording of Fleetwood Mac's *Rumours*," Johnny Black, *Q*, May 1997

Check Out Time
Interviews: Jimmy Robinson, Michael Braunstein, Chris Stone, Bill Szymczyk, Devon Kellgren

"Home Away from Home Studio," *LA Times*, Oct. 11, 1975

"Don Henley, Eagles' Complete Discography: Don Henley Looks Back," David Browne, *Rolling Stone*, June 10, 2016

Don Henley, *60 Minutes*, Steve Kroft, 2002

Is it Six Yet?
Interviews: Bill Szymczyk and Joe Walsh

Birth of a Record, Hotel California, NAMM Convention 2016, with David Goggin

"Bill Szymczyk and Phasing," "Classic Tracks: The Eagles 'Hotel California'," Richard Buskin, *Sound on Sound*, Sept. 2010

"Behind the Song, 'Life in the Fast Lane'," Jason Scott, *American Songwriter*, 2019

Don Henley, *History of the Eagles*, documentary, Jigsaw Productions, 2013

TAPE 40
Where's Sly?
Interviews: Rob Fraboni, Cathy Callon, Tom Flye, Phil Ryan, Chris Stone, Pete Slauson

TAPE 41
The Long Ranger
Interviews: Chris Stone, David Hewitt

Audio Recording for Profit: The Sound of Money, Chris Stone with David Goggin, Focal Press, 2000

On the Road: Recording the Stars in a Golden Era of Live, David W. Hewitt, Backbeat Books, Nov. 2021

TAPE 42
Studio Tan
Interviews: Joe Travers, Michael Braunstein, Davey Moire, Chris Stone

Zappa: A Biography, Barry Miles, Grove Press, 2004

TEXT SOURCES

The Wiz
Interviews: Lee Kiefer, Ed Freeman, Chris Stone, Lucian K. Truscott IV
"Inside the Hotel California," by Lucian K. Truscott IV, *New Times*, Aug. 5, 1977
Zoned Out
Interviews: Chris Stone, Jimmy Robinson, Gloria Stone, Eddie Kramer
G-L-O-R-I-A
Interviews, Chris Stone, Gloria Stone, Samantha Stone, Al Kooper, Bill Szymczyk, Michael Braunstein
The Last Party
Interviews: Lucian K. Truscott IV, David Strick, Jimmy Robinson
"Inside the Hotel California," by Lucian K. Truscott IV, *New Times*, Aug. 5, 1977, editor, John Lombardi
"How Did Gary Kellgren Die," *Laurel Canyon: The Inside Story of Rock and Roil's Legendary Neighborhood*, Michael Walker, Macmillan, 2010
K-Hole
Interviews: Jim Keltner, Chris Stone, Robert Margouleff, Monti Rock III, Michael Braunstein, Loreana Wrench, Jimmy Robinson, Neil Hausman, Ray Corey, *Southland Crime Report, LA Times*, July 22, 1977
Art Garfunkel interview, *Rolling Stone*, June 3, 1976,
Ronnie: The Autobiography, Ronnie Wood, Macmillan, 2008
"Monti Wants to Rock You—Again," Dave Good, *San Diego Reader*, Nov. 4, 2011
"Johnny Depp's Hidden Castle," John Ponder, *West Hollywood History*, Oct. 2, 2022
"How Ketamine Went from the Battlefield to the Dancefloor," Sam Kelly, *Science*, Sept. 11, 2020

TAPE 43
Gary's Church
Interviews: Jim Keltner, Jimmy Robinson, Michael Braunstein
Fire & Rain
Interviews: Chris Stone, Nance McManus, Bob Edwards Gloria Stone
Gloria Stone, letter to her mother, Jan. 8, 1978
Backstage Passes & Backstabbing Bastards, Al Kooper, Hal Leonard Corp., 1998
"Rose of the Record Plant," Lunching with Bonzai, David Goggin, *Mix*, Feb. 1984
Goodbye, Little Rock and Roller, Marshall Chapman, St. Martins, 2011

TAPE 44
Where's Jimmy?
Interviews: Jimmy Iovine, Thom Panunzio, Shelly Yakus, Lori Burton, Frank Stefanko, John Hanti
Bruce Springsteen, *The Promise: The Making of Darkness on the Edge of Town*, directed by Thom Zinny, Thrill Hill Productions
Jimmy Iovine, *The 37th Annual Rock & Roll Hall of Fame Induction Ceremony,* Saturday, Nov. 5, 2022, Microsoft Theater in Los Angeles, CA
"In the Studio: An Interview with Legendary Engineer Shelly Yakus," Bruce Borgeson, Prosoundweb.com, Nov. 13, 2013
"New York '77, New Wave, Disco and the Yankees Ruled in the Year of Mix's Birth," Blair Jackson, *Mix*, Oct. 1, 2007
"Patti Smith: The Field Marshall on Portobello Road," Vivien Goldman, *Sounds*, Nov. 6, 1976
"Power of Three," *Goodnight L.A.*, Kent Hartman, Da Capo Press, 2017
Up on the Roof
Interviews: Frank Stefanko, Martyn Goddard
"Blondie in Camera," catalog, Mirandy Gallery, London
Classic Tracks: Blondie, "Hanging on the Telephone," Sound On Sound, Richard Buskin, June 2008

TAPE 45
Nanosecond in Time
Does the Noise in My Head Bother You?: A Rock 'N' Roll Memoir, Steven Tyler, HarperCollins, 2004
Rocks: My Life in and out of Aerosmith, Joe Perry, Simon & Schuster, 2014

TAPE 46
. . . But You Can Never Leave
Interviews: Jack Douglas, Arlene Reckson, Paul Prestopino, Steve Marcantonio, John Hanti, Thom Panunzio
"John Lennon: The Last Interview," *Rolling Stone*, Jonathan Cott, Dec. 23, 2010 (interview conducted Dec. 5, 1980)
John Lennon 1980: The Last Days in the Life, Kenneth Womack, Omnibus, 2020
Starting Over: The Making of John Lennon and Yoko Ono's Double Fantasy, Ken Sharp, MTV Books, 2010
"Record engineer recalls fun times

with Lennon," *Traverse City Record Eagle*, Dec. 12, 1988
"Willie Nile shares new details on the night John Lennon was killed," Willie Nile, Interview with WTOP, Jason Fraley, Mar. 30, 2017
The John Lennon Piano, *Sotheby's Auction Catalog*, June 24, 2014
Wall of Pain, Dave Thompson, Omnibus Press, 2009
"Eight Days in the Studio with John Lennon and Yoko Ono," *Nashville Public Television*, Nov. 18, 2010
"Classic Tracks: John Lennon and Yoko Ono's 'Watching the Wheels,'" Matt Hurwitz, *Mix*, Dec. 8, 2010
On the Road: Recording the Stars in a Golden Era of Live, David W. Hewitt, Backbeat Books, Nov. 2021

Epilogue
ThePlantNYC.com
Mix, Apr. 1, 2004
"Classic Tracks: Prince and the Revolution's 'Purple Rain,'" Dan Daley, *Mix*, Jan. 1, 2009
"A New Place to Score," *Millimeter*, May 1986
"The Day the Music Died," Rip Rense, *Mix*, Mar. 1986
"The Record Plant's Last Jam. Third Street Farewell," *Pro Sound News*, Feb. 7, 1986
"Chris Stone Departs LA Record Plant as Chrysalis Becomes Sole Owner," *Pro Sound News*, Sept. 1989
"The Record Plant is Growing," David Goggin, *Mix*, 1988
"Record Plant Co-Founder Chris Stone Dies at 81," *UltimateClassicRock.com*, Sept. 12, 2016
"Sausalito's historic Record Plant may rock 'n' roll again soon," Paul Liberatore, *Marin Independent Journal*, Nov. 5, 2020
"Call of the Wild: The Rise & Fall of the Record Plant Studio," Jim Welte, JimWelte.com, Jan. 8, 2010
If These Halls Could Talk: A Historical Tour through SF Recording Studios, Heather Johnson, Bookpatch, 2019
"Narcotics Agents Seize Studio," Maura Therman, *Marin Independent Journal*, Sept. 13, 1985
"Running the Record Plant in Sausalito," Richie Unterberger, *Into the Mix, KQED*, Nov. 21, 2016

374

Illustration Credits

Every effort has been made to locate and credit copyright holders of the material reproduced in this book. The author and publisher apologize for any omissions or errors, which can be corrected in future editions.

a = above, **b** = below, **c** = center, **l** = left, **r** = right

2 © Bob Gruen/www.BobGruen.com; **7** Photograph by David Strick, courtesy Redux Pictures; **10** Photograph by Willis Hogan Jr., courtesy of the Museum of Pop Culture (MoPop); **16** Courtesy John Townley Collection; **21a** Photograph by Charles Steiner / Getty Images; **21b** © Charles Steiner 1967; **26a** Photograph by Eddie Kramer, courtesy Eddie Kramer Archive; **26b** Photograph by Bettman Archives / Getty Images; **31** Courtesy Chris Stone Archive; **37** Photographs by Jay Good, courtesy Frank White Photo Agency; **48** Courtesy Chris Stone Archive; **51a** Photograph courtesy of Barry Feinstein Photography; **51b** Courtesy Chris Stone Archive; **67** Photo-reproductions by Heidi Antman; **74–75 a–b, l–r:** *White Light / White Heat*, the Velvet Underground, Verve, photograph: Billy Name, design concept: Andy Warhol, design: Acy Lehman; *We're Only in It for the Money*, Frank Zappa, Verve, photograph: Jerry Schatzberg, artwork: Cal Schenkel; *Lumpy Gravy*, Frank Zappa, Verve, artwork: Cal Schenkel, art direction: Frank Zappa; *Electric Ladyland*, Jimi Hendrix, Reprise, photograph: Karl Ferris, art direction: Ed Thrasher; *Traffic*, Traffic, Island, United Artists, photograph: Gered Mankowitz & Richard Polak, design: Jim Capaldi; *The Soft Machine*, The Soft Machine, ABC Probe, design: Byron Goto, Eli Allman & Henry Epstein; *The Fool*, The Fool, Mercury, artwork: Simon Posthuma & Marijke Koger-Dunham; *All the Friendly Colours*, Hedge & Donna, Capitol, photograph: Summerwind; "ABC," Jackson 5, Tamla Records (French edition); *Climbing!*, Mountain, Windfall Records, photograph: Gail Collins, art direction: Beverly Weinstein; *Band of Gypsys*, Jimi Hendrix, Capitol, photograph: Jan Blom, design: Vicktor Kahn; *Woodstock: music from the Original Soundtrack*, Cotillion Records, photograph: Burk Uzzle; *James Gang Rides Again*, James Gang, ABC records, design: Bob Lockhart; *Runt*, Todd Rundgren, Ampex, photo: Bruce Laurance, design: Bob Cato; *Chunga's Revenge*, Frank Zappa, Bizzare/Reprise, photograph: Phil Franks, design and illustrations: Cal Schenkel; *Indianola Mississippi Seeds*, B. B. King, ABC Records, photograph: Ivan Nagy, design: Robert Lockart; *We Got to Live Together*, Buddy Miles, Mercury, photograph: Burnell Caldwell, art direction: Des Strobel, design: Richard Germinaro; *Watcha Gonna Do*, Denny Doherty, Dunhill, photograph: Barry Feinstein & Philip Melnick, art direction: Tom Wilkes & Philip Melnick; *Dave Mason & Cass Elliot*, Dave Mason & Cass Elliot, Blue Thumb, photograph: Clive Arrowsmith; *Paper Airplanes*, Jimi Hendrix, Yellow Dog Records, design: based on original photo by Barry Wentel; *Funky Nothingness*, Frank Zappa, Zappa Records, photograph: John Williams, art direction & design: Michael Mesker; **76** Photograph by Henry Diltz, courtesy Henry Diltz; **88a** Photograph by Michael Ochs Archives/Getty Images; **88b** Courtesy Bob Margouleff; **104** Photographs courtesy of Barry Feinstein Photography; **107 a–b, l–r:** *Cry of Love*, Jimi Hendrix, Legacy, artwork: Nancy Reiner; *Who's Next*, The Who, Decca, photograph: Ethan Russell, art directions: John Kosh; *Labelle*, Patti Labelle, Warner Brothers Records, photograph: Bob Gruen, illustration: Arnold Skolnick; *Imagine*, John Lennon, Apple, artwork: Yoko Ono; *Fly*, Yoko Ono, Apple, artwork: John Lennon; *American Pie*, Don McLean, United Artists Records, photograph: George Whiteman; *Rainbow Bridge*, Jimi Hendrix, Reprise, photograph: Daniel Tahaney, design: The Pineal Playhouse; *Concert for Bangladesh*, George Harrison, Apple, photograph & design: Tom Wilkes & Barry Feinstein; *Nine to the Universe*, Jimi Hendrix, Reprise, art direction: Tim Ritchie; *Valleys of Neptune*, Jimi Hendrix, Legacy, photograph: Linda McCartney, artwork: Jimi Hendrix; *People, Hell and Angels*, Jimi Hendrix, Legacy, photograph: Gered Mankowitz, design: Phil Yarnall & Smay Design; *Both Sides of the Sky*, Jimi Hendrix, Legacy, photograph: Mike Berkofsky, design: Phil Yarnall & Smay Design; **108** © Bob Gruen/www.BobGruen.com; **112** All photographs courtesy Chris Stone Archives; **120** © Bob Gruen/www.BobGruen.com; **126a** Schematic courtesy John Storyk, illustration redrawn by Adrian Cartwright; **126b** Courtesy John Storyk; **137** Courtesy Chris Stone Archive; **144** Courtesy Chris Stone Archive; **149** Courtesy Chris Stone Archive; **152** Stevie Wonder performing 'Living For the City' at Record Plant, 1973, promotional footage; **159a** Courtesy Chris Stone Archive; **159b** Photograph by Michael Ochs Archive/Getty Images; **164** Courtesy Chris Stone Archive; **167al** Courtesy Chris Stone Archive; **167ar** Photograph by Michael Ochs Archives/Getty Images; **167b** Photograph by David Goggin, courtesy David Goggin; **182** Photographs by Richard Creamer/Michael Ochs Archives/Getty Images; **198** © Bob Gruen/www.BobGruen.com; **199a** © Bob Gruen/www.BobGruen.com; **199b** © Ron Pownall, courtesy Ron Pownall; **201a–b, l–r:** *Stephen Stills*, Stephen Stills, Atlantic, photograph: Henry Diltz, art direction: Gary Burden; *The Morning After*, The J. Geils Band, Atlantic, photograph: Stephen Paley, design: Sam Cooperstein; *Cold Spring Harbor*, Billy Joel, Family Productions, photograph: Jerry Abramowitz, art director: Irwin Mazur; *There's a Riot Going On*, Sly and the Family Stone, Epic, photograph: Stephen Paley, art director: John Berg; *Gonna Take a Miracle*, Laura Nyro & Patti LaBelle, Columbia, photograph: Stephen Paley, art direction: Gary Burden; *Something/Anything?*, Todd Rundgren, Bearsville, design concept: Todd Rundgren; *Music of My Mind*, Stevie Wonder, Tamla, photograph: Gaetano, artwork: Daniel Blumenau; *The Pope Smokes Dope*, David Peel & The Lower East Side, Nibelung Records, artwork: Jeffrey Levy, art direction: Robert L. Heimall; *Still Bill*, Bill Withers, Sussex Records, photograph: Hal Wilson, art direction: Maurer Productions & Michael Mendel; *Some Time in New York City*, John Lennon & Yoko Ono, Apple, sleeve design: Michael Gross, sleeve concept: John Lennon & Yoko Ono, cover concept: Allan Steckler, Cal Schenkel, John Lennon & Yoko Ono; *Elvis as Recorded at Madison Square Garden*, Elvis Presley, RCA Records, art direction: Roger Semon; *School's Out*, Alice Cooper, Warner Brothers Records,

375

ILLUSTRATION CREDITS

photograph: Robert Otter, design: Craig Braun; **202–203 a–b, l–r:** *Vol. 4*, Black Sabbath, Vertigo, photograph: Keith McMillan, design: Bloomsbury Group; *Talking Book*, Stevie Wonder, Tamla, photo: Robert Margouleff; *Homecoming*, America, Warner Brothers Records, photo: Henry Diltz, design: Gary Burden; *Elephant's Memory*, Elephant's Memory, Buddah Records, photograph: Peter Beard, design: Michael Gross; *Crazed Hipsters*, Finnigan & Wood, Blue Thumb, photograph: Charles Bush 7 Caryl Berle, design: Alan Sekuler & Ruby Mazur; *Approximately Infinite Universe*, Yoko Ono, Apple Records, photograph: Bob Gruen & Iain MacMillan; artwork: Bettina Rossner, John Lennon & Yoko Ono; *Life in a Tin Can*, Bee Gees, RSO Records, design & collage: David Larkham, cover concept: John Youssi; *Billion Dollar Babies*, Alice Cooper, Warner Brothers Records, photograph: David Bailey, art direction: Greg Allen & Hugh Brown; *Fresh*, Sly and the Family Stone, Epic Records, photograph: Richard Avedon, design: John Berg; *New York Dolls*, New York Dolls, Mercury, photograph: Toshi; *Innervisions*, Stevie Wonder, Tamla, illustration: Efram Wolff; *3+3*, Isley Brothers, T-Neck/Epic Records, photograph: Don Hunstein, design: Ed Lee; *Mind Game*, John Lennon, Apple Records, artwork: John Lennon; *Laid Back*, Gregg Allman, Capricorn Records, artwork: Abdul Mati Klarwein; *Wake of the Dead*, Grateful Dead, Grateful Dead, artwork: Rick Griffin; *Adventures of the Panama Red*, New Riders of the Purple Sage, Columbia, design: Toots And Toots, artwork: Lore and Chris; *Ridin' The Storm Out*, REO Speedwagon, Epic, photograph: Bob Jenkins, type & design: Jimmy Wachtel; *Rock 'n' Roll Animal*, Lou Reed, RCA Records, photograph: Dalrymple, art direction: Acy Lehman; *Kansas*, Kansas, Kirshner, artwork: John Steuart Curry, design: Ed Lee; *Get Your Wings*, Aerosmith, Columbia, art direction: Joel Zimmerman; *I've Got My Own Album to Do*, Ron Wood, Warner, photograph: Dick Polak; *Nightmares . . . and Other Tales*, The J. Geils Band, Atlantic, artwork: Jean Lagarrigue, design: Pam & Peter of AGI; *David Live*, David Bowie, RCA Records, photograph: Dagmar; *Rock 'n' Roll*, John Lennon, Capitol, photograph: Jurgen Vollmer, art direction & design: Roy Kohara; **204** Photograph by Fin Costello/Redferns; **207** Courtesy Chris Stone Archive; **210a** Photograph by Henry Diltz, courtesy Henry Diltz; **210b** Photograph by Tom Hill/WireImage; **221** Photographs by David Gahr/Getty Images); **224** © Bob Gruen/ www.BobGruen.com; **231a** Courtesy Brandon Wallis/National Music Centre; **231b** Courtesy Bob Margouleff; **236** Photograph by Jeffrey Mayer; **241** © Lynn Goldsmith; **256** © Yoko Ono Lennon; **264–265 a–b, l–r:** *On the Border*, the Eagles, Asylum, artwork: Beatian Yazz, art direction & design: Gary Burden & R. Twerk & Company; *Second Helping*, Lynyrd Skynyrd, Sounds of the South / MCA, illustration: Jan Salerno; *Fulfillingness' First Finale*, Stevie Wonder, Tamla, design & illustration: Bob Gleason; *Small Talk*, Sly and the Family Stone, Epic, photograph: Norman Seeff, design: John berg & John Van Hamersveld; *Pussy Cats*, Harry Nilsson, RCA Records, art direction: Acy Lehman; *Walls and Bridges*, John Lennon, Apple Records, photograph: Bob Gruen, art direction: Roy Kohara; *Souvenirs*, Dan Fogelberg, Full Moon / Epic Records, photograph: Henry Diltz, art direction & design: Gary Burden; *John Dawson Winter III*, Johnny Winter, Blue Sky Records, photograph: Richard Noble, design: Teresa Alfieri; *Rufusized*, Chaka Khan & Rufus, ABC Records, photograph: Norman Seeff, design: Earl Klasky; *Zaire '74*, production: Hugh Masekela & Stewart Levine; *Phantoms of Paradise*, Paul Williams, artwork: John Alvin & Anthony Goldschmidt Graphic Design Ltd., art direction: Roland Young; *Young Americans*, David Bowie, RCA Records, photograph: Eric Stephen Jacobs; *Two Sides of the Moon*, Keith Moon, MCA/Polydor, photograph: Jim McCrary & Robert Failla, artwork [cover concept]: Bruce Reiley, Gary Stromberg, John, Keith & Skip; art direction: George Osaki; *Toys in the Attict*, Aerosmith, Columbia, illustration: Ingrid Haenke, design: Pacific Eye & Ear; *One of These Nights*, the Eagles, Asylum, photograph: Tom Kelley, art direction & design: Gary Burden; "Lyin' Eyes," the Eagles, Asylum; *One Size Fits All*, Frank Zappa. DiscReet, design: Cal Schenkel; *Born to Run*, Bruce Springsteen, Columbia, photograph: Eric Meola, design: Andy Engel & John Berg; *Stone Alone*, Bill Wyman, Rolling Stones Records, photograph: Bill King, cover concept: Pierre LaRoche; *A Star is Born*, Barbra Streisand & Kris Kristofferson, photograph: Francesco Scavullo, art direction: Seiniger and Associates; *A Toot and a Snore*, John Lennon & Paul McCartney, Mistral Music, designer: unknown. Cover based on *Revolver*, the back cover of *Imagine*, and the 1979 compilation album *The Songs Lennon and McCartney Gave Away*; **266** Photograph by Richard E. Aaron/Redferns; **272a** courtesy Chris Stone Archive; **272b** Photograph by Bruce Steinberg/Getty Images; **276–277** The Regents of the University of California, licensed under a Creative Commons Attribution 4.0 International License; **282** Photographs by Elyse Lewin; **289a** Photograph by Fin Costello/Redferns; **289b** © Bob Gruen/www.BobGruen.com; **301** Photographs by Herbie Worthington III, Courtesy of Ken Caillat; **320** Courtesy of Michael Braunstein; **328a** Photograph by David Strick, courtesy Redux Pictures; **328b** photographer unknown; **331** Contact sheet by David Strick, courtesy Redux Pictures; **337 a–b, l–r:** *I Can Stand a Little Rain*, Joe Cocker, A&M Records, photograph: Steve Vaughan, design: Chuck Beeson, art direction: Roland Young; "You Are So Beautiful," Joe Cocker, A&M Records, photograph: Steve Vaughan; *Hearts*, America, Warner Brothers Records, photograph: Henry Diltz, art direction & design: Gary Burden; *The Tubes*, The Tubes, A&M Records, photograph: Harry Mittman, design: Michael Cotton & Prairie Prince, art direction: Roland Young; *Kiss Alive!*, KISS, Casablanca Records, photograph: Fin Costello, design Dennis Woloch; *Don't Fear The Reaper*, Blue Öyster Cult, Columbia, *Bongo Fury*, Frank Zappa, DiscReet Records, photograph: John Williams, design Cal Schenkel; *Lazy Afternoon*, Barbra Streisand, Columbia Records, photograph: Steve Schapiro, design: Nancy Donald; *Nighthawks at the Diner*, Tom Waits, Asylum Records, photograph: Norman Seeff, design: Cal Schenkel; *High on You*, Sly Stone, Epic Records, photograph & art direction: Herbie Greene, design Andy Egel & John Berg; *Rufus featuring Chaka Khan*, Rufus & Chaka Khan, ABC, design: Bill Naegels & Rod Dyer, illustration: Bill Imhoff; *Pablo Cruise*, Pablo Cruise, A&M Records, design: Junie Osaki, illustration: Charlie Wild, art direction: Roland Young; **338–339 a–b, l–r:** *New Riders*, New Riders of the Purple Sage, Columbia, design: Rod Dyer, art direction: George Osaki; *Paris*, Paris, Capitol, art direction: Roy Kohara; *Attitudes*, Attitudes, Dark Horse Records, art direction: Fabio Nicoli, artwork: Nick Marshall; *Destroyer*, KISS, Casablanca, design: Dennis Woloch, artwork: Ken Kelly; *Cry Tough*, Nils Lofgren, A&M Records, photograph & design: Ed Caraeff; *Rocks*, Aerosmith, Columbia Records, photograph: Scott

ILLUSTRATION CREDITS

Enyart, design: Pacific Eye & Ear; *Good Singin' Good Playin'*, Grand Funk Railroad, MCA Records, photograph: Gary Heery & Norman Seeff, art direction: George Osaki; *Songs in the Key of Life*, Stevie Wonder, Tamla / Motown Records, art direction: Curtis McNair; *Radio Ethiopia*, Patti Smith, Arista Records, photograph: Judy Linn, design: Nancy Greenberg & Patti Smith; *Hotel California*, the Eagles, Asylum Records, photograph: David Alexander, art direction: John Kosh; *Cheap Trick*, Cheap Trick, Epic Records, photograph: Jim Houghton, design: Paula Scher; *Rumours*, Fleetwood Mac, Warner Brothers Records, photograph: Herbert Worthington, design: Desmond Strobel, lettering: Larry Vigon; *On Earth as it is in Heaven*, Angel, Casablanca Records / Mercury, photograph: David Alexander, design concept: David Joseph & Susan Munao, artwork: (Angel Logotype) Bob Petrick; *A Period of Transition*, Van Morrison, Warner Brothers Records, photograph: Ken McGowan, art direction & design: Mike Doud & AGI Hollywood, design concept: Van Morrison; *CSN*, Crosby, Stills & Nash, Atlantic Records, photograph: Joel Bernstein, art direction & design: Gary Burden & R. Twerk & Co.; *A Piece of the Rock*, Monti Rock III, Everest Records Archive Of Folk & Jazz Music, photograph: Sharon Weisz, design: Paul Gross; *Bat out of Hell*, Meat Loaf, Cleveland International / Epic Records, cover concept: Jim Steinman, design: Ed Lee, artwork Richard Corben; *Broken Blossom*, Bette Midler, Atlantic Records, photograph: George Hurrell, design: Bob Defrin; *Running on Empty*, Jackson Browne, Asylum Records, art direction & design: Jimmy Wachtel; *Live in New York*, Frank Zappa, DiscReet Records, photograph: Dweezil Zappa; *Studio Tan* Frank Zappa, DiscReet Records, art direction: John Cabalka, design: Rod Dyer & Vartan, illustration: Gary Panter; *Hot Rats III / Sleep Dirt* , Frank Zappa, DiscReet Records, art direction: John Cabalka, illustration: Gary Panter; *Orchestral Favorites*, Frank Zappa, DiscReet Records, art direction: Rick Serrini, design & illustration Gary Panter; *Bruce Springsteen & the E Street Band Live 1975–1985*, Bruce Springsteen & the E Street Band, Columbia Records, photograph: Neal Preston, art direction: Sandra Choron; **340** Photograph by Martyn Goddard, courtesy Martyn Goddard; **344** Courtesy Chris Stone Archive; **350** Photographs by Frank Stefanko, courtesy Frank Stefanko; **351a** © Lynn Goldsmith; **351b** Photograph by Frank Stefanko, courtesy Frank Stefanko; **355a** Photo by Roberta Bayley/Redferns; **355b** Photograph by Martyn Goddard, courtesy Martyn Goddard; **357** Photographs by Henry Diltz, courtesy Henry Diltz; **362a** Photograph by Allan Tannenbaum, courtesy Allan Tannembaum; **362b** © Bob Gruen/www.BobGruen.com; **366–367 a–b, l–r:** *Eddie Money*, Eddie Money, Wolfgang, Columbia Records, photograph: Gary Heery, design concept: Mick Brigden, design Tommy Steele; *A Song*, Neil Sedaka, Elektra Records, photograph: Bill King, art direction & design: Tony Lane; *Street Hassle*, Lou Reed, Arista Records, *Easter*, Patti Smith, Arista Records, photograph: Lynn Goldsmith; *For You*, Prince, Warner Brothers Records, photograph: Joe Giannetti, art direction: Jeff Farmakes, design: Prince; *Heaven Tonight*, Cheap Trick, Epic Records, photograph: Reid Miles, design: Jim Charne & Paula Scher; *Darkness on the Edge of Town*, Bruce Springsteen, Columbia Records, photograph: Frank Stefanko; *Parallel Lines*, Blondie, Chrysalis Records, photograph: Edo Bertoglio, art direction & design Ramey Communications, lettering: Jerry Rodriguez; *Thoroughfare Gap*, Stephen Stills, Columbia Records, photograph: Jim McCrary, design John Berg & Stephen Stills; *Jaded Virgin*, Marshall Chapman, Epic Records, photograph: Bill King, design: Ed Lee & Phyllis H.B.; *Bloodbrothers*, Dictators, Asylum Records, photograph: Chris Callis, art direction: Johnny Lee & The Dictators; *Come Together*, Aerosmith, Columbia Records; *Damn the Torpedoes*, Tom Petty and the Heartbreakers, Backstreet Records / MCA Records, photograph: Glen Christensen, art direction: Tommy Steele; *Willie Nile*, Willie Nile, Arista Records, photograph: Christine Olympia Rodin, art direction: Ron Kellum; *Double Fantasy*, John Lennon & Yoko Ono, Geffen Records, photograph: Kishin Shinoyama, art direction: John Lennon & Yoko Ono artwork art hotel: Christopher Whorf; "Walking on Thin Ice," John Lennon & Yoko Ono, artwork art hotel: Christopher Whorf; "Watching the Wheels," John Lennon & Yoko Ono, photograph: Paul Goresh; *She's So Unusual*, Cyndi Lauper, Portrait, photograph: Annie Liebovitz, art direction, design concept & design: Janet Perr; *Sports*, Huey Lewis and the News, Chrysalis, artwork: Bennett Hall, design: Bunny Zaruba; "Purple Rain," Prince, photograph: Ron Slenzak, Ed Thrasher & Associates, art direction: Prince, design: Laura LiPuma; *Load*, Metallica, artwork: Andres Serrano, design Andie Airfix; *Supernatural*, Santana, Arista, art direction: Carlos Santana & Su. Suttle; *Palace Theater, Albany, 1977*, Bruce Springsteen and the E Street Band, photograph: David Gahr, design: Michelle Holme; *Lemonade*, Beyoncé, Parkwood / Colombia, photograph: frame from the music video for "Don't Hurt Yourself."

Index

Illustrations are in **bold**.

A

A&M 103, 184, 187–9, 279, 353
A&R Recording 57, 58, 174, 259
Abaddon 25
ABC/Dunhill Records 50, 52
Adams, Jack 36, 53–4, 61, 81, 82, 84, 284
Adler, Lou 184, 186
Aerosmith: "Come Together" 358, **366**; *Get Your Wings* 194–9, **203**; live recordings 163; *Rocks* **338**; *Toys in the Attic* 254, 262–3, **265**; "Walk This Way" 262–3
Africa concerts 238–9
air hockey 297–9
Ali, Muhammad 125, 238
Alice Cooper (band). *See* Cooper, Alice
All the Friendly Colours (Hedge & Donna) **74**
Allen, Rustee **159**
Allman, Gregg **203**
America (band) **202**, **357**; *Hearts* **337**, 358; "Ventura Highway" 128
Ampex 106, 113, 133–4, 250
Angel **339**
Animals 40; "The House of the Rising Sun" 89
Apostolic Studios, Greenwich Village 15, **16**
Appel, Mike 348
Apple Records 92, 93, 142, 233
Aronowitz, Al 225
Arthur, Brooks 259
Ascher, Ken 223, 252
Atlantic Studios 348
Attitudes 279, **338**
Automatic Double Tracking (ADT) 98
Azoff, Irving 209, 211

B

Badfinger 233
Baez, Joan **26**
The Band 100
Band of Motherfuckers (BOMF) 257
Beach Boys 63–4; *Pet Sounds* 14
Bearsville Studios 134
Beatles 68, 96, 165–6; *Sgt. Pepper's Lonely Hearts Club Band* 14, 20, 356–8
Beats headphones 175, 188
Beck, Jeff 24, 151
Bee Gees **201**, 249
Bergeron, Victor 14
Beverly Hills Hotel 79, 304
Beyoncé 365; **367**
Bittan, Roy 261
Black Sabbath 139, **202**
Black Truck 165

Blondie **355**; *Parallel Lines* 354–6, **366**
Blood, Sweat & Tears 163
Bloodbrothers (The Dictators) 349, **366**
Blue Öyster Cult **367**, 352
Bond, Angelo 213
Bongiovi, Tony 349
Boone, Pat 89–90
bootleg recordings 39–40, 216–18, **265**
Bowie, David 166, 237, 250, 254, **264**; *David (Bowie) Live* 163, **203**
Braunstein, Michael 110, 235, 248, 251, 278, 305, 315, **320**, 333–5
Brewer, Don **320**
Bronstein, Stan 121
Brown, David "DB" 315
Browne, Jackson **339**
Brown, James 125, 237, 238, 239, **241**
Bruce, Jack 213
Buckingham, Lindsey 299
Burdon, Eric 42; "Sky Pilot" 32, 33
Burton, Lori 56–7, 58, 81, 171, 183–5, 186, 187, 255, 259, 352–3

C

Caillat, Ken 299, 300, 302, 303
Calbi, Greg 226, 261, 353
Cale, John 19
Callon, Cathy 269, 310–13
Capitol Records 94
Caribou Ranch 134
Carmen, Eric 222
Casady, Jack 34
Castle development and residence 274–5, 303, 307, 319, 323–5, **328**, 330–2
CBS Records 179, 279
Cecil, Malcolm: background 89–90; images of **88**, **152**; *Innervisions* (Wonder) 178–9; Isley Brothers 179–80; *Talking Book* (Wonder) 150–1; TONTO 87, **88**, 89, 297; Wonder master tapes 128, 150, 229–30; Wonder sessions 124–5
Chad Mitchell Trio 84
Chaikin, Peter 212, 227–8
Chandler, Chas 35
Chapman, Marshall 343, 345, 346, **366**
Chapman, Mike 354, 356
charity concerts 92, 93, 99–100, 142
Cheap Trick **338**, 346, **366**
"Cherry, Cherry" (Diamond) 33
Chrysalis Records 358, 366
Ciao! Manhattan (film) 85
Cicala, Jade 171, 186
Cicala, Roy: background 36, 56–7; Brazil 365, 366; character 360; *Concert for Bangladesh* album 101; death of Hendrix 72; divorce 360; family 171, 183–4, 220; hires Iovine 174–5; images of **120**, **362**; learns about RP S 122; Lennon and Ono sessions 95, 96–8, 99, 117, 118, 119–22;

Lennon sessions 183, 184–6, 187, 223, 225–6, 252–4, 258; RP NY management 84, 130–1; RP NY ownership 131–2, 143, 169–70, 220, 254–5, 352–3, 360, 364; working methods 57–8, 59–60, 85, 121
Clapton, Eric 38, 102, 103, 249
Clemons, Clarence 261
Cocker, Joe 312, 313; "You're So Beautiful [to Me]" **337**, 269
Cohen, Herb 319
Columbia Records 85–6, 195
Concert for Bangladesh (Harrison) 92, 93, 99–105, **107**, 160, 200
Cooper, Alice: *Billion Dollar Babies* 161, 163, 172, 175, **202**, 287; Hollywood Vampires **182**, 206; images of **182**; *Muscle of Love* 195; *School's Out* 131, 160, 172, **201**, 287
Corey, Ray 335–6
Cosby, Bill 125
Coury, Al 223
Creedence Clearwater Revival 115
Crenshaw, Marshall 78
Criss, Peter **289**
Criteria Studios 134, 249, 273, 306, 309
Crosby, David 63–4, 114
Crosby, Stills, Nash (CSN) 317; *CSN* **339**
Crosby, Stills, Nash & Young (CSNY) 63–4; "Find the Cost of Freedom" 64; "Ohio" 63–4
Crystal Recording Studios 124, 296–7
Curtis, King 98

D

Daltrey, Roger 83
Damn the Torpedoes (Petty) 353, **367**
Dashut, Richard 299
Dave Mason & Cass Elliot **75**
Davis, Clive 140, 158, 179, 200, 245
Davis, Jesse Ed 185–7, 216, 223, **224**, 252
Davis, Miles 40
Davis, Patti 248
Diamond, Neil 33
Dick Charles Recording 33, 105
The Dictators 349, **366**
digital recording 250–1, 322
DIR Broadcasting 162
Dire Straits 353
Doherty, Denny **75**
Dolby 130, 132
Dolenz, Micky **182**, 206
Donahue, Raechel 113–14, 116, 138
Donahue, Tom 113–16, 142, 145, 155, 256, 279
"Don't Bogart Me" (Fraternity of Man) 27
Douglas, Jack: Aerosmith sessions 194–200, 254, 262–3, 358; Alice

378

INDEX

Cooper sessions 175; Hendrix sessions 61; hires Hubach 161; images of **199**; Joel sessions 106; joins RP 36, 58–9; Lennon and Ono sessions 95–8, 123, 141, 171, 359–61, 363–4; New York Dolls sessions 173, 175; *Who's Next* recording sessions 81–4

Douma, Lillian Davis 68, 71, 94, 101

Dowd, Tom 211

drugs at RP 35, 59, 69, 86, 105, 111, 123, 154, 155, 212, 271, 279, 290, 291–2, 300, 310–13

drum machines 79

Dunbar, Ronald 213

Dylan, Bob 18, 29, **76**, 102, 117; *Bringing It All Back Home* 17

E

Eagles: *Barnstorm* 209; *On the Border* 208, 209–12, **210**, **264**; "Hotel California" 208, 303–6; *Hotel California* 294, 303–4, 306, 307–10, **338**; "Life in the Fast Lane" 34, 307, 308–9; *One of These Nights* 247–50, **265**; pinball machine 213; "Tequila Sunrise" 114; *Their Greatest Hits* 294–5

earthquakes 125

Edwards, Bob 344

Electric Lady Studios 40–1, 56, 60, 71–2, 73, 124, 254

Elephant's Memory 117, 118, 119–21, 141, 142, **202**

Elliot, Cass **75**

Elvira 342

Emerick, Geoff **357**

EMI 98, 184

Entourage restaurant, Los Angeles 236

Epic Records 140, 158

Errico, Greg 79

Estrada, Roy **21**

Evans, Mal: background 143; death 285; Lennon and McCartney session 216, 217; Moon sessions 232–3; relationship with Hughes 166, 284–5; Spector gun 190, 192

Eventide 122, 250

Everly Brothers 24

Ezrin, Bob: Alice Cooper sessions 131, 160, 172–3, 174–5; character 174–5, 287; Germano relationship 171, 255; images of **289**; KISS sessions 286–91; recommends Douglas 194

F

False Start (Love) 62

Fantasy Records 115

Farrell, Wes 66–8

Felder, Don 212, 248, 304, 306, 308

Feldman, Marty 263

Ferrante, Dennis 97, 118–19, 222

Finnigan & Wood **202**

fire extinguishers 59–60

Fireball pinball machine **207**, 208, 213

Fischbach, John 296–7

Fleetwood Mac 24, 271; *Rumours* 294, 295, 299–303, **338**

Fleetwood, Mick 267, 299, 302

Flo & Eddie 232, 233

Flye, Tom: *Concert for Bangladesh* tapes 103; hired for RP S 122, 140, 154–5; Lothar and the Hand People 84–5; McLean sessions 80, 86–7; RP S drugs bust 311–12; Stone police raid 192–3; Stone sessions 156–8, 244, 246; Woodstock tapes 102–3

Flying Burrito Brothers 46

Fogelberg, Dan 209, 247, **264**

The Fool 68, **74**

Foreman, George 238, 239

Foster, David 168, 232, 268–9

Fraboni, Rob 310–13

Frampton, Peter 162, 314

Fraternity of Man 27

Freeman, Ed 85–7, 190–1, 291–2, 321

Frehley, Ace **289**

Frey, Glenn 213, 295, 305, 308–9

Frost, Craig **320**

G

Gaines, Kristianne 9, 322, 332–6

Galesi Estate 160–1

Gately, Michael 206, **207**, 208, 248, 303

Geffen, David 364

Germano, Eddie 170, 171–2, 174–5, 220, 254–7

Ginsberg, Allen 117

Gitomer, Phil 315

Goddard, Martyn 354

Godsey, Austin 216

Goffin, Gerry 33

Gonna Take a Miracle (Nyro & LaBelle) 117, **201**

Good Singin,' Good Playin' (Grand Funk Railroad) 317, **338**

Gordon, Robert 349

Gordy, Berry 68, 124, 150, 275

Grade, Lew 257

Graham, Bill 115

Grand Funk Railroad 317, **338**

Grateful Dead **203**

GREED 65–6, **67**, 93

Greenwich, Ellie 173–4

groupies 111

Gruen, Bob 361

H

Hair (musical) 28, 30–2

Halverson, Bill 64

Hamill, Pete 192

Hamilton, George 30, **31**

Hardin, Tim 85

Harrison, George: "Bangla Desh" 94; borrowing Kellgren's car 66;

Concert for Bangladesh 91, 92, 93, 99–105, **104**, **107**, 160, 200; "Deep Blue" 94; "Far East Man" (Harrison & Wood) 166; home studio 166; images of **76**, **104**; *Living in the Material World* 166, 168; not at RP NY opening party 30; Sausalito 268–9; TONTO 128

Harry, Debbie **340**, 354, **355**

Hausman, Neil 334, 335

Haymer, J.W. 285

Hearst, Patty 250

Hefner, Hugh 44

Heider, Wally 92, 93–4, 115, 141, 302

Hellfire Club 55, 111

Hendrix, Jimi: "All Along the Watchtower" (cover) 28, 36; *Band of Gypsys* **74**; bootleg recordings 39–40; "Burning of the Midnight Lamp" 27; death 72; Electric Ladyland party 72; *Electric Ladyland* 6, 5, 35–6, **74**; first visit to RP NY 27–9; images of **10**, **26**, **37**; invitation to RP LA opening party 46–7; last RP NY session 63; leaves RP 71; *Paper Airplanes* **75**; posthumous albums **107**; The Scene jam sessions 24; studio costs 39, 40, 47, 56, 60, 71; "Star-Spangled Banner" (cover) 24–5, 47, 62–3; visits RP LA 62; "Voodoo Chile" 35–6, 215; work with Kramer 34–5

Henley, Don 295, 304, 308, 309

Hensel, Bruce 298

Hewitt, David 163, 257, 314–15

Hidley, Tom: background 57, 316; hires Cecil 90; RP LA design 44–5, 69–70; RP NY renovation 55, 70; RP S design 145; speaker designs 42–3, 50–2

Hit Factory 33, 130, 255–7, 296, 359–60

Holland, Dave 39

Hollywood Vampires **182**, 185, 206

Hopkins, Nicky 223

Howe, Bones 278

Hubach, Frank 161, 162, 163

Huey Lewis and the News 365, **367**

Hughes, Bob/Bobby 36, 106, 284

Hughes, Fran 36, 71, **144**, 166, 233, 283–4

I

Interscope Records 175, 353

Iovine, Jimmy "Shoes": Alice Cooper sessions 175–6; background 173–4; images of **351**; Lennon sessions 184–6, 188, 225, 253; Petty sessions 353; Smith sessions 347–8, 349–52; Springsteen sessions 259–62, 347–9

Isley Brothers: "That Lady" 128, 179; *3+3* 180, **202**

"Itchycoo Park" (Small Faces) 33

379

INDEX

J

J. Geils Band 50, 163, **201**, **203**, 307

Jackson 5 66; "ABC" 124

Jackson, Michael 150, 228, **231**, 296

Jagger, Mick 45, **120**, 141, 166; "Too Many Cooks (Spoil the Soup)" 213–15

James Gang 49–50, **74**

James, Rick 366

James, Tommy 106

Jasper, Chris 180

Jenkins, Arthur 252

Jett, Joan 354

Joel, Billy 66, 83, 125; *Cold Spring Harbor* 105–6, **201**

Johansen, David 263

John, Elton **224**, 225, 254

Johns, Andy **344**

Johns, Glyn 86, 209, 211

Johnson, Ben 15

Johnson Brothers 150

Jones, Quincy 150, 187

Jones, Tom **362**

Joplin, Janis 114

K

Kama Sutra Records 66

Kansas **203**

Kapralik, David 78–80, 140

Kaylan, Howard 111, 232, 233

Kellgren, Devon 111, 305

Kellgren, Gary: accident 138, 139, 141; analog switch to digital 250–1; appearance 23, 29, 329; background 23–4; Beatles and Stevie Wonder bookings 91, 92–3; buys Ancky's LA house 138; car and license plate 65–6, **67**, 93, 132, 134, 324, 327; Castle idea and residence 274–5, 303, 307, 319, 323–5, **328**, 330–2; character 22, 43, 54, 68, 69, 153, 243–4, 319, 322–7; children 111, 322; *Concert for Bangladesh* album 101, 102–3; deal with Roberts 273, 323, 325, 326, 327; death 9, 332–6, 342–3; first meets Stone 12–13, 14–15; first visit LA 43; founding of Record Plant 6; Gary's Book 303; images of **1**, 31, **31**, **37**, **51**, **144**, **328**, **331**; Jagger super-session 215; Jim Keltner Fan Club Hour 168, 216; Joel sessions 105–6; kidney stone 332; Mayfair Studios work 18–20, 22, 24–5, 27–8; move to LA 55, 66; relationship with Hendrix 38, 39, 73; RP LA design requirements 42–3, 44–6, 49, 69–70, 111; RP LA opening party 47; RP NY opening party 29–32; RP NY sale 41; RP S design requirements 122, 134, 146–7; RP S proposal 113–15, 116, 132–3, 136–8; Sly Stone sessions 243, 245–6; Spector gun 189; Truscott interview 8–9, 327,

329, 343; visits London 165–6; Warner Bros. meetings 54–5; working methods 20, 22, 32–4, 68, 69, 138, 139, 150, 319, 321–2; Zappa relationship 330; Zappa sessions 318

Kellgren, Mark 111

Kellgren, Marta: employed at American Airlines 43; friendship with Gloria Stone 12; Gary's accident and aftermath 138, 139; Gary's death 334–5; images of **31**; Jagger super-session 214; move to LA 55; names Record Plant 25–7; opinion on Gary's car 66; receives Harrison call 92

Kellgren, Aleda Michelle 44, 73

Keltner, Jim: Harrison sessions 94; house band 168; images of **167**, **224**; Jagger super-session 213, 215; Kellgren's death 333, 342; Lennon and McCartney session 217–18; Lennon sessions 187–8, 223, 252; Spector gun 190

Keys, Bobby 213, 223, 232

Khan, Chaka **337**; *Rufusized* (Rufus and Chaka Khan), **264**; "Tell Me Something Good" (Rufus and Chaka Khan) 128

Kiefer, Lee 49, 106, 111, 138, 148, 189

King, B. B. 50, **51**; *Indianola Mississippi Seeds* 52, **75**

King Biscuit Flower Hour 162, 163

King, Carole 52, 213; *Tapestry* 85, 184 "The Locomotion" (Goffin & King) 33

King, Deni 284

King, Don 284

KISS 314, **338**; *Destroyer* 286–91, **337**

Kooper, Al: images of **210**, **344**; Jacuzzi sessions 110, 236; Jagger super-session 213; Lynyrd Skynyrd sessions 208, 212; name mixup 131; New York studio scene in 60s 25; nitrous oxide 292–3; RP LA fire 343, 346; Stone sessions 246

Kortchmar, Danny "Kootch" 168, 213–14, 232, 279

Kramer, Eddie 34–5, 36, 40, 61, 68, 85, 323–4

Krebs, David 195

Krepps, Clair 18, 24–5, 41

Kristofferson, Kris: *A Star is Born* (Streisand & Kristofferson) **265**

KROQ 273

KSAN radio station 115–16, 155, 158

Kunkel, Russ 52

L

LaBelle, Patti 81, 82, **107**, 117, **201**

Ladd, Jim 113–15

Ladinsky, Gary 212

Lambert, Kit 82, 83

Landau, Jon 258, 259, 261, 348, 349, **351**

Lauper, Cyndi 366, **369**

Leadon, Bernie 248–9, 308

Leber, Steve 194

Lee, Arthur 62

Lefsetz, Bob 287

Lennon, John: Abbey Road 33; *A Toot and a Snore in '74* (Lennon & McCartney bootleg) 216–18, **265**; birth of Sean 258; death 258, 363–4; *Double Fantasy* (Lennon & Ono) 95, 258, 359–61, **367**; FBI investigations 123, 142; "Happy Xmas (War is Over)" 119; images of **2**, **108**, **120**, **182**, **221**, **224**, **256**, **362**; "Imagine" 91, 94; *Imagine* 95–9, **107**, 358; invitation to RP S opening party 143, 145, 147–8; Jagger super-session 214–15; last RP session with McCartney 216–18, **265**; live performance recording 141; meets Stevie Wonder 181; *Mind Games* 176, 183, **203**; moves to Hit Factory 258; *The One-to-One Concert* 142; pianos 68, 83, 222–3, 361; relationship with May Pang 172, 354; relationship with Yoko Ono 171, 186–7, 257–8; *Rock 'N' Roll* 181–3, 184–6, 188–92, **203**, 228–19, 220, 223, 252–4, 259; *Shaved Fish* 258; *Some Time in New York City* (Lennon & Ono) 117–18, 119–22, 142, 150, 170, **201**, 360; *Walls and Bridges* 220–6, 232, **264**; "You Can't Catch Me" 321

Levine, Stewart 238, 239, 240–2

Levy, Morris 183, 252

live performance recording: Bowie 163, **203**; growth of tours 279–80, 314–15; Presley **201**; Sly Stone failure 270; Springsteen 348; Tom Flye 141; *Zaire '74* 238–42. *See also Concert for Bangladesh*; studio trucks; Woodstock tapes and album

live radio concerts 114–16, 158, 162, 163

Lofgren, Nils 292, **338**

Los Angeles: Mount Kalmia Castle, Sunset Boulevard 274–5, **275–6**; night life 44; studio. *See* Record Plant LA studio

Lothar and the Hand People 84–5

Love (band) 62

Lynyrd Skynyrd **210**; *Second Helping* 208, 212, **264**

M

McAllister, Kooster 161–2

McCann-Erickson ad agency 82

McCartney, Linda 216

McCartney, Paul 96, 165–6, 228; *A Toot and a Snore in '74* (Lennon & McCartney bootleg) 216–18, **265**; *Band on the Run* (McCartney

INDEX

and Wings) 358; "Live and Let Die" 216; *Red Rose Speedway* (McCartney and Wings) 168
McCracken, Hugh 52
McDermott, John 25, 38
McLaughlin, John 39
McLean, Don 80, 85; "American Pie" 86–7, 155; *American Pie* 84, **107**
McManus, Bill 238
McVie, Christine 299, 300
McVie, John 299
Madinger, Chip 148, 253–4
Mahavishnu Orchestra 163
Mann, Rose 284, 298, 303, 345–6
Marcantonio, Steve 361–4
Margouleff, Bob: asked to move to RP S 153; *Fulfillingness' First Finale* (Wonder) 227–8; images of **88**, **152**; *Innervisions* (Wonder) 178–9; Isley Brothers 179–80; Lothar and the Hand People 84–5; Mediasound 90; respects Kellgren opinions 321–2; *Talking Book* (Wonder) 150–1; TONTO 87, 89; Wonder master tapes 128, 150, 229–30; Wonder sessions 124–5
Marron, Jim 40
Mars, Bruno 365
Martin, George 20, 356–8, 365
Martini, Jerry **159**
Masekela, Hugh 237, 238, 242
Mason, Dave **75**, 317
Mayer, Roger 35, 72, 122
Mayfair Studios, New York 13, 14, 18–20, 27
Maysles, Albert 238
MCA 232, 233
MCI 249
Meat Loaf 352; *Bat Out of Hell* **339**
Mediasound 87, 90, 130
Merritt, Bob 191, 285
Messina, Jay 196, 197, **199**, 200, 288
Metallica 365
Midler, Bette **339**
Miles, Buddy: death of Hendrix 73; Hendrix sessions 39–40; images of **26**, **144**; Jacuzzi sessions 110; RP LA sessions 236; RP S opening party 148; RP S proposal 113, 114, 115; The Scene jam sessions 24; *We Got to Live Together* 73, **75**
Mitchell, Dave 145, 155
Moire, Davy 318
Monck, Chip 100, 180, 238, 278
Money, Eddie **366**
Montrose, Ronnie 148
Moon, Keith 83, 103, 185, 188, 206, **234**; *Two Sides of the Moon* 232–5, **265**
Morris, Cris 300
Morrison, Jim 24
Morrison, Van 269, **272**, 273, **339**
Mothersbaugh, Mark 110
Motown 124, 150, 177, 179, 229, 295
Mottau, Eddie **224**

Mount Kalmia Castle, Sunset Boulevard 274–5, **275–6**
Mountain 165; *Climbing!* **74**, 83
Muntz, Earl "Madman" 42

N
Nash, Graham 63–4, 68
National Music Centre, Calgary, Canada 230
New Riders of the Purple Sage 311, 314, **338**; *Adventures of Panama Red* 155, **203**
New Times magazine 6, 8–9
New York Dolls 173, 174–5, 194, **202**
New York Philharmonic 98
New York studio. *See* Record Plant NY studio
Nicks, Stevie 299, 300, **301**, 353
Nighthawks at the Diner (Waits) 278, **337**
Nile, Willie 363, 364, **367**
Nilsson, Harry: console damage 188; Hollywood Vampires 185, 206; images of **182**, **221**; Jagger super-session 213; Lennon sessions 216, 219; *Pussy Cats* 220, 222–3, 232, **264**
914 Studios 258–9
nitrous oxide 292–3, 312
Nyro, Laura 117, **201**

O
Olazabal, Gary 180, 181, 216, 217, 296, 297, 288
Olympic Studios, London 34–5
The One-to-One Concert 142
Ono, Yoko: *Approximately Infinite Universe* 141, **202**; *Double Fantasy* (Lennon & Ono) 95, 258, 359–61, **367**; *Feeling the Space* 171; *Fly* **107**, 118; images of **108**, **120**, **201**, **362**; *Imagine* 94, 96, 97, 99; invitation to RP S opening party 143, 145, 147–8; Lennon's death 363–4; live performance recording 141; opinion of Cicala 57; recording sessions 118–19; relationship with Lennon 171, 186–7, 257–8; *Some Time in New York City* (Lennon & Ono) 117–18, 119–22, 142, 150, 170, **201**, 360
Owens, Stephani 79

P
Pablo Cruise **337**
Pacific High Recording 115
Pang, May 172, 181–3, 186, 190, 214, 216, 253, 257, 354
Panunzio, Thom 348, 349, 352, 353, 361–3, 364
Paris (Paris) 271, **338**. *See also* Welch, Bob
Parsons, Gram 45
party invitations 29, **31**, 46–7, **48**, 143, **144**, 326
Paul, Les 33

Paul, Steve 24
PCP 79
Peek, Dan **357**
Peel, David 123, **201**
People magazine article 280–3
Perry, Joe 195, 196, **199**, 262–3, 358
Perry, Richard 214–15
Peters, Dale 50
Petty, Tom 353, **367**
Phantom of the Paradise (Williams) 228, **264**
phasing 33–4, 122, 309–10
phone tapping 122, 123
pinball machine **207**, 208, 213
platinum albums 294
Playboy Club, Sunset Boulevard 44
Plotkin, Chuck 349, **351**
Poco 163
Power Station 349
Presley, Elvis 141, **201**, 343
Preston, Billy 230, 257
Prestopino, Paul 98, 171, 361
Pridgeon, Fayne 38
Prince: *For You* 347, **366**; "Purple Rain" 365, **367**

Q
quadraphonic-sound recording 127

R
radio concerts. *See* live radio concerts
Ragavoy, Jerry 254
Rainbow Bar & Grill, Sunset Boulevard 206, 306, 319
Ramone, Phil 57, 58, 83, 174, 259
Ramone, Tommy 36
Raspberries 117, 122, 222, 352
Reckson, Arlene 59, 99, 109, 118, 122, 360
Record Plant: analog switch to digital 250–1; The Book 283–4; foundation 6; initial funding 17; name 25–7; ownership 30; stock options 117
Record Plant LA studio: bedrooms 110–11, **112**, **282**; buzz lock 105, 208; carpenters 235; Chrysalis Records purchase 358, 365; Crosby, Stills, Nash & Young 64; design 6, 42–3, 44–5, **48**, 49, 68–9, 125–7; Eagles sessions 208–12, 247–9, 305–68, 307–10; fire 343–6; Harrison sessions 94; Hendrix visits 62; images of **112**, **126**, **137**, **207**; Jacuzzi 68–9, 110, 127, **282**; Jagger super-session 213–15; Jim Keltner Fan Club Hour 168, 215, 216–17, 278, 279; Lennon sessions 216–19; live radio concerts 115–16; Moon sessions 232–5; opening party 46–9, 326; parties 206; *People* magazine article 280–3; rebuilt and then moved 365; speakers 50, 62; Spector gun 188–92; Studio C 178, 180–1, 278, 297–8, 342; Walsh sessions 233; Wonder

381

INDEX

sessions 91, 124–5, 127–8, 150, 151–3, 226–9, 296–8; Zappa sessions 317–18

Record Plant NY studio: Aerosmith sessions 195–9, 262–3; Blondie sessions 354; Cicala buyout 169–70; Cicala ownership 131–2, 143, 169–70, 220, 254–5, 352–3, 360, 364; Cicala work methods 57–8; closure 365; design 6, 28–9, 130; Hendrix sessions 34–6; images of **26**; KISS sessions 286–91; Lennon and Ono sessions 94, 95–9, 117–19, 141, 142–3, 170–1, 359–64; Lennon sessions 252–4; opening party 29–32; piano 83, 98–9, 197, 222–3, 225, 361; recording costs 39, 40; renovation 55, 70, 82; rooftop 60–1, **350**, 353–4; sale to TVC 41, 90; soundproofing 40; Springsteen sessions 259–62, 347–9; Studio C 60, 85; training program 59–60, 172–3, 174–5; Warner Bros. purchase 53–5, 113, 115, 123; White Truck extra studio 162; *Who's Next* recording sessions 81–3

Record Plant Remote 163, **164**, 165

Record Plant Sausalito studio: bedrooms 246; design 6, 133–4, 143–7, 155, 245–6, 271; drugs bust 310–13; Fleetwood Mac sessions 299–302; images of **149**, **159**; Miles and Donahues proposal 113–15; opening party 143, **144**, 145–8, 155; reopening 365; Sausalito Bay Road house purchases 268–9; Sly Stone sessions 140–1, 155–6, 243–5, 270; "Tom & Tom" 80, 101, 140, 141, 154–5, 178, 192; Wonder sessions 296; Wyman sessions 271–3

recording techniques: digital 250–1, 322; phasing 33–4, 122, 309–10; quadraphonic-sound 127; slapback 121, 189; tape slicing 20, 86–7. *See also* live performance recording

Redding, Noel 35, 36

Reed, Lou 17, 349, **366**; *Rock 'n' Roll Animal* 163, **203**

REO Speedwagon **203**, 270

Revlon 12–13

Revson, Ancky 15–17, 30, 32, 47, 113, 135–6, 236–7, 325

Revson, Charles 13, 15, 32

Richards, Keith 45

Richo, John 20

Riperton, Minnie: "Lovin' You" 128, 228; *Perfect Angel* 228

Ripp, Artie 66, 105–6

Roberts, Ken 79, 140–1, 157, 244, 246, 270, 273

Robinson, Cynthia **159**

Robinson, Jimmy 36, 82, 271, 303–4, 305–6, 329–30, 334–6, 342

Rolling Stones 45, 114, 162, 271

Ross, Diana 150

Ross, Steve 53–5, 113, 122–3, 135, 269

Rufus **337**; *Rufusized* (Rufus and Chaka Khan) 232, **264**; "Tell Me Something Good" (Rufus and Chaka Khan) 128

Rumble in the Jungle 238

Rundgren, Todd 36, 77, 173, 175; *Runt* **75**; *Something Anything* 117, **201**

Rush, Tom 85

Russell, Gray 353

Russell, Leon 52, 273

Rutan, Grange 66

Ryan, Phil 311–13

S

San Francisco 113, 115. *See also* Record Plant Sausalito studio

Santana 62, **367**

Sarnoff, Albert 169

Sausalito Bay Road house purchases 268–9

Sausalito studio. *See* Record Plant Sausalito studio

The Scene nightclub 24, 25, **26**, 35, 38

Scheiner, Elliot 174

Schier, Phil 45–6, 62, 187, 213

Schmidt Horning, Susan 22

Scott, Tom 93–4, 101, 140, 143–5, 238–9

Seals and Crofts 163

Sebastian, John 232

Sedaka, Neil 358, **366**

Sedgwick, Edie 85

Shankar, Ravi 92, 103, 128

Shoes, Jimmy. *See* Iovine, Jimmy "Shoes"

Silverspoon 285

Silverstein, Abe 55, 135, 169–70, 171

Simmons, Gene **289**, 290

Simon and Garfunkel 18

Simon, Carly 85, 117

Simon, Paul 222

Sinatra, Frank 42

Sinclair, John 142

Sir Monti Rock III 333, 336, **339**

slapback 121, 189

Slauson, Pete 312

Slick, Grace 113

Sly and the Family Stone: *Fresh* 156–8, 192, **202**; *Greatest Hits* 79; *Small Talk* 243, **264**; *There's a Riot Goin' On* 79, **201**

Small Faces 33

Smith, Albert E. 66

Smith, Patti 72, **338**, 347, 348; "Because the Night" 349, 352; *Easter* 348, 349–52, **366**

Soft Machine 34, **74**

Sony Music 365

Soul Power 242

Sound City 353

Sounds of Silence (Simon and Garfunkel) 17–18

Source restaurant 274

Souvenirs (Fogelberg) 247, **264**

speakers 42–3, 50–2, 62

Spector, Phil: *Concert for Bangladesh* album 101, 102–5; guns 187–92; Harrison sessions 94; images of **104**; invitation to RP LA opening party 47; Lennon sessions 92, 96–8, 119, 121, 181–3, 185, 187–92, 321; Lennon tapes 218–19, 220; RP LA toilets 128; RP NY receptionist 90

Spinal Tap 278

Springsteen, Bruce: *Born to Run* 258–62, **265**; *Bruce Springsteen & the E Street Band Live 1975–1985* **339**; *Darkness on the Edge of Town* 261–2, 347–9, 354, **366**; images of **204**, **350–1**; live recordings 163, **339**, 348, **367**

Stallworth, Paul 168, 232, 279

Stanley, Paul 288, **289**

Starr, Ringo 165, 166, **167**, 168, 206, 232

Stasiak, Corky 288, 290

Steckler, Allen 94, 97, 100, 103, 105, 147–8

Steely Dan 232, 296

Stevens, Penn 162

Stevens, Rick 365

Stewart, Rod 110, 280, 325

Stigwood, Robert 358

Stills, Stephen 64, 100, **201**, 249, 251, 273, 317, 345, **366**

Stolaroff, Myron 133–4

Stone, Chris: Africa concerts 238–42; background 12–13, 14; cable TV proposition 269–70; car and license plate **67**, 70; character 325–6; Clapton recovery for concert 102; death 365; first meets Kellgren 12–13, 14–15; first visit LA 43; hires Cicala 57; hires Schier 45; images of **31**, **137**, **144**, **272**; Kellgren's Castle idea 274–5; Kellgren's death 333, 334, 336; leasing equipment 70; raises funds for first studio 17; RP LA fire 343, 346; RP LA gun 139, 141; RP LA opening party 47; RP NY opening party 29–32; RP NY potential repurchase 123, 129–30; RP NY sale 41; RP S drugs bust 311–12; RP S proposal 113–16, 132–3, 136; Sly Stone management 270; suggests booking Stevie Wonder 91; Szymczyk stereo 52–3; visits London 165–6; Warner Bros. meetings 53–5

Stone, Gloria 12, 68, 69, 99–100, 102, 322, 325–6, 343–6

Stone, Mike D. 45, 64

Stone, Samantha 325

Stone, Sly: armed robbery 244; background 113; drugs bust 310–13; first visit to RP 62; *High on You* **337**; images of **159**, **272**;

382

INDEX

introduced to Kellgren 78, 80; Jacuzzi sessions 110; management changes 270; master tapes 156, 158; police raid 192–3; RP LA sessions 79, 80, 139–40, 151–3; RP S introduction 115; RP S sessions 140–1, 156, 243–6, 292; Wyman sessions **272**, 273. *See also* Sly and the Family Stone
Storyk, John 41, 71–2, 125
Streisand, Barbra *A Star is Born* (Streisand & Kristofferson) **265**, 278; La*zy Afternoon* 278, **337**
Strick, David **328**, 329–30
Stronach, John 233
studio trucks 92–4, 100, 101, 155, 160–5, 178, 298–9, 314–15, 346
studios: cost to build 15; New York 1972 situation 129–30. *See also specific studios*
Sunset Sound 166, 232
synesthesia 28
Szymczyk, Bill: Eagles sessions 208–12, 247–50, 306, 307–10; images of **51**, **210**; meets Kellgren 33–4; RP LA sessions 50, 52–3; Walsh sessions 134, 233, 236

T
tape machines 14, 34, 35, 40, 43, 90, 98, 106, 121
tape slicing 20, 86–7
Taplin, Jonathan 102–3
Television Communications Corp (TVC) 41, 54, 70, 113, 115, 122–3
Ten Years After 163
"The Locomotion" (Goffin & King) 33
"The Pope Smokes Dope" (Peel) 123, **201**
Thoener, Dave 260–1
Thompson, Dave 189
Tommy James and the Shondells 106
TONTO (*also known as* TONTO's Expanding Head Band) **88**, 89, 90–1, 124, 127, 128, 151, **152**, 230, **231**, 297; *Zero Time* 87
Tork, Peter 43–4
tours, growth of 279–80
Tower of Power 246, 273
Tower Records 177
Townshend, Pete 83–4
Trader Vic's 14–15
Traffic 24, **74**
Travers, Joe 317, 318
Trident restaurant, Sausalito 113, 114, 115–16, 142
trucks. *See* studio trucks
Truscott, Lucian K., IV 6, 8–9, 306, 326–32, 343
TTG Studios 42, 43, 316
The Tubes **337**
TVC. *See* Television Communications Corp
Tyler, Steven 196–7, **198–9**, 263, 358

U
U2 353
unions 170
United Artists 85

V
Van Scyoc, Gary 118–19, 121
Velvet Underground 17, 20; *Banana* 19; "Sunday Morning" 19; *White Light/White Heat* 18–20, **74**
video 237
Vol. 4 (Black Sabbath) 139, **202**
Volman, Mark 232
Voormann, Klaus 216, 223, **224**, 232, 252

W
Waits, Tom 278, **337**
Wally Heider Studios 63–4, 94, 302
Walsh, Joe: Caribou Ranch 134; images of **266**; James Gang 49; joins Eagles 306, 308; live recordings 163; meets Kellgren 52; Moon sessions 232, 233–5; *So What* 233, 236; *Souvenirs* 247; Szymczyk and the Eagles 209, 211; Wyman sessions 273
Warner Bros. 53–4, 71, 113, 115, 122–3, 135, 169–70, 279, 318
Watcha Gonna Do (Doherty) **75**
Wayne, Edith 214
Webb, Jimmy 66
Weinberg, Max 261, 349
Welch, Bob 271, 273. *See also* Paris
Werman, Tom 346
West, Leslie 83
Westlake Monitors 52
When We Were Kings 242
White Truck 160–5, 314–15, 348
Whitford, Brad 196
Whitney Studios 317
The Who 81–4, 163; *Lifehouse* 82; *Quadrophenia* 84; *Who's Next* 82–3, **107**
"Wild Horses" (Flying Burrito Brothers) 46
Williams, Paul 264
Williams, Robin 114
Wilson, Brian 232
Wilson, Dennis 47
Wilson, Devon 38, 73
Wilson, Tom: Africa concerts 237, 238; asks for Revson investment 236–7; character 20; encourages Hendrix and Kellgren connection 24, 25; hiring of Eddie Kramer 34; images of **21**; Kellgren use of bungalow 113; production range 17–18, 27, 78–9; RP LA opening party 47; RP NY opening party 30, **31**; RP publicity 280; Sly Stone 78–9; work with Ripp 66
Wings 168
Winter, Johnny 24, 200; *John Dawson Winter III* 222, **264**
Winwood, Steve 71

Withers, Bill **201**; "Lean on Me" 133
Wolf, Peter 222
Womack, Bobby 139
Womack, Ken 360
Wonder, Stevie: accident 180, 212, 227; air hockey 297–8; death of Hendrix 72–3; Electric Lady Studios 124; *Fulfillingness' First Finale* 227–8, **264**; images of **152**, **231**, **282**; *Innervisions* 150, 177–9, **202**; Jacuzzi sessions 110; Lennon and McCartney session 217; "Living for the City" 151, 179; master tapes ownership dispute 229–30; meets John Lennon 181; move to LA 122; *Music of My Mind* 125, 127, **201**; records RP LA arguments 285; RP LA sessions 91, 124–5, 127–8, 150, 151–3, 226–9; *Songs in the Key of Life* 294–8, **338**; "Superstition" 151, 156; *Talking Book* 127, 148, 150, 151, **202**; TONTO 87, 89, 91, 230; "You Are the Sunshine of My Life" 151
Wood, Ron (*also known as* Ronnie) 273, 336; "Far East Man" (Harrison & Wood) 166; *I've Got My Own Album to Do* 166, **203**
Woodstock tapes and album 47, 61–3, **74**, 85
Wrench, Loreana 334
Wright, Syreeta 128
Wyman, Bill **272**; *Stone Alone* **265**, 271

Y
Yakus, Shelly: Alice Cooper session 131, 161; background 58; character 59–60; hires Iovine 174, 175; images of **225**; Lennon and Ono sessions 96, 97, 99; Lennon sessions 122; Petty sessions 353; Raspberries sessions 117, 352; Smith sessions 352; Winter sessions 200, 222
Young, Neil 63–4
Young Rascals 56

Z
Zaire '74 238–42, **264**
Zandt, Steve Van 261
Zappa, Frank: *Bongo Fury* 314, **337**; *Chunga's Revenge* **75**; *Funky Nothingness* **75**; images of **21**, **74**, **75**, **320**; Jacuzzi sessions 110; Kellgren relationship 330; leaves Warner Bros. 318–19; *Live in New York* **339**, live recordings 314, **337**, **339**; *Lumpy Gravy* 20, **74**; *One Size Fits All* 236, **265**, 317; own studio 13–14, 319; RP studio designs 15, 316; *Studio Tan* 317–18, **339**; TTG Studios 42; *We're Only in It for the Money* 13, 19–20, 22, **74**
Zarin, Michelle 158, 269

Acknowledgments

The following "witnesses" shared their thoughts, memories and memorabilia with the authors:

Al Kooper, Al Schmitt, Allan Steckler, Andy Neill, Apollo Cavallo, Arlene Reckson, Benjamin Schultz, Bill Halverson, Bill Szymczyk, Bob Edwards, Bob Gruen, Bob Merritt, Bobbi Marcus, Brooks Arthur, Bruce Hensal, Cathy Callon, Chris Crosby Morris, Chris Stone, Craig Alberino, Cris Morris, Daniel Barbieri, Danny Kortchmar, David Hewitt, Davey Moire, David Strick, Dave Thoener, DB Browne, Dee Willoughby, Deni King, Devon Kellgren, Dick Hunt, Dominick Costanza, Donna Pekkonen, Doug Simon, Ed Freeman, Eddie Kramer, Fran Hughes, Frank Hubach, Frank Stefanko, Frederick Woodruff, Gail Zappa, Gary (Olazabal) Adante, Gary Ladinsky, Gary Van Scyoc, Gloria Stone, Grange Rutan, Guillermo Rodiles, Henry Diltz, Howard Sherman, Jack Casady, Jack Douglas, Jade Cicala, James Sandweiss, Jay Messina, Jim Keltner, Jim Scott, Jimmy Robinson, Joe Travers, John Hanti, John Markland, John McDermott, John Richo, John Storyk, John Townley, Jonathan Taplin, Katherine Weiss, Ken Caillat, Ken Womack, Kooster McAllister, Lee Kiefer, Lillian Davis Douma, Loreana Wrench, Lori Burton, Lou Lindauer, May Pang, Malcolm Cecil, Mark Mothersbaugh, Marta Kellgren, Martyn Goddard, Michael Braunstein, Michael Verdick, Michelle Zarin, Mike D. Stone, Monti Rock III, Nance McManus, Nina (Urban) Bombardier, Norman Dlugatch, Paul Broucek, Paul Prestopino, Peter Chaikin, Peter Slauson, Phil Jamtas, Phil Ryan, Philip Schier, Raechel Donahue, Ray Corey, Ray Goldman, Ray Gomez, Richard Buskin, Rick Sanchez, Rick Smith, Rob Fraboni, Robert Margouleff, Roger Mayer, Ron Nevison, Samantha Stone, Saul Davis, Scott Stogel, Shelly Yakus, Steve Price, Steve Smith, Steve Marcontonio, Stewart Levine, Susan Schmidt Horning, Todd Rundgren, Tom Allom, Tom Flye, Thom Panunzio, Tom Scott, Tom Werman, Vic Briggs

The authors would like to thank Chris Stone who told us his stories during countless backyard interviews but who also wanted everyone else to be heard. Thank you to the families of Gary, Chris and Roy, with special thanks to Gloria Stone, Marta Kellgren, Devon Kellgren, Lori Burton, Jade Cicala and Craig Alberino who reviewed this manuscript. This work was made possible through the support and contributions of Susie Porter, Steve Harvey, Fred Goodman, Christopher Walsh, Ira Mayer, Heidi Antman, Sam Nachimson, Bill Szymczyk, Max Porter, Sophie Sperber and KamranV.

Captions for additional illustrations

Page 2: John Lennon photographed at the Record Plant NY studio in 1972.

Page 10: Jimi Hendrix at the Record Plant NY studio on April 21, 1969.
With audio engineer Gary Kellgren behind the board, the session resulted
in the song "Room Full of Mirrors."

Page 76: George Harrison and Bob Dylan performing live at the Concert
for Bangladesh held at Madison Square Garden on August 1, 1971.

Page 108: John Lennon with Yoko Ono (holding John's favorite candy bar)
and Elephant's Memory band members at Record Plant NY in 1972.

Page 204: Bruce Springsteen performs on stage as part of the Born to Run
tour in October 1975.

Page 266: Eagles guitarist and recording artist Joe Walsh performs on
stage at a concert with the band in 1980.

Page 340: Blondie's lead singer, Debbie Harry, photographed in the studio
at Record Plant NY in 1978.